MW00991006

THOMAS OF CANTIMPRÉ:
THE COLLECTED SAINTS' LIVES

THOMAS OF CANTIMPRÉ:
THE COLLECTED SAINTS' LIVES

Abbot John of Cantimpré,
Christina the Astonishing,
Margaret of Ypres,
and Lutgard of Aywières

Edited and with an Introduction by

Barbara Newman

Translations by

Margot H. King and Barbara Newman

BREPOLS

British Library Cataloguing in Publication Data

Thomas, de Cantimpre, ca. 1200–ca. 1270
    The collected saints' lives : Christina the Astonishing, Lutgard of Aywieres, Margaret of
Ypres and Abbot John of Cantimpre. – (Medieval women : texts and contexts ; 19)
    1. Christina, Mirabilis, Saint, 1150–1224 2. Lutgardis, Saint, 1182–1246 3. Margaret, of
Ypres, 1216–1237 4. John, Abbot of Cantimpre
I. Title II. Newman, Barbara, 1953– III. King, Margot H.
270.5'0922

ISBN-13: 9782503520780

© 2008, Brepols Publishers n.v., Turnhout, Belgium

D/2008/0095/116
ISBN: 978-2-503-52078-0

Printed in the E.U. on acid-free paper

CONTENTS

LIST OF ABBREVIATIONS

AASS	J. Bolland and others, *Acta sanctorum*, 3rd edn, 68 vols (Paris: Palmé, 1863–1925)
Archives du Nord	*Archives historiques et littéraires du Nord de la France et du Midi de la Belgique*, ed. by A. M. Dinaux, A. J. G. Le Glay, and A. N. Leroy, 16 vols (Valenciennes: Bureau des Archives, 1829–57)
BHL	*Bibliotheca hagiographica latina antiquae et mediae aetatis*, 2 vols (Brussels: Société des Bollandistes, 1949)
BUA	*Thomas of Cantimpré, Bonum universale de apibus*, ed. by Georges Colvénère (Douai: Beller, 1627)
CCSL	*Corpus christianorum: series latina* (Turnhout: Brepols, 1953–)
CSEL	*Corpus scriptorum ecclesiasticorum latinorum* (Vienna: Gerold, 1866–1974)
DNR	*Thomas of Cantimpré, Liber de natura rerum*, ed. by Helmut Boese (Berlin: de Gruyter, 1973)
DS	*Dictionnaire de spiritualité ascétique et mystique, doctrine et histoire*, 17 vols (Paris: Beauchesne, 1932–95)
Gallia Christiana	*Gallia Christiana, in provincias ecclesiasticas distributa*, 16 vols (Paris: Palmé, 1715–1865; repr. Farnborough: Gregg, 1970)

MB	*Monasticon Belge*, 8 vols (Bruges: Abbaye de Maredsous, 1890–)
MGH.SS	*Monumenta Germaniae historica: Scriptores rerum germanicarum* (Hannover: Hahn, 1826–)
PL	J-P. Migne, *Patrologiae cursus completus: series latina*, 221 vols (Paris: Migne, 1861–64)
RB	*Regula Sancti Benedicti: The Rule of St Benedict in Latin and English*, ed. by Timothy Fry (Collegeville, MN: Liturgical Press, 1981)
VA	*Vita Abbreviata or Vita Antiqua: 'Vita Sancte Lutgardis Virginis et Monealis' [sic]*, ed. by Guido Hendrix, *Cîteaux*, 29 (1978), 162–74
VCM	*Thomas of Cantimpré, Vita Christinae mirabilis*, ed. by J. Pinius, in AASS, 24 July, V, pp. 637–60
VJC	*Thomas of Cantimpré, Vita Ioannis Cantipratensis*, in 'Une oeuvre inédite de Thomas de Cantimpré, la "Vita Ioannis Cantipratensis"', ed. by Robert Godding, *Revue d'histoire ecclésiastique*, 76 (1981), 241–56 (introduction); 257–316 (text)
VJMM	*Vita Ioannis de Monte-Mirabili*, ed. by Constantin Suysken, in AASS, 29 September, VIII, pp. 186–235
VLA	*Thomas of Cantimpré, Vita Lutgardis Aquiriensis*, ed. by G. Henschen, in AASS, 16 June, III, pp. 187–209
VMO	*James of Vitry, Vita Mariae Oigniacensis*, ed. by A. Raysse, in AASS, 23 June, V, pp. 547–72
VMO-S	*Thomas of Cantimpré, Vita Mariae Oigniacensis, Supplementum*, ed. by A. Raysse, in AASS, 23 June, V, pp. 572–81
	Mary of Oignies: Mother of Salvation, ed. by Anneke B. Mulder-Bakker (Turnhout: Brepols, 2006). Includes translations of the VMO by Margot H. King (pp. 33–127) and the VMO-S by Hugh Feiss (pp. 129–65)

VMY   *Thomas of Cantimpré, Vita Margarete de Ypres*, in 'Les
                       Frères Prêcheurs et le mouvement dévot en Flandres
                       au XIIIe siècle', ed. by G. Meersseman, *Archivum
                       Fratrum Praedicatorum*, 18 (1948), 106–30

CHRONOLOGY
THOMAS OF CANTIMPRÉ
(*c.* 1200–*c.* 1265/70)

c. 1180	Augustinian house of Cantimpré founded near Cambrai
c. 1200	Thomas of Cantimpré born at Bellingen near Brussels
1206–17	Educated in Cambrai
1215/16	First encounters James of Vitry as a crusade preacher
1215/16	James of Vitry's *Life of Mary of Oignies* (1177–1213) composed
1216–27	James in Holy Land as Bishop of Acre
1217	Thomas enters Augustinian house of Cantimpré
1218	First Franciscan house in region founded at Valenciennes
1223–28	***The Life of Abbot John of Cantimpré*** (*c.* 1155–*c.* 1205/09) composed
1224	First Dominican house in region founded at Lille
1228	Dominican house established at Leuven
1228	Thomas becomes confessor at cathedral of Cambrai
c. 1228–30	Thomas meets Lutgard of Aywières
1229	James of Vitry becomes cardinal of Tusculum
c. 1229–32	Thomas's ***Supplement to the Life of Mary of Oignies*** composed
1232	Thomas moves to Dominican community at Leuven
1232	***The Life of Christina the Astonishing*** (*c.* 1150–1224) composed
c. 1237–40	Thomas at Dominican *studium generale* in Paris

c. 1230–40	***Liber de natura rerum*** (On the Nature of Things) composed
1240	Death of James of Vitry
1240	Thomas returns to Leuven
c. 1240–43	***The Life of Margaret of Ypres*** (1216–37) composed
1240–46	Thomas travels widely on preaching circuit
1246	Thomas acting as lector and subprior at Leuven
1246–48	***The Life of Lutgard of Aywières*** (1182–1246) composed
1250–51	Thomas studying at Cologne with Albertus Magnus
c. 1256–63	***Bonum universale de apibus*** (Book of Bees) composed
c. 1265–70	Death of Thomas of Cantimpré

INTRODUCTION

Barbara Newman

B orn around 1200, Thomas of Cantimpré grew up with the thirteenth century to become one of its liveliest chroniclers. In his long career as a preacher and confessor, the Dominican completed three major literary projects. His encyclopedic *Liber de natura rerum* (*On the Nature of Things*), written in the 1230s, is a compendium of natural science assembled as a preaching aid. Hugely successful in its time (more than 160 manuscripts survive), it supplied material for the still better-known encyclopedias of Albertus Magnus and Vincent of Beauvais. In a very different kind of preachers' guide, the *Bonum universale de apibus* (*Book of Bees*, or *The Universal Good, c.* 1256–63), Thomas gathered edifying, often spine-tingling tales from his pastoral ministry to provide sermon exempla.[1] Like the collections of other thirteenth-century preachers (James of Vitry, Caesarius of Heisterbach, Stephen of Bourbon), Thomas's anecdotes reveal more about his variegated social and religious world, demons and all, than they do about ethics. This extremely popular work is extant in about sixty manuscripts and several printed editions, the most recent dating from 1627. Medieval French and Dutch versions also exist, as well as a modern French translation.[2]

---

[1] The title may have been inspired by a sermon James of Vitry preached to beguines around 1228, in which he contrasted the spider, whose venom turns good things into poison, with the bee that makes everything sweet. See *Sermones vulgares*, second sermon to virgins, Paris, Bibliothèque nationale de France, MS lat. 17509, fol. 147; cited in Joseph Greven, 'Der Ursprung des Beginenwesens: Eine Auseinandersetzung mit Godefroid Kurth', *Historisches Jahrbuch*, 35 (1914), 26–58 (p. 48). See also the chapter on bees in DNR.

[2] *Les Exemples du 'Livre des abeilles': une vision médiévale*, trans. by Henri Platelle (Turnhout: Brepols, 1997).

But modern taste in medieval texts usually differs from that of
contemporaries, and Thomas of Cantimpré is no exception.[3] Although his saints'
lives enjoyed nothing like the grand success of *De natura rerum* and the *Book of
Bees*, it is for his hagiographic dossier that he is now best remembered. The
collection comprises four and a half works, so to speak — the 'half' being his
Supplement to the Life of Mary of Oignies. The others are his *Lives* of Abbot John
of Cantimpré, Christina the Astonishing, Margaret of Ypres, and Lutgard of
Aywières, all presented here in annotated English translations. The *Life of John
of Cantimpré* has been freshly translated from the edition of Robert Godding.
The women's *Lives* are based on versions by Margot King, first published in the
Peregrina Translations Series but extensively revised by the editor of this volume.
The footnotes to the women's *vitae* are King's and the notes to *John of
Cantimpré* are Godding's, except where specified by the initials [BN]. Thomas
of Cantimpré's *Supplement* can be found in another Brepols volume, *Mary of
Oignies: Mother of Salvation*, along with James of Vitry's original *Life* of that
saint and other historical and liturgical texts.[4]

The Life and Works of Thomas of Cantimpré

Thomas of Cantimpré's writings afford a rich, constantly shifting panorama on
his turbulent world. Commanding three languages — his native Dutch or
Flemish (*theutonicus*), the neighbouring French vernacular (*lingua romana*), and
the Latin of his scholastic training — Thomas embodied many of the salient
religious and intellectual trends of his age. Although we lack a biography of this
prolific biographer, we can infer a rough chronology of his life from what he tells
us in his works, especially the *Book of Bees*.[5] Born into the lower nobility in

---

[3] I cite here 'Murray's Law', which deserves to be better known: 'the more widely copied
a work was in the late Middle Ages the less likely it is to enjoy a modern critical edition'. See
Alexander Murray, 'Should the Middle Ages Be Abolished?', *Essays in Medieval Studies*, 21
(2004), 1–22 (p. 14). Online at http://muse.jhu.edu/journals/essays_in_medieval_ studies/
vo21/21.1murray.pdf.

[4] *Mary of Oignies: Mother of Salvation*, ed. by Anneke Mulder-Bakker (Turnhout: Brepols,
2006).

[5] For this outline I have drawn on Henri Platelle, 'Le Recueil des miracles de Thomas de
Cantimpré et la vie religieuse dans les Pays-Bas et le Nord de la France au XIIIᵉ siècle', in *Actes
du 97e Congrès national des sociétés savantes, Nantes, 1972*, 2 vols (Paris: Bibliothèque nationale,
1977–79), I, pp. 469–98; Alfred Deboutte, 'The *Vita Lutgardis* of Thomas of Cantimpré', in

Bellingen, near Brussels, Thomas owed his vocation to the sins of his father, a knight who held a fief from Richard the Lion-Heart. Characteristically turning his own story into an exemplum, Thomas reveals that his father made a penitential pilgrimage to the Holy Land, where he confessed his sins to a hermit in the mountains near Jerusalem. The hermit must have been impressed, for he told the knight that he had little hope of expiating his faults unless he raised a son for the priesthood.[6] Thus the young Thomas was sent to a cathedral school, probably Cambrai, where he studied from 1206 to 1217.[7] At the age of about fourteen he met James of Vitry, a cleric then attached to the priory of Oignies, whose preaching made an indelible impression. On completing his studies Thomas entered the Victorine abbey of Cantimpré at the gates of Cambrai, attracted by the still-glowing reputation of its founder, Abbot John. With his passion for preaching, Thomas would probably have joined a mendicant order if he had been just a few years younger. But the mendicants had not yet established themselves in the Low Countries, although they would very soon do so. The Franciscans founded their first house in the region at Valenciennes in 1218, just a year after Thomas became a regular canon. Six years later, the Dominicans established their first northern house at Lille, and in 1228, they founded the convent at Leuven that Thomas would enter in 1232.

In the meantime, the young canon was quickly promoted to the rank of confessor with plenary powers under the bishop of Cambrai. This meant that he had the right to absolve even 'reserved' sins beyond the scope of parish clergy, such as sexual offences that sorely tested his own chastity. In this pastoral crisis

---

Hidden Springs: Cistercian Monastic Women, ed. by John Nichols and Lillian Thomas Shank, 2 vols (Kalamazoo: Cistercian Publications, 1995), I, pp. 255–81; and Robert Sweetman, 'Thomas of Cantimpré: Performative Reading and Pastoral Care', in *Performance and Transformation: New Approaches to Late Medieval Spirituality*, ed. by Mary Suydam and Joanna Ziegler (New York: St Martin's Press, 1999), pp. 133–67. I was unable to consult Thomas Grzebien, 'Penance, Purgatory, Mysticism and Miracles: The Life, Hagiography, and Spirituality of Thomas of Cantimpré (1200–1270)' (unpublished doctoral dissertation, University of Notre Dame, 1989). Readers should be aware that many of the dates in Thomas's life are conjectural, and scholarly reconstructions differ.

[6] BUA II.53.32, pp. 513–14. Thomas adds that whenever he neglected to sing mass for his father, his spirit appeared to him in dreams, pleading and displaying his wounds.

[7] In BUA I.19.10, p. 74, Thomas says only that he was educated in a 'cathedral city'. Deboutte, Sweetman, and Simons (n. 9 below) identify it as Cambrai; Platelle and Godding prefer Liège. I choose Cambrai because it was there that Thomas entered religious life as soon as he completed his schooling.

he appealed to his close friend and confidante, the nun Lutgard of Aywières, whom he may have met through James. By her prayers, he says gratefully, he won the grace of listening unmoved to even the most sordid sins.[8]

Thomas also discovered his bent for hagiography at a young age. He began the *Life of John of Cantimpré* when he was only twenty-three, working on it intermittently for five years — though for some reason he laid it aside before completing the final chapter on John's death, which he added more than forty years later while awaiting his own. Even though John inspired no lasting cult, Thomas's youthful work is an immensely interesting text, revealing its author's love of drama and his inability to resist a seductive anecdote. Abbot John (*c.* 1155–1205/10) was a fiery, charismatic preacher who disputed with Cathars, campaigned against usury, and converted a surprising number of nobles, as well as repentant moneylenders, to apostolic poverty. Around 1180 he founded the house of canons at Cantimpré, and in 1183 he secured its affiliation with Saint-Victor in Paris. Although Thomas entered too late to have known John personally, he did know his successor and many of his converts, so it was from extensive oral history that he composed this sprawling *vita*, a monument to his own as well as his subject's evangelical zeal. The *Life of John* was essentially complete by 1228 — the same year as the canonization of St Francis and the appearance of Thomas of Celano's *Vita prima*. These two *Lives* are kindred in spirit, though hardly in influence, for the sole manuscript of *John of Cantimpré* (*c.* 1496) was not edited until 1981.

Much more famous are Thomas's contributions to female hagiography, a subgenre that flourished in the thirteenth-century Low Countries as never before.[9] In fact, *mulieres religiosae* already figure prominently in our author's sole masculine *vita*. The prioress of Prémy (Cantimpré's sister-house) earns extravagant praise, and Thomas even gestures toward a *vita* for the recluse Yburgis: 'because of its greatness her life demands a work of its own and the

---

[8] VLA II.38.

[9] For overviews see Simone Roisin, *L'Hagiographie cistercienne dans le diocèse de Liège au XIIIᵉ siècle* (Louvain: Bibliothèque de l'Université, 1947); Brenda Bolton, '*Vitae Matrum*: A Further Aspect of the *Frauenfrage*', in *Medieval Women*, ed. by Derek Baker (Oxford: Blackwell, 1978), pp. 253–73; Margot H. King, 'The Desert Mothers Revisited: The Mothers of the Diocese of Liège', *Vox Benedictina*, 5 (1988), 325–54; Bernard McGinn, *The Flowering of Mysticism: Men and Women in the New Mysticism (1200–1350)* (New York: Crossroad, 1998), pp. 158–66; Walter Simons, *Cities of Ladies: Beguine Communities in the Medieval Low Countries, 1200–1565* (Philadelphia: University of Pennsylvania Press, 2001), pp. 36–48.

leisure to write it'.[10] For want of such leisure, Yburgis has been doomed to oblivion, since Thomas chose instead to advance the saintly causes promoted by his role model, James of Vitry. James had written an influential *Life* of his friend, the ascetic and mystic Mary of Oignies (1177–1213), not long after her death. Mary's life had included both active ministry to lepers and contemplative solitude, making her a beloved exemplar of the early beguine movement (though not its 'founder', as she is sometimes misleadingly called). No sooner had he completed her *Life*, however, than James abandoned the diocese of Liège (as Thomas saw it) to pursue a high-powered ecclesiastical career, first as Bishop of Acre in the crusader states (1216–27), then as Cardinal of Tusculum (1229–40). Shortly after James accepted the second position, Thomas penned his *Supplement*, ostensibly to add further miracles and anecdotes about Mary, though more pointedly to rebuke his erstwhile mentor in her name. Thomas begged James to leave Rome and return to his true vocation as pastor to the flocks of beguines at Liège, as he insisted Mary would have wished.[11] But in that purpose he failed, for the cardinal remained at the curia until the end of his life. In James's absence, therefore, Thomas did his best to fill his shoes, not only as a preacher and pastor, but also as a tireless promoter of religious women.

Having completed his *Supplement to the Life of Mary* just before he moved to Leuven in 1232, Thomas wrote the *Life of Christina the Astonishing* just afterward, taking care to cite James's own eulogy for the 'unforgettable virgin' in his prologue. In this *Life*, Thomas took the risk of sanctifying a colourful, wildly eccentric woman who, on his own testimony, was more often taken for a demoniac. Having to all appearances died around the age of thirty-two, Christina of Sint-Truiden (1150–1224) came back to life at her funeral mass, levitated to the roof of the church, and would not come down until she was exorcized by the priest, while the congregation fled in terror. This amazing spectacle was only the beginning of her career of ingenious self-torture, in the course of which she threw herself into baking ovens, boiling cauldrons, and icy rivers, curled up like a hedgehog in treetops, prayed standing on fence posts, suspended herself voluntarily on the rack and the gallows, broke the chains in which her alarmed relatives bound her, and survived in the woods on miraculous milk that exuded from her own virginal breasts — all to deliver souls from the torments of purgatory, or so Thomas claims. Eventually Christina calmed down enough to spend several years with a recluse, Jutta, who taught her some Latin

---

[10] VJC I.15.

[11] VMO-S IV.22–27, in *Mary of Oignies*, pp. 160–65.

and nurtured her prophetic abilities. Her fortune turned when the local count, Louis II of Loon, became a devotee and offered her patronage in return for prayers, and in later life she was a frequent visitor (though never a nun) at the convent of St Catherine in Sint-Truiden. Thomas's sensational *vita*, scarcely longer than a pamphlet, was for centuries derided as a monument of naive credulity. But medieval readers loved it. Twelve manuscripts are extant, in addition to Dutch and Middle English translations.[12] Recently Christina has come into her own once more as a fascinating example of medieval women's ecstatic, corporeal, and performative piety.

Around 1237 the Dominicans sent Thomas for further study at St Jacques, their *studium generale* in Paris, where he stayed for two or three years and worked on *De natura rerum*. An anecdote in the *Book of Bees* mentions the Talmud-burning ordered by Louis IX in 1239, which Thomas witnessed.[13] Returning to Leuven in 1240, the year of James of Vitry's death, he passed through Ypres, where an earnest conversation with his colleague Zeger (or Siger) of Lille inspired him to write the *Life of Margaret*.[14] The young Margaret of Ypres (1216–37) had been as sheltered and reclusive as Christina was flamboyant and public. Raised by her bourgeois mother and an uncle, the girl was a pious child, but fell in love at eighteen and seemed well on her way to marriage when she encountered Friar Zeger, a Dominican from Lille, who had come to Ypres on a pastoral mission. As the *vita* has it, a single conversation sufficed for Margaret's radical and irrevocable conversion. From then on she loved only Christ and Zeger. Much to her mother's chagrin, she embarked on the life of a recluse in her family home, maintaining a devout (or sullen) silence and fasting ferociously. Rewarded with mystical gifts, Margaret had already started to attract devotees when she took ill with the horrific malady that would carry her off before her twenty-first birthday. It was from Zeger that Thomas gleaned most of the material for his

---

[12] For the rhymed Middle Dutch version ascribed to Willem van Afflighem, see *Leven van sinte Christina de Wonderbare, in oud-dietsche rijmen*, ed. by J. H. Bormans (Ghent: Annoot-Braeckman, 1850); for the prose version see Broeder Geraert, *Sinte Kerstinen heiligen leven*, in *Sinte Lutgart, Sinte Kerstine, Nederrijns Moraalboek*, ed. by Maurits Gysseling and Willy Pijnenburg (The Hague: Nijhoff, 1987), pp. 104–53. For the Middle English text see 'Þe Lyfe of Seinte Cristyne þe Mervelous', in 'Prosalegenden: Die Legenden des MS. Douce 14', ed. by Carl Horstmann, *Anglia*, 8 (1885), 119–34. Jennifer Brown is preparing a new edition for Brepols.

[13] BUA I.3.6, pp. 17–18.

[14] VMY Prologue. Simons suggests that the *vita* was not completed until 1243: *Cities of Ladies*, pp. 39 and 171, n. 17.

vita, though he supplemented his colleague's report with the reminiscences of surviving family members. If Margaret's rather formulaic *Life* lacks the extravagance of Christina's and the initiative we see in John of Cantimpré and Mary of Oignies, it may be because the girl never had a chance to grow up. We cannot know what she might have become, given a stronger constitution or a more temperate piety. In her three years as an apprentice saint, however, Margaret supplies a striking, even frightening, example of a malleable young woman in the hands of an immensely determined confessor.

Thomas of Cantimpré's interest in holy women intersected with the growing pressure on Europe's Jews in another, much briefer, hagiographic notice from the *Book of Bees*. This exemplum recounts the conversion of a young Jewish girl from Leuven, Catherine née Rachel, who escaped from her outraged family by taking the veil at the Cistercian nunnery of Vrouwenpark (Parc-aux-Dames). The incident, also recorded by Caesarius of Heisterbach, occurred between 1218 and 1221, though Thomas may not have learned of it until he settled in Leuven.[15] Back at his home convent, we find him serving as lector and subprior by 1246, all the while preaching and hearing confessions throughout the large, populous sees of Cambrai and Liège, with forays into the neighbouring dioceses of Tournai and Thérouanne. Thomas also stayed in close touch with Lutgard, writing her *vita* at his own initiative soon after her death. The *Life of Lutgard of Aywières* (1182–1246) is Thomas's most mature, sophisticated *vita* and also his most intimate, for he considered Lutgard his spiritual mother, just as James had regarded Mary of Oignies — even to the point of claiming the same relic, a finger, after the holy woman's death. In fact, Thomas acknowledges that he composed Lutgard's *vita* because he needed a gift to offer the abbess of Aywières in exchange for this treasured talisman.[16] His determination to promote her cult

---

[15] Caesarius of Heisterbach, *Dialogus miraculorum*, 2.25, ed. by Joseph Strange, 2 vols (Cologne: Heberle, 1851), I, pp. 95–98; BUA II.29.20, pp. 295–99; Aviad M. Kleinberg, 'A Thirteenth-Century Struggle over Custody: The Case of Catherine of Parc-aux-Dames', *Bulletin of Medieval Canon Law*, n.s. 20 (1990), 51–67; *Other Middle Ages: Witnesses at the Margins of Medieval Society*, ed. by Michael Goodich (Philadelphia: University of Pennsylvania Press, 1998), pp. 26–31. Goodich translates a fifteenth-century composite text printed in AASS, 4 May, I, pp. 537–39. See also Henri Platelle, 'L'Image des Juifs chez Thomas de Cantimpré: De l'attrait à la répulsion', in *Mélanges à la mémoire de Marcel-Henri Prévost: Droit biblique, interprétation rabbinique, communautés et société* (Paris: Presses Universitaires de France, 1982), pp. 283–306.

[16] VLA III.19.

is suggested by his eagerness to secure the relic as well as his account of posthumous miracles, a hagiographic feature slighted in his other *vitae*.

The daughter of a noblewoman and a prosperous burgher, Lutgard was born in the Flemish town of Tongeren. At the age of twelve her parents committed her to a small beguinage at Sint-Truiden, where she came to know Christina the Astonishing. About twelve years later the women, by then Benedictine nuns, elected her prioress, but, preferring contemplation to administration, Lutgard decided to become a Cistercian in order to evade the office. Naturally enough, she first chose the Flemish-speaking convent of Herkenrode, but Christina and a clerical friend, John of Liroux (Lierre), both advised her that if she wanted to escape leadership permanently, it would be wiser to choose a French-speaking monastery, where a lack of fluency would make her ineligible to govern. Hence she entered the convent of Aywières instead of Herkenrode, and for the rest of her life studiously (or as Thomas says, miraculously) avoided learning any more than the bare minimum of French. Nonetheless, at Aywières Lutgard became an exemplary nun, celebrated for mystical gifts that included the powers of healing and exorcism. But her special grace lay in releasing multitudes of souls from purgatory through compassionate prayers and fasts. Toward the end of her life, blindness was heaped on her other mortifications. With her German contemporary, Gertrude of Helfta, she was among the earliest devotees of the Sacred Heart of Christ.

It was about 1250, not long after finishing Lutgard's *vita*, that Thomas spent a year at the recently founded *studium generale* in Cologne. There he attended the lectures of Albertus Magnus on Aristotle and made the acquaintance of Thomas Aquinas, a fellow Dominican, though hardly a like-minded one. In the final phase of his career, Thomas of Cantimpré was appointed a preacher general for the province of Teutonia. During his last fifteen or twenty years he travelled widely on pastoral missions, at the same time gathering the exempla that constitute the *Book of Bees* — some from his own experience, others from oral tradition, still others from written sources. The work was launched in response to an initiative of the Dominican General Chapter in 1256, asking friars to compose just such collections for the benefit of future preachers, and finished by 1263.[17] In his old age Thomas belatedly completed his *Life of John* at the request of Anselm, then abbot of Cantimpré, and returned it to the canons with a poignant letter of dedication: 'I beseech you in closing, dearest brothers, that

---

[17] Platelle claims that Thomas continued to add new material as late as 1268, but the example he cites (BUA II.57.42, p. 568), actually took place in 1258: 'Le Recueil', p. 475.

when you hear of my death, you will do me the kindness of offering the same rites that are customary for a deceased brother among yourselves. For even though I am now a friar of a different order, yet I lived among you as your brother without scandal or hatred, as I trust, for fifteen years and more. But now, suffering the daily pain of arthritis and gout, I believe I shall not live much longer.'[18] Although we have no notice of Thomas's death, it must have occurred *c.* 1265–70.

Thomas and the 'Great Awakening' of the Thirteenth Century

The many-faceted transformation that Giles Constable christened 'the reformation of the twelfth century', and M.-D. Chenu its 'evangelical awakening', bore its ripest fruit in such urbanized regions as northern Italy and the Low Countries, where Thomas lived and worked.[19] As the locus of economic power in those areas shifted from the great feudal barons to the merchant class, the much-touted 'rise of capitalism' generated a great deal of new wealth, along with new opportunities for conspicuous consumption. Economic theory still lingered far behind practice, leaving moralists to gape in dismay at the 'unnatural' ability of coins to breed more coins.[20] But the new mercantile wealth also generated more visible disparities between rich and poor, who rubbed shoulders in the crowded towns as they could not in rural villages, overshadowed by the towering keeps of their lords. With the recognition of these vast disparities came protest, that mighty engine of renewal. Even as merchants' sons threw off their rich robes to tramp across the Umbrian hills with the *Poverello*, crushing money underfoot like dung, merchants' daughters surreptitiously opened their pantries to beggars and refused to eat the flesh of cattle obtained

---

[18] VJC Prologue.

[19] Giles Constable, *The Reformation of the Twelfth Century* (Cambridge: Cambridge University Press, 1996); Marie-Dominique Chenu, 'The Evangelical Awakening', in *Nature, Man, and Society in the Twelfth Century*, ed. and trans. by Jerome Taylor and Lester K. Little (Chicago: University of Chicago Press, 1968), pp. 239–69. On parallels between the two regions see Alcantara Mens, *L'Ombrie italienne et l'Ombrie brabançonne: Deux courants religieux parallèles d'inspiration commune* (Paris: Études Franciscaines, 1967).

[20] John T. Noonan, *The Scholastic Analysis of Usury* (Cambridge, MA: Harvard University Press, 1957); Lester K. Little, *Religious Poverty and the Profit Economy in Medieval Europe* (Ithaca: Cornell University Press, 1978); Jacques Le Goff, *Your Money or Your Life: Economy and Religion in the Middle Ages*, trans. by Patricia Ranum (New York: Zone, 1988).

through usury. Evangelical preachers like John of Cantimpré cheered them on, singing the praise of these new voluntary poor who did what they could — never enough, but more than nothing — to help the legions of involuntary poor.[21]

Yet not even the most extreme poverty, chastity, ascetic toil, or missionary zeal sufficed to distinguish the 'living saints' of the evangelical movement from their great rivals, the Cathars, who cultivated the same virtues with equal ardour. Catholic saints needed something more — and that something, for Thomas as for James of Vitry, lay in their fervent devotion to the priesthood.[22] Priests, after all, had the awesome power to command the Almighty, changing bread at a word into the flesh of the infant God — a food for which the saints hungered beyond all measure. By their eucharistic visions and ecstasies, holy women proved how wrong the heretics were to deny such grace.[23] Further, priests could administer the sacrament of penance, which had power to move heaven and earth, for by it demons lost their prey and souls eluded the grasp of hell. Here too living saints offered priests their aid. Not only were their own confessions frequent, scrupulous, and tearful — a very model of penitential practice; but, in addition, through their prophetic gifts they revealed unconfessed sins, shamed the hard-hearted, and encouraged the faint-hearted. By enduring heroic penance far beyond what their sins required, they also released hundreds of poor souls from purgatory.[24] Finally, priests could spread the divine word through

---

[21] Jean Longère, 'Pauvreté et richesse chez quelques prédicateurs durant la seconde moitié du XIIᵉ siècle', in *Études sur l'histoire de la pauvreté*, ed. by Michel Mollat, 2 vols (Paris: Sorbonne, 1974), I, pp. 255–73. On differences between elite and non-elite charity toward the poor see Sharon Farmer, *Surviving Poverty in Medieval Paris: Gender, Ideology, and the Daily Lives of the Poor* (Ithaca: Cornell University Press, 2002).

[22] John Coakley, 'Friars as Confidants of Holy Women in Medieval Dominican Hagiography', in *Images of Sainthood in Medieval Europe*, ed. by Renate Blumenfeld-Kosinski and Timea Szell (Ithaca: Cornell University Press, 1991), pp. 222–46; Jo Ann Kay McNamara, 'The Rhetoric of Orthodoxy: Clerical Authority and Female Innovation in the Struggle with Heresy', in *Maps of Flesh and Light: The Religious Experience of Medieval Women Mystics*, ed. by Ulrike Wiethaus (Syracuse, NY: Syracuse University Press, 1993), pp. 9–27; Dyan Elliott, *Proving Woman: Female Spirituality and Inquisitional Culture in the Later Middle Ages* (Princeton: Princeton University Press, 2004), pp. 47–84.

[23] Caroline Walker Bynum, *Holy Feast and Holy Fast: The Religious Significance of Food to Medieval Women* (Berkeley: University of California Press, 1987). See also Peter Browe, *Die eucharistischen Wunder des Mittelalters* (Breslau: Müller & Seiffert, 1938); Edouard Dumoutet, *Corpus Domini: Aux sources de la piété eucharistique médiévale* (Paris: Beauchesne, 1942).

[24] Jacques Le Goff, *The Birth of Purgatory*, trans. by Arthur Goldhammer (Chicago: University of Chicago Press, 1981), pp. 318–26; Brian Patrick McGuire, 'Purgatory, the

preaching, a medium of immense authority and no small entertainment value. Although few holy women dared to preach directly in defiance of canon law, saints could uphold 'their' preachers with prayer, advise them on delivery, and furnish those compelling exempla that were, for many hearers, the most memorable parts of a sermon.[25] These then were the distinctive traits of the Netherlandish holy women: ardent devotion to the Eucharist, visions and raptures, penitential asceticism, purgatorial piety, and evangelical zeal, all carried to theatrical extremes that reinforced the old hagiographic adage of *admiranda sed non imitanda*.[26]

Scholars have devoted intensive study to the new forms of religious life that emerged in the late twelfth and early thirteenth centuries, especially the beguine movement. In northern France, the Low Countries, and the Rhineland, beguine communities seemed to appear out of nowhere and proliferate with astonishing speed. By the mid-thirteenth century, princely patrons such as Louis IX in France and Countesses Jeanne and Marguerite in Flanders had taken the lead in founding and endowing major houses.[27] But the first beguine generations were

Communion of Saints, and Medieval Change', *Viator*, 20 (1989), 61–84; Barbara Newman, 'On the Threshold of the Dead: Purgatory, Hell, and Religious Women', in her *From Virile Woman to WomanChrist: Studies in Medieval Religion and Literature* (Philadelphia: University of Pennsylvania Press, 1995), pp. 108–36; Robert Sweetman, 'Thomas of Cantimpré, *Mulieres Religiosae*, and Purgatorial Piety: Hagiographical *Vitae* and the Beguine "Voice"', in *A Distinct Voice: Medieval Studies in Honor of Leonard E. Boyle, O.P.*, ed. by Jacqueline Brown and William P. Stoneman (Notre Dame: University of Notre Dame Press, 1997), pp. 606–28.

[25] Nicole Bériou, 'Femmes et prédicateurs: La transmission de la foi au XIIe et XIIIe siècles', in *La Religion de ma mère: Les femmes et la transmission de la foi*, ed. by Jean Delumeau (Paris: Cerf, 1992), pp. 51–70; Bériou, 'The Right of Women to Give Religious Instruction in the Thirteenth Century', in *Women Preachers and Prophets through Two Millennia of Christianity*, ed. by Beverly Mayne Kienzle and Pamela Walker (Berkeley: University of California Press, 1998), pp. 134–45; Claire Waters, *Angels and Earthly Creatures: Preaching, Performance, and Gender in the Later Middle Ages* (Philadelphia: University of Pennsylvania Press, 2004).

[26] Richard Kieckhefer, *Unquiet Souls: Fourteenth-Century Saints and Their Religious Milieu* (Chicago: University of Chicago Press, 1984), pp. 13–15; Caroline Walker Bynum, *Metamorphosis and Identity* (New York: Zone, 2001), pp. 51–53.

[27] Theo Luykx, *Johanna van Constantinopel, Gravin van Vlaanderen en Henegouwen* (Antwerp: Standaard-Boekhandel, 1946); G. Meersseman, 'Jeanne de Constantinople et les Frères Prêcheurs: À propos d'un livre récent', *Archivum Fratrum Praedicatorum*, 19 (1949), 122–68; Penelope Galloway, '"Discreet and Devout Maidens": Women's Involvement in Beguine Communities in Northern France, 1200–1500', in *Medieval Women in Their Communities*, ed. by Diane Watt (Toronto: University of Toronto Press, 1997), pp. 92–115;

far from respectable. As a variety of theological, demographic, and institutional studies have demonstrated, one hallmark of this age of religious ferment was an unusual degree of flexibility and improvisation in one camp, met by rumbles of suspicion and repression from another.[28] But the fault lines do not neatly divide older from newer orders or regulars from extraregulars, much less women from men. Rather, the new evangelical spirit fostered the growth of a supple but vulnerable network of *mulieres religiosae* and *viri spirituales*, including secular clerics such as James of Vitry, Dominicans such as Thomas of Cantimpré, and Cistercians such as Caesarius of Heisterbach and Goswin of Villers.

Women, who tended to pass from one mode of religious life to another as circumstance dictated, can be harder to classify. Thus Mary of Oignies moved from chaste marriage to hospital work with the lepers at Willambrouk to contemplative leisure at Oignies — all without taking vows or modifying her penitential ardour.[29] Christina the Astonishing spent her life as a humble cowherd until her premature death and resurrection. Then, after a longish period as a freelance holy woman, she stayed for nine years with the recluse Jutta at Loon (or Borgloon), though without formal enclosure. When her patron, Count Louis, died in 1218, she left Loon to divide her time between 'the desert' and the Benedictine convent in her home town, Sint-Truiden, where she was finally buried. Lutgard, whose life followed the most traditional pattern, was professed

---

Simons, *Cities of Ladies*, pp. 98–100, 104–09.

[28] The most important work in English is now Simons, *Cities of Ladies*. Three influential older studies are Herbert Grundmann, *Religiöse Bewegungen im Mittelalter* (Berlin: Ebering, 1935; 2nd edn Darmstadt: Wissenschaftliche Buchgesellschaft, 1961), trans. by Steven Rowan as *Religious Movements in the Middle Ages [...]* (Notre Dame: University of Notre Dame Press, 1995); Alcantara Mens, *Oorsprong en Betekenis van de Nederlandse Begijnen Begardenbeweging. Vergelijkende studie: XII^{de}–XIII^{de} eeuw* (Antwerp: Standaard-Boekhandel, 1947); and Ernest W. McDonnell, *The Beguines and Beghards in Medieval Culture, with Special Emphasis on the Belgian Scene* (New Brunswick: Rutgers University Press, 1954). On Cistercian links see Simone Roisin, 'L'Efflorescence cistercienne et le courant féminin de piété au XIIIe siècle', *Revue d'histoire ecclésiastique*, 39 (1943), 342–78; on Dominicans see G. Meersseman, 'Les Frères Prêcheurs et le mouvement dévot en Flandre au XIIIe siècle', *Archivum Fratrum Praedicatorum*, 18 (1948), 69–105 (with text on pp. 106–30); and on Premonstratensians, see Carol Neel, 'The Origins of the Beguines', *Signs*, 14 (1989), 321–41. On fluidity between early beguines and recluses see Anneke B. Mulder-Bakker, *Lives of the Anchoresses: The Rise of the Urban Recluse in Medieval Europe*, trans. by Myra Heerspink Scholz (Philadelphia: University of Pennsylvania Press, 2005), pp. 130–34.

[29] On her marriage see Dyan Elliott, *Spiritual Marriage: Sexual Abstinence in Medieval Wedlock* (Princeton: Princeton University Press, 1993), pp. 239, 253–54, 258–59.

at the same convent but spent most of her career as a Cistercian. Nevertheless, the cloister did not limit her circle of friends and clients, which included not only James of Vitry and Thomas of Cantimpré, but also Jordan of Saxony, Master General of the Dominicans,[30] and any number of beguines and recluses. As for the short-lived Margaret of Ypres, she is often described as a Dominican tertiary because of her confessional relationship with Friar Zeger. But this status was never formalized by adoption of a habit, so she could equally well be characterized as a domestic recluse or beguine. In short, Thomas and the people we meet in his *vitae* do not seem to have worried overmuch about the distinction of orders or the formal markers of profession. It was this very liminality that vexed their critics, who did not like anomalies in the orderly scheme of things. In particular, they did not like *apostolas*, or women in ministry, whether they were advising distinguished clerics, tending lepers, or having inconvenient ecstasies in their parish church.[31] The only proper ministries for a woman, in the eyes of religious conservatives, were raising children at home or praying behind convent walls.

Ministry performed by the wrong people, of course, has always been dangerous. To risk an analogy, in the early twenty-first century we see churches bitterly divided over such issues as women's ordination, clerical celibacy, gay clergy, and same-sex unions. Attitudes on these gendered issues disclose a gaping rift between the Christian Left and the Christian Right, running deeper than the old battle lines between Anglicans and Lutherans, Methodists and Presbyterians, or even Catholics and Protestants. Eight hundred years ago, the hot-button issues already included the ministry of women, along with extraregular religious life, lay preaching, mendicancy, apostolic poverty, frequent communion, and

---

[30] In VLA III.3, Thomas says that 'Lutgard had an amazing love for this venerable man [Master Jordan …] and he confided in her above all women, making her the mother and nourisher of the whole Order of Preachers'.

[31] Both James of Vitry and Thomas of Cantimpré address such critics. James tells Bishop Fulk of Toulouse in VMO Prologue, 4 (in *Mary of Oignies*, p. 43): 'You have seen and marvelled at those shameless men […] who, hostile to all religion, maliciously slandered the religious life of these women and, like mad dogs, railed against customs which were contrary to theirs.' Cf. VLA III.5: 'May that vile slanderer blush for shame — he who said and wrote that people who record the fantastic visions of insignificant women (*muliercularum*) should be considered profane!' See also Renate Blumenfeld-Kosinski, 'Satirical Views of the Beguines in Northern French Literature', in *New Trends in Feminine Spirituality: The Holy Women of Liège and Their Impact*, ed. by Juliette Dor, Lesley Johnson, and Jocelyn Wogan-Browne (Turnhout: Brepols, 1999), pp. 237–49.

ecstatic revelations. Then, as now, the line between those who generally favoured such things and those who opposed them cut deeper than the 'denominational' differences of Cistercians, Franciscans, Dominicans, and secular clergy. Within each order there was a gap, sometimes wider, sometimes narrower, between supporters of the lay religious movement and foes. These internal divisions, which could split even individual houses, explain an otherwise baffling discrepancy between the official positions of religious orders, which were often hostile, and the spotty enforcement of their General Chapters' decrees against devoting more resources to the *cura mulierum*, or pastoral care of women.[32]

But analogies have their limits, and it would be a grave mistake to consider the *mulieres religiosae* and their clerical allies as constituting a 'Christian Left' in the modern sense of religious tolerance or pacifism. The struggle against heresy was, of course, not only theological but military. Even if Thomas felt that James of Vitry had abandoned his pastoral mission in Liège, James himself perceived a clear continuity between his championship of the staunchly pro-clerical beguines and his later work as a crusade preacher and Catholic bishop in the Muslim and Orthodox East. It is no coincidence that he dedicated his *Life of Mary of Oignies* to Fulk of Toulouse — first troubadour, then Cistercian monk, finally militant anti-heretical bishop, who had come to the Low Countries in the first place to solicit funds and knights for the Albigensian Crusade.[33] Later in his career, James would enrich the priory of Oignies with precious relics and other spoils of the East, and Lutgard of Aywières was among the many correspondents to whom he sent dispatches from the Holy Land.[34] Thomas shared James's sense of urgency in the anti-Cathar campaign as well as his support for the Crusades. His hero, John of Cantimpré, was instrumental in the death sentence of at least one Cathar, early in his career,[35] and Lutgard fasted against heretics for seven

---

[32] For a sweeping but trenchant assessment of the religious orders' approaches to women, see Jo Ann Kay McNamara, *Sisters in Arms: Catholic Nuns through Two Millennia* (Cambridge, MA: Harvard University Press, 1996), Chs 10 and 11.

[33] Dyan Elliott, 'The Beguines: A Sponsored Emergence', in her *Proving Woman*, pp. 47–84; Ulrike Wiethaus, 'The Death Song of Marie d'Oignies: Mystical Sound and Hagiographical Politics in Medieval Lorraine', in *The Texture of Society: Medieval Women in the Southern Low Countries*, ed. by Ellen Kittell and Mary Suydam (New York: Palgrave Macmillan, 2004), pp. 153–79. On Fulk's career see Nicole Schulman, *Where Troubadours Were Bishops: The Occitania of Folc of Marseille, 1150–1231* (New York: Routledge, 2001).

[34] *Lettres de Jacques de Vitry, 1160/1170–1240*, ed. by R. B. C. Huygens (Leiden: Brill, 1960), pp. 79–97.

[35] VJC I.9. John's role is perhaps deliberately left vague.

years, perhaps in response to what she heard from James.[36] Christina the Astonishing, who knew prophetically when Jerusalem fell to Saladin in 1187, rejoiced at the news because of the impending Third Crusade. In the words Thomas puts in her mouth, she exulted with Christ 'because he has given so many men the occasion by which they might be saved [...] Men shall shed their blood in this affair of the Holy Land and they, in turn, shall repay the death of Christ with great devotion.'[37]

We can set many of Thomas of Cantimpré's distinctive traits in relief by comparing him with other hagiographers of his general milieu. One feature that distinguishes the whole array of Netherlandish *vitae*, setting these *Lives* apart from earlier hagiography, is their overwhelmingly pastoral character. *Vitae* often had institutional aims; many were written to enhance the prestige of religious houses or orders by advertising the holiness of their founders. This, to be sure, was one purpose of the *Life of John of Cantimpré*. Thomas took pains in this *Life* to glorify not only the abbot, but also his first brethren, his successor, his illustrious converts, and his prioress at the sister-house of Prémy. Likewise, *vitae* often served to reinforce existing saint cults or inaugurate new ones by attracting pilgrims to miracle-working shrines. We can see traces of this intention in the *Lives* of Mary of Oignies and Lutgard, with their emphasis on the writers' eagerness to secure holy relics. But even in these *vitae*, and all the more in *Christina the Astonishing* and *Margaret of Ypres*, local prestige and cult are subordinated to another end — the pastoral teaching to be drawn from the saints' deeds and sufferings. Thomas was first and last a preacher who used all genres — anecdotes, saints' lives, even natural science — to craft edifying, unforgettable lessons. Just as the *Book of Bees* is filled with hagiographic tales, his *vitae* are no less crammed with what his contemporary, Stephen of Bourbon, called *materia praedicabilis*.[38] From these texts a preacher could glean memorable tales about the urgency of penance, the majesty and intimacy of Christ's eucharistic presence, the evil of usury, the malice and vulnerability of demons, the pains of purgatory, and the benefits of prayer. In their original form the *vitae* enjoyed uneven success: we have twelve Latin manuscripts of Christina, nine of Lutgard, three of Margaret, and just one of John of Cantimpré. Yet Christina's

---

[36] VLA II.2.

[37] VCM 32–33.

[38] Étienne de Bourbon [Stephen of Bourbon], *Tractatus de diversis materiis praedicabilibus*; abridged trans. by A. Lecoy de La Marche in *Anecdotes historiques, légendes et apologues, tirés du recueil inédit d'Étienne de Bourbon* (Paris: Librairie Renouard, 1877).

Life was also translated into Dutch and English, Lutgard's into Dutch and French, and Margaret's into German, indicating a readership beyond the author's fellow Dominicans.[39] Even this vernacular evidence cannot tell us how many laymen and women heard the exploits of one or another saint used to reinforce the point of a sermon.

This emphasis on the anecdotal may account for one key difference between Thomas's *vitae* and his most important model, the *Life of Mary of Oignies*. James organized his first book around the saint's virtues and ascetic disciplines, while his second is structured by the seven gifts of the Holy Spirit listed in Isaiah 11. 2. Thomas used no such schemes. In *Lutgard* and his late prologue to *John of Cantimpré*, he mentions three spiritual stages corresponding to beginners (*incipientes*), advanced students (*proficientes*), and adepts (*perfecti*), but this structure bears less theological weight than one might think.[40] His main organizing device is simply a loose chronology, aided by the clustering of thematically related anecdotes on usury, prophecy, healing, and so forth. Obviously, Thomas has a religious agenda, but it is to be found more in his individual anecdotes than in any ambitious theological scheme imposed on his material.

Simone Roisin, the first scholar to write expressly on 'Thomas of Cantimpré's hagiographic method', discerned the author's own spiritual development in the increasingly inward focus of his *vitae*. On her reading, Thomas stressed external wonders in the *Supplement to Mary of Oignies* and *Christina the Astonishing*, ascetic virtues in *Margaret of Ypres*, and mystical graces in *Lutgard of Aywières*.[41] She ascribes this shift to Cistercian influence, arguing that in the 1230s, in between *Christina* and *Margaret*, Thomas must have read the trilogy of *vitae* by his contemporary Goswin of Bossut, cantor at the Cistercian house of Villers. Goswin's *Lives* commemorate the nun Ida of Nivelles (d. 1231), the lay brother

---

[39] I cite these figures, with my thanks, from Jennifer Carpenter's unpublished database on manuscripts of the Netherlandish *vitae*.

[40] But see Margot King's notes to the VCM and VLA, in which she argues that the stages of both saints' *Lives* correspond to the animal, rational, and spiritual phases in William of Saint-Thierry's analysis of the contemplative soul's development.

[41] Simone Roisin, 'La Méthode hagiographique de Thomas de Cantimpré', in *Miscellanea Historica in Honorem Alberti de Meyer*, 2 vols (Louvain: Bibliothèque de l'Université, 1946), I, pp. 546–57.

Arnulf (d. 1228), and the monk Abundus of Huy (d. 1239).[42] The hypothesis is plausible, for Lutgard's *Life* recalls Ida's in many respects, although their similarities surely owe much to the women's own spirituality as Cistercian nuns. Less predictably, the extravagant penances of Christina the Astonishing can be compared with the almost equally extreme (and incredible) ascetic feats Goswin ascribes to the lay brother Arnulf of Villers. Both the lives and the *Lives* of these two saints are contemporary. But in this case, the parallels suggest not so much literary influence as a correlation between ferocious corporeal penance and a saint's lay status (rather than gender, as argued in earlier discussions).[43]

More broadly, Thomas of Cantimpré shares two of the three hallmarks of Goswin's spirituality that I identified in a preface to his *vitae*.[44] These are a sense of transparency about the inner life and a focus on community. Both hagiographers valued such mystical experiences as visions, revelations, and ecstasies, and more strikingly, both shared a confidence that these extraordinary states could be communicated with ease, whether in words or in direct, telepathic access to the souls of others. Further, both wrote for and about a broadly conceived network of spiritual friends transcending the boundaries of language, gender, and religious profession, as noted earlier. But Thomas was in one sense less optimistic than Goswin. The Cistercian seldom worried about false visions or demonic delusions, whereas the Dominican, a grizzled veteran of the confessional, had a much keener sense of the possibilities for spiritual self-deception. Even so, stories of false spirituality and delusion are much more common in the *Book of Bees* than in the saints' *Lives*.[45] Yet Thomas was unfazed by the miraculous, a concept he used freely. Events are forever occurring *miro modo*, 'in a wondrous way', yet the author's constant refrain is *Quid miri?* 'Why marvel?' The rhetorical question introduces a scholastic or exegetical gloss on the significance of the miracle.

---

[42] *Send Me God: The Lives of Ida the Compassionate of Nivelles, Nun of La Ramée, Arnulf, Lay Brother of Villers, and Abundus, Monk of Villers, by Goswin of Bossut*, ed. and trans. by Martinus Cawley (Turnhout: Brepols, 2003).

[43] Compare Martha Newman, 'Crucified by the Virtues: Monks, Lay Brothers, and Women in Thirteenth-Century Cistercian Saints' Lives', in *Gender and Difference in the Middle Ages*, ed. by Sharon Farmer and Carol Braun Pasternack (Minneapolis: University of Minnesota Press, 2003), pp. 182–209.

[44] Barbara Newman, Preface to *Send Me God*, pp. xlvi–xlvii.

[45] Elliott, *Proving Woman*, pp. 250–53.

Not surprisingly, scholars have devoted much attention to Thomas's views on gender. He was not immune to some widely held misogynist beliefs of his culture, such as the oft-cited notions that women cannot keep silent, but can extort any secret from the hearts of men.[46] In his *Life of Lutgard*, Thomas mentions the saint's early menopause as a sign of her liberation from 'the nuisance with which God tamed pride in the sex of Eve'.[47] Yet, despite sharing such conventional views, Thomas himself was no misogynist. As Katrien Heene has noted, his *vitae* are 'populated with virtuous women: pious widows, abbesses, nuns, recluses and noble laywomen all pass in revue.' But no stereotypical 'bad women' appear, and in fact, villains of either sex are rare: 'there are no men nor women who are vicious by nature, but only people in distress who need the saint's help'.[48] John of Cantimpré is never tempted by a seductress, that stock figure in masculine *vitae*. Rather, it is Lutgard who has to foil an attempted rape. Sometimes worldly women obstruct the saints' efforts: Christina the Astonishing is — understandably — chained by her sisters, who believe she is mad and wish to keep her from harming herself, while Margaret of Ypres' bid for holiness is initially opposed by her mother. But in both cases, the misguided family members eventually come around. Similarly, a noblewoman whom Margaret rebukes for oppressing her peasants soon repents and lightens their burden.

As a witness to the charismatic authority of *mulieres religiosae*, John Coakley finds Thomas's position close to his mentor's: 'Like James he sees holy women as, in effect, marking a boundary of priestly authority by displaying powers that lie beyond the priest's grasp'.[49] In Coakley's view, Thomas is somewhat more cautious than James in affirming those powers. If so, it may be in part because

---

[46] VJC II.3 and III.2; VLA III.19; Alexandra Barratt, 'Language and the Body in Thomas of Cantimpré's *Life* of Lutgard of Aywières', *Cistercian Studies Quarterly*, 30 (1995), 339–47 (pp. 346–47).

[47] VLA II.21.

[48] Katrien Heene, 'Hagiography and Gender: A Tentative Case-Study on Thomas of Cantimpré', in '*Scribere sanctorum gesta*': *Recueil d'études d'hagiographie médiévale offert à Guy Philippart*, ed. by Étienne Renard and others (Turnhout: Brepols, 2005), pp. 109–23 (p. 115).

[49] John Coakley, 'Thomas of Cantimpré and Female Sanctity', in *History in the Comic Mode: Medieval Communities and the Matter of Person*, ed. by Rachel Fulton and Bruce Holsinger (New York: Columbia University Press, 2007), pp. 45–55 (p. 55). On relationships between clerics and holy women see also John Coakley, *Women, Men, and Spiritual Power: Female Saints and Their Male Collaborators* (New York: Columbia University Press, 2006), and *Gendered Voices: Medieval Saints and Their Interpreters*, ed. by Catherine M. Mooney (Philadelphia: University of Pennsylvania Press, 1999).

his friend Lutgard was a cloistered nun, unlike Mary of Oignies, while Margaret remained under Zeger's tight control, so neither had the same opportunities for transgression. But Christina, whom no one could control, went so far as to hear Count Louis's deathbed confession, at his own request, in lieu of a priest. This famous incident unnerved Thomas so much that he felt a need to remind readers that Christina had no power to absolve the count. All she could do was pray for him and share his purgatorial torments.[50] Nevertheless, no jealousy of clerical prerogatives kept Thomas from telling this story, which he could easily have suppressed, as a testimony to the saint's merits.

Inevitably, of course, Thomas perceived his female saints from a distance. Despite his warm admiration, each holy woman remains in some sense a marvelous Other. Most illuminating in this regard is Karen Glente's comparison of Thomas with a later Dominican hagiographer — Catherine of Gueberschwihr or Unterlinden, author of the nuns' early fourteenth-century sister-book.[51] Glente shows that, where Thomas sought to arouse *admiratio*, Catherine wrote expressly to encourage *imitatio*. As a sister belonging to the same house as her subjects, she clearly identified with the earlier nuns in much the way Thomas identified with his founding abbot, John of Cantimpré, rather than his female saints. Although both Thomas and Catherine emphasize visions and miracles, Catherine ascribes greater agency to her holy women: they take initiatives and the grace of God responds, whereas Thomas views God as the initiator and the woman as respondent. This pattern appears especially in the image of Christ as wooer. One way Thomas tried to accommodate the otherness of Margaret and Lutgard was by invoking the fashionable paradigm of bridal spirituality, which might (or might not) have been as much his own projection as their experience. Thus he constructs Margaret's conversion as a rivalry between her potential husband, a carpenter, and 'the eternal Lover of human souls', who — acting through Zeger — 'espoused her by a hidden calling and did not permit her to be carried off by another lover'.[52] Once her affections had been successfully

---

[50] VCM 44–45.

[51] Karen Glente, 'Mystikerinnenviten aus männlicher und weiblicher Sicht: Ein Vergleich zwischen Thomas von Cantimpré und Katherina von Unterlinden', in *Religiöse Frauenbewegung und mystische Frömmigkeit im Mittelalter*, ed. by Peter Dinzelbacher and Dieter Bauer (Cologne: Böhlau, 1988), pp. 251–64. For the sister-book see 'Les "*Vitae Sororum*" d'Unterlinden', ed. by Jeanne Ancelet-Hustache, *Archives d'histoire doctrinale et littéraire du moyen âge*, 5 (1930), 317–509.

[52] VMY 5.

transferred to the friar, Margaret worried that she was offending God because 'she loved her spiritual father more than anybody or anything she had in the world', but Christ reassured her that she had nothing to fear on that account.[53] Similarly, Christ has to woo the young Lutgard away from a noble suitor by coming to her in the first of many visions and displaying his wounds: 'Do not seek any longer the caresses of unseemly love. Here you may perpetually contemplate what you should love and why you should love it.'[54] A devout matron then prophesies that Lutgard will become a second Agnes — citing the virgin martyr who proclaims in a well-known liturgical text, 'I am betrothed to him whom the angels serve, at whose beauty the sun and moon marvel [...] I love Christ into whose chamber I shall enter, whose Mother is a virgin, whose Father knows not woman.'[55] As brides of Christ, Lutgard and Margaret become immediately comprehensible within the terms of male-authored hagiographic convention. Interestingly, the lower-class, untamable Christina is never cast in this role.

In a 1989 article on James of Vitry's *Life of Mary*, Michel Lauwers raised what is now a familiar question about medieval women: how far can we ever understand their spirituality on the basis of male constructions of it?[56] As I have indicated, no *vita* is ever an 'innocent' biography in the sense of having no theological or pastoral agenda. Without corroborating evidence, we can never truly know whether it was Margaret herself, Zeger of Lille, or Thomas of Cantimpré who first fashioned her as a bride of Christ, much less whether Christina truly performed all the bizarre feats ascribed to her with the intention of liberating souls. Yet Robert Sweetman has published a convincing reply to Lauwers, arguing that even if Thomas of Cantimpré constructed his saints to promote particular ends, those very ends were shaped by religious women's

---

[53] VMY 25.

[54] VLA I.2.

[55] Antiphon and Responsory for the Feast of St Agnes, 21 January, Roman Breviary. See *The Hours of the Divine Office in English and Latin*, 3 vols (Collegeville, MN: Liturgical Press, 1963), I, pp. 1705, 1707. These texts were also used for the Common of Virgins and for women's monastic profession. Cf. Jacobus de Voragine, *The Golden Legend: Readings on the Saints*, trans. by William Granger Ryan, 2 vols (Princeton: Princeton University Press, 1993), I, p. 102.

[56] Michel Lauwers, 'L'Expérience béguinale et récit hagiographique: À propos de la *Vita Mariae Oigniacensis* de Jacques de Vitry (vers 1215)', *Journal des savants*, 11 (1989), 61–103. See also John Coakley, 'James of Vitry and the Other World of Mary of Oignies', in *Women, Men, and Spiritual Power*, pp. 68–88.

influence on his own piety. The clearest case in point is his abiding interest in purgatory — a concern largely absent from his early *De natura rerum* and *John of Cantimpré*,[57] but crucial to his *Supplement to the Life of Mary*, central in *Christina* and *Lutgard*, and still prominent in the *Book of Bees*. Nor does Thomas in these texts view purgatorial suffering from the contemporary scholastic or homiletic angles discussed in Jacques Le Goff's *Birth of Purgatory*, which covers the same period. Rather, his treatment is intensely personal: 'Purgatory is the face of the beloved dead, a face that seeks a boon of the living, a boon that, when given, gives itself in return.'[58] This kind of 'haunted personalism', Sweetman argues, is not a devotion Thomas imposed on the *mulieres religiosae* but one that he learned from them, for it is also found in James's *Life of Mary* and other female *vitae* from the diocese of Liège, including Juette of Huy and Juliana of Mont-Cornillon. Yet Margaret of Ypres, a woman of Flanders rather than Brabant, seems not to have shared this concern. In his purgatorial piety, therefore, Thomas may be a reliable witness to a mode of spirituality distinctive to the holy women of Liège.

Abbot John of Cantimpré: A Northern Francis

Even though Thomas of Cantimpré's first hero was not destined to become a miracle-working saint, he remains an outstanding exemplar of the late twelfth-century evangelical movement. John was ordained a priest in 1177, but 'still a young man' when he visited the abbey of Saint-Victor in 1183, so he was probably born around 1155. At that time of enormous expansion within the clerical ranks, ecclesiastical careers lay open to talent, offering upward mobility for young men of promise. Thus John, though born to artisan parents 'who lived by the work of their hands', somehow managed to study theology in Paris (I.1–3). Perhaps his schooling was financed by the same parish priest who, upon his return, recommended him to the bishop of Cambrai for ordination. While still a deacon, the young John had already earned a reputation for brilliant anti-heretical preaching when his preferments began. His first chapel at Cantimpré, initially a hospital, was endowed by a prosperous burgher as a chantry for his deceased son. Further endowments by the bishop of Cambrai (Roger of Wavrin) and the castellan (Hugh III of Oisy) gave John enough land and revenues to

---

[57] The one exception is VJC II.1, an anecdote concerning the saint's mother.

[58] Sweetman, 'Thomas of Cantimpré, *Mulieres Religiosae*, and Purgatorial Piety', p. 612.

establish a house of regular canons, observing the Augustinian Rule, and soon he decided to affiliate with the Victorines of Paris.

Interestingly, the famous abbey required yet more fund-raising 'because a house that still lacked sufficient material foundations could be shaken by ill fortune and the religious reduced to public begging, to the disgrace of the whole order' (I.14). For a champion of poverty, John was remarkably successful in attracting donations, and with help from his patrons, he succeeded in this mission. So Cantimpré with its first six canons became a daughter of Saint-Victor in 1183. Nevertheless, we should not envision these men as contemplative scholars in the lineage of Hugh and Richard of Saint-Victor. Even after John was raised to the rank of abbot, a dignity that came with his new affiliation, he did not devote himself to leisured writing and liturgical prayer. Rather, he immediately resumed his work as a circuit-riding preacher, 'visit[ing] the cities, villages, castles, and towns just as he had always done, taking pains for the salvation of souls' (I.18). His zeal was great but his health poor, allowing Thomas an unforgettable vignette: when the diminutive abbot once found himself without a horse but felt too fatigued to walk, he rode two miles on the shoulders of a brawny servant to the village where he was meant to preach (II.10). From the vantage point of a preaching friar like Thomas, John looks very much like a Dominican *avant la lettre*.

Allowing for some hyperbole intrinsic to the genre, Thomas paints a credible and individual portrait of his subject, for he had access to numerous informants who still remembered him vividly. Brother Julian, whom Thomas identifies as a close friend, recalls that when Dom John preached against heretics in Cambrai, 'heavenly grace seemed to flash from his mouth like a bolt of lightning. Thunderstruck by his urgency, all the people were in such ecstasy that their hair stood on end. Without delay this divine horror, transfused into their souls, brought a great many to eternal salvation' (II.11). The preacher's charismatic presence so awed the crowds, Thomas claims, that no sooner would he ascend the pulpit and announce his theme 'than everyone would already be stricken with compunction and dissolved in tears' (II.9). But his way with the nobility was gentler, and he persuaded a great many knights and lords to 'follow the naked Christ' — some evidently to join the Third and Fourth Crusades. Although John never glorified poverty for its own sake in Franciscan style, he loathed economic oppression in all its forms, both the older feudal mode and the newer commercial mode. 'With the greatest urgency and persistence', Thomas writes, 'he attacked people devoted to usury and unjust profit-taking, for there were many of them who oppressed the urban poor' (II.12).

Active a generation before Francis, who cast off his father's clothes around the time of John's death (*c.* 1206), Dom John agreed with such contemporary moralists as Peter the Chanter, William of Auxerre, Robert of Courçon, and James of Vitry that moneylending was an intrinsically vicious and exploitive trade.[59] Insisting on full restitution before he would absolve a usurer, John favoured public spectacle as a means of shaming. In a dramatic scene that anticipates Franciscan hagiography, Thomas describes a 'typical' conversion:

> Some were so conscience-stricken at his preaching, knowing there was no justice in them, that they publicly stripped off their clothes down to their bare shame, moved by repentance for their former lives, and utterly renounced all that they had. Congratulating these penitents, John would embrace them as members of his family, and indeed his own children. Turning to the people he used to say, 'Who will clothe my children who have made themselves poor and naked for Christ's sake?' At this word you would see nobles and distinguished people competing with each other to throw off their garments. You would see tunics and cloaks flying through the air from the violence of those who threw them, naked men clothed and overwhelmed, and the people shouting to heaven with a mighty voice. Seeing this the blessed man dissolved in tears and said to the people, 'Rejoice and be glad, brothers, for there is greater joy in heaven over these who repent than over ninety-nine righteous who need no repentance.' (II.12)

Thomas singles out two of John's most spectacular conversions for full treatment, one of a feudal lord, the other of an urban moneylender. Both narratives include ceremonies of public penance for the restitution of plundered goods. John of Montmirail, the converted baron, is lauded at such length that his deeds constitute a mini-*vita* embedded in the larger one.[60] As lord of Oisy in succession to Hugh III, this John had been notoriously cruel, but after conversion he took to piety with a vengeance. Upon finding a leprous priest at a hospice in Provins, he took 'no account of the leprosy, the wounds, the sores, the pus, or the dripping blood, [but] fell upon the man, all afire with the spirit of God, and caressed the face and hands that had once devoutly offered the singular sacrifice' (II.8b). Whenever he saw a eucharistic procession, John knelt before the sacrament in the mud — remaining miraculously undefiled by filth.

---

[59] Little, *Religious Poverty*, p. 39. For later scholastic critiques and some defences, see pp. 178–83, as well as Noonan, *The Scholastic Analysis of Usury*. Le Goff, in his *Your Money or Your Life*, includes numerous exempla against usurers similar to those in the VJC.

[60] Thomas borrowed from an earlier *Vita Ioannis de Monte-Mirabili* composed by a monk of Longpont (AASS, 29 September, VIII, pp. 186–235). Although much of his material comes from this text and its continuations, he also interviewed a knight, Philip of Montmirail, who had been close to John.

But it was only after he had become a Cistercian at Longpont in 1209 that he performed his most dramatic penitential act. Returning to his old fiefdom in his new monastic garb, he encouraged three hundred grave-diggers in the cemetery of Cambrai to ridicule him, then passed on to the town of Havrincourt 'where almost all the people of the land had assembled so that he could make restitution to them' (II.8b). For this ceremony a huge mound of silver had been heaped on a table, presumably in the public square. John knelt down before it, raised his eyes and hands to heaven, and begged rich and poor alike to forgive him before he disbursed the cash. As he did so, 'it was not enough for him to bestow a kiss of peace on their faces unless his holy kiss touched the feet of someone of the very meanest class'. When an elderly woman, 'abhorring her lord's great humility', withdrew her hand from his proffered kiss, he bestowed it on her foot instead, triumphantly completing the rite. In relating these events, Thomas is more impressed by John's ostentatious humility than by his peasants' claim to justice: the old woman whom the prince-monk deigns to kiss remains 'despicable' in the writer's eyes. Nevertheless, such spectacular displays served more than one purpose. The peasants regained a portion of their due, John of Montmirail won the salvation of his soul, John of Cantimpré earned points in heaven, and the onlookers were mightily edified by an exemplum come to life.

One of John's converted moneylenders, Alard, carried the ritual theatre of penance even further. After restoring all the properties he had exacted through usury and distributing the rest of his money to the poor, he requested that a pit be dug beneath the threshold of his house so that he could be pulled out of it naked, with a rope around his neck. 'To set an example for others', Thomas writes, 'John shrewdly granted this request' (II.13). Stripped to his skin before the public, Alard performed his penitential drama of death and rebirth. As he was being led in procession by the rope, he realized that he was still wearing a little fur cap which he violently hurled to the ground, saying, 'I do not have even this much that I can rightly call my own'. The spectators, of course, wept buckets as they saw Alard re-clothed in donated garb. When the penitent arrived at church, he was released from the rope as a sign of absolution, but immediately took up the cross in its stead. Thomas concludes his tale of 'that happy beggar who was transformed from a rich man into a pauper, or rather from a pauper into a millionaire' in heaven, by celebrating his holy end. After traveling with the party of Count Baldwin IX on crusade, Alard died under the open sky in Jerusalem, stung incessantly by wasps, whom he welcomed with the remark that he was 'worthy of even harsher stings'.

Rituals of stripping and re-clothing figured in many sectors of medieval life. We might compare a knight's ceremonial arming, a nun's clothing in the habit, a monarch's coronation, a new bride's adoption of the wimple. But unlike the others, this rite centres less on the dignity of the new garb than on the liminal moment of nakedness: *nudus nudum Christum sequi*, in Jerome's famous phrase.[61] As Henri Platelle has shown, the original 'paraliturgy' devised by Alard for his conversion also draws on a judicial source.[62] When a man committed the mortal sin of suicide in his own house, a hole was dug beneath his door and his body dragged out by a rope, so as not to defile the sacred threshold (*limen*, as in the anthropological concept of 'liminality'). In emerging from his own house by this means, Alard signifies his ritual suicide as a usurer so that he can be reborn from the womb of the earth as a penitent. Like St Francis and Angela of Foligno after him, he so revels in his penance that each new humiliation represents a further step toward sanctity, culminating in his wretched but unmistakably holy death.

Vignettes like these, for all their theatricality, illustrate a radical program of reform. They were not merely feel-good gestures, thirteenth-century photo opportunities that left lives essentially unchanged, for the poor got real restitution for their losses, and by the end of the ritual, the rich were no longer rich except in grace. From their better-known Franciscan analogues, we learn how powerfully hearts and minds could be kindled by such spectacles as a naked moneylender led by a rope or a repentant lord kissing the feet of his peasants. Although Thomas of Cantimpré was not above paying compliments to pious nobles, whom he greatly preferred to merchants, he himself was no friend of wealth and power. In the *Book of Bees* he traced the origin of kings to Nimrod, the mighty hunter of Genesis 10, as the first man who 'began to oppress and rule subjects by force; then kings arose and subjected the whole world to unjust laws'. The same passage goes on to quote Augustine's maxim from *The City of God*:

[61] The formula goes back to Jerome, *Epistulae*, Ep. 125 ad Rusticum monachum (PL 22:1085): 'Si habes substantiam, vende et da pauperibus. Si non habes, grandi onere liberatus est, nudum Christum, nudus sequere.' For other examples in Jerome see Achard de Saint-Victor, *Sermons inédits*, ed. by Jean Châtillon (Paris: Vrin, 1970), pp. 259–60. See also Giles Constable, '"Nudus nudum Christum sequi" and Parallel Formulas in the Twelfth Century: A Supplementary Dossier', in *Continuity and Discontinuity in Church History: Essays Presented to George Hunston Williams*, ed. by F. Forester Church and Timothy George (Leiden: Brill, 1979), pp. 83–91.

[62] Henri Platelle, 'Conversions spectaculaires et langage symbolique (Cambrai XIIᵉ siècle): De la polyvalence des symboles', *Bulletin philologique et historique* (1980), 27–38.

'what are great kingdoms but great robberies?'[63] But Thomas's pessimism about the violence of worldly power was balanced by an even greater optimism about the power of apostolic preaching and example. He and his abbot John truly believed in the beatitudes: they believed that those afflicted with a hunger and thirst for justice could be satisfied here and now; that the eternal fate of the powerful lay in the hands of the meek; that the poor in spirit would not only receive the kingdom of heaven, but enact it on earth. As a testament to that faith, the *Life of John of Cantimpré* might well be the most radical of Thomas's *vitae*.

It is also, beyond doubt, the most solidly anchored in its social world. Alongside the spectacular conversions of the rich and powerful, Thomas includes a few sentences on Brother Geoffrey, who was so merciful that in winter, he would rip the thick lining out of his own coat to stuff the boots of the poor; and he designed a special toilet seat for the disabled, perhaps the first such invention on record (I.15). 'Nota humile officium', as an early modern reader remarked in the margin. The same reader was fascinated with other period details that make this *vita* such a rich historical source, among them the exquisitely woven floral crown that Robert Mauvoisin wears at a Christmas court — green even in the dead of winter, as in a scene from Chrétien de Troyes (II.9). To illustrate John's gifts as a confessor, Thomas presents us with a thief who kneels in feigned penitence to steal the abbot's purse, but is instead converted to real penance by his exhortations (II.21). In another exemplum on penance, we meet a brother and sister suspected of killing a rich merchant they have entertained as a guest. Sentenced to the ordeal of hot iron, each one first submits to the sacrament of penance. When the bandages are removed from their hands a few days later, the brother's burns have festered, while his equally guilty sister's have healed — because she had the wisdom to choose Dom John as her confessor. Thus the sister is immediately set free, the brother put to death (II.6). Although the tale is told to exalt the power of John's prayers, it is more likely to suggest why ordeals were outlawed by the Fourth Lateran Council only a few years later. Lepers appear as well, not just to be ostentatiously kissed by John of Montmirail, but as part of an even more grisly judicial scene: we learn that murderers were buried alive and guarded until sunset, after which the town lepers were permitted to dig them up and strip off their clothes (II.8b).

---

[63] BUA II.33.I, pp. 370–71; Augustine, *De civitate Dei*, IV.4, ed. by Bernard Dombart and Alphonsus Kalbin, in CCSL 47, p. 101; Platelle, 'Le Recueil', pp. 483–84, 496.

In the last book of the *vita*, Thomas presents John in a new role as counselor to Marie of Champagne, young wife of the crusading Count Baldwin IX of Flanders. This Marie was a granddaughter of Eleanor of Aquitaine and daughter of the more famous Marie of Champagne (d. 1198) who patronized Chrétien and other literary figures. Baldwin's wife Marie, like her younger contemporary, St Elizabeth of Hungary, was a princess renowned for piety and charity. Thomas credits her saintliness to his hero: 'During a brief period after [John] began to visit her, he led her to such sublime perfection that she would often rise from her bed before dawn, content with only a single maid, to visit poor sick people in the neighbouring villages, walking barefoot to distribute alms' (III.3). Dom John resisted his role as confessor to the countess, afraid that court favour would blunt his freedom to rebuke sin. But he nonetheless assisted at the birth of Marie's daughter Jeanne, the future countess of Flanders, in 1199/1200. Thomas also credits John with a role in the troubling events of the Fourth Crusade, the same expedition on which the ex-moneylender Alard died. After the diversion of that crusade in 1204, when its Venetian leaders decided to sack Constantinople instead of proceeding to Jerusalem, Baldwin of Flanders was elected as Latin Emperor of the east. According to Thomas, whose knowledge of the events is hazy, Baldwin summoned Marie to join him in the imperial city after his election, and she in turn called a council of vassals to help her decide whether to obey that command or more prudently remain at home, guarding her land and daughters. Her barons advised the latter course except for John, who 'steadfastly resisted the advice of all' and urged wifely obedience (III.5). It was this counsel that Marie accepted, Thomas says. But he might have been less eager to magnify John's role had he recalled how the affair turned out. In reality Marie, who had herself taken the crusaders' cross, took ship for the Holy Land even before Baldwin's election, only to die of the plague in Acre in August 1204. In April 1205, less than a year after his election, Baldwin was captured and killed by the Bulgars.[64]

It was at this point in the tale that Thomas laid down his pen, and by the time he resumed his task more than forty years later, his informants were long gone. So his brief, formulaic account of John's death may be largely hagiographic invention. We do not even know its date. Thomas merely notes that Cambrai was under interdict at the time (1205–10), and he earlier states that the abbot

---

[64] Robert Lee Wolff, 'Baldwin of Flanders and Hainaut, First Latin Emperor of Constantinople: His Life, Death, and Resurrection, 1172–1225', *Speculum*, 27 (1952), 281–322 (pp. 288–90).

died before John of Montmirail entered Longpont, which he did in the spring
of 1209. But the coda to this *Life* contains one indisputable fact: John died and
was buried, not with his brothers at Cantimpré, but with his sisters at Prémy.
That in itself is a testament to the role that *mulieres religiosae* now played on the
evangelical scene.

Christina the Astonishing: A Woman Possessed

In sharp contrast to the *Life of John of Cantimpré*, which despite its hagiographic
goals manages to be a plausible biography situated in a realistic social world, the
Life of Christina has proved all but impervious to history. It even begins like a
fairy tale: once upon a time there were three orphaned sisters. They decided that
the oldest should devote herself to prayer, the second look after the house, and
the youngest pasture the cows — and of course, it was the humble cowherd who
received God's grace. The level of plausibility hardly rises with Christina's
miraculous resurrection and superhuman feats of penance. Even by the standards
of hagiography, much of her behaviour seems not so much saintly or idealized
as just plain weird. It is little wonder that Thomas gave her the sobriquet of
mirabilis, 'the Astonishing', or that his first critical reader, Simone Roisin, called
this *Life* a 'tissue of extravagances', childishly obsessed with marvels.[65] Yet, as we
have seen, it was the most successful of all Thomas's *vitae*, inspiring not only
vernacular translations but also the high regard of such theologians as Denis the
Carthusian and, later, Cardinal Bellarmine.[66] Since the *Life of Christina*
presupposes such a wide gap between *admiranda* and *credenda* (there can be no
question of *imitanda*!), it will be helpful to approach it from two distinct angles,
first locating its heroine within ordinary space and time as best we can, and only
then exploring Thomas's theological project.

   What, concretely, can we say about Christina's life beyond the realm of
mirabilia? First, she can be reliably linked with three places. One is the
Benedictine monastery of St Catherine's in Sint-Truiden, where Lutgard was a
nun from about 1194 to 1206. Christina was on close terms with many of the
sisters there: she commiserated with one whose father fought in the deadly battle

---

[65] Roisin, 'La Méthode hagiographique', p. 553.

[66] Margot H. King, 'The Sacramental Witness of Christina *Mirabilis*: The Mystic Growth
of a Fool for Christ's Sake', in *Peace Weavers*, ed. by Lillian Thomas Shank and John Nichols
(Kalamazoo: Cistercian Publications, 1987), pp. 145–64 (p. 147).

of Steppes in October 1213 (Ch. 29), and when an apostate nun repented and begged for readmission, Christina's influence persuaded the community to reinstate her, although they had initially refused (Ch. 30). As we have seen, Christina also knew Lutgard, for she was among those who advised her in 1206 to leave Sint-Truiden for Aywières in order to escape her office of prioress. When Lutgard hesitated to move to French-speaking territory where she would be, in effect, a foreigner, Christina cited the proverb, 'I would rather be in hell with God than in heaven with the angels without God'.[67] In the last year of her life, 1223–24, Thomas says Christina stayed 'more frequently' at St Catherine's (Ch. 46), where a nun named Beatrice — one of our author's informants — reported that she herself had called the deceased Christina back from death a second time to satisfy her curiosity about something (Ch. 51–53).

Between 1239 and 1248, Thomas of Cantimpré returned to Sint-Truiden and interviewed another Thomas, abbot of the male community there, who supplied him with an addendum to Christina's *Life*. This story is of considerable literary interest. It features Christina physically enacting a dialogue between soul and body, alternately beating her breast and kissing the soles of her feet as she played the two roles in turn (Chs 47–49). Whether or not she actually did this, the tale attests to a continuing cult (and folkloric tradition) about Christina at least fifteen years after her death. Finally, the *vita* mentions two translations of the saint's relics. In 1231, when the nuns of St Catherine's moved from Sint-Truiden to Nonnemielen, they opened Christina's grave and took her body with them. Thomas claims that a sweet odour wafted from the tomb and miracles of healing occurred, though he declines to recount them (Ch. 54). In 1249 the relics were translated a second time, ostensibly at the revelation of an angel who made this request to the convent priest, conspicuously refusing to speak to the prioress (Chs 57–59). This anonymous postscript shows, first, that Christina's cult had made it to the quarter-century mark (a miracle took place on this occasion as well); but also that the cult was controversial, for the prioress and perhaps others had no wish to promote it.

The second place with which we can link Christina is the cell of a recluse, Jutta, in the town of Borgloon. Thomas says he travelled a long way to interview Jutta, his main source for the *vita*, and notes that Christina stayed with her for nine years (Ch. 38). Frustratingly, he neglects to say which years they were. The same Jutta was a close friend of Lutgard, who spent at least two weeks with her,

[67] VLA I.22.

sharing ecstatic experiences.[68] Walter Simons speculates that 'Jutta's and Christina's fame [...] attracted several female apprentices to the cells' at their church in Borgloon, perhaps contributing to the foundation of a beguinage there.[69] As Anneke Mulder-Bakker has pointed out, the vocations of 'beguine' and 'recluse' overlapped. Despite its forbidding name, a reclusorium was a permeable place where guests were free to come and go; it often served as a kind of retreat house for other pious women.[70] During her time with Jutta, Christina also frequented the court of Count Louis II of Loon (1197–1218), whose castle was not far from the recluse's cell. Louis considered Christina his spiritual mother and received both religious and political advice from her. On one occasion, for example, she warned him that the Duke of Limburg was plotting treachery against him — in the duke's very presence, if we can trust Thomas's account (Ch. 43). It was this familiar relationship that underlay Louis's request to have Christina, rather than a priest, as the auditor of his deathbed confession (Ch. 44), and her subsequent promise to share his purgatorial sufferings (Ch. 45).

Castle, nunnery, and recluse's cell, then, mark the institutional boundaries of Christina's world. Though she could never be constrained within even the semiregular discipline of a beguinage, let alone a nunnery, many of her practices recall those of other *mulieres religiosae*. For instance, the irreproachably monastic Lutgard, like Christina, also prophesied, interceded for souls in purgatory, experienced ecstasies, gave spiritual counsel, and advised men of power. Christina's assistance to the dying (Ch. 27) was among the most common and urgently needed ministries of beguines, who were the hospice workers of their day. More surprisingly, perhaps, she knew Latin. We find her chanting the Psalms (Ch. 16), singing the *Te Deum* at St Catherine's (Ch. 36), answering questions about Scripture, albeit 'unwillingly and rarely' (Ch. 40), and improvising Latin chant during her exquisite solo performance of matins (Ch. 39). This Latinity may have been completely oral, for Thomas says she had no knowledge of letters (Ch. 40). But it need not have been miraculous, for Christina could have learned liturgical Latin from the nuns of Sint-Truiden as well as the beguines and recluses of Borgloon. All these activities sketch the portrait of a recognizable human being, and the friendship of Lutgard, Count Louis, Jutta, and the nuns of St Catherine's suggests that, at least during the second half of her long life, Christina was trusted and accounted sane by many.

---

[68] VLA I.16.

[69] Simons, *Cities of Ladies*, p. 43.

[70] Mulder-Bakker, *Lives of the Anchoresses*, pp. 70–72, 197.

She was also among the holy women eulogized by James of Vitry, who first called her to the attention of Thomas.[71]

What, then, are we to do with the 'other' Christina — the woman so Other that fire could not burn, nor waters drown, nor death hold her? We are, of course, free to believe that Thomas invented these stories out of sheer sensationalism; or that he was, at best, naively credulous of current folklore; or else that the uncanny events really happened, marking Christina's life as a sustained, miraculous intervention of God in the world. But if none of these answers satisfy, this *vita* poses the most challenging conundrum of any. In a 1998 *Speculum* article, I offered, for the first time, an account that attempted to meld Thomas's theological program with a reconstruction of the historical Christina's experience. Interpreting her in the light of thirteenth-century beliefs about spirit possession, including the anecdotes Thomas himself records in the *Book of Bees*, I suggested that in the early years after her 'death and resurrection', Christina was widely accounted a demoniac rather than a saint.

> Orphaned at an early age, [...] Christina fell sick with an unknown illness and lay comatose for so long that her sisters believed she was dead and arranged for her burial.[72] But her unexpected return to life at the funeral was dramatic enough to make her an instant celebrity, a female Lazarus whose resurrection could be explained only in supernatural terms, whether demonic or divine. Unfortunately, however, the coma had masked considerable brain damage, and Christina never fully recovered but began to show signs of severe mental disturbance — antisocial behaviour, violent self-mutilation, peculiar and repellent choices in food and dress. Judging her to be insane and/or possessed by demons, the citizens of [Sint-Truiden] took the usual measures: restraining her with chains and fetters, imprisoning her 'for her own good', making a public spectacle of her, attempting to exorcise the unclean spirits. None of these tactics helped. So, when the young *obsessa* was not being maintained on bread and water in her dungeon, she was reduced like other disabled men and women to a life of begging. Hers was the mendicancy, not of a St Francis, but of the ordinary poor, subject at whim to the pity, charity, or scornful abuse of the fortunate.[73]

[71] VMO Prologue, 8, cited in full in VCM 1.

[72] In 1998 I stated that Christina was a teenager at the time of her 'first death'. But if the received date of *c.* 1150 for her birth is correct, she would have been about thirty-two. See VCM 54 and Anneke Mulder-Bakker, 'The Prime of Their Lives: Women and Age, Wisdom and Religious Careers in Northern Europe', in *New Trends*, ed. by Dor and others, pp. 215–36 (pp. 218–19).

[73] Barbara Newman, 'Possessed by the Spirit: Devout Women, Demoniacs, and the Apostolic Life in the Thirteenth Century', *Speculum*, 73 (1998), 733–70 (p. 766). This article has been abridged as 'Devout Women and Demoniacs in the World of Thomas of

I still believe that some version of this scenario comes as close as we are likely to get to the historical figure behind the *vita*.[74] During a period of flamboyant mental illness after her near-death experience, Christina gave every sign of spirit possession — but, as Nancy Caciola has recently shown, it was extraordinarily hard for contemporaries to interpret 'possessed behaviours', which could point ambiguously to either divine or demonic agency.[75] Nowhere is this ambiguity more telling than in Christina's case. Thomas openly acknowledges that people thought her to be 'filled with demons' (Ch. 9, 17), and he reports two attempts at exorcism. The first priest, after finishing her abortive funeral mass, uses the sacrament to 'force' Christina's body down from the ceiling of the church, where it has remained immobile as if held aloft by diabolical agency (Ch. 5). The second 'adjure[s] her by the name of Christ' to emerge from the Meuse, where she has spent days on end in the icy water; and at the sacred name she is 'forced to come out' (Ch. 12). Interestingly, this priest is described as the one 'who took care of her' (*qui ejus curam gerebat*) — a phrase that could simply denote her parish priest, but is more likely, I think, to denote a custodian for someone who was not mentally competent. Finally the monks and nuns of Sint-Truiden, alarmed by the crowds who gather to watch Christina and fearing that their 'beastly minds [...] might convert these divine deeds into demonic activity' (*malignam operationem*), hold a public prayer service asking God to restore her to 'the usual human state' (Ch. 20). The upshot is a successful self-exorcism. 'Violently stirred by a spirit' (or the Spirit), Christina enters a church, finds an open baptismal font, and totally immerses herself in it (Ch. 21). Afterwards her behaviour is calmer, if never quite 'normal', and she no longer abhors the stench of humans so much that she feels compelled to pray from treetops and church spires.

The ambiguity of Christina's spirit possession also extends to the way Thomas describes her specific behaviour. Her alternating torments in fire and water, as well as stretching on instruments of torture (Ch. 13), evoke the

---

Cantimpré', in *New Trends*, ed. by Dor and others, pp. 35–60.

[74] Amy Hollywood has taken issue with this account, largely because of my attempt to recuperate the word 'hysteria' in describing Christina and other possessed persons. In Hollywood's view, this term is tainted beyond repair by centuries of misogynist abuse. But it is not central to my reading, and I hope this revised account responds to her objections. Hollywood, *Sensible Ecstasy: Mysticism, Sexual Difference, and the Demands of History* (Chicago: University of Chicago Press, 2002), pp. 241–47.

[75] Nancy Caciola, *Discerning Spirits: Divine and Demonic Possession in the Middle Ages* (Ithaca: Cornell University Press, 2003), especially Ch. 1.

punishments of purgatory as they were represented in contemporary otherworld visions. In her notes to the translation, Margot King cites parallels from one such text, the *Visio Lazari*. As both James of Vitry and Thomas of Cantimpré believed, Christina's mission was precisely to suffer the torments of purgatory here on earth, both to deliver the souls of the dead and to move the living to penitence. But there are other, disturbingly ambivalent elements here too. Christina's self-mutilation, her lament among the tombs (Ch. 13), and her superhuman strength, enabling her to break any chains (Ch. 9, 18), recall the infamous Gerasene demoniac whose unclean spirit tells Christ, 'My name is Legion' (Mark 5. 1–13). On the other hand, Christina can walk on water as Christ himself did (Ch. 10); she hangs herself between thieves on the gallows, recalling his Passion (Ch. 13); she miraculously escapes from prison as Peter and Paul did (Ch. 18) and, like the Virgin Mary, she experiences miraculous lactation (Ch. 9). Throughout the first half of the *vita*, therefore, she functions as a supremely ambivalent sign, a call to discernment. Then, as now, people see in her what they want to see — saint, madwoman, hapless beggar, virtuoso performer — or, as Thomas claims, an immortal soul revealing its destiny in the mortal flesh.

How, then, do we link the uncanny heroine of the first half of the *vita* with the respected holy woman of the second? One rather pedestrian way is to speculate that, after a period of uncontrolled frenzy, Christina's mental health improved to the extent that she could control her self-destructive impulses by channeling them into spiritually useful, socially valued acts of intercession and penance. Thomas himself suggests as much by pointing to her baptismal immersion as a turning point. From that time on, God 'moderate[d] his miracles in Christina' (Ch. 20), and/or cast out the demons that had possessed her. In his earlier account, James of Vitry offered the parallel observation that 'after she had performed penance in so many ways, she lived in peace' and became a psychopomp, leading the souls of the dead to purgatory or heaven 'without any harm to herself'.[76] This reading almost suggests a shamanic initiation: after an initial otherworld journey followed by arduous feats of physical endurance, Christina won the ability to travel at will between the worlds, guiding others on their own journeys. Her oral teaching on purgatory suggests a kind of insider's knowledge: 'Demons, she said, presided over those in torment, but those who were handed over to the demons to be tortured knew that the more cruelly they were afflicted by them, the shorter their torments would be' (Ch. 28).

---

[76] VCM 1 and VMO Prologue, 8.

Purgatory, of course, is the grand theological theme of this *vita*, as theologians have recognized since at least the sixteenth century.[77] Robert Sweetman offers the most compelling recent explanation of Thomas's purgatorial theology as conveyed through the exemplum of Christina's life.[78] In Sweetman's words, the saint is entrusted with a 'preaching apostolate' that enables her to proclaim by example what the Church will not let her teach from any pulpit. As Thomas asks in his peroration,

> What else did Christina cry out during her entire life except to do penance and be ready at every hour? This she taught with many words, with tears, with lamentations and boundless cries, and with the example of her life. This, indeed, she taught more insistently and shouted louder than anyone we have heard of before or since (Ch. 56).

Her torments, whether inflicted directly by God or by demons with God's permission, have the exemplary value of making purgatory visible here and now (thus frightening sinners into penance), at the same time that her merits deliver souls already held there (much like the fasts and tears of other *mulieres sanctae*). The very grotesquerie of the *vita* increases its exemplary value, for it was well known that bizarre and violent images impressed themselves more firmly on the memory.[79] In a more recent contribution, Sweetman clarifies the theological rationale for Christina's ability to survive such torments. Because she has already died and returned to life, she possesses a glorified body like those that, according to Aquinas and other schoolmen, the blessed would enjoy after the general resurrection.[80] Graced with the four 'dowries' of subtlety, clarity, agility, and impassibility, Christina can rise into the air and perch in trees like a bird (Ch. 5, 15, 20), pass through rivers and walls in her material body (Ch. 10, 46), produce angelic song by mysterious, non-vocal means (Ch. 35, 49), and survive lethal punishments without a bruise or burn on her flesh (Chs 11–14, 18). Yet, although she is not physically harmed by these sufferings, she does experience

---

[77] King, 'The Sacramental Witness', p. 147, citing Robert Bellarmine and F. X. Shouppe (1893).

[78] Robert Sweetman, 'Christine of Saint-Trond's Preaching Apostolate: Thomas of Cantimpré's Hagiographical Method Revisited', *Vox Benedictina*, 9 (1992), 67–97.

[79] Sweetman, 'Christine of Saint-Trond's Preaching Apostolate', pp. 79–80; Mary Carruthers, *The Book of Memory: A Study of Memory in Medieval Culture* (Cambridge: Cambridge University Press, 1990; repr. 1996), pp. 134, 245.

[80] Sweetman, 'Thomas of Cantimpré, *Mulieres Religiosae* and Purgatorial Piety', pp. 619, 627, n. 64; Caroline Walker Bynum, *The Resurrection of the Body in Western Christianity, 200–1336* (New York: Columbia University Press, 1995), pp. 100, 131–32.

pain just as disembodied souls in hell and purgatory do, for otherwise her torments would have no redemptive value.

Seen from these varied angles, the *Life of Christina* proves to be a remarkably subtle and supple text. In it Thomas of Cantimpré achieved a kind of double-coding: the 'simple' (such as readers of the medieval Dutch and English translations) would find in it a truly astonishing and unforgettable reminder of God's wonders, as well as the need for penance, while more theologically educated readers could understand it as a sophisticated treatise on purgatory.[81] Further, I hope to have shown that even in this most otherworldly of *vitae*, we can glimpse the dim outlines of a historical person — a woman whose terrifying mental illness at first prompted her relatives to take drastic repressive measures, such as were customarily used to restrain persons possessed by demons. But, thanks to the enlightened pastoral care of such women as Jutta and the nuns of Sint-Truiden, as well as the sympathetic appreciation of clerics like James of Vitry, this 'demoniac saint' was enabled to recover and develop into a spiritual guide whose prophetic and ecstatic gifts came to be valued at the highest levels of her society.[82]

Margaret of Ypres: Teenaged Ascetic

The brief and, one is tempted to say, tragic life of Margaret of Ypres unfolds in a more ordinary setting. As in Christina's *Life*, however, Thomas enables us to see from two perspectives simultaneously. Reading with pious eyes, we discover an exemplary *mulier religiosa*, embodying all the traits that contemporaries would expect to find in a saint. But the *vita* is anecdotal enough to furnish a pair of secular lenses as well, through which we glimpse a troubled, rebellious teen trying to carve out her own niche in what she clearly saw as an oppressive matriarchal family.

Born of 'respectable' bourgeois parents in Ypres, Margaret lost her father at the age of four and may have spent the rest of her life trying to replace him. At

---

[81] For a similar case of double-coding in exemplary texts, see Kate Greenspan, 'Lessons for the Priest, Lessons for the People: Robert Mannyng of Brunne's Audiences for *Handlyng Synne*', *Essays in Medieval Studies*, 21 (2004), 109–21. Online at http://muse.jhu.edu/journals/essays_in_medieval_studies/v021/21.1greenspan.pdf.

[82] In 'Possessed by the Spirit', p. 767, I assigned most of the credit for Christina's recovery to her 'clerical friend', whoever he might have been. I would now ascribe a greater role to her female associates, especially the nuns of St Catherine's and Jutta of Borgloon.

first she was sent to an unnamed nunnery, where she learned letters and acquired the foundations of the fiercely ascetic and eucharistic piety she would manifest later on. Given her devout character, she might happily have professed monastic vows, but without a father's income, she may have lacked a sufficient dowry. After an unspecified period with the nuns, Margaret went with her mother, a maiden aunt, and two sisters to live with her uncle, a priest. During her childhood in this celibate household, she fasted on bread and water twice a week and scourged herself regularly with thorns, a good earnest of afflictions to come. When she was eighteen, Margaret's uncle died and she flirted briefly with 'the world', in the person of an attractive young carpenter who could have made a fine husband. Thomas ties himself in knots of self-contradiction as he describes the youthful saint's feelings (Ch. 5), stating that she conceived 'a most burning love' and 'talked with him alone very often' (so we can understand her heroic virtue in breaking off the friendship), yet in spite of her affection, she experienced no 'filth of lustful desire' and 'was never defiled either in will or in inclination' (so we know her virgin purity remained intact). But a providential meeting with the Dominican Friar Zeger quickly cured this passion. Called to conversion, Margaret renounced the world on the spot, made a vow of chastity, and experienced her first vision of Christ. Like other virgin saints, 'for the rest of her life, never would she feel even the first stirrings of temptation in her flesh' (Ch. 7).

Whether through necessity or choice, Margaret worked out her sainthood in her family home, not without struggle. Thomas casts her as a sacred Cinderella, cruelly misused by her mother and estranged from her worldly sisters — yet in spite of this abuse, it is she who earns the undying love of Christ the Prince. Margaret's mother constantly rebukes her for this or that domestic peccadillo, while her sisters are forever accusing her to Friar Zeger, who replaced both father and lover in the girl's affections. Since the Dominicans had as yet no friary in Ypres, it seems that Zeger lodged in the family's home during his frequent pastoral missions in their town,[83] making him not only Margaret's confidant, but a pivotal figure in the conflicts spurred by her conversion. These are refreshingly ordinary, in contrast to the endless marvels in Christina's *Life*. One day Margaret carelessly broke a wooden goblet and sent it to her carpenter friend, hoping he could fix and return it before her mother discovered the loss; and so he did. But the girl, noticing a lack of peace in her prayers the next day, ran to Zeger for confession and consolation. Sensibly enough, the friar explained that even

---

[83] Meersseman, 'Les Frères Prêcheurs', p. 72.

though Margaret had meant no harm, the youth could reasonably take this incident as encouragement for his suit. Horrified, the girl 'blushed profusely' and resolved never to see him again (Ch. 10).

It is impossible to miss the streak of adolescent rebelliousness in Margaret. Alexandra Barratt points out that *vitae* like hers glorify 'behaviour within the family that today would be labelled as dysfunctional at best, seriously disturbed at worst'.[84] Or in Margot King's words, this *vita* shows

> how far removed we are from the thirteenth century in our perception of saintly behaviour. What to us is called anorexia was to them a lifetime of miraculous self-mortification. Where today we would see in Margaret's silence the infuriating behaviour of a sulky and self-absorbed teen-age girl, they would see a soul turned in upon its Creator.[85]

Thomas uses this silence as a stick to beat contemporary monks and nuns, who cannot compete with Margaret's virtue; yet the example he gives can only evoke sympathy for her long-suffering family. When Margaret's mother complained to Zeger that her daughter would not deign to speak to anyone in the house, the friar ordered her under obedience to converse after lunch every day 'for as long as it took to recite the Seven [Penitential] Psalms' (Ch. 13). In other words, domestic civility is to be her new penance. The girl complies with the letter of this command while totally flouting its spirit:

> Obedient to her father in all things, she spoke as she had been directed, but of absolutely nothing except God. If they discussed anything else in her presence, any ordinary subject or gossip, at once she turned away and fell asleep. Whenever her mother compelled her to sit and talk longer than the appointed time, she obeyed her by sitting there, but promptly slumped down against the wall, and her face and hands would turn livid.

The rhetoric of sainthood slips, barely masking the classic picture of an alienated teen. If her mother nagged Margaret to help with the housework, 'to keep the peace she would snatch up a distaff or some such thing to work — and then fall into ecstasy', until her exasperated parent finally yielded and 'gave Christ's beloved fawn her freedom' to pray as long as she liked (Ch. 14). In a typically passive-aggressive response, the girl once found a bowl of raw eggs in the kitchen waiting to be cooked for dinner. 'Thinking they were eggshells', she threw them

---

[84] Alexandra Barratt, 'Undutiful Daughters and Metaphorical Mothers among the Beguines', in *New Trends*, ed. by Dor and others, pp. 81–104 (p. 81).

[85] Thomas de Cantimpré, *The Life of Margaret of Ypres*, trans. by Margot H. King (Toronto: Peregrina, 1995), Introduction, p. 11.

out 'so it would look as if she had done something useful and constructive on a day she had devoted to prayer' (Ch. 15).[86] Her mother of course was furious — giving Margaret a chance to perform the 'great and stupendous miracle' that all the king's horses and all the king's men could not have achieved. Restored by prayer to their pristine state, the now-hallowed eggs are boiled and distributed in a kind of domestic Eucharist, shared by all except Margaret — who predictably hides in her room and fasts.

Even more deeply than she resented her mother, Margaret adored her spiritual father. Zeger, of course, was Thomas of Cantimpré's chief source for the *vita*, so we see their relationship only retrospectively through the friar's eyes; but even so, it seems clear that the girl's entire life after conversion revolved around Zeger's affection, direction, and approval.[87] When he was present, she hung on his every word (Ch. 13); if he was absent, she consulted his inner, spiritual presence for comfort and counsel (Ch. 24). Thomas even finds proof of saintly patience in Margaret's granting 'permission' for the friar to leave her sickbed to answer urgent summons from the bishop and the countess (Ch. 14)! On one occasion, she longs so desperately for Zeger's presence that she 'lift[s] up her eyes toward Lille', where he is attending a meeting at the friary, and clairvoyantly sees her spiritual father 'with her bodily eyes' (Ch. 34). Thomas takes this episode seriously as a case of miraculous physical vision across a distance of five leagues, prompting him to a long scientific excursus on optics and the perspicacity of the lynx. When Zeger says a mass for Margaret, she is aware of it before he tells her (Ch. 30), and he alone is the confidant of her visions and revelations. In return, her prayers shower divine grace on his preaching (Chs 32–33), much as Mary of Oignies had done for James of Vitry.[88] Margaret has enough self-awareness to wonder if her love for the friar 'was against the Lord in some way' because 'mutual love and frequent conversation between a man and a woman seem suspicious to our superiors' (Ch. 25) — not surprisingly, given Dominican ambivalence about the *cura mulierum*. In 1228, less than a decade earlier, the order had categorically forbidden 'the pastoral care of nuns or any other women'.[89] So the saint heroically promises never to speak to Zeger again if Christ should forbid it. Instead, the Lord assures her that nothing the friar commands

---

[86] For provocative comments on this incident see Barratt, 'Undutiful Daughters', p. 85.

[87] Compare Coakley, 'Friars as Confidants', pp. 226–28.

[88] VMO II.69, in *Mary of Oignies*, p. 99.

[89] [C]*ura vel custodia monialium vel quarumlibet aliarum mulierum*: Meersseman, 'Les Frères Prêcheurs', p. 93.

will ever harm her — a locution Zeger puts to the test by ordering Margaret to walk a league with him on Easter after four days of fasting (Ch. 26). Her supernatural strength confirms God's promise and thus sets a divine seal of approval on their bond.

The kind of piety that Margaret practiced, Zeger directed, and Thomas held up for emulation is a textbook model of the devotional program shared by Cistercians, Dominicans, and *mulieres sanctae* in the Low Countries. This is the pattern Caroline Walker Bynum so clearly delineated in *Holy Feast and Holy Fast*, and Margaret illustrates virtually every aspect of eucharistic feasting, penitential fasting, and other afflictions described there.[90] She receives a precocious first communion at the age of four, being supernaturally enlightened about Christ's real presence in the sacrament (Ch. 2); communicates every fortnight as an adult, which would have been considered extraordinary at the time (Ch. 11); experiences intense scruples over her worthiness to receive the Lord's body (Ch. 28); finds physical strength in the Eucharist even when she is able to eat nothing else (Ch. 40); and receives the sacrament from Christ himself when no priest is available to serve her (Ch. 24). Her fasting is prodigious, beginning in childhood (Ch. 3); she not only fasts on bread and water every Wednesday and Friday, on the vigils of saints, and all through Lent, but spends days on end without eating at all, drinks next to nothing, and rarely notices if food is present (Ch. 16). Margaret also forgoes sleep (Ch. 17), zealously scourges herself (Chs 4, 16), and prays ceaselessly, reciting both the canonical hours and four hundred Our Fathers and Hail Marys with genuflections every day (Chs 20–21). Remarkably, Thomas not only holds up her lay piety as a model to shame negligent monks and nuns, but proclaims that she endured all these mortifications 'without self-destruction' (Ch. 17) — yet he also reports her constant illnesses, including the horribly debilitating malady that kept her bedridden for a year before she died at twenty. Her edifying deathbed scene occupies no fewer than eleven chapters, about a fifth of the *vita*.

One missing element is the charitable feeding of others, or indeed, other-directed behaviour of any kind. Thomas notes that Margaret does, like Mary of Oignies, attempt to beg so as to imitate Christ's poverty, but her spiritual father strictly forbids it — with the exception that she can receive small donations from her parish priest to pass along to lepers (Ch. 22). Although she becomes the centre of a coterie of spiritual friends, both men and women, we rarely see her interceding for others, except once when her sister nearly dies in childbirth (Ch.

---

[90] Bynum, *Holy Feast and Holy Fast*, especially pp. 115–21.

27). In contrast to Lutgard, she does not perform healings or exorcisms, offer spiritual direction,[91] or release souls from purgatory through her prayers. In short, Margaret dies too young to attain spiritual maturity but remains a perpetual daughter, firmly under her father's thumb. Consequently, Thomas presents her less as a charismatic woman than as a penitent of the type that would later come to be called a 'victim soul'. Zeger's interest in her seems almost proprietary: Karen Glente aptly compares him to 'an older, experienced husband who rejoices that he has been able to awaken the love of his young, innocent bride'.[92] After her death, it is Zeger who eagerly secures her relics, using the saint's once putrefied but now shining white headdress as a miraculous talisman (Ch. 54).

The only exception to this pattern is a chapter so atypical that it might almost have been lifted from the *Life* of John of Cantimpré. Zeger had introduced Margaret to a 'noble lady from the ruling family', almost certainly the future countess Marguerite of Flanders, in order to secure the saint's prayers. Stunningly, however, the girl averts her eyes in disdain, saying the Lord has just revealed that all prayers for this noblewoman would be vain 'because her hands are filled with blood: every day she plunders my poor by her taxes' (Ch. 29). Of course the lady is appalled and Zeger too professes shock, asking his daughter 'in the name of Christ whether the Lord had most expressly used the word "taxes"'. Margaret replies, 'I swear to you in the name of Christ our Lord that never in my life until today have I heard the word "taxes" in divine revelation'. The mere mention of them arouses horror, like an outburst of profanity at mass — but it works. Threatened with divine retribution, Marguerite lightens her peasants' burden and restores much of what she had plundered, if not quite so ostentatiously as John of Montmirail or Alard the moneylender. The incident is significant because Marguerite would not only go on to become a devotee of the young saint, competing with Zeger for her relics (Ch. 54), but also a significant patron of beguines and other *mulieres sanctae*.[93]

---

[91] VMY 36 is somewhat contradictory on this point; Margaret is vaguely said to admonish sinners and encourage the righteous on the basis of her visions, which she shares with no one except her spiritual father so as to 'preserve her reputation'.

[92] Glente, 'Mystikerinnenviten', p. 254.

[93] Galloway, '"Discreet and Devout Maidens"', pp. 100–03; Simons, *Cities of Ladies*, pp. 98–99, 105.

Lutgard of Aywières: Patron of Purgatory

Lutgard's *vita*, Thomas of Cantimpré's most mature work in the genre, has earned the status of a classic in mystical hagiography, and its subject is the only one who, thanks to the Cistercians, ever enjoyed a significant cult. As her 'spiritual son', Thomas had ready access to Lutgard and her associates. But the text also represents his most systematic effort to stylize a holy life according to standard models of spiritual progress, so the empirical Lutgard often disappears behind icons of the ideal Cistercian nun and the perfected bride of Christ. Perhaps the clearest expression of Thomas's attitude toward his subject occurs in I.15:

> Although she seemed and indeed was rather uncultivated and very simple (*rudis quodammodo et simplicissima*) in common speech, yet in private spiritual conversations, never from anyone's lips have I heard more genuine, more ardent, or more decisive words in accord with the spirit of truth — to such an extent that I often accounted myself to be quite uncultivated and dull (*rudem prorsus et hebetem*) in my understanding of her speech.

In other words, Lutgard was a profound but unpretentious soul — a quality masked by the rhetorical contortions of hagiography.

Thomas formally divides this *vita*, like John's, into three books that purportedly represent Lutgard as a spiritual beginner (*inchoans*), an advanced contemplative (*proficiens*), and a perfected saint (*perfecta*). These stages may be based on William of Saint-Thierry's anatomy of the mystic's progress in his *Exposition on the Song of Songs*, where the bridal soul advances from its 'animal' or purely natural, psychological condition through a 'rational' stage to the fully 'spiritual' state of perfection.[94] But they also coincide with the major periods in Lutgard's life: her childhood and youth at St Catherine's, her adult life as a Cistercian at Aywières, and her last illness, death, and posthumous miracles. Strikingly, most of Lutgard's distinctive mystical experiences are described in Book I when she is still a 'beginner'.[95] Book II, which claims to represent Lutgard 'resting in the sleep of contemplation', in fact depicts her remarkably active

---

[94] See Margot King, 'The Dove at the Window: The Ascent of the Soul in Thomas de Cantimpré's Life of Lutgard of Aywières', in *Hidden Springs*, ed. by Nichols and Shank, I, pp. 225–53. Thomas's debts to William, Augustine, Gregory the Great, and Bernard of Clairvaux are identified in King's notes to the translation.

[95] J.-B. Lefèvre, 'Sainte Lutgarde d'Aywières en son temps (1182–1246)', *Collectanea Cisterciensia*, 58 (1996), 277–335 (p. 314).

ministry as a spiritual adviser, healer, prophet, intercessor, exorcist, and peerless comforter of the afflicted. Beyond this division, Thomas subdivides Lutgard's life through the device of her three seven-year fasts — the first for the conversion of Albigensian heretics (Cathars), the second for sinners in general, and the third to avert some great scourge threatening the Church, probably a feared alliance between Frederick II and the Tartars. These fasts demonstrate Lutgard's holy austerity even as they enable Thomas to schematize her advancement without providing an exact chronology.

Thomas first met Lutgard between 1228 and 1230, when she was a mature woman in her forties and he, some eighteen or twenty years younger.[96] The anecdotes in the first half of the *vita*, before he knew her, would have been based on her own memories, supplemented by those of a confessor, Friar Bernard, whose distinction as penitentiary to Pope Innocent IV added plausibility and lustre to the tales. As Jean-Baptiste Lefèvre has noted, Thomas took a keen interest in the development of individuals, but much less in that of communities. He thus projects the condition of both St Catherine's and Aywières as he knew them at the time of writing (*c.* 1246) onto the early, formative stage of both communities. Hence he anachronistically portrays the twelve-year-old Lutgard, her dowry lost through the ruin of a local merchant, joining 'the order of St Benedict' in 1194 at the highly respectable (*honestissimum*) monastery of St Catherine's in Sint-Truiden — the same house where Christina the Astonishing would become a regular guest. At the time, however, this community was simply a small group of beguines. It is clear that the women of St Catherine's were not cloistered or life-professed, since Lutgard both entertained suitors there and rode out to visit her sister and her close friend, the recluse Jutta of Borgloon.[97] In her later reminiscences, some of these teenaged adventures become turning points in the young mystic's ultimate choice of divine over earthly love. Once, while conversing with her boyfriend, she experiences a sudden epiphany of Christ displaying his bloody wounds and promising her 'the delights of total purity' (I.2), so she emphatically sends the suitor packing. A second rejected suitor, a knight, encounters Lutgard on horseback in the woods en route to her sister's house, and attempts to rape her. Publicly shamed by the hue and cry, she identifies with the humiliated Christ and unveils her face to the gawking crowd, offering her spurned modesty as a sacrifice.

---

[96] Lefèvre, 'Sainte Lutgarde', p. 320.

[97] Ibid., pp. 297–98.

Only when Lutgard and her sisters received the formal consecration of virgins from the bishop of Liège (some time between 1200 and 1205) did they adopt the Benedictine rule and become officially nuns — electing Lutgard, much to her dismay, as their prioress. Since she could have been little more than twenty at the time, the election suggests her forceful personality as well as a relatively high social status. Her spiritual charisms had also become manifest, to say the least. According to Thomas, while still at St Catherine's Lutgard levitated (I.10), glowed with celestial radiance as she prayed (I.11), received the gift of healing (I.12), sucked divine sweetness from Christ's wounded side (I.13–14), oozed miraculous oil from her fingertips (I.16), and sang her responsory solos with ravishing beauty because Christ, in the form of a lamb, drew the melody out of her mouth (I.19).[98] These are all hagiographic topoi, of course, though this makes it more rather than less likely that the fervent convert's intimacy with Christ would express itself in such forms. Such literal, concrete representations of inner experience are indispensable to the genre, as Amy Hollywood has shown:[99] if Lutgard had merely *felt* she were floating midway between earth and heaven, this would carry far less conviction than if 'the whole community' manifestly *saw* her 'elevated two cubits into the air'.

The most significant experience Thomas recounts in Book I is an edifying dialogue between Christ and Lutgard about spiritual gifts (I.12). Disillusioned with her grace of healing because the needy crowds disturbed her prayer, Lutgard asked Christ to replace it with a 'better' gift, namely understanding of the Psalter. But this gift too disappointed her, until finally, like the fisherman granted three wishes in a folktale, she settled on the correct choice — an exchange of hearts with Christ. Thomas interprets this as full mystical union — 'the union of an uncreated with a created spirit through a surplus of grace', just as St Paul had written: 'whoever clings to God is made one spirit with him' (I Corinthians 6. 17). The exchange of hearts became the dominant motif in St

---

[98] On Lutgard's spiritual development see the three articles in *Hidden Springs*, ed. by Nichols and Shank: Amandus Bussels, 'Saint Lutgard's Mystical Spirituality', pp. 211–23; King, 'The Dove at the Window', pp. 225–53; and Deboutte, 'The *Vita Lutgardis*', pp. 255–81. See also Thomas Merton, *What Are These Wounds? The Life of a Cistercian Mystic, Saint Lutgarde of Aywières* (Milwaukee: Bruce, 1950).

[99] Amy Hollywood, *The Soul as Virgin Wife: Mechthild of Magdeburg, Marguerite Porete, and Meister Eckhart* (Notre Dame: University of Notre Dame Press, 1995), pp. 27–39.

Lutgard's later iconography, and would soon be echoed in the writings of other mystics such as Gertrude of Helfta and Mechthild of Hackeborn.[100]

It is not clear how long Lutgard served as prioress, but she did not relish the role. As Thomas says, 'she considered that a most grave injury had been done to her' by the election (I.20), deciding that her only escape would be to move to another house. Canon law permitted such transfers only if they involved moving to a stricter order; thus Lutgard, as a Benedictine, would have to become Cistercian. In the diocese of Liège alone, fifteen Cistercian nunneries were founded between 1200 and 1229, and sixteen more between 1230 and 1240.[101] But although some individual abbots — notably at Villers — were enthusiastic about women's spirituality, the General Chapter was notoriously resistant to the *cura monialium*.[102] Hence many female communities at the time were 'Cistercian in spirit but not in law', and among these was the tiny group that Lutgard joined in 1206, in the village of Les Awirs near Liège. About the same time she entered, the community petitioned to join the Cistercian order, but they were not officially received until 1210. In 1211 they moved from their original site to Lillois in the duchy of Brabant, under the patronage of a nobleman named Iwan de Raive, whose relative Marie became the first abbess.[103] Only a few years later the women moved again, this time to the fief of Couture-Saint-Germain, which they renamed Aywières after their initial site. In short, between 1205 and 1215 Lutgard moved not once but three times, living amid the bustle of constant construction, but Thomas says nothing of all this mundane activity.

What he does say is considerably stranger. When Lutgard initially decided to seek a Cistercian monastery, she inclined toward the recently founded Herkenrode, since the sisters there were Dutch- or Flemish-speaking as she was. But her spiritual director, John of Liroux, pressed her to choose the francophone Les Awirs — a counsel reinforced by Christ and Christina the Astonishing (I.22). On Thomas's account, the nun recognized the wisdom of their advice when several of the newly incorporated Cistercian houses 'longed to have Lutgard as abbess had she learned even a little French' (II.1). But, having fled the burden of

---

[100] André Cabassut, 'Coeurs, changement des', in DS II.2, cols 1046–51.

[101] Lefèvre, 'Sainte Lutgarde', p. 281.

[102] Sally Thompson, 'The Problem of the Cistercian Nuns in the Twelfth and Early Thirteenth Centuries', in *Medieval Women*, ed. by Baker, pp. 227–52. A decree of the 1228 General Chapter, prohibiting the incorporation of further nunneries into the Order, proved ineffective.

[103] Lefèvre, 'Sainte Lutgarde', pp. 311–12.

office once, she had absolutely no intention of shouldering it again, so she stubbornly refused to master the language — or rather, the Virgin Mary granted her a kind of miraculous disability. Though she moved to Les Awirs at twenty-four, her mind still agile, 'yet in the forty years she lived among French-speaking companions, she could barely learn more French than she needed to ask for bread correctly when she was hungry' (II.1). We need not take Thomas's remarks at face value, however, for as Alexandra Barratt remarks, the whole *vita* displays 'an uneasy and paradoxical relationship between Lutgard, language, and languages, of which Thomas himself fails to make sense'.[104] Granted, as Cistercians the nuns would have kept long periods of silence, communicating chiefly by sign language. But there were nevertheless periods of recreation and necessary business during which, in the course of four decades, Lutgard would have had ample occasion to learn the native tongue. Indeed, at one point the nuns were visited by a depressed woman in desperate need of the consolation only Lutgard could give — yet this visitor spoke only French. To the sisters' astonishment, the two women conversed privately at some length, after which the greatly relieved guest asked, 'Why did you say that this most holy lady was Flemish? Indeed, I have found by experience that she is quite French!' (II.40). Thomas regards this incident as a miracle of glossolalia, cancelling out the previous 'miracle' of linguistic incompetence. What seems more likely is that Lutgard did acquire some proficiency, but concealed it as far as possible — certainly from Thomas and probably from her sisters as well — until any danger of election as abbess or prioress was safely past. When absolutely necessary, however, she could perform well enough in French, as in conversing with the depressed woman and, on another occasion, with the francophone bishop of Cambrai (II.40).

Lutgard's relation to Latinity was even more vexed, as suggested by the odd account of her first requesting, then rejecting, an ability to understand the Psalter because she 'had not made as much progress in this grace as she had expected' (I.12). Thomas provides an Augustinian explanation: 'the reverence of a veiled mystery is the mother of devotion, what is hidden is the more avidly sought, and what is concealed is looked upon with more veneration.'[105] But he

---

[104] Barratt, 'Language and the Body', p. 340.

[105] Compare Augustine, *De doctrina Christiana*, IV.8.22. In D. W. Robertson Jr's translation, Scripture often speaks 'with a useful and healthful obscurity for the purpose of exercising and sharpening [...] the minds of the readers [...] and stimulating the desire to learn': *On Christian Doctrine* (New York: Macmillan, 1958), p. 132.

also has Lutgard ask the Lord, 'What use is it to me to know the secrets of Scripture — I, an unlettered, uncultivated, and uneducated nun (*idiotae et rusticae et laicae moniali*)?' Was this emphatic assertion of 'simplicity' essential to Lutgard's self-understanding, or did it rather fulfill Thomas's definition of what it meant to be a holy woman? Since Lutgard had been prioress of St Catherine's for at least a year and chanted the Divine Office every day of her life, she could hardly have been *illitterata* in the sense of 'knowing no Latin', though she may well have been diffident about her own abilities. Even more paradoxical are the accounts of her mystical locutions: Christ speaks to her in Latin, which she allegedly does not understand, yet she is able to remember and repeat these locutions verbatim to the 'more lettered nuns' who interpret them for her (II.8, II.10, II.20) — presumably in French which, if we believe Thomas, was equally problematic. In particular, she asks her closest friend, Sybille de Gages, who at one point looks up a gloss on the Psalter to confirm what Lutgard has learned through *intellectio spiritualis* (II.33). It is possible that in comparison with Sybille, who could use the tools of biblical scholarship and composed Lutgard's epitaph in elegant leonine verse (III.20), the mystic genuinely felt that her Latin skills were deficient. Barratt suggests that 'for her the non-rational, non-symbolic dimensions of language — language as sound and rhythm, the physical, aural, and tactile experiences of forming syllables, pronouncing, chanting, and singing — were more fulfilling than language in its symbolic dimension of communicating meaning'.[106] Or perhaps she was like a shy American student in Paris, whose college French only comes to life under the stimulus of a few drinks — except that in Lutgard's case, the stimulus was ecstatic prayer.

In Book II, Thomas mingles further mystical graces with accounts of Lutgard's ministry to the living and the dead. Although he likes to represent her in bridal terms, frequently explaining her experiences as illustrating verses from the Song of Songs (II.43, III.9), her own piety seems to have been more Passion-centred than nuptial. Hearing 'the cry of Christ's wounds' as they perpetually bleed for the ones he calls 'my sinners' (II.6, II.9), Lutgard becomes a co-redemptrix, devoting herself to urgent prayer, tears, and fasting to avert the Father's ever-threatening wrath.[107] Her prayers expect immediate and explicit replies, and when God does not promptly answer with a reassuring vision or locution, she redoubles her efforts, at one point asking to be erased from the

[106] Barratt, 'Language and the Body', p. 342.

[107] In II.9 Christ explicitly asks Lutgard to 'surrender yourself wholly to me for my sinners', just as he surrenders himself wholly to the Father in the Eucharist.

book of life unless a particular client's sin is remitted (III.15). These clients came from far and wide. Lutgard heals the eating disorder of one sister and the deafness of another (II.20, 22); cures a matron's epileptic son (II.28); reads the heart of a young recluse who is too embarrassed to confess to a priest (II.37); secures the return of a Franciscan friar after twelve years of apostasy (II.35); and serves as spiritual mother to a knight who, after a series of financial reverses, becomes a monk at Afflighem (II.24). James of Vitry was part of her network: it may have been he who urged her to intercede against the Cathars (II.2), and she knew him well enough to discern his private temptations. At one point, Thomas notes, James had begun to neglect his preaching out of obsession with a certain *mulier religiosa* whom he loved 'not lustfully but with an all too human love' (II.3). Wary of this relationship, Lutgard prayed relentlessly until the preacher was 'liberated' from his willful blindness. Thomas himself, as we have seen, called on Lutgard's help to resist unclean thoughts while hearing confessions (II.38).

The mystic's special charism, however, lay in her apostolate to the dead.[108] Though purgatorial piety was common in her milieu, Lutgard stands out as a uniquely gifted intercessor — a grace Thomas underscores by twice recalling Mary of Oignies's prophecy that 'the world has no more faithful or efficacious intercessor than Lady Lutgard in [...] delivering souls from purgatory' (II.9, III.8). Visits from the recently departed were not only expected (III.5); they could even be commanded (II.12), and it was not rare for spiritual friends to make a pact that whoever died first should appear to the survivor (II.8). Such apparitions facilitated suffrages to speed the dead person's way into heaven, but they could also pack a political wallop, for the length of purgatorial 'sentences' faithfully intimated the gravity of a friend's, patron's, or enemy's sins. In the *Vita Lutgardis* these messages are loud and clear. John of Liroux, the saint's spiritual father — who died on a mission to the Curia to defend religious women — appears to her at the very moment of his death, already clad in his tri-coloured celestial robes (II.8). Jordan of Saxony, St Dominic's successor as Master General, died suddenly in a shipwreck in 1237. His spirit predicts Lutgard's own demise (albeit nine years early) and reveals that he now 'shine[s] among the choirs of apostles and prophets' (III.3). James of Vitry endures a mere three days in purgatory (III.5), which Thomas doubtless felt he deserved for abandoning his pastoral work in Liège to accept the cardinal's hat. Duchess Mary of Brabant, a daughter of King Philip Augustus, is 'rescued from the pains of purgatory beyond all

---

[108] Newman, 'On the Threshold of the Dead'.

expectation' (II.36) because of her devotion to the Virgin. On the other end of
the spectrum, Lutgard's married sister fares less well, for the saint hears her
'horrible and lamenting voice' in mid-air, pleading for mercy (II.13). Simon, the
Cistercian abbot of Foigny, confesses that he would have faced forty years in
purgatory because of his 'bitter zeal towards his subjects', were it not for
Lutgard's powerful aid (II.4). Yet even she can barely save the most egregious
sinner — Pope Innocent III, whom Thomas evidently loathed. Lutgard sees the
late pope's spirit 'surrounded by an enormous flame' as he reveals that, because
of three grave sins, he 'will be tortured by the most atrocious punishments until
the day of the Last Judgement' (II.7). This apparition allows Thomas to have his
cake and eat it too, for it reveals Lutgard's supreme power and compassion (she
'afflicted herself with wondrous pain' for the departed), while titillating the
reader with forbidden and subversive knowledge. 'Note well, reader', the
Dominican writes, 'that Lutgard revealed these three reasons to me, but I will
shroud them over out of reverence for so great a pontiff'.[109]

Needless to say, Lutgard herself not only glides straight into paradise, but
delivers a whole flock of sinners from purgatory as her compassionate spirit
passes by (III.21). Thomas dwells lovingly on her death, which comes complete
with angelic visions, prophecies, fond partings, and miraculous cures. Most
revealing is the author's personal quest for a relic. Years before Lutgard's passing,
Thomas began to lobby the abbess, nuns, and lay brothers of Aywières for this
privilege. Not surprisingly, the holy woman learned what he intended and gently
teased her protégé, insisting that instead of the hand he had requested, her little
finger would suffice for him (III.19). After some jockeying over the saint's body,
Thomas managed to secure the finger, but he had to bargain for it: Abbess
Hadewijch shrewdly denied his pleas until he came up with an attractive
counter-offer — he would write Lutgard's *vita* in exchange for her relic. 'Let no
envious person snap at me', says Thomas defensively, for after all, relics had been
cut from the bodies of Mary of Oignies and Elizabeth of Hungary before either
was canonized. This hint suggests his hope that Mary and Lutgard would soon
follow Elizabeth onto the official calendar of saints. Although this never
happened, the Cistercians unofficially promoted Lutgard's cult, as evidenced by
translations of her *vita* into Middle Dutch (both verse and prose) as well as

[109] Margot King suggests plausibly that one of these sins was Innocent's ban on new
religious orders, thus frustrating James and Thomas's hopes for the beguines. See VLA II.7
below.

French.[110] In 1578, the church and convent in Aywières were badly damaged by war, and in the process of rebuilding, Lutgard's relics were rediscovered and solemnly elevated (1616). In 1656, the Cistercian Order granted the saint a major feast (16 June), leading to an international expansion of her cult.[111] Having patiently accepted the blindness of her last years (III.1), Lutgard is venerated as a patron of the blind, and the hamlet of Aywières is still a modest pilgrimage site. The monastery itself was dissolved in the French Revolution.

A Textual Note on the Vita Lutgardis

A fifteenth-century *Passionale* now in Brussels (Bibliothèque royale de Belgique, MS 7917) contains fifty short *vitae, passiones*, and other items pertaining to female saints. The manuscript originally belonged to St Jerome in Utrecht, a house of the Brethren of the Common Life founded in 1475, and later to the Bollandists.[112] Its twenty-eighth item (fols 116ra–121rb) is an abridged version of the *Vita Lutgardis*, preserving all the saint's visions but omitting the prologue, numerous concrete events, posthumous miracles, and most of Thomas's exegesis and commentary. In a 1978 article in *Cîteaux*, Guido Hendrix maintained that this text was a 'primitive version' of the *vita*, written immediately after Lutgard's death and soon expanded.[113] Margot King accepted this hypothesis in the notes to her original 1987 translation, speculating on the brief text's authorship and comparing it with the complete *vita*. In 1996, however, J.-B. Lefèvre argued convincingly that the anonymous text was in fact not Thomas's original draft but a late medieval abridgment.[114] I accept Lefèvre's reasoning and have accordingly modified King's notes on this point. Hendrix's acronym VA (for Vita Antiqua) can now be interpreted as Vita Abbreviata.

---

[110] Guido Hendrix, 'Primitive Versions of Thomas of Cantimpré's *Vita Lutgardis*', *Cîteaux*, 29 (1978), 153–206 (pp. 158–60).

[111] Lefèvre, 'Sainte Lutgarde', pp. 327–29.

[112] Joseph van den Gheyn, *Catalogue des manuscrits de la Bibliothèque royale de Belgique*, 13 vols (Brussels: Lamertin, 1901–09), V, pp. 163–65.

[113] Hendrix, 'Primitive Versions'. The article includes editions of the short *vita* (pp. 162–74) as well as the French translation (pp. 175–206).

[114] Lefèvre, 'Sainte Lutgarde', pp. 292–96.

THE LIFE OF ABBOT JOHN OF CANTIMPRÉ

Translated by Barbara Newman

CHRONOLOGY
THE LIFE OF ABBOT JOHN OF CANTIMPRÉ
(*c*. 1155–*c*. 1205)

c. 1155	Birth of John in Cambrai
1177	Construction of John's first chapel at Cantimpré, west of Cambrai
1180	Canons transferred to St-Saviour by the gift of Hugh III, lord of Oisy
1182	Priory of Bellingen attached to Cantimpré
1183	Cantimpré affiliated with St-Victor; John elevated to rank of abbot
1186	Marriage of Marie of Champagne to Baldwin IX, heir of Flanders and Hainaut
1189/90	Death of Hugh of Oisy; John of Montmirail inherits his lordship
1191	Contested election in diocese of Cambrai; Jean d'Antoing appointed bishop by Emperor Henry VI
c. 1193	John of Cantimpré resigns his abbacy and is succeeded by Matthew
1194	Baldwin IX becomes count of Flanders
1195	Baldwin becomes count of Hainaut
1199/1200	Birth of Jeanne of Constantinople, daughter of Baldwin and Marie, later countess of Flanders
1202	Birth of Marguerite, sister of Jeanne and her successor as countess

1204	Fourth Crusade; Venetians sack Constantinople; Baldwin elected and crowned as emperor; Marie travels to Holy Land and dies in Acre
1205	Emperor Baldwin captured and killed by Bulgars
1205–10	Cambrai under interdict; death of John of Cantimpré (before 1210)
1209	John of Montmirail enters Cistercian abbey of Longpont
1212	Death of John of Montmirail
1212	Marriage of Jeanne of Constantinople, countess of Flanders, to Ferrand of Portugal
1213	Death of Mary of Oignies
1214	Sisters of Prémy canonically separated from brothers of Cantimpré
1217	Thomas enters Cantimpré as a regular canon
1218	Death of Abbot Matthew of Cantimpré, successor of John
1222	Death of Peter II of Corbeil, archbishop of Sens
1224	Foundation of Dominican convent at Lille
1227	Foundation of Cistercian abbey of Marquette
1228	Abbey of Marquette richly endowed by Jeanne and Ferrand
1223–28	***The Life of John of Cantimpré*** written except for final chapter
c. 1263–70	Thomas completes final chapter and dedication

PROLOGUE

To the most reverend father in Christ, Anselm, by the grace of God abbot of Cantimpré,[1] and the whole sacred community: Friar Thomas, least of the Order of Preachers in Leuven, offers the service of reverence due them.

The venerable Gerald, prudent governor of your house in Bellingen,[2] has come to me on your behalf, asking for the biography that I composed long ago at your house when I was scarcely twenty-three years old and inexperienced in writing.[3] But since I had not yet finished this book when I was living with you, I sent for a scribe, and in the space of scarcely a day, I finished what remained to be said about the death of the blessed John, your abbot and founder. Dearest masters and brothers, receive the little gift that I send you, for I do not think you should spurn what is lacking to the origins of your foundation.

The present book on the life of the blessed abbot John is divided into three parts: the stages of beginning, progress, and consummation. The first book is called the initial stage because it describes his birth, childhood, and adolescence. The second represents the stage of progress in which, having attained the higher path of charity, he clings to the embraces of Rachel by way of contemplation.[4]

---

[1] Anselm, ninth abbot of Cantimpré, between 1260 and 1305: *Gallia Christiana*, III, p. 163.

[2] Bellingen (province of Brabant, arr. Hal-Vilvorde, cant. Hal, comm. Pepingen), priory dependent on Cantimpré.

[3] II Corinthians 11. 6. The rhetoric of this prologue should be compared with that of the VLA.

[4] Rachel, the second wife of Jacob (Genesis 29–30), allegorically represents the contemplative life, while Leah symbolizes the active life. Cf. Augustine, *Contra Faustum*, 22.52.58, in CSEL 25–1, pp. 645–46, 654. The image is central to the *Benjamin minor* of Richard of Saint-Victor, Cap. 2–3, in PL 196:2–3.

The third is called the consummation in which, having come to old age[5] with limbs wearied by daily labour, he shakes off the coils of the flesh and flies freely to the world above.

I beseech you in closing, dearest brothers, that when you hear of my death, you will do me the kindness of offering the same rites that are customary for a deceased brother among yourselves. For even though I am now a friar of a different order, yet I lived among you as your brother without scandal or hatred, as I trust, for fifteen years and more. But now, suffering the daily pain of arthritis and gout,[6] I believe I shall not live much longer. Farewell, and may almighty God keep you safe and mindful of me. Amen.

---

[5] *Decrepita etas*: for Thomas this is the sixth age, beginning at seventy. See DNR I.83, p. 81.

[6] *Langore arthetice et podagre:* cf. DNR I.68, p. 71.

BOOK I

*Of John's birth, education, and ordination to the diaconate**

1. As the present world draws near to its setting and proclaims by diverse signs that the end of all things is at hand, while the charity of many grows cold,[7] the spheres are darkened, and the shadows of iniquity everywhere hide the face of the earth, yet he who shut up the stars beneath a seal[8] and bade them shine where he would to promise perpetual thrones to mortals, for whose sake Lucifer, the first morning star, was thwarted in his pride, has caused John to arise as a new daystar amid the shadows of twilight, which until now have grown ever thicker. I may indeed call him a daystar in every way, he who has nobly illumined the holy Church throughout the world by his deeds, his words, and his merits.[9] He was born in the city of Cambrai; his father was called Alelinus and his mother Theoberga. Both his parents were upright people[10] who lived by the work of their hands. They had enough to satisfy their needs and nothing by way of riches. Born to these parents, the infant boy showered gifts upon their cares.

---

* Chapter titles have been inserted by the translator unless otherwise noted.

[7] Matthew 24. 12. Cf. BUA II.1.23, p. 124.

[8] Job 9. 7.

[9] This chapter undoubtedly draws inspiration from Augustine's commentary on the book of Job (which also contains many other biblical quotations present in the VJC), as well as Gregory the Great's *Moralia in Job*. See Augustine, *Adnotationum in Iob liber I*, Cap. 31–38, ed. by Joseph Zycha, in CSEL 28–2, pp. 576–607; Gregory, *Moralia in Job*, 9.8, 10.18, 11.50, 16.67, in CCSL 143, pp. 460–62, 561–63; and 143a, pp. 625, 846–47.

[10] Luke 1. 6.

2. In the course of time divine grace shone out in him in accord with his name, so that heavenly virtue might in this way reveal a sign of his hidden calling. When his gracious mother used to tell this story to his brothers and sisters, from whom I in turn heard it, she said that when she poured out her tears and prayers in church before the image of God's mother Mary, praying for the son whom she especially loved, she used to repeat the angelic greeting time and again. Once as she was praying and repeating the words 'blessed are you among women', a divine voice gently replied in her ears, 'blessed is the fruit of your womb'.[11] A marvellous response indeed, and surely a marvellous thing worthy of a miracle! Is this not marvellous, that you most graciously bless the fruit of a little woman's womb with the same blessing by which the whole world especially blesses you, who alone are good[12] — you, the fruit of the Virgin's womb? But he who once humbly imparted a share in his own name to Peter, the foundation stone of the Church, and even now distributes the gifts of his Spirit to his faithful,[13] indeed blessed our John magnificently with his own special benediction to declare his remarkable future virtue and grace.

3. The child, then, was sent to school and learned to read. Having acquired a sufficient knowledge of grammar in his native country, he thought it appropriate and fitting to go to Paris, the mother of all arts, for he had an easy grasp of all subjects and a brilliant mind. There he first studied dialectic and became expert in the disciplines of theology, until at last family business compelled him to return home. Although he lived alone for a while in a small house, he did not remain hidden. For a man named Henry, a parish priest in the city of Cambrai, came to know of his reputation for good works and befriended him with urgent prayer and eager desire. Finding him to be devoted to sober living, constantly studying the Scriptures, inclined to prayer, and distinguished in other virtues, he approached the bishop of the city, whom he knew well, and thoughtfully recommended the young man. The bishop did not hesitate to advance the affair, and at a suitable time he had him ordained as a deacon. Compelled from now on to preach the word of God, he exhorted the faithful to eternal life.

[11] Luke 1. 42.

[12] Luke 18. 19.

[13] Cf. Augustine, *Retractationes*, 1.20.2, in CSEL 36, pp. 97–98.

How he preached against the heretics in Cambrai

4. Strengthened by the exercise of preaching, John confounded the heretics by whom the city of Cambrai was foully defiled at that time. He called publicans and sinners[14] entangled in vices back to the practice of virtues and true worship. It is hard to believe how effectively he sowed the seed of the divine word and bore fruit among the people — especially hard for a prelate charged with the office of priesthood or the authority of an archimandrite. But John at that time did well enough in the rank of a deacon. It was rare in those days to find anyone in the country who would admonish the people with the word of salvation, but almost everyone, priests and clerics alike, busied themselves to fill their purses. The people, ignorant of justice, strayed miserably like sheep without a shepherd, sick with the swelling of pride, scattered in enmity and sedition as in the mountains.[15] Therefore oppressive wolves, breaking into the Lord's sheepfold, proceeded boldly and savagely to kill and destroy.[16] Because God in his mercy, taking pity on the ruinous sickness of his people, had chosen this man in the sight of all, like another John to correct their morals or another Augustine to confound their errors,[17] the priests of the churches, kindled by the flames of envy, harshly attacked him with the scurrilous darts of their tongues. The heretics meanwhile raged with the dangerous madness of hatred.[18] But the steadfast young man was not frightened by the slander of his enemies nor by their threats, for the efficacy of God's collaboration had only made him stronger.

---

[14] Matthew 9. 10–11, 11. 9.

[15] Cf. III Kings 22. 17; Deuteronomy 1. 43; Augustine, *Enarrationes in Psalmos*, 97. 9, ed. by Eligius Dekkers and Iohannes Fraipont, in CCSL 39, p. 1377.

[16] Cf. John 10. 1, 10, 12; Matthew 7. 15; Acts 20. 29.

[17] The parallel with John the Baptist is underlined at many points: *novum luciferum* (I.1), *secundum nomen eius* (I.2), *benedictus fructus ventris tui* (I.2). Augustine is by far the author most cited by Thomas in all his works.

[18] These heretics, mentioned several times in the VJC, are probably the Cathars. Their presence is attested in the diocese of Cambrai in the twelfth century, but hitherto few traces of their activity in the town had been noted before the great repression by Robert le Bougre in 1236. See M. Grisart, 'Le Catharisme dans le Nord de la France', *Cahiers d'études cathares*, 2ᵐᵉ sér., 3–4 (1959), 24–40 (p. 29); Arno Borst, *Les Cathares* (Paris: Payot, 1974), p. 90, n. 3.

How the first chapel at Cantimpré was established

5. Around that time an honoured citizen was mourning inconsolably, having lost a son whom he had dearly loved. In great agitation he sought counsel from many people, asking how he could establish a special memorial to commend the soul of his dead son. A discerning man advised him to build a chapel in a suitable place and have John, a man of outstanding life, ordained chaplain there to celebrate masses for the dead man's soul, for his salvation and that of his family — and also to preach the word of God to the people, who would flock there from all quarters. Wonderfully comforted, that honourable citizen sought out the man who was so widely famed, explained his desire, and asked for his consent. When John considered the place that was being offered him by God — truly by God, fit for his purpose in every way — he rejoiced in the hope of peace[19] and agreed to the man's request. Without delay a chapel was constructed on the west side of the city and a stipend established for its clergy.[20] John, worthy of greater dignity, was ordained priest of the place, supported by the authority of the bishop. There he preached to the people who gathered from all sides. The name of the place was Cantimpré, so called from *cantus in prato*, because the young people of the city used to go walking there to enjoy its charm, singing of shady loves.[21] But now, by a change of the right hand of the Most High,[22] worldly pride was confounded by the abolition of sins in the very place where it had once delighted in wickedness.

6. Not long afterward two young clerics named Matthew and Walter, conspicuous for their chastity and good morals, joined in fellowship with John. Matthew, from the town of Inchy-en-Artois,[23] hailed from a distinguished

---

[19] The word *pax* is charged with meaning for Thomas. In the BUA, citing Augustine, he enumerates no fewer than seven types of peace: BUA II.14.3 and 5, pp. 205, 207.

[20] According to a charter of 1177, this was a hospital chapel: Archives du Nord, 37 H 26, 96; see A. Le Glay, *Glossaire topographique de l'ancien Cambrésis* (Cambrai: Deligne, 1849), pp. 65–66.

[21] For other versions of the same etymology see Guillaume Gazet, *L'Histoire ecclésiastique du Pays-Bas* (Arras: Guillaume de la Rivière, 1614), p. 83; A. Clément-Hémery, 'Notice sur les communautés des femmes établies à Cambrai avant la Révolution', *Mémoires de la Société d'émulation de Cambrai*, 10 (1826), 141–83 (p. 179, n. 4). For 'shady loves' cf. Augustine, *Confessiones*, ed. by Martin Skutella (Stuttgart: Teubner, 1969).

[22] Psalm 76. 11.

[23] Inchy-en-Artois, dép. Pas-de-Calais, arr. Arras, cant. Marquion.

military family. Walter, from the village of Buissy,[24] was born of respectable parents. I will have more to say later concerning these men.[25]

Around the same time John's father died and he took his widowed mother into his house.[26] Being utterly free of avarice, he wished to share by giving to everyone and receiving from virtually no one. But a man who gives everything away and receives no income usually incurs such poverty that he lacks even bread for his own needs. Yet the prophet 'does not see a just man forsaken, nor his household begging for bread'.[27] Nor could John be easily forsaken by Christ, who is the Truth:[28] how could he not 'add these things also' to one who sought his kingdom so perfectly?[29] When some of the faithful learned through vigilant inquiries of John's poverty, they took it on themselves to prepare the food he needed in season and leave it at night in a wood-burning stove outside the man of God's house. There his disciples would find it in the morning without the knowledge of John, who had no idea who was doing this. As similar tales were circulating far and wide by rumour, it happened that a matron rich in character and wealth lay dying at Arras. Being divinely inspired, she left John a huge piece of property in her will, so large that he could support himself on its annual income. Thanks to this excellent woman's devotion, some of the faithful were able to purchase seven bushels of grain with the tithes from this property.[30] These revenues were, in a sense, the original cause of the blessed John's holy enterprise in assembling a congregation of brethren.

Of a miraculous vision of St Gregory

7. At around that time Libertus, a young man of amazing simplicity and innocence, joined the venerable companions. Once on the feast of St Gregory,[31] as he was assisting Dom John at mass in the little chapel, he looked up after the

---

[24] Buissy, dép. Pas-de-Calais, arr. Arras, cant. Marquion.

[25] See VJC I.15.

[26] John 19. 27.

[27] Psalm 36. 25.

[28] John 14. 6.

[29] Matthew 6. 33.

[30] Cf. the charters of Hugh III of Oisy, 1179 (Archives du Nord, 37 H 31, 114) and Roger of Wavrin, 1180 (Archives du Nord, 37 H 31, 115); Le Glay, *Glossaire topographique*, p. 72.

[31] 12 March.

Gospel reading to see a man of supreme beauty, adorned with the papal insignia, standing at the blessed John's right hand. There he remained without moving until the service ended.[32] When it was over the holy pope disappeared. Thus one who is now immortal showed how the man he attended should be revered among mortals. Lest anyone presume to doubt this miracle because of its greatness, he should know I heard it from the mouth of Libertus himself, whose merits are so great that the reader can trust him without hesitation. Nevertheless, was it so difficult or marvellous for Christ to bear witness to his servant's saintliness by making a glorified saint visible to the spirit? Was this difficult for Christ, who has established ministries of angels to attend wherever the sacrament of his body is celebrated throughout the world? So I think it is no great digression to insert this exemplary tale into the lesson.

Of a miracle concerning the celebration of mass

8. From the venerable archdeacon Walter of Antwerp, a man conspicuous for knowledge and virtue, I learned that in his day there had been an old priest in Brabant who, though chaste in body, could not believe in the angelic ministry said to be present at the celebration of mass. At the church where this priest was vicar, the high altar was erected above a stone vault. Beneath it in the crypt was another altar. One day the old priest was about to celebrate mass at the high altar, where he had come after the Gospel to consecrate the body and blood of Christ, when with his bodily eyes he saw such a great host of angels — above, below, before, and beside him — that no human reckoning could count them.[33] Stricken with terror by this vision he fell flat on his back, the chalice still in his hands. Then there occurred an awesome and marvellous wonder. As the chalice spilled before the altar, the stone could not bear the force of Christ's blood, but gave way with a loud crack and split down the middle. Thus it made a path for the dripping blood to pass into the crypt below and find a place worthy of its dignity on the lower altar, there to be poured out in the sacrament. So the blood sank down to the altar, and the crack in the vault opened with no less power and

---

[32] Although the theme of the 'Mass of St Gregory' dates only to the fourteenth century, the holy pontiff is linked to many other eucharistic miracles. See Louis Réau, *Iconographie de l'art chrétien*, 3 vols (Paris: Presses universitaires de France, 1958), III.2, pp. 614–15.

[33] A classic theme. Cf. Browe, *Die eucharistischen Wunder*, pp. 5–12. Nomenclature for miracles of this kind can be found in G. B. Bagatta, *Admiranda orbis Christiani*, 2 vols (Augsburg: Bencard, 1700), I, pp. 51–52.

glory than when the blood poured out from the Lord's side and caused an earthquake on Calvary.[34] But this much must suffice on these matters. Now let me return to the life of John which I have set out to relate.

How John confounded a heretic and converted the nobleman Walter of Flos

9. One day the venerable John was returning from the city as usual after preaching a sermon in which he earnestly attacked the heretics. On the way back he met an old man of long-standing malice, who was publicly said to be an adherent and teacher of the nefarious error. When this man vomited out the blasphemous poison he had kept so long in his heart, he was summoned into court, but not defeated. Rather he was defended by many. But his case was later transferred to the see of Reims, where the heretic was defeated and condemned and paid the penalty for his error.

10. It is well known in the city and the countryside that Baldwin, a monk of the Holy Sepulchre in Cambrai,[35] was a religious and pious man in every way. He used to visit the blessed John early in his religious career and was well acquainted with his actions, so it is from him that I learned the story I am about to tell. Around the time the heretic I mentioned was condemned, the contagion of heretical depravity had spread so widely, not only among the citizens of Cambrai but also among the surrounding nobles, that the heretics had a defender among the chief men of the region. Walter of Flos,[36] a nobleman, was sharp-minded and clever in argument. One day he came to tempt the servant of God, and after he had proposed many partisan questions and received answers to all of them, he began to discuss the more subtle and profound mysteries of our faith. The blessed John, who was wary in such matters, rightly suspected Walter of heretical leanings. For the conversation finally came around to this: the knight openly admitted that he did not believe in the everyday sacrament of the altar, nor could any verbal explanation satisfy him unless he saw with his fleshly eyes what he so thoroughly disbelieved. After saying this the knight returned home. The blessed John had no little compassion on him, for, aside

---

[34] John 19. 34.

[35] The Benedictine abbey of St-Sepulchre, erected at Cambrai in 1064 by Bishop Lietbert. See *Gallia Christiana*, III, p. 118.

[36] An act of January 1211 records a donation by Mathilde, widow of Watier du Flos: Le Glay, *Glossaire topographique*, p. xxix.

from the crime of his unbelief, he was quite distinguished in his actions. So John gave himself wholly to the Lord, offering prayers and tears for this man. Three days later the knight returned and was present when the servant of Christ celebrated mass. At the time of the elevation, Walter suddenly beheld in the priest's hands a boy of such elegant beauty that he could by no means doubt this was the newborn Child who had once descended from heaven into the Virgin's womb for the salvation of humankind.[37] The beautiful sight was wondrous in every way — yet this was nothing and no one other than the One who is daily hidden beneath the veil of bread.[38] Seeing this wonder, the man fell prostrate in fear, and when the saving mystery was completed he threw himself at the feet of the holy priest. Begging his forgiveness, Walter appeared so utterly transformed that he abandoned the pomp of the world, and walking barefoot, he took up the cross and followed the naked, crucified Christ to Jerusalem.[39] Such were the fruits of the blessed John's fasting, such the efficacy of his prayers.

Of a miracle concerning twin boys who died after receiving baptism

11. I will recall another magnificent story about a knight because, although it does not pertain to my narrative, it is worth including to confirm our faith. These things happened around the same time. A knight's wife was pregnant and gave birth to twins. Since they were small and feeble, baptism was sought at once. The godparents had not yet reached the church when the vital spirit of one child flickered out and he seemed to be dead — although he was still secretly alive, as it later turned out. The priest hurried to baptize both infants, even though the status of one was in doubt. They had scarcely been brought home when the second child died. Both were carried once again to the church. One child was buried in the churchyard and the other, since it was believed to have

---

[37] An extremely widespread theme. Cf. Browe, *Die eucharistischen Wunder*, pp. 100–11. Thomas of Cantimpré was himself the witness of a miracle of this type, the famous miracle of St-Amé at Douai: BUA II.40.2, pp. 399–401.

[38] Exodus 16. 13–31.

[39] An expression of Jerome, very common in the eleventh through thirteenth centuries. Thomas could have read it, notably in James of Vitry, VMO II.45, in *Mary of Oignies*, p. 81. Cf. Matthäus Bernards, 'Nudus nudum sequi', *Wissenschaft und Weisheit*, 14 (1951), 148–51; Réginald Grégoire, 'L'Adage ascétique "Nudus nudum Christum sequi"', in *Studi storici in onore di Ottorino Bertolini*, ed. by Ottavio Banti and others, 2 vols (Pisa: Pacini, 1972), I, pp. 395–409.

died before baptism, was carried out to the fields for burial.[40] But as the priest
with the godparents was performing a funeral to honour the knight, the man
who held the infant's body in his arms suddenly heard a kind of muttering in the
casket, like the voice of a little child whimpering. Before he could be sure of the
unexpected voice, it fell silent, so he diligently put his ear to the body to see if
he would hear it again. Without delay he heard the child speaking more clearly
now and complaining, 'You do me an injury, for I was baptized just like my
brother'. Astonished at this voice, the man with the child called his companions
and the priest and declared that the infant was speaking. The priest drew near,
opened the casket, and adjured the child in the name of Christ to speak again.
The boy said, 'You do me an injury, for I was baptized just like my brother'.
Carrying him back to the church with great joy, the priest summoned the father
and the faithful and told them what had happened. At once the knight invited
his relatives and the nobles of the region and prepared a sumptuous funeral.
When the mass was completed with due honour, the boy was committed to the
grave. Baldwin, whom I mentioned earlier, told me this story which he heard
from those who witnessed it. But enough: let us return to our purpose.

How the castellan Hugh of Oisy endowed John's foundation at Cantimpré

12. Many people in those days followed the venerable John so ardently that
they could not bear his absence for even a short time. Among these was a widow
of Douai named Iueta, who was chaste, sober, and of marvellous faith. Having
abandoned her worldly goods because of the blessed John's teaching, she went
to live with her mother. Now John had not yet lived four years in Cantimpré
when, by Christ's divine inspiration, he announced that he wanted to fight the
good fight there in the habit of a religious order, for he had long ago conceived
this plan in his mind. When the venerable Hugh of Oisy, the castellan of
Cambrai[41] — an extremely noble and powerful man — learned of this, he went
to visit Christ's servant, whom he revered with great affection. Upon seeing his
abode, which seemed rather unsuitable for a foundation, Hugh provided some
land adjacent to the church of Saint Saviour on its right side, much more than
necessary for the founding of a religious house. After the houses on this land had

---

[40] A marginal note reads, 'Puer mortuus sine baptismo sepelitur extra terram sanctam' ('A
child who dies without baptism is buried outside of holy ground').

[41] Hugh III of Oisy, castellan of Cambrai (*c.* 1170–89/90).

been moved and a small chapel built to honour the glorious Virgin Mary, John took up residence there with his disciples. Without delay the venerable Roger, bishop of Cambrai,[42] was summoned and dedicated the place in everlasting glory, giving it the same name as the previous location.[43] This honourable bishop had previously offered the reverend John another place for his foundation, but, acting on wiser counsel, John preferred to yield to Hugh of Oisy as chief lord of the region.[44]

13. As the news of this foundation spread far and wide through the region, two well-regarded priests from Brabant flocked to John's company. These two men, Martin and Hilliard, had acquired a little chapel with some other small properties, and they too had planned to build a monastery. But they abandoned this plan because of John's holy reputation and submitted themselves wholly to his rule.[45] At the same time, with many exhortations John converted a certain Robert, distinguished in mind and reputation, from the seductive snares of the world and joined with him in an everlasting pact. After Robert another man of Brabant named Julian, born of very respectable parents, threw in his lot with the rest.

How John and Matthew went to Paris to be affiliated with the canons of Saint-Victor

14. Strengthened by the spirit of God, the blessed John had accepted the venerable Matthew as his first disciple, but Matthew now became his colleague,

---

[42] Roger of Wavrin, bishop of Cambrai (1178–91).

[43] A charter of Roger of Wavrin from 1180 records the donation of Hugh of Oisy, exempts the land from all tithes and parochial rights, and authorizes the construction of a church there: Archives du Nord, 37 H 1, 1; see A. Bruyelle, 'Abbaye de Notre-Dame de Cantimpré, et église de St-Sauveur, paroissiale de Cantimpré', *Archives du Nord*, n.s. 5 (1844), 300–11 (pp. 300–01).

[44] 'Voluit nobis ad fundandum dare locum sed ad maiorem ecclesie nostre utilitatem domino Hugoni de Oiziaco utpote terre principi in hoc dando voluit cedere' ('[The bishop] wished to give us [land] to found a religious house, but for the greater utility of our church, [Dom John] wished to yield to Lord Hugh of Oisy as prince of the region in this donation'): Necrology of Cantimpré, 23 November (Archives du Nord, 37 H 29). This seventeenth-century copy does not permit us to affirm with certainty that the necrology predates the VJC, but certain signs nevertheless point in that direction.

[45] This is the origin of the priory of Bellingen. Cf. the charter of Roger of Wavrin from 1182: Bruyelle, 'Abbaye de Notre-Dame de Cantimpré', pp. 301–02. The two priests are there called Martin and Léardice.

for he had risen to the rank of priesthood. With him John hastened to visit the distinguished religious community of Saint-Victor in Paris,[46] explained his burning purpose, and begged to be received into the society of that order and subjected to its holy institutions. But the honourable men were prudent in every way. When they recognized the poverty and neediness of the new foundation, they deferred John's desire for a while because a house that still lacked sufficient material foundations could be shaken by ill fortune and the religious reduced to public begging, to the disgrace of the whole order. Then the honourable men I named earlier — Bishop Roger of Cambrai and Hugh of Oisy, castellan of Cambrai, with some other nobles of the region — heard that John and his companions could not be admitted to the Victorine order because of their poverty, so they took counsel and made donations. The bishop gave the right to present clergy and the parish revenues[47] of the church of St Saviour outside the walls; Hugh, an annual income in grain; and others, the tithes of the church of Cantimpré.[48]

Then the devout confessor returned to Paris with his colleague and demonstrated that his house had received further income, so the obstacle was removed. But those most reverent men, who were extremely shrewd in business matters, gave a memorable answer. 'It is obvious', they said, 'that monastic life is everywhere in a state of decline. Every house seeks its own, and the love of many has grown cold.[49] As for you, even if you have now collected enough revenue to satisfy your needs, what you have is by no means sufficient for other contingencies that can unexpectedly threaten a monastery which is still poor.[50] So you will stay here with us for a while and learn the usages of the order until divine providence visits you from on high.' Since the brethren comforted the blessed man and his companion with this response, they agreed to remain at Saint-Victor. There too John, in accord with the meaning of his name, did not

---

[46] The abbey of canons regular of Saint-Victor at Paris. See Fourier Bonnard, *Histoire de l'Abbaye royale et de l'ordre des chanoines réguliers de Saint-Victor de Paris*, 2 vols (Paris: Savaète, 1904–08); Jean Chatillon, 'Canonici regolari di San Vittore', in *Dizionario degli Istituti de Perfezione*, 10 vols (Rome: Paoline, 1975), II, pp. 124–34.

[47] *personatum cum presbiteratu.*

[48] Cf. the charter of Roger of Wavrin, 1183 (Archives du Nord, 37 H 31, 117); Le Glay, *Glossaire topographique*, pp. 74–75.

[49] Cf. Philippians 2. 21 and Matthew 24. 12.

[50] Although Cantimpré was a house of regular canons, Thomas never uses the term *canonici*. He calls John's companions *viri* or *fratres*, but refers to their house as a *monasterium*. [BN]

lack divine grace. Rather, it became clear to all that heavenly virtue had made its dwelling place in him. His modesty, his dovelike simplicity,[51] and his sober, unaffected, timely wisdom astonished them all so much that even though he had not yet earned the respect due to age, being still a young man, he amazingly came to be cherished as a father, not only by the brethren of Saint-Victor, but also by the abbot and brethren of Sainte-Geneviève.

Thus it came about that before he had completed sixteen months there, the most reverend abbot of Sainte-Geneviève and some of his brethren went to the abbot and community of Saint-Victor[52] to express their displeasure that the devout man had not yet been received. They maintained that it was indecent to defer such a pious, humble, and patient desire any longer: the request John had made some time ago should be swiftly granted. The abbot was not disappointed in his pleas, but gratified at once by the abbot and brethren of Saint-Victor. They met and sent a letter by John's hand to the venerable Roger, bishop of Cambrai, directing him by the authority of the order to profess John and his brethren in perpetual vows under the rule of St Augustine and the institutions of Saint-Victor.[53] Thanking them graciously, John and his companion returned home with great joy and told the bishop what had happened. The bishop rejoiced with him and set a date to conclude the matter. When the day came, the blessed John stepped forth with only six brothers, who humbly bowed their necks and received the yoke of the order with the yoke of God, professing perpetual vows under the rule of St Augustine and the institutions of Saint-Victor.[54] It is hard to imagine all the sighs and tears that were shed on that occasion.

Now, for the sake of posterity, I think it fitting to record the names of those six who joined the order with their blessed father, and to tell what kind of men they were.

---

[51] Matthew 10. 16.

[52] The communities of St-Victor and Ste-Geneviève had been closely linked since 1148. See Bonnard, *Histoire de l'Abbaye royale*, I, pp. 160–71; P. Féret, *L'Abbaye de Sainte-Geneviève et la Congrégation de France*, 2 vols (Paris: Champion, 1883), I, pp. 101–09. At the time of John of Cantimpré's sojourn in Paris, around 1183, the abbot of Ste-Geneviève was none other than Stephen of Tournai.

[53] The institutions of St-Victor have been preserved in the *Liber ordinis*: see *De antiquis Ecclesiae ritibus*, ed. by Edmond Martène, 4 vols (Antwerp: [n. pub.], 1736–38), III, pp. 252–91.

[54] Cf. the charter of Bishop Roger of Wavrin, 1183 (Archives du Nord, 37 H 1, 5); André Le Glay, *Mémoire sur les archives des églises et maisons religieuses du Cambrésis* (Lille: [n. pub.], 1852), pp. 73–74.

On the first six men received into the order with John*

15. *Dom Matthew.* I set the venerable Matthew first as the most distinguished both in birth and in morals. Among his other shining virtues, he was notable for humility and sobriety, which made him appear so gracious that he was revered by the humble and the powerful alike. After the outstanding father of our foundation, he governed the community as its second abbot.[55] I saw him myself in the early days of my conversion, when he was already worn with age, so I can speak with certainty as an eyewitness. Even after he had laid down the burden of office, full of years and merits and oppressed by the severe, frequent illnesses that plagued him until his death, he never withdrew his advice or support from sinners who wished to repent. Rather, he was eager to hear confessions and comfort the desolate, striving zealously to multiply the Lord's talent with the interest of souls.[56] In such things he did not spare himself until the blood that ran down from his half-dead limbs moistened his footprints. Since he who has lived well always dies well, as Augustine says,[57] we saw Matthew both living well and dying well. When his venerable body was brought to be washed by the brothers, it blossomed as bright and pure as a lily. Who would have believed that this body had been foul with scabies and dripping with corruption? Yet divine power was manifest in such a man. He died around the seventy-first year of his age, on 6 February 1218.

Walter. After Matthew came Walter, a man endowed with marvellous wisdom, who never stopped working for the growth of the house with incredible patience and virtue, from the flower of his youth until the end of his life. He deserved to see the fruit of his labour on earth and receive its reward in heaven. I saw him at the very end of his days, when he was neither ready to give up his work nor able to continue it.

---

* Chapter heading appears in the manuscript. [BN]

[55] An Abbot Matthew is mentioned in 1199: *Monuments pour servir à l'histoire des provinces de Namur, de Hainaut et de Luxembourg, Collection de chroniques belges inédites*, ed. by Frédéric de Reiffenberg, 8 vols (Brussels: Hayex, 1844–74), II: *Cartulaire de l'abbaye de Cambron*, ed. by J. J. De Smet (1869), p. 742, and again in 1204 and 1207: Archives du Nord, 36 H 66, 36 H 223; Aubertus Miraeus and J.-Fr. Foppens, *Opera diplomatica et historica*, 4 vols (Louvain: Denique, 1723–48), I, p. 732.

[56] Cf. Matthew 25. 14–30; VMO I.38, in *Mary of Oignies*, p. 74.

[57] Augustine, *De disciplina christiana*, 12.13, ed. by R. vander Plaetsein, in CCSL 46, p. 221; cf. BUA II.2.5, p. 128.

Robert. In the third place Robert distinguished himself. He had been worldly in his illustrious youth, but the blessed John converted him to the religious life by constant exhortation. Holding the office of subprior, Robert is said to have been so devout that he could scarcely ever restrain his tears. The venerable Nicholas, fourth abbot of the church of Cantimpré, brilliant in virtue and letters, composed an epigraph in verse for this man:[58]

> Here lies that venerable father Robert, a man
> Endowed with nature's gifts and heaven's grace,
> Patient, humble, stable, chaste, and mild,
> Wise and well-pleasing to Christ in all ways.

Julian. The fourth was my close friend and compatriot Julian. Born of a distinguished family in Brabant, he was a man of wonderful devotion who lived a very pious life. About three years before he died I heard this marvellous and noteworthy tale from his lips, but he compelled me to say nothing about it as long as he remained in the body. From an early age he had an immoderate fear of sin, although he kept his conscience pure. One night, as he lay in the infirmary and rose at the sound of the bells, he was making his way across the cloister to church when suddenly the devil, the enemy of humankind, came to meet him. With a horrible voice he said, 'Where are you going? What are you seeking? Why do you labour in vain? You cannot be saved!' The man was disturbed beyond measure by this voice, yet in this state of mind he continued on to matins. After the service he went out again. Being tormented for a long while in great spiritual anguish, at last by a divine impulse he remembered the Lord's mercies,[59] and dissolving in tears, he raised his eyes and hands to heaven with these words: 'I know, Lord, I know and am truly certain that if you consider my innumerable sins, your justice will judge that I have no share in your kingdom. Yet I also know and I am no less certain that, being merciful and compassionate,[60] you do not despise those who return to you. Although I am a slave to sins, yet since I have long hoped to be well disposed toward you, I beg that if, in your foreknowledge, you know that I will do worthy penance and come into your glory, you will deign to reveal it to me by some sign, for I am

---

[58] *Epit. Ioannis Belethi: Anzeiger für Kunde der deutschen Vorzeit* (Nürnberg: Germanisches Museum, 1835–83), N.F.14 (1867), p. III.

[59] Isaiah 63. 7.

[60] Psalms 85. 15, 102. 8, 110. 4, 111. 4, 144. 8; James 5. 11.

desolate and as far from hope as I can be.'[61] He had scarcely finished these words when suddenly, raising his eyes above, he saw the sky open up like a wheel, and his surroundings sparkled like sunlight. The vision remained without change for the space of an hour, and by giving such proof of the divine condescension, it comforted the man approved by God and gave him better hope.[62] Though I heard this from his own mouth, I can also call as a witness our prior, the venerable Briccius, who heard him tell the same story as he lay at the point of death. If any reader is amazed by this, he would be no less amazed by other things I could tell about him, which I omit for the sake of brevity.

Martin. The fifth was Martin from Brabant, who was converted from the secular life by Yburgis, a most holy virgin. This Yburgis was our sister in our house at Bellingen, where, as a recluse shut up in stone walls, she led an angelic life upon earth. Taking only a little food, carefully weighed and measured, she was reported to be so chaste that she was frequently visited by the delightful company of angels and learned many celestial secrets. Her marvellous life and merit requires me to write much more about her, but because of its greatness her life demands a work of its own and the leisure to write it.[63] As for Martin, among his other splendid virtues he is said to have had such great faith that he once confidently promised an adversary that a candle would be lighted by miracle to disprove a slander against him.

Hilliard and Geoffrey, who followed him. The sixth was Hilliard who, after making a show of righteousness for a while among the others, showed in the end what kind of man he was and returned to his vomit.[64] Yet the fall of one among so many excellent men should not scandalize anyone. For their house was not greater, in fact not nearly as great, as the habitation of Christ, in which eleven good men tolerated the thief and liar Judas. Nor was it better than heaven itself, from which the angels fell.[65]

---

[61] Ezekiel 6. 14.

[62] The same story is retold in BUA II.52.5, p. 483; hence the notice devoted to Julian by Arnoldus de Raisse, *Ad Natales Sanctorum Belgii Ioannis Molani Auctarium* (Douai: Avroy, 1626), fol. 381.

[63] Perhaps this is the same recluse mentioned in BUA I.23.2–3, pp. 92–94. [No trace remains of any *Vita Yburgis* by Thomas, but this comment anticipates his interest in the hagiography of holy women. BN]

[64] II Peter 2. 22.

[65] Cf. VLA II.35.

So a certain Geoffrey from Flanders took the place of Hilliard — a very good-looking man, wonderfully adorned with the jewels of all virtues, but especially compassion. He showed himself humble and devoted not only to his brothers but also to the sick, even among the serfs. For those who suffered from painful infirmity in their legs, he devised a special kind of toilet seat to assist their natural purgation.[66] Toward the poor he was so merciful and kind[67] that in wintertime, he furtively removed the thick linings from his own tunic and coat and stuffed them into the boots of the needy. See what a wonderful life he led! He was no less wonderful in the leaving of it. As he lay dying in our house at Bellingen, the common people, summoned by one of the brothers, flocked to church to gather at his bedside. With a warm fervour he exhorted them to everlasting joy, breathing out his very soul in the living testimony of his voice, and by the holy desire with which he showed them the way, like one who knew it well, he proved that he himself was about to enter that joy.

This is the sixth man who, with five others just as distinguished, joined the venerable John at the beginning of our foundation, like the six arms of a candelabra joined to one trunk.[68] Many people were amazed that these seven men — so excellent in beauty, so noble in merits, so resplendent in virtue — had come together with one spirit at one time for a single work. Men of this calibre could not easily have been found in those days, when the way of justice was corrupted almost everywhere, in every rank among every people, unless the divine Spirit had gathered them. It was indeed divine providence that arranged such stones in our foundation, on whose firmness so great a building could rise securely to the heights. These seven men, therefore, like the seven lamps in the tabernacle,[69] shone with a sevenfold grace. They are like seven golden candlesticks or seven stars,[70] encircling this church of ours like the throne of divine majesty with never-setting light. Even now, although they have died, they encircle and illumine it still more blessedly.

But here let me end this narrative and return to our John, whose honour and glory were even greater and will remain, by the grace of God, to set an example for posterity.

---

[66] A marginal comment reads 'Nota humile officium' ('note the humble office').

[67] Ecclesiasticus 2. 13.

[68] Exodus 25. 35.

[69] Apocalypse 4. 5.

[70] Apocalypse 1. 12, 16, 20.

How Libertus left the community but was helped in temptation by John's prayers

16. After the blessed John and the men I have named had by God's consent received the yoke of the order, that Libertus whom I mentioned earlier, along with a certain Fulco, developed an aversion to monastic life and left the house and company of the others. Breaking his original vow of chastity, Fulco scandalized the wicked world by his fall. But the blessed John's prayers and exhortations induced him to repent, and afterwards he lived a chaste religious life. Purified by his tears, he rose to the rank of priesthood. As for Libertus, he accepted the office of subtreasurer in the greater church of St Mary. Not long after he departed, he received proof of the holiness of that man whose company he had just timidly forsaken. One night, having risen at dawn, he was seized by a great, unbearable anxiety as he lay prostrate in prayer. As his mind was shaken more and more violently by temptations, he fell to trembling all over and, by some divine impulse, cried out in a horror-stricken voice, 'Dom John is praying for me!' He had not yet fully returned to himself when, once again, he trembled with terror, and again he fearfully exclaimed in the same voice, 'Dom John is praying for me!' But as I myself learned from him, he did not know why he said this. Rather, at the moment when he was stricken with sudden fear and trembling, this spontaneous cry broke from his lips without his knowledge.

A few days later Libertus came to visit John and they exchanged greetings. The man of God said to Libertus, 'I believe that something bad happened to you not long ago, my son, for the other day I found myself praying to the Lord for you more than usual'. The priest asked, 'What day and time was that?' John told him, and Libertus recognized that it was at exactly that hour when he felt imperilled by temptations and, suddenly horror-stricken, broke out in the words I have recorded. It is worth noting that blessed John did not lack the divine Spirit, by which he was able to know what happened in his absence, nor did the divine Judge esteem his merits lightly when he revealed his prayers by such a powerful sign. I heard this story, as I have said, from the priest Libertus himself.

How the fame of the house at Cantimpré spread throughout the region

17. So the venerable priest John had achieved his purpose. He served the Lord at Cantimpré in poverty and humility, with his chosen religious brethren, under the canonical rule. As their fame spread, not only in Cambrai but also in Arras, Douai, and other nearby towns and villages, powerful noblemen and devout matrons, both humble and exalted, learned of John's holy reputation by sight, hearsay, or personal experience, and offered countless donations of gold, silver, precious vestments, revenues, and estates to endow and enrich the new plantation. So the temporal possessions of the house were multiplied beyond belief, yet the blessed John paid little or no attention. He even refused many of the gifts that were offered to him, for he wished to have a house not glorious in riches, but genuine in virtues. For his own part, he devoted himself to prayer, study, and preaching. Intent on hearing confessions, he cared about nothing so much as how to instruct the scrupulous conscience. People throughout the region flocked to him every day. So the community was held in such reverence, along with the man who made it holy, that everyone wanted to claim John as their advocate. Those troubled by misfortune sought his comfort; those beset by anxiety awaited his counsel; those assaulted by temptations begged for his support; those oppressed by the weight of sins received his absolution. Such needs have weighed on his successors from that day even to the present. But they think it a pleasure to bear this toil because most of them are aflame with zeal for souls, and at harvest time their labours will bear much fruit, for people are being saved every day.

How Dom John was appointed abbot by Bishop Roger of Cambrai

18. Not long after the blessed John and his companions were received into the order, a very religious and pious man named Herbert, abbot of Saint-Aubert in Cambrai,[71] gathered the noble and powerful men of the city and went to Bishop Roger of Cambrai. Without John's knowledge, they earnestly begged the bishop to raise the holy man to a higher dignity and appoint him abbot of his foundation, for he was still languishing in the humble office of prior. They said this would be useful to the foundation and help it grow, nor could anyone despair of the house if it had such a man styled with the title of abbot. Delighted by this request, the bishop gave the brothers license to elect such an abbot as the divine Spirit would ordain among them. In accord with their pious desire, the blessed John was elected unanimously. Despite his strenuous resistance, he was nevertheless elected and presented to the bishop, nor did he have a chance to

---

[71] The abbey of canons regular of St-Aubert. The abbacy of Herbert (whose name is given in certain acts as 'Hubert') is attested from 1185; the last mention of his predecessor, Amaury, dates from 1182 (*Gallia Christiana*, III, pp. 154–55). Thomas's allusion gives the impression that Herbert was abbot from 1183 on.

decline or refuse. Rather, before an assembly of the nobles and powerful men of the region, he was blessed by the bishop and raised to the more dignified office of abbot.[72] It happened that Fulco, whom I mentioned a little earlier, had been suffering from quartan fever for about four years, but when John received the episcopal blessing he was suddenly cured.

It is hard to conceive the urgency and vigilance, the fear and trembling,[73] with which Abbot John strove for the salvation of his subjects. How gracious it was to see the humility and kindness, the modest and holy reverence,[74] with which he governed them! Seldom in his whole career as abbot was he compelled to use harshness. Once, when a certain brother had rebelled with stubborn disobedience, he sequestered him from the company of his brethren for a while because it would have been unfitting to let any vice take root in such a new house, especially the vice of rebellion or disobedience. So it was necessary and wholesome to chastise this evil from the outset with a rather harsh punishment. Indeed, though I praise John for treating his subjects so kindly and gently, it would have been a vice in him if he had given scope to any other vice — for it is no less wrong to squelch justice in one's community than it is to exercise harshness without mercy. The truth is, John's disciples were such that his kindness never became an occasion for laxity, nor did his justice or severity ever become a burden.

After he became abbot he had the same zeal for souls as before, the same devotion. Making a circuit of the region, he used to visit the cities, villages, castles, and towns[75] just as he had always done, taking pains for the salvation of souls. If he lacked a vehicle he went on foot, and if any act could reveal even greater humility, the devout and humble man performed it — with apologies to those who cavil at such things. But now, having drawn this volume of my narrative out to great length because its story is so full, I will end the first portion here so that readers may renew their study more agreeably with new material.

---

[72] The elevation of Cantimpré to the rank of abbey can be dated to 1183. Cf. the charter of Roger of Wavrin, 1183: 'ibidemque abbas canonice ordinetur' ('let him be canonically ordained as abbot in the same place'): Archives du Nord, 37 H 1, 5; Le Glay, *Mémoire sur les archives*, pp. 73–74.

[73] Ephesians 6. 5, 18.

[74] Colossians 3. 12.

[75] Matthew 9. 35.

Of the death of Dom John's mother and how she was received into heaven

1. Not long after the Lord's servant John became abbot of his congregation, his good and pious mother died. After her death a monk named Vacellus, devoted to contemplation, was praying before the altar in church when suddenly an eagle with glorious, radiant feathers appeared to him and lifted his spirit as if on its shoulders to a broad, beautiful region. There St Benedict came to meet the monk and led him to even more beautiful and lofty places. When the saint had shown him the many mansions Christ had prepared for his faithful there in accord with their merits,[76] the monk suddenly heard the voice of a woman giving thanks on high. He asked St Benedict, 'Master, whose voice is it that I hear giving thanks so gladly?' Benedict answered, 'This is the mother of Dom John of Cantimpré, who was recently delivered from purgatorial fire by the prayers of her devoted son. Now she thankfully exults in heaven with the souls of the faithful.' After the monk had seen many other things in that place, he returned to the human realm on the same eagle that had brought him there. Privately expounding his vision, he also revealed what he had learned about John's mother. Because the monk who saw these things was a man of such holiness, authority, and merit, I would judge it wicked and impious not to believe him and those who knew him well. Therefore these little verses were inscribed on John's mother's tomb:

> A simple dove without guile lies buried in this soil.[77]
> Theoberga was her name, in morals without blame,

---

[76] John 14. 2.

[77] *Epit. Frederici Leodiensis episcopi*: MGH.SS 25, p. 97; cf. VLA III.17.

The happy mother of this church's father.
Beneath this dust she lies, yet to the skies
She flew from purgatorial fires, released by prayers,
As vision shows. Let none marvel that a faithful son,
True in life as in belief, could by his worth achieve
This grace, blessed then in prayer, today in power.

How Dom John intervened with the emperor during an episcopal schism

2. The first book of Kings records that, when the Lord sent a prophet to Eli the priest to rebuke his sons, the prophet said to him among other things, 'Whoever honours me, I will glorify him'.[78] Because Abbot John, beloved of God and men,[79] took care to honour God in and through all that he did, God glorified him daily even upon earth among the powerful and the humble alike; and now he glorifies him in everlasting life with the contemplation of the beatific vision.

Now Bishop Roger of Cambrai, whom I have mentioned before, took the sign of the Cross and journeyed to the Holy Land of the Lord's resurrection. There he fell asleep in the Lord and made a blessed end. But a serious and disgraceful schism arose among the clergy of Cambrai over the election of a new bishop. Some of them — the wiser part — chose the archdeacon of that church, the venerable John of Arras, a very handsome man, outstanding for his chastity; but others elected the master of the school, conspicuous for his high birth. As both candidates hastened to the emperor with great pomp and circumstance to ask for the regalia, as custom demands, the archdeacon and bishop-elect John took the abbot Dom John to court with him on account of his excellent reputation.[80] At that time the empire was governed by Henry VI, the son of Emperor Frederick the Great — a most Christian man, vigorous in mind and

---

[78] I Samuel 2. 30.

[79] Ecclesiasticus 45. 1.

[80] Roger of Wavrin died in the Holy Land in 1191. The election that followed pitted the archdeacon Jean d'Antoing (who was also dean of Arras) against the scholar Wautier, chancellor of Cambrai. Both appealed to the emperor, whose right to decide for the *sanior pars* in case of a division within the chapter had been recognized by the Concordat of Worms. Henry VI (1190–97) pronounced in favour of Jean d'Antoing. These events are recounted by Gislebert de Mons, who makes no mention of John of Cantimpré in his *Chronicon Hanoniense: La Chronique de Gislebert de Mons, Recueil de textes pour servir à l'histoire de Belgique*, ed. by Léon Vanderkindere (Brussels: Kiessling, 1904), pp. 256, 267–68.

arms, and superbly educated in letters.[81] When the blessed John had obtained an audience with the emperor, he addressed him in words like these: 'It is yours, lord, to exercise judgement and justice, for you are set over the kingdom. Christ's bride, the Church, has been commended to your care: she prays for you in the Psalms and says, "Lord, save the King".[82] For you she pours forth her prayers and supplications to the Lord. In the unique sacrifice of our redemption, you occupy a special place every day; for your sake the sacrifice of Christ's flesh and blood is offered on the altars. Therefore it is your role as emperor to defend and protect Christ's bride to the best of your ability, to provide for her members with sound government, and to guard the Lord's church throughout the world in the unity of faith[83] and peace, for by her prayers you can attain both serenity in your present kingdom and everlasting glory in the kingdom that is to come.'

Delighted with these and other remarks of the holy John, the emperor inquired diligently to find out who this man was, so small in body yet so magnificent in integrity. The bishop-elect John, for whose sake the blessed John had come to court, replied, 'This, lord, is a man outstanding for holiness and virtue in every way, the teacher and light of our province, through whom God works wonderfully for the salvation of souls'. The emperor said, 'Truly, splendid virtue is hidden in his small body!' So after this, because the outcome of the election was contested in both civil and canon law, the glorious emperor approved the election of John, the former archdeacon, and gave him the regalia.

How the sisters' house was established at Prémy under the prioress Iueta

3. After his mother's death Abbot John, a discreet pastor and prudent overseer, began to fear potential complaints if the sisters continued to live with the brothers in one monastery, even if they were outside the walls; for the prophet says 'it is good and pleasing for brothers' — not brothers and sisters — 'to dwell together in unity'.[84] Therefore he gave orders to build a suitable

---

[81] The literary activity of Henry VI is attested by contemporaries: H. M. Schaller, 'Heinrich VI', in *Neue Deutsche Biographie*, 22 vols (Berlin: Duncker & Humblot, 1953–), VIII, pp. 323–26.

[82] Psalm 19. 10.

[83] Ephesians 4. 13.

[84] Psalm 132. 1.

dwelling for them at a place called Prémy.[85] But when this was done the sisters themselves were afraid, as women usually are, to live so far away from men. This is not surprising because in those days, malicious bandits used to prowl around the country, robbing and murdering people. So the man of God went to consult the Lord in prayer before his mercy seat. Without delay he received an answer from the Lord in his spirit: the sisters should enter the place prepared for them and have no fear, knowing they would be protected in all things by divine aid and guarded by the defence of heaven. At once, giving thanks to the mercy of God, he summoned Iueta, whom I mentioned in the first book[86] — for she was prioress at that time — with the other sisters, and informed them that they could move safely to their new place. The prioress, who discerned from John's face as he was speaking that he had received some message about this move, asked him in private what he had seen or felt. For nothing to do with the holy man could escape the prioress's shrewd observation, and with her blandishments she extorted this secret, like so many others, from his heart.[87]

Iueta was a woman magnificent in virtue and marvellous in faith, a most fervent admirer of the blessed John's actions. Outstanding in morals as in birth, she watched over him like a mother, for in the flower of her youth, she had renounced abundant worldly riches and pleasures because of his preaching. Imitating her example, other noble and distinguished matrons and virgins joined her in the observance of a religious rule. Among these were the very noble Anastasia de Croisilles[88] and the distinguished Mathilda, wife of the great nobleman Thomas of Fontaines, along with many others who, spurning worldly power and glory, chose to live under the saint's rule and teaching.

I learned of the following miracle concerning Mathilda from Dom Matthew, our second abbot.

[85] Prémy, cant. and arr. of Cambrai. See Archives du Nord, 50 H. The authors of the *Gallia Christiana* (III, p. 166) assign the approximate date of 1185 to the foundation, but without evidence to justify it.

[86] Cf. VJC I.12. Gazet mentions (without citing his source) a woman named Eufenne, sister of John of Cantimpré, as first 'abbess': *L'Histoire ecclésiastique du Pays-Bas*, p. 92. This reference is adopted from Gazet (with 'abbess' corrected to 'prioress') in *Gallia Christiana*, III, p. 166.

[87] Thomas here turns what were normally misogynist topoi (e.g., women are naturally fearful and skilled at extorting secrets from men) to the praise of a woman. [BN]

[88] An Alard de Croisilles appears among the first benefactors of Cantimpré: Miraeus and Foppens, *Opera diplomatica et historica*, I, p. 732; André Le Glay, *Revue des Opera Diplomatica de Miraeus* (Brussels: Hayez, 1856), p. 77.

4. While the sisters were still living in the monastery, it was their custom to rise at night for matins. But Prioress Iueta often required Mathilda to stay in bed when the vigils were unusually long and her body was frail, for she was a woman of very delicate health. One night it happened that the light in their dwelling went out while the sisters were at matins and Mathilda was resting in bed. When she saw this she got up at once and ran to the kitchen, but found no fire there, and it was forbidden for the sisters to knock at the brothers' gate by night. So she fell humbly before the Lord in prayer and begged him with tears, 'Look at our sisters, Lord! See your handmaids who have risen from sleep, breaking the quiet of night to offer you the sacrifice of mortification and prayer. After such a long, cold vigil, how are they to return in darkness? How can they find their way back to bed without light? Your servants should not rest in darkness, nor is it fitting for them to walk in darkness. Act then, Lord! Graciously show us your mercy: let your power rekindle the lamp!'[89] She had scarcely finished her prayer when at once the lamp was divinely rekindled and shone with celestial light. Nor was it difficult or marvellous for God to display so great a miracle in so small a thing, for he does not consider what is asked so much as the intensity of desire with which the devout, worthy woman sought what he granted. Not only Dom Matthew but also Brother Walter — second among the first six whom I listed above — was a reliable witness of this event.

5. About the time the convent moved to Prémy, as I have heard, another of our sisters was praying one night when she was seized by the divine Spirit and rapt into ecstasy. She saw a great horde of demons converging at the gate as, with a mighty assault, they tried to break down the door and demolish everything. But at once St John the Evangelist, the patron saint of that house, appeared and banished the whole multitude of cruel fiends. It was surely fitting and right for the blessed evangelist John to defend the chaste community of virgins against the ferocious, malignant assaults of the demons, for he himself preserved his virginal integrity and protected Christ's virgin mother, who was commended to his care because he too was a virgin.[90] I heard this from several members of our community and especially from the prioress, venerable Iueta.

Such then are the noble origins of the church of Prémy; such are the beginnings of that holy convent. The marks of our holy father sparkle in and

---

[89] Psalm 17. 29.

[90] *Responsorium Officii S. Ioannis*, in R.-J. Hesbert, *Corpus antiphonalium officii*, IV, no. 6454, in *Rerum ecclesiasticarum documenta, Series maior, Fontes 7-12* (Rome: Herder, 1963-79). Cf. BUA II.29.3, p. 275.

through everything, and everywhere the seeds of meritorious works, sown by his holy hand, sprout and flourish. So let me now return to him as my central figure and recall my mind, which has strayed to other matters — even though it was I who sent it wandering.

Of a brother and sister who underwent a judicial ordeal for murder

6. In the city of Cambrai a brother and sister, living in the same house, received a very wealthy merchant as their guest. Imagining how rich they would be if they killed him and having no fear of so great a crime, they cheerfully murdered the man in his bed and hid his body in the earth. But there is nothing covered that will not be revealed, nothing hidden that will not be made known,[91] so a rumour arose among their neighbours that these two were guilty of the crime. Even though there was no definite proof, they were suspected because of circumstantial evidence. Arrested and put in prison, they were compelled to undergo the ordeal of hot iron because there were no witnesses to the truth. So, as the custom is in such ordeals, they received a stay of execution and the brother chose the bishop of Cambrai, while the sister chose the blessed John as a confessor. As soon as God's saint had learned her secret, she threw herself at his feet, stricken with compunction, and confessed that she was guilty of homicide. The compassionate John, pitying her anguish, wept and comforted her, urging her to trust in Christ's mercy, and absolved her of the crime. On the day set for the ordeal, people gathered to watch the spectacle as they usually do in such cases. Both the brother and the sister were brought forth and completed the ordeal, and afterward their palms were sealed with bandages.[92] A few days later, when the seals were removed and the hands of both suspects were displayed, the brother's were burned by the fire and covered with lesions, but the sister's appeared much healthier and her skin was clearer. Without delay, the brother was made to pay the penalty of the crime and the sister was set free.[93] Who can doubt that it was through the blessed John's protection that her guilt was not disclosed by the ordeal, and the hand stretched out in retribution by the divine

---

[91] Luke 12. 2. Cf. BUA I.24.3, pp. 97–98; II.27.2, p. 265.

[92] A marginal note reads 'Nota morem sigilli in probationibus' ('note the custom of sealing in ordeals').

[93] Caesarius of Heisterbach tells the story of a heretic branded by red-hot iron who, upon agreeing to confess, sees the burn progressively disappear as he proceeds with his confession: *Dialogus miraculorum*, III.16, I, p. 132.

majesty was withdrawn?[94] Indeed, when he absolved her of sins by his priestly authority, he also absolved her of punishment by his prayers. I learned this from Baldwin, the monk of the Holy Sepulchre.

Of a pilgrim miraculously saved from shipwreck

7. To this chapter I will add a similar miracle which rumour has diffused throughout the city. But as a greater witness to its truth I cite Dom Matthew, our second abbot. I once heard Father Matthew say that some pilgrims, returning from Jerusalem by sea to their homes in France, had been sailing with favourable winds when suddenly the sky darkened. Thunder and lightning descended and a great storm arose at some distance, imperilling everyone's life. As the danger increased and the rising waves threatened to sink the ship, all the passengers began to undress and throw themselves into the sea, hoping they could perhaps swim to land somewhere. Among them was a citizen of Cambrai named William, who had renounced the world through the preaching of the holy father John. This man waited longer than he should have to undress, and having no time to remove his clothes carefully, he tried in great anguish to tear the fustian tunic he was wearing. But the cloth was new and very strong, and his attempt failed. Seeing this, he despaired of his life until he remembered his spiritual father and cried out, 'O John, most holy father, you who freed my soul from the still graver peril of eternal death, if you are aware that I now stand in peril of death, free me quickly by your prayers'. Saying this, he set his hand to the tunic again and this time, without difficulty, he tore it off as if it were made of rotten straw. At once, gaining confidence from this omen of his escape, he climbed a mast and leapt off, entrusting himself to the sea. As he was tossed about by the gale, seeking now the depths and now the heights, yet full of confidence because of the preceding miracle, he poured out his prayers to the Lord. 'O God', he said, 'you delivered me from my troublesome clothes by the merits of your servant John. Now again, Lord, deliver me from the waves of the sea so that, saved by your power, I may live to praise your great wonders, and to see with my eyes the man by whose merits I do not doubt you will help me.' The man was not disappointed in his hope, his prayer, or his devotion, for on the third day he was tossed ashore without injury and returned in good health to his home. Going to Cantimpré, he told the venerable John and the rest of the

---

[94] Cf. Psalm 54. 21.

brothers all that had happened to him.[95] But the holy man, endowed with all virtues including humility, replied that God had shown his miraculous power not by his merits, but according to the man's faith.

How Dom John escaped unharmed after falling into a snowy ditch

8. The blessed John was once travelling to our house of Bellingen in Brabant with the venerable Matthew — later our second abbot, but then prior of the monastery — and the cleric Fulco, whom I mentioned in the first book. It was winter and snow covered everything. Allured by the solitude he loved, John had left his travelling companions behind and was riding ahead by himself to have his mind free for the Lord. With his mind and eyes intent on heaven, he loosed the reins of his horse and suddenly fell into a deep ditch full of snow. The others galloped up and shouted from the edge of the pit, but there was nothing they could do. In fact, they could not even see or hear the man they were trying to help, because the abyss had filled up with snow driven by the wind. But then, amazingly and unexpectedly, John appeared, still on his horse, and managed to reach the edge of the pit. It is no wonder that almighty God saved him from such a fall, for through him he had saved many thousands from the calamity of the eternal abyss.

8b. *On Lord John of Montmirail and his virtues**

After this Hugh of Oisy, the noble castellan of Cambrai, and his daughter both died. She was the only child he had with the noble Margaret, daughter of Count Thibaut the Great of Chartres, who is now countess of Blois. After her death, John of Montmirail, a man extremely vigorous in arms, inherited the lordship of Oisy.[96] This lord, a nobleman famed for his great cruelty and power,

---

[95] In VMO-S IV.20, Thomas tells a similar story about James of Vitry: *Mary of Oignies*, pp. 157–58.

* As this chapter is not numbered in the manuscript, we conventionally give it the number 8b. A marginal note reads 'De Johanne de Montmirail octo paginae et amplius' ('eight pages and more about John of Montmirail'). [The chapter heading is in the manuscript. BN]

[96] Hugh III of Oisy died in 1189/90. A notice is devoted to him in the necrology of Cantimpré on the date of 30 August (not 20 as in the note of Aubertus Miraeus, *Notitia ecclesiarum Belgii* (Antwerp: Cnobbarum, 1630), p. 461). His wife Marguerite was the daughter

was said to have been converted by John, the blessed servant of God, so that he became as gentle as a lamb. I have heard that his conversion came about through some horrible sign, but I have not been able to investigate or prove the story. This much, however, I have received as absolutely certain. By constant exhortation John led the knight to such a sublime degree of perfection that he restored all the goods and riches he had violently extorted from his subjects, and the fragrance of his humility and sanctity wafted throughout France and Germany.[97]

This astonishing act of atonement is reported: he once humbly kissed a leper whose face was foul and horrible, with pus gushing from his mouth, and removed his own garment to clothe the man.[98] And at the castle of Provins in Champagne, in a religious house that cares for the poor, he found a leprous priest whose whole body was covered with wounds and sores. As soon as he went in to see him, he remembered that the priest had once held the ministry of sacrificing Christ's body and blood. Taking no account of the leprosy, the wounds, the sores, the pus, or the dripping blood, he fell upon the man, all afire with the spirit of God, and caressed the face and hands that had once devoutly offered the singular sacrifice, moistening them with his tears. The priest himself bore witness to this and so did those in the house with him, who had seen the noble prince's face smeared with blood and pus.[99] Truly he was one of those mountains of which David joyfully exclaims in the Psalms, 'Touch the mountains and they will smoke'.[100] Did not the touch of divine love kindle the fire that sent the incense of such fragrant virtue wafting into the nostrils of pious minds? Was he not a mountain who lifted his lofty peak above all clouds,

---

of Thibaut IV of Chartres (Thibaut II of Champagne), called the Great. According to Miraeus, both died without children (ibid., p. 504). The lordship of Oisy and the castellany of Cambrai therefore passed to John of Montmirail, who was the son of André, lord of Montmirail (dép. Marne, arr. Épernay) and la Ferté-Gaucher, and his wife Hildiarde, sister of Hugh III of Oisy. See VJMM I.28–33, pp. 190–91.

[97] The *Vita Ioannis de Monte-Mirabili* (VJMM) was written by a monk of Longpont (BHL, 4415, I, p. 654). In a manuscript from Cîteaux, it received diverse additions known as *Auctaria*; these were edited by A. Manrique, in *Cisterciensium seu verius ecclesiasticorum annalium* (Lyon: Boissat & Anisson, 1642–59), III, and partially reprinted by the Bollandist Suysken in the *Commentarius praevius* preceding the text of the VJMM in the AASS.

[98] Cf. VJMM II.19–20, p. 222.

[99] Cf. VJMM II.22, p. 223.

[100] Psalm 143. 5. Cf. VMY 21.

making himself a mirror for the whole world to imitate? But read what follows and you will be amazed.

The knight Philip of Montmirail was a man altogether just, holy, religious, and devout. Placing his hope in the goodness of God alone as a foundation, he built four excellent monasteries of virgins by the power of faith with virtually no material support, not counting all the virgins and continent women — as many as three hundred, they say — whom he set up to live chaste and holy lives without joining a religious order.[101] He was so vigilant for the salvation of souls that he can rightly be numbered with the men of old 'by the folly of whose preaching God made the wisdom of this world foolish to save those who believe'.[102] The most noble prince John cultivated Philip with the highest reverence and honour, as was truly fitting and right. It is from him that I learned the story I am about to tell.

Philip was passing through the royal city of Paris with Prince John, accompanied by a large throng of knights and followers. The venerable John Varas, archdeacon of the church of Châlons-sur-Marne, was also there.[103] Now a priest, bearing the sacraments of Christ, was riding in John's direction along a very muddy street. As soon as Prince John heard the customary bell that was sounded before him, he at once yielded the way so the priest would have a less muddy route for his passage. Not only that, but he got off his horse and humbled himself in the mud, kneeling before Christ in the filthy street. Long after the priest had passed, the prince rose to his feet, and his clothes had remained clean amid the filth so that, by this miracle, the virtue of a man who

---

[101] Philip of Montmirail is known to us only through a brief allusion by Étienne de Bourbon [Stephen of Bourbon], *Anecdotes historiques*, ed. by de la Marche, pp. 20–21, and a passage in the BUA (II.38.2, pp. 391–92), where he is said to have founded eight monasteries of Cistercian nuns and placed more than five thousand beguines at Christ's service. (These movements were closely linked at this period.) The term *beguina* does not appear in the VJC because it still had a pejorative sense, with heretical connotations; the beguines called themselves *virgines* or *continentes*. Cf. J. Van Mierlo, 'Béguins, Béguines, Béguinages', in DS I, cols 1344–45.

[102] I Corinthians 1. 20–21. Cf. BUA I.3.2, p. 14; II.29.18, p. 293; II.48.1, p. 435.

[103] The necrology of the priory of St-Martin-des-Champs mentions a *Johannes, archidiaconus Cathalaunensis* on the date of 19 November (a thirteenth-century notation). See A. Molinier and Auguste Longnon, *Recueil des Historiens de la France, Obituaires: Obituaires de la Province de Sens*, 4 vols (Paris: Imprimerie nationale, 1902–23), I–I, p. 469.

humbles himself from the filth of pride, which defiles almost all powerful men of the world, might shine as a bright example.[104]

The knight Philip told another story about John of Montmirail, no less miraculous. It was the holy prince's custom that, whenever he saw an image of Christ, the blessed Virgin, or any other saint that had been set up in the road to collect alms, he got off his horse at once and knelt humbly in worship. One day, without looking around, he crossed a bridge by which there stood an image of the blessed Mary, Mother of God, perhaps set up for the repair of the bridge. He had not passed far beyond it when he looked back and saw the image. Immediately he descended onto the bridge, where he knelt down in supplication before the image, not facing it but on the right side — and by divine permission the Virgin seemed to turn toward the prince with a kindly smile to show her approval. How fitting that the man who prostrated himself so humbly before irrational matter to honour the living God should be honoured rationally by a sublime miracle![105]

Another miracle worthy of admiration is reported about him. A citizen of Cambrai had killed a young man in a wretched accident, with no malicious intent, and according to the ancient laws of the city, he was condemned to death as soon as the judge, the magnates, and the people learned what had happened. The devout and religious prince, who was then at Prémy with the brothers, returned in haste and humbly begged that the innocent man be set free. The people refused. He repeated his plea. Again they refused. The prince was persistent; prostrate on the ground, he begged with redoubled force that the innocent man should be freed. But the foolish and furious people, not fearing to spurn the prayers of such a great man, who was also their castellan, cried all the more urgently that a murderer could by no means be released. The prince yielded to the people's stubbornness and returned to Prémy. So a pit was dug and the condemned man was buried alive, diligently guarded by the people until evening. After the guards had left, the lepers, who had gathered as their custom is to strip the dead man of his clothes, began to dig. At once the man they thought to be dead cried out to the diggers as a free man, 'Be careful! I am alive and I will wait for you peaceably.'

---

[104] The same story is told by Caesarius of Heisterbach, *Dialogus miraculorum*, IX.51, II, p. 206. On the liturgical customs described here see Peter Browe, 'Die Sterbekommunion im Altertum und Mittelalter', *Zeitschrift für katholische Theologie*, 60 (1936), 1–54 and 211–40 (pp. 40–42).

[105] Cf. VJMM I.11, p. 220.

The news spread swiftly and people came running. When the prince heard of it, he too returned. The escaped man recounted the mighty works of God:[106] he had been guarded by St James, the apostle to whom he had entrusted himself, standing on one side of his head, but the person standing on his other side resembled the prince. He said he had never rested more cheerfully, and indeed this seemed clear to everyone. Afterward the prince wanted to take the man and his whole family into his household, but he refused and made a pilgrimage of thanksgiving to Santiago in Spain. After his return he lived many years longer.[107] Who will deny that the devout prince's humility deserved this reward from the supreme Judge — that a man in such grave peril of death should be kept unharmed by an angelic guard in his own likeness? For his humility must have had no small value in the eyes of divine majesty, since a prince of such great power and glory had prostrated himself at the feet of such a disgraceful public to deliver an innocent man.

After the death of the blessed father John of Cantimpré, John of Montmirail left his princedom, his worldly glory, and his wife and children to follow Christ more perfectly[108] and entered the Cistercian abbey of Longpont as a monk.[109] There he was observed to be so humble and perfect that, whenever he could secretly find a fit time and place, he used to polish the weak brothers' shoes. When he was reproached for this by some noblemen who came to visit him and heard of it, he replied with a remarkably gracious speech: 'If secular princes knew there was any sweetness to be found in polishing shoes, I tell you, they would never let their servants perform this task, but they would do it themselves when it had to be done.'[110] Indeed he spoke truly — but only if they could taste that sweetness with the heart's palate![111]

---

[106] Ecclesiasticus 36. 2, 13.

[107] Cf. *Auctaria*, in *Cisterciensium*, ed. by Manrique, III, p. 146; reprinted in AASS (see above, n. 97).

[108] Matthew 19. 21, 29.

[109] Longpont, dép. Aisne, arr. Soissons, cant. Villers-Cotterêts. The abbey, a daughter house of Clairvaux, was founded in 1132. John of Montmirail received the habit there from the hands of Abbot Gauthier d'Ochies (1201–19) on the feast of the Ascension in 1209 or 1210 (VJMM VII.131-32, p. 206, and VIII.135-37, p. 207), probably in 1209 if we accept the chronology proposed by Thomas (see below, n. 121).

[110] Cf. VJMM III.46, p. 227.

[111] Cf. Augustine, *In Epistolas Ioannis ad Parthos*, Prologue, in PL 35:1977; VMO II.89, in *Mary of Oignies*, pp. 111–12; VMO-S III.17, p. 155; BUA II.46.2, p. 427.

How John of Montmirail made restitution to his former subjects

After he had already become a monk, he was visiting his former home, the principality of Oisy, to restore stolen goods to his people. When he had reached a place from which he could look out over the land that had once been his, he sighed from the bottom of his heart and asked the monk who was attending him, 'Master, do you know what I'm thinking?' 'No', said the monk. 'It seems to me', John said, 'that the people of this land, who were once subject to my wretched self in my evil days, ought to assemble and tie a rope around my neck and drag me through the countryside like a captured thief, for in those days I was not ashamed to seize their goods and lay waste to their land'. What a truly humble and lofty man he was — humble in himself and lofty in the Lord his God! Let each reader judge for himself what he would think if he had fallen from such glory into such lowliness. I dare not judge on behalf of others, but as for myself, I know how I would feel. The eyes of the Lord have seen my imperfection:[112] I have thought I was more worthy of glory than I was to be dragged through the land with a rope. Yet this humble and glorious prince deemed himself worthy of such a judgement; and the lower he was in his own eyes, the greater he stood in the eyes of God.[113]

He next passed through the city of Cambrai, where he had formerly been castellan. The workmen in the public cemetery, commonly called gravediggers[114] — more than three hundred of them — were moved by the usual levity which none of them lack. They shouted with uproarious laughter as he passed, 'Look at the monks! Look at the monks!' That blessed and marvellous man, delighted by their laughter, removed his cowl and shouted merrily, 'Laugh all you like! Laugh at the fool from Montmirail!' At the sound of his humble voice their clamour ceased and the whole crowd fell silent as if they had lost the use of their tongues, not because they knew who he was — for they had no idea — but because the voice of one who humbles himself gains power.[115]

Finally he arrived at the town of Havrincourt,[116] where almost all the people of the land had assembled so that he could make restitution to them for the goods he had once seized. Beside the table where a huge mound of silver had

---

[112] Psalm 138. 16.

[113] Luke 9. 48, 22. 26.

[114] *botharios*.

[115] Cf. Psalm 67. 34; VJMM III.43, p. 227.

[116] Havrincourt, dép. Pas-de-Calais, arr. Arras, cant. Bertincourt.

been piled, he knelt and raised his hands and eyes to heaven, begging every one of the people, both poor and rich, to forgive him the sins he had committed. He even kissed their feet and hands so that nothing would be lacking to his sublime humility. The money was for the restitution of stolen goods, the humble prayers and kisses for the injuries and violence he had done. Who has ever heard or seen such things? Who has ever seen such a great man, such a prince, beg forgiveness of his former peasants with prayers and soften them with kisses? It was not enough for him to bestow a kiss of peace on their faces unless his holy kiss touched the feet of someone of the very meanest class. There was one little old woman, poor and despicable. After he had satisfied her with restitution for her goods, the humble prince seized her hand and wanted to kiss it. But the woman, abhorring her lord's great humility, tried to withdraw her hand as best she could, so he released the hand and immediately seized her foot. What he could not do with her hand, he completed with a devout kiss on her foot.[117]

How many glorious proofs he gave of his holy humility! These are so great and unheard-of in all ages that almost no one could hear or read of such radiant deeds, whether among the ancients or the moderns. But it would take too long and, to tell the truth, it would be impossible to write down all that is said about this prince. So, having recorded just a few of his memorable deeds, let me pass on to his most glorious death.

After this refined, elegant man had been fighting the Lord's battles for three years in the monastic habit, so that Christ might crown him with the diadem of his everlasting kingdom in recompense for all he had renounced for his sake, John hastened to his departure.[118] On the day he was delivered from the burden of his flesh and passed into everlasting glory, a monk of ripe years and merits was praying intently at the abbey of Igny.[119] Suddenly ravished in spirit, he heard a choir singing joyful psalms in heaven.[120] When he asked the cause of their gladness, he was answered that the humble John of Montmirail had passed from the world, and for that reason the celestial citizens were rejoicing so festively. Without delay the monk arose and struck the tablet of the dead. Hearing the sound, the monks rushed to the infirmary, but finding that no one had died,

---

[117] This passage (beginning *Aderat et quedam annicula*) is found almost verbatim in the *Auctaria*, III.304.1, a passage not reprinted in the AASS (see above, n. 97).

[118] Cf. VJMM IV.59–61, p. 230.

[119] Igny, dép. Marne, arr. Reims, cant. Fismes, comm. Arcis-le-Ponsart. The abbey, a daughter house of Clairvaux, was founded in 1128.

[120] Cf. Lamentations 5. 14.

they asked the monk why he had struck the tablet. The brother told them, 'John of Montmirail has passed from the world today'. But no one believed him. Even as they were saying that the old man had been deluded by a dream, a messenger was sent from the abbot to announce the news, and he confirmed the exact day and hour when the monk said the blessed man had died.

Some miracles concerning St Mary of Oignies

The precise day and hour of his passing were also revealed by the Lord to a religious woman living far away — St Mary of Oignies, whose life was written by the venerable James, bishop of Acre, with outstanding eloquence. James was with Mary at the time and she told him, leaping up with immense joy.[121] Even though this is not written in her life, it is widely believed beyond any doubt. For that most reverent man neglected to write a great many things about Mary lest he tire his readers with excess, or lest the incomprehensible greatness of her miracles become an odour of death rather than life in the hearts of unbelievers.[122] For example, he does not mention that she crossed the river Sambre with dry feet,[123] nor that she entered a church through closed doors while still living in a solid mortal body, or many other things which utterly surpass human faith — unless we believe Christ when he says, 'All things are possible to one who believes'.[124] Yet that most discerning, eloquent man told these and many similar things to his household and his spiritual friends, and he acknowledged that he had not written even a tenth part of St Mary's life because there were many who would not believe it.

---

[121] Since Mary of Oignies died on 23 June 1213, the death of John of Montmirail would have to be placed in 1212, according to the chronology of Thomas, in lieu of the previously accepted date of 1217.

[122] II Corinthians 2. 16. Cf. Jerome, *Commenarius in Danielem*, Prologue, in PL 25:494; VMO-S Prologue, p. 137; VMY 27; BUA II.38.I, p. 390.

[123] Cf. VMO-S II.9, p. 147. Christina Mirabilis is similarly supposed to have walked across the Meuse at Liège: VCM 10.

[124] Mark 9. 22.

Of Dom John's wonderful method in converting noblemen to Christ

Since I have strayed very far from the purpose of my narrative — albeit fittingly and usefully — let me now return to the story I set out to write. Yet I have recounted this much about the eminent nobleman so that the world may see all the more sublimely what great and glorious spiritual fruits our John brought forth in his life. For this indeed was the blessed man's special glory, that the seed of his word sprang up with such power, the labour of his teaching was compensated with such rewards. John of Montmirail was not the only nobleman converted by the blessed man's preaching or admonition. France, most noble in its chivalry, and Flanders and Hainaut with their distinguished knights, many of whom he converted to devotion, still rejoice and boast rightly of his fame. In recalling and converting such men from the pomp of secular knighthood to the light yoke of humility,[125] he had a method that was plainly wonderful. When he first began to speak with them in a friendly way, he did not abhor and condemn their deeds in lofty disdain, as some do, but after attracting them with humble and gracious talk, he drew them gradually away from their accustomed sins. He did not bring out the surgical knife and insert it harshly before he had cut away all the corrupt matter, but waited until he found them well prepared, their minds confirmed and strengthened by frequent admonition. Let me demonstrate this more clearly by the example of one striking action.

9. Once as the blessed man was going to France, a large assembly of nobles had gathered at the court of a certain prince for the Christmas festival. The venerable father John was summoned to the same court for some reason and welcomed there amid general rejoicing. After he had given sincere thanks for this hospitality, which did him such fitting honour, his eyes lit on a powerful prince, Robert Mauvoisin,[126] who surpassed the rest in beauty, apparel, chivalry, and

---

[125] Matthew 11. 29–30.

[126] Robert II Mauvoisin, probably the scion of a family from the French Vexin. See *Histoire de l'Empire de Constantinople sous les Empereurs François*, ed. by Charles Du Fresne Du Cange, 2 vols (Paris: [n. pub.], 1657), I, p. 258, cited by Jean Longnon, *Les Compagnons de Villehardouin. Recherches sur les croisés de la quatrième croisade* (Geneva: Droz, 1978), p. 121. After his conversion, recounted by Thomas, he took part in the Fourth Crusade. See Villehardouin, *La Conquête de Constantinople*, VII.109, ed. by Edmond Faral (Paris: Société d'édition 'Les Belles Lettres', 1938), pp. 10, 110, 112, then in the Albigensian Crusade, in which he played an important role: Petri Vallium Sarnaii, *Historia Albigensis*, 129, 154, 286, 304, 336, ed. by P. Guébin and E. Lyon, 8 vols (Paris: Champion, 1926–39), I, pp. 133–34, 159, 283; II, pp. 4, 34–35. He died on 16 November, most likely in 1214: ibid. I, p. 133, n. 1. The date of 1217 is less probable: Longnon, *Les*

noble elegance, so he turned his steps and mind toward this man. Laying his hands on the prince's head, John praised the crown he was wearing, which he had most curiously and exquisitely fashioned for himself out of herbs and flowers.[127] 'My son', he asked, 'where did you get this vernal crown at this time of year? It suits you well, as a knight devoted to the world, to wear such elegant attire at this place and time. But if you turned toward the everlasting delight of Christ's verdant paradise of bliss, how much better it would suit you to be crowned with the diadem of his perpetual and immortal glory! For this crown passes with the season, and in time it will dry up and wither. But the other, enduring to eternity, glorifies its wearer with verdure and fragrance alike.' In these remarks, he brilliantly showed the knight what curiosity and value such ornaments have and demonstrated that temporal things should be little prized in comparison with the eternal, since by exchanging our transient goods we can acquire the dignity of everlasting ones. On hearing this the prince, turning inward with vehement self-reproach, marvelled at John's holiness and eloquence, and began to cultivate him with heartfelt affection and listen seriously to his words and admonitions. Not long afterward he renounced the pomp of the world and entered the service of Christ, the King of all, with a devotion worthy of imitation and praise.

I have recounted this one example to show the wonderful way he had of calling noblemen to Christ, but also to correct those who beat their plowshares into swords,[128] who think they can overcome the world with pompous words or stinging rebukes — when the holy fathers of old, the apostles, set out to conquer the world with humility and gentleness rather than disdainful eloquence or provocative speech. For if Christ had wanted to use his eternal power to vanquish the world, he would not have chosen illiterate laymen, as Luke testifies in the Book of Acts, but summoned thousands of thousands, twelve hundred thousand angels, to come to his aid.[129] But his kingdom is not of this world, for he came to serve, not to be served, and he has chosen what is weak in the world to confound the strong. He has chosen what is abject and contemptible to overturn the powers that be, as if they had never been.[130] Indeed, if we consider his words

---

Compagnons, p. 122.

[127] A marginal note reads, 'Coronae florum in solemnitatibus capite gestatae etiam hyeme' ('floral crowns worn on the head at feasts even in winter').

[128] Joel 3. 10.

[129] Cf. Daniel 7. 10; Matthew 26. 53; BUA II.19.1, p. 226.

[130] Cf. John 18. 36; Matthew 20. 28; I Corinthians 1. 27–28; VMY 2; VLA I.1.

and deeds upon earth, we will find no sign of cruelty, no word of insult or invective. On the contrary, he says to his disciples, 'Learn from me, for I am gentle and humble of heart'.[131] And through the prophet he says, 'On whom shall I rest, if not one who is humble and peaceful?'[132] Therefore the man of whom I speak, as a diligent imitator of Christ and his followers, tamed the proud minds of men with kindness and humility of spirit. This is the gracious method he used to overcome and humble the minds of the nobility for Christ.

Toward the common crowds he seemed so holy and marvellous, as if superhuman, that a kind of apostolic dignity shone out in him. When he was about to preach to the people, he would no sooner ascend the pulpit or chair and announce the theme of his sermon than everyone would already be stricken with compunction and dissolved in tears. For the gravity of his face and a certain angelic majesty in his eyes displayed the grace of wonder-working virtue, which none of his audience could escape without being put to shame. Hence this universal and miraculous truth: no matter where he sowed the seeds of the divine word, a joyful, evergreen crop always sprang up, and he most efficaciously bore abundant fruit in the salvation of souls. Everywhere were the offshoots of his preaching, everywhere the seeds of his words were sprouting, and rightly so. If you want to know the full extent of his zeal, see now how he behaved when ill.

How Dom John rode on the back of his servant for want of a horse

10. Once when he was feeling weak and fatigued, Father John was sitting quietly at home,[133] sad and mournful. One of the servants, Conrad — a good and faithful man — asked, 'Why are you so depressed, master?' Father John replied, 'Here I sit idle and quiet at home while souls redeemed by the blood of Christ are going to hell!' — 'And why is that?' Conrad asked. 'Because I have no means of transport and I'm not strong enough to make my rounds on foot, preaching the word of God.' Smiling, the servant answered, 'If it suits you, I'm ready to carry you on my shoulders wherever you want to go, instead of a horse.' At once the holy abbot leaped up with a zealous and fervent spirit, saying, 'Indeed it suits me! Carry me, and I will be no more ashamed before human eyes than I am in the sight of God.' Without delay the servant — an enormous man who was very

---

[131] Matthew 11. 29; cf. BUA 1.4.1, p. 19.

[132] Compare Isaiah 66. 2 (Vetus Latina).

[133] John 4. 6.

strong — took the saintly abbot on his shoulders, and weighed down with this holy burden, carried him about two miles to the village of Fontaine-Notre-Dame.[134] Descending from his rational horse, John entered the church. The people had gathered because it was a feast day, and he preached all the more effectively, by God's gift, in that he had been brought the more humbly for that purpose.

What blessed humility, what genuine charity, what a memorable deed, the more magnificent because it is so rare! Indeed, supremely rare! Who ever heard of a man doing such a thing after receiving the title of abbot? For that matter, I have never heard of anyone doing it before. I confess that I take so much special pleasure in this deed not because it is unusual, but because it is pious. So it is not absurd or unworthy that the blessed John's preaching, so vehement, zealous, and fervent, bore such a harvest among the people. As St Augustine said, he who does not burn cannot kindle a fire.[135] Conversely, he who burned with love kindled a fire with his preaching.

Of the marvellous fruits of his preaching

11. In Cambrai more than any other city, castle, or town, his preaching met with brilliant success, bearing fruit as for one who pressed on with continual clamour, so to speak, in season and out of season.[136] In the church of St Saviour outside Cambrai there hung a huge, sonorous bell that was permanently designated for this purpose: on a morning when the holy man was going to preach to the people, the bell was rung by the faithful at the second or third hour.[137] Whenever it sounded, people from all over the city gathered in great numbers, as was fitting. John put heretics to flight and exposed them publicly, turning the peoples' minds against their doctrine through disputations. For example, he once entered a church of Saint-Martin in Cambrai[138] to preach and

---

[134] Fontaine-Notre-Dame, five kilometres from Cambrai (dép. Nord, cant. and arr. Cambrai). A marginal note reads 'Fontanae villa ad quam Johannes humeris defertur' ('the village of Fontaine to which John was carried on someone's shoulders').

[135] Augustine, *Sermo* 234, in PL 38:1117; *In Epistolas Ioannis ad Parthos*, Prologue, in PL 35:1977.

[136] II Timothy 4. 2.

[137] A marginal notes reads 'Magna Campana pluries pulsata pro concione' ('the Great Bell often rung for assembly').

[138] The parish church of St-Martin in Cambrai.

had begun to dispute the heretics before the assembled people, proceeding one by one through the sacraments. There he ignited such ardent faith that according to my source, brother Julian — one of our first seven brothers, who was present at the time — heavenly grace seemed to flash from his mouth like a bolt of lightning. Thunderstruck by his urgency, all the people were in such ecstasy that their hair stood on end. Without delay this divine horror, transfused into their souls, brought a great many to eternal salvation through compunction.

12. With the greatest urgency and persistence he attacked people devoted to usury and unjust profit-taking,[139] for there were many of them who oppressed the urban poor. He would by no means absolve those who wished to repent until they had fully restored the wealth they had taken by fraud, or at least done so to the best of their ability. Some were so conscience-stricken at his preaching, knowing there was no justice in them, that they publicly stripped off their clothes down to their bare shame, moved by repentance for their former lives, and utterly renounced all that they had. Congratulating these penitents, John would embrace them as members of his family, and indeed his own children. Turning to the people he used to say, 'Who will clothe my children who have made themselves poor and naked for Christ's sake?' At this word you would see nobles and distinguished people competing with each other to throw off their garments. You would see tunics and cloaks flying through the air from the violence of those who threw them, naked men clothed and overwhelmed, and the people shouting to heaven with a mighty voice. Seeing this the blessed man dissolved in tears and said to the people, 'Rejoice and be glad, brothers, for there is greater joy in heaven over these who repent than over ninety-nine righteous who need no repentance'.[140] With such remarks he provoked the whole people to astonishing compunction and praise of God.

How the moneylender Alard was converted and made full restitution

13. Among these penitents was one Alard, called Priest, well known for the wealth he had gained through usury and fraud.[141] This man burned in such a

---

[139] Cf. Psalm 71. 14.

[140] Luke 15. 6–7.

[141] *Alardus, presbiter cognominatus.* He may have been an unbeneficed priest who took up moneylending for want of other employment and thus came to be known by the surname of Prestre or Le Prestre. [BN]

fervour of penitence that, after restoring the goods and properties he had exacted through usury and distributing the rest of his money to the poor, he made a request of the blessed John. He asked that a pit be dug beneath the threshold of his house and that he be pulled out of it naked with a rope around his neck, so that he might go forth poor and naked from his house as one who knew he possessed nothing of his own. To set an example for others, John shrewdly granted this request. So the clergy and people of the city were assembled and this moneylender Alard, stripped of his clothes, descended into the pit beneath his threshold. At the blessed John's command, one of the brothers approached, tied a rope around his neck, and pulled him out naked — as naked as he had come from his mother's womb.[142] At once the naked man was dressed in clothes presented to him and led in procession to the church of the Blessed Virgin Mary, surrounded by throngs of clergy amid great praise to Christ. I will not pass over this remarkable incident: as he was being led along, he realized that he had a little fur cap on his head[143] and violently threw it off, casting it to the ground with the words, 'I do not have even this much that I can rightly call my own'. A great crowd of spectators were present, weeping abundantly. Who could contain his tears before such a piteous spectacle? Even the vicious cruelty of our mutual alienation could hardly bear the sight. After this procession Alard was led into the church, and as a sign of spiritual absolution, he was released from the material rope around his neck. Upon receiving the cross to go on pilgrimage to Jerusalem, he was set in a place of eminence right next to the blessed John as a solemn spectacle.

Then the dean of the cathedral, Master Adam — a man deeply learned in human knowledge and divine law[144] — rose by his authority to preach to the people. 'It is fitting to feel joy and wonder, my brothers', he said, 'because today Christ has deigned to work a greater miracle in this man than when he raised

---

[142] Job 1. 21.

[143] 'Calamistrum, quod huram uulgariter uocant'. This passage is illuminating for our knowledge of medieval Latin. The word *calamistrum* normally designates a curling iron. On the basis of a text from 1206, the *Mittellateinisches Wörterbuch* (Munich: Beck, 1959–), II, p. 50, recognizes another meaning, rather vague, accompanied by a question mark: an *ornamentum capitis quoddam*. This meaning is clarified by the word *hura*, which designates a *pileus uillosus*, a fur cap (Charles Du Fresne Du Cange, *Glossarium mediae et infimae latinitatis*, 10 vols (Niort: Favre, 1883–87), IV, p. 266). A marginal note reads 'Calamistrum quem Huram dicunt'.

[144] Adam's tenure as dean is attested from 1192 to 1219: *Gallia Christiana*, III, p. 70.

Lazarus from the dead after four days in the tomb.[145] For he who raised Lazarus in the body has raised Alard in mind; and although such a thing is more common, it is yet more wonderful. For Lazarus was raised in the body to suffer death once more, but Alard has been raised in the mind to be granted everlasting life. It was greater therefore for Christ to quicken the soul of a man dead in spirit to make him live forever, than to raise a man dead in the body only to die again.' As soon as the dean had expounded this theme to the best of his ability, he fell silent as if suddenly mute. Signalling to the blessed John to rise and finish the sermon, he sat down again, full of shame. Rising at his signal, John bowed his head humbly to the dean to relieve his shame a little and said, 'Pronounce some theme that I am to speak about'. When the dean had whispered a sentence into his ear, this most discerning man, adorned with every virtue, said as joyfully as if he had been taught some great new wisdom, 'My sons, I have brought my bucket to this gushing fountain and filled it to my capacity to share this eloquence with you.' With these words he continued the sermon of divine praise at length. Then, bringing the matter to a close with fitting eloquence, he returned home amid great exultation and praise from all.

Now let us return to that happy beggar who was transformed from a rich man into a pauper, or rather from a pauper into a millionaire, for by renouncing what was not his own, he came to possess the treasures of a good conscience and the riches of an eternal promise through hope. After all the events I have recounted, on the very same day that he despised such great possessions, he went begging alms from house to house to the greater shame of the devil, who had once seduced him with riches. In this abjection he managed to tame the inhuman monster of pride, for he did not deny that he had been its captive when he used to glory in the abundance of his goods. So in this steadfast virtue, overwhelmed by more transitory human praise than his conscience could bear, he was commended by the blessed John to the noble Count Baldwin of Flanders,[146] who transported him overseas. Afterwards he closed his life with a blessed end in the holy land of Jerusalem. Those who were present at his death, it is said, reported that as he lay dying beneath the open sky in the heat of the sun, the wasps buzzed incessantly about his mouth and bit his face with their importunate stings. His attendants tried to drive them away, but the dying man said to them as best he could, 'Let them be! I am worthy of even harsher stings.' As soon as he had breathed forth his spirit in marvellous fervour, there was such a sweet fragrance

---

[145] John 11. 1–46.
[146] Baldwin IX, count of Flanders and (VI) of Hainaut (1195–1205).

that it proved beyond doubt he had passed into glory, where a scent no breath can blow away yields its sweetness to all.[147]

Other exempla concerning usurers

14. The blessed John steadfastly refused gifts and donations from moneylenders and publicly preached that everyone should refuse them, especially churches. He said churches could by no means be enriched for long through such possessions, but instead they would be justly impoverished. The patrimony of Christ does not mix with unjust gains, for it is written, 'A little leaven corrupts the whole lump'.[148] Therefore the donations of thieves and moneylenders are pernicious to the recipients, provoking God's vengeance in the dwindling of spiritual goods. As for this, I have heard a story about the nearby monastery of Vaucelles.[149] The money of a late usurer from Arras was being stored there, either to distribute to the poor or for some other good and necessary reason, I assume, although I don't know what it was. Far be it from men of such holiness and religious vows to have kept such impure goods against their conscience! One day when the monk Walter of Belmont, famous for his saintliness, was praying near the chest where the money was kept, he saw with open eyes a devil seated on it, and asked him why he was sitting there. The devil answered, 'I am sitting here with just cause to guard what is mine'. Horror-stricken, the monk told his abbot what he had seen. He in turn, horrified by this vision, returned the heap of money to Arras.[150]

15. John used to say that burial in the churchyard should be absolutely denied to moneylenders who persevered in their sins, lest the sanctified ground of the faithful be polluted by the filth of such demonic vessels to the detriment of holy, undefiled Mother Church.[151] Let me insert a useful story that shows his virtue in this matter. It happened once that he had travelled far away for some urgent

---

[147] Augustine, *Confessiones*, 10.6.8, p. 154.

[148] I Corinthians 5. 6; Galatians 5. 9.

[149] Vaucelles, dép. Nord, arr. Cambrai, cant. Marcoing, comm. Crèvecoeur-sur-Escaut. The Cistercian abbey, a daughter house of Clairvaux, was founded in 1131.

[150] The same story is retold in BUA II.26.4, p. 260.

[151] The Third Lateran Council decreed in 1179 that 'notorious usurers are not to be admitted to the communion of the altar, nor, if they die in that sin, to receive Christian burial'. [BN] See *Concilium Lateranense*, III.25, in *Conciliorum oecumenicorum decreta*, ed. by Giuseppe Alberigo, 3rd edn (Bologna: Istituto per le scienze religiose, 1973), p. 223.

reason, and in the meantime a very rich moneylender, one of the most powerful men in the city, fell sick and went the way of all flesh. His relatives, the leading nobles of the city, brought his corpse to the church of Cantimpré to whitewash his sins and gain a mark of honour. For the church of Cantimpré had this special privilege: anyone who could obtain burial or commemoration of his death there presumed he would win great benefit for his soul through the suffrage of the brothers' prayers. By Christ's gift this custom persists even today. So the brothers, excessively swayed by the nobles' authority and the crowd of people, received the dead man in their church, albeit unwillingly — especially since it was not the custom in churches then to deny burial to such people. Having dug a grave in the cemetery, they began the funeral mass. When it was over and the body was about to be carried out from their midst, the abbot suddenly returned! As soon as he heard that the body of this moneylender had been brought for burial, he hastened to the churchyard with swift steps and commanded that the grave be filled with earth again. When the reverend father's arrival was announced in church, all the mourners were shaken at once with fear and trembling.[152] Quickly removing the body of their dead kinsman, they fled any way they could. In fact, they well knew that Abbot John was unbending in the rigour of his justice, nor could he be swayed by threats or compliments. Rightly so! For I will recall another story I heard from people whose good faith I do not doubt, showing why the blessed man burned with righteous zeal against such sins.

16. I heard a great and memorable man say there was an abbot, black in life as in habit,[153] who buried the body of a moneylender in his churchyard for the sake of a bribe. Immediately the enemy of mankind, the devil, began to attack the monks as they walked through the cloister at night, telling them all that he would have dominion over them as long as they retained that man, a follower of his own religion. At once the abbot dug up the obscene body and had it removed for burial in the fields. But even then the devil did not rest, for the monks still kept the riches of his late devotee. Then the abbot, compelled by necessity rather than devotion, commanded that the money be brought out and buried in the earth with the corpse of its owner.

---

[152] Cf. Psalm 2. 11, 54. 6; I Corinthians 2. 3; II Corinthians 7. 15; Ephesians 6. 5.

[153] Here as in his other works, Thomas hardly seems to appreciate the Benedictines. Cf. Elie Berger, *Thomae Cantipratensis Bonum Universale de Apibus quid illustrandis saeculi decimi tertii moribus conferat* (Paris: Thorin, 1895), p. 44.

17. In the town of Brussels in Brabant, a cleric had risen one night for matins and was passing through the cemetery en route to the church of St Gudula, the holy virgin,[154] when he stumbled on the open grave of a man who had just been buried. Filthy dogs had surrounded the grave, torn out the entrails and viscera of the wretched corpse, and most horribly fouled the whole area.[155] On seeing this the cleric ran to the church as fast as he could, but as soon as he saw the reassuring light, his strength failed him because of the fantastic vision. Afterward, when he had come to himself and regained his strength, he took some of the bystanders with him, bringing a light, and approached the foul spectacle of the corpse. When he arrived, those dogs of darkness immediately left the body and fled at the presence of light. It is no wonder, brothers, that they received such power to insult the corpse and pollute the consecrated ground of the cemetery with such filth! By this example men should learn to dread such shame, having seen the punishment revealed by such an open judgement of God against their comrade.

How Dom John exorcized a usurer's widow vexed by a demon in the form of a lapdog

18. The memorable father used to say of such people, 'It is extremely hard for them as long as they have kept anything that rightly belongs to another. But if they give up their illicit profits, they can be delivered from the devil's bondage.' If it is true that 'when the cause ceases, the effect will cease', so too if the cause persists, the effect will persist. For the cause of their bondage is the seizure of someone else's rightful property, and when a person has subjected himself to sin, he has made himself a slave to the devil. As Augustine testifies, 'by whatever thing a person is bound, he has become a slave to that thing',[156] and no one is delivered except by breaking the chain that binds him. The chain in this case is the seizure of another's rightful goods, and such people cannot be freed from the devil's bondage unless the chain of unjust possession that binds them has first

---

[154] The collegiate church of Ste-Gudule, Brussels.

[155] For similar scenes see BUA I.24.4, p. 99 (a traitor exhumed and torn apart by dogs) and II.30.5, p. 322 (a nun of wicked life exhumed and torn apart by a sow and her piglets).

[156] Augustine, *De civitate Dei*, IV.3, ed. by Dombart and Kalbin, in CCSL 47, p. 101 (cf. II Peter 2. 19). See also BUA II.33.1, p. 370.

been broken. To make this point more clearly I must not withhold the following story, even though some foolish people may think it injures the blessed John.

In the city of Cambrai there was a widow named Katherine, of respectable morals, who daily gave great alms to Christ's poor. Formerly she used to practice usury with her late husband, making a profit from filthy lucre. Although she had restored most of the money to those they had injured, she nevertheless kept much for her personal use, following the advice of certain people to her own harm. For many days and nights, the devil had vexed this woman in the form of a little dog, which could not be removed by making the sign of the cross, sprinkling with holy water, or any other act of sanctification. Instead, the evil guest remained with her at all times, lying on her bed at night and sitting in her lap by day. It was invisible to everyone: only the woman herself could see it. After she had been taken to the shrines of many saints, yet was still not free from her wicked companion, she was finally brought to God's servant John to be helped by his prayers. Although he rightly felt great trepidation, he was overcome by the tears of many people and promised to do what he could.

Foreseeing the difficulty of the affair, he asked his brothers and sisters and many religious people of approved life to pray urgently for several days. When they had done so with great devotion, Christ's servant came forth. The woman was there too and so was the whole community of brothers, offering great supplication. The abbot first bade the deacon to recite the sacred Gospel lesson that begins, 'Jesus, lifting his eyes, said, "Father, the hour has come: glorify your Son"', and so forth.[157] He meanwhile was praying in tears with the brothers. After the lesson John approached the widow and adjured the demon that had long frequented her to depart. But it persisted. Again he prayed and adjured the demon which still remained; it would not be moved, for the time had not yet come.[158] Either the woman was not yet worthy to receive compassion, or if she was worthy, this took place by a secret sign from God that she might be purified by such temptation. Then Christ's holy servant turned to his brothers and said, 'You see what happens! Either I am unworthy that my prayer should be heard, or else this woman, who I truly believe is not yet fully purged of unclean profit, has been left by God's providential judgement to be tried by the cleansing punishment of this horrible company. This is what I have often proclaimed to the people: it is very hard for such sinners to be freed from the devil's bondage

[157] John 17. 1.
[158] John 7. 6.

as long as they possess anything that is not theirs by right.' With such remarks he exhorted the widow to amend her life and returned home.

Brothers, let none of the faithful deem that this affair detracts from the blessed John's merits. Bear in mind that with sure faith we hold St Paul to have been a holy apostle of Christ, worthy in every way, yet when he asked the Lord three times to remove an angel of Satan that troubled him, his wish was not granted.[159] So if Paul, the teacher and apostle of the nations, Christ's chosen vessel,[160] prayed for himself and was not heard, why should this incident detract from Abbot John's merits? As far as the outward eye could tell, he had great compassion and prayed to the Lord graciously and devoutly enough, in the name of the poor Christ, for relief from this affliction. Indeed, we must believe that when God's discerning servant prayed thus, what he intended was the eternal salvation of the one for whom he prayed. Nor would he have wished to be heard in any other way unless the result of his prayer would advance her salvation. Praying in this way, therefore, he was heard after all because he intended the widow's progress toward salvation, and it was expedient for her to suffer the enemy's assault to obtain a peaceful life in the future. Even though she was not set free, Christ's servant obtained his goals through the many ways he preached and the memorable deeds performed as a result. Although I have recorded very few of these, what I have said must suffice because a great deal still remains to be written.

Of his grace as a confessor and how he converted hardened sinners

19. Now, brothers, what shall I say about the unique grace John showed those who confessed to him? He was a wonderful man who used a clearly wonderful method. Because of this grace, both acquaintances and strangers flocked to him from the furthest parts of the province. Although they had confessed their sins and transgressions to many others, even very learned and spiritual men, they believed they had made no progress toward perfection until they had obtained the grace of this blessed man. In fact, the divine mercy had granted John an extraordinary grace in this regard to advance people's salvation. To say nothing of other genuinely wonderful things, I will tell only one story, which plainly reveals the singular gift he had with the most stubborn, hard-hearted sinners. For

---

[159] II Corinthians 12. 7–8.
[160] Acts 9. 15.

when they confessed their sins without weeping, he himself dissolved in tears first and did what they should have done. By his own example he showed what they needed to do, in his mercy having compassion on the weak. In this way he dissolved stony minds into tears and compelled the stubborn to despise the wrongs they had done so that hardly anyone came to him, no matter how hard-hearted, without leaving much improved. As a witness to this, some of our brethren tell the following tale.

20. A certain woman, goaded by the Enemy and burning in the fires of lust, was roaming through the countryside. She had been taken by her religious relatives to many men of virtuous life, but was not subdued. Finally she was brought to Christ's servant so that, by his conversation and prayers, he might bend her to penitence. With the reverent grace of his speech, he gently admonished her to reject the acts of the dissolute flesh and shudder to perpetrate such a foul offence. But the wretched, miserable woman spurned his pleading and compassionate words, as well as his warnings, and despised his wholesome counsel with a wild expression. He, on the other hand, shedding his habitual tears for the poor woman, urged her to consider the uncertain hour of death, the ordeal of the dread Judgement, the wrath of the Judge, and the flames of everlasting fire. Nevertheless, she persisted in her hardness of heart and became even more rebellious than when she came. Seeing this, the blessed man left the woman at once and ran into the church. Standing before the altar, aflame with the zeal of charity, he assumed a posture of complaint before the Lord and burst out with these words: 'What is this, Lord? What is this? You have redeemed the whole world by shedding your blood, and still you shut up your mercy in your wrath! If there is such iniquity in me that I do not deserve to be heard, nevertheless save your creature![161] But if there is some crime in her on account of which she does not deserve your mercy, graciously forgive it for my sake and for those who have trusted me for the sake of your name. Surely I labour in vain to convey the words of your truth if your help is lacking, for without you I can do nothing good, I accomplish nothing.[162] Act then, Lord! Arouse and summon this woman! Illumine, kindle, and soften her! Let her now love you and run to you.'

He had scarcely finished speaking when the woman, not so much wretched as pitiable, suddenly ran in with a great cry, as if seized by some impulse, and threw herself in tears at the holy father's feet, exclaiming, 'Forgive me, father! Have mercy and receive me in repentance! I see the wrath of God hanging over

[161] Cf. Psalm 76. 10, 7. 4, 138. 24; Genesis 4. 13.
[162] Romans 7. 18–19.

me unless you intercede!' Then he smiled, both consoled and consoling, and said, 'So you confess that you can be conquered, and indeed you are conquered! Rightly so, for God is stronger, and it never profited anyone to kick against his goad.'[163] Thus the learned scribe, entering the treasuries of divine mercy, brought forth riches new and old[164] for the woman and offered her the sacred remedies of penance. Having heard her confession, with Christ's help he transformed her from a vessel of contempt into a vessel of honour and grace.[165]

21. There was a hardened thief, very skilled in his malicious craft. Suspecting that the blessed John carried a purse of money, he sank to his knees in feigned penitence so that, while God's saint was intent on admonishing him, he might slyly steal the money he suspected. But while God's servant was addressing the thief and inviting him with tears, as usual, to accept the mercy of God, all of a sudden he was divinely inspired! The one who had come to take was himself taken and ensnared by the blessed man's words. Falling at his feet, he confessed the purpose that had brought him there in a lengthy confession. Thus he who had come as a predator in evil was preyed upon by goodness, and he who had come to snatch another's goods was snatched from the Evil One's bondage and restored to himself. There are many more stories like this about John's divine gifts; I could relate them in a prolix but useful narrative. But since I must hasten on to other matters, I pass over many more such deeds in silence.

Of his ascetic labours and spiritual martyrdom

22. Because this most devout servant of God burned inwardly with amazing ardour, he tormented his body outwardly with savage, uninterrupted labour. He could by no means have survived very long without harming himself unless he had sometimes done what his spirit found burdensome, yielding to his flesh through the corruption of nature itself. He ordered his life and work in such a way that he was always praying, reading, preaching, or hearing confessions, and he took no more time for himself than he needed to indulge in sleep or food. His fasts were frequent, his nourishment sparing, his bed hard, his vigils long. Afflicted by these crosses, his limbs were strained by continuous toil. This was his outer life. But inwardly his ardent spirit was tormented the more keenly the

---

[163] Acts 9. 5.

[164] Matthew 13. 52. Cf. VMO-S III.16, p. 154.

[165] II Timothy 2. 20–21.

more he longed to be dissolved and be with Christ.[166] He was urgently constrained on one hand by concern for his neighbours, among whom scandals were increasing, and on the other by the desire to see Christ, whom he bore constantly in mind. Suspended thus between hope and fear in an agony of spiritual martyrdom, he found himself exalted on one side on the rack of expectation, burned on the other by the fires of scandal. In this way he afflicted his body outwardly and his spirit inwardly. Since the age of physical martyrdom is now over, there remained to him only spiritual affliction of the will. But his sufferings were relieved chiefly and wholly by the solace the Lord sometimes gave him in the sweetness of quiet contemplation. Without this comfort his spirit could not have nurtured the flesh, nor the flesh the spirit, for with spirit and flesh alike he exulted in the living God.[167] Indeed, it is said by those who knew him best — and I truly believe it — that his inner eyes never turned away from contemplating a spiritual vision, no matter how his outer eyes were occupied. He abounded so powerfully and wonderfully in the gift of tears that scarcely anyone can remember him preaching or praying without tears — and never did he celebrate mass without them. I will say more about this gift at a suitable time and place.

How Dom John, though sick with dropsy, sang at the vigil of Christ's Nativity

23. His health ruined by these and many similar practices which have not yet come to light, this fervent man fell gravely ill with dropsy. Indeed, it was not fitting for the One who did not spare his own consubstantial Son[168] to leave an adopted son without a scourge. For truly, as Augustine testifies, he disciplines every son like his own.[169] So Abbot John, swollen with dropsy, suffered extreme pain in his abdomen, legs, and feet, as is typical with this disease. As this plague grew worse and worse every day, it happened that one Christmas Eve he was suffering in the infirmary, already close to death. The venerable Matthew, who

---

[166] Philippians 1. 23.

[167] Psalm 83. 3.

[168] Romans 8. 15, 23, 32.

[169] Augustine, *Enarrationes in Psalmos*, 36.2.4, ed. by Dekkers and Fraipont, in CCSL 38, p. 350; *In Psalmum* 37.23, pp. 397–98; *In Psalmum* 88.2.2, in CCSL 39, p. 1234; *In Psalmum* 118.13, in CCSL 40, p. 1707; *De peccatorum meritis et remissione*, II.16.25, ed. by Carolus Urba and Joseph Zycha, in CSEL 60, p. 98. Cf. Hebrews 12. 6, Proverbs 3. 1, and VMO I.40, in *Mary of Oignies*, p. 75.

would be his successor but was then prior of the monastery, and another of the brothers were sleeping so they could keep the night vigil. At midnight, shaking off sleep, the abbot heard his brothers chanting matins, weak both in number and in strength, for they were so exhausted by the burden of the order, as well as their own continual secret devotions, that their voices in psalmody sounded but feebly. The pious pastor, moved with diligent compassion for his sons, sat up in bed as best he could and began to weep profusely. His caretakers ran up and asked him what was the matter or what he wanted. He said to them, 'I want you to help carry me to church'. They asked, 'Why?' Then he said, the tears rising again, 'Don't you hear how weak our brothers sound on this sacred night of Christmas? We must help them!' They did not take his words seriously, thinking they came from weakness of the brain, so they took him in their arms and compelled him to lie down again. But he was of perfectly sound mind and demanded persistently that he should be carried to church. Seeing this and marvelling beyond measure, they led the most devout servant of Christ to church and arranged him in his chair, supported by cushions on either side.

A wonderful thing happened! As soon as he had prayed to the Lord, he was strengthened with such vigour that he was able to lift his voice like a resounding trumpet in a marvellous song of exultation and confession,[170] and he spurred them all on in a kind of pious competition to prolong the psalmody and elevate the chant. Upon seeing the power and grace of God so unexpectedly, they were inspired to more solemn praise of the holy Nativity of Christ. Hearing this, who would not be amazed by such a miracle of divine power? Christ, standing over Peter's mother-in-law, rebuked the fever, and raising her to her feet, he at once strengthened the woman he had healed to serve those who were reclining at table.[171] Now the same Christ, who is the power of God and the wisdom of God,[172] showed equal might in raising our father, who might have been suffering from a still more perilous illness, for his own praise and service. By this deed he declared himself to be the one of whom the prophet said, 'he frees the lame and raises up those who are cast down'.[173]

[170] Psalm 41. 5.

[171] Luke 4. 38–39.

[172] I Corinthians 1. 24.

[173] Psalm 145. 7–8.

How he resigned the office of abbot

24. Because the blessed servant was eager to imitate his Lord as far as anyone can, he chose to follow him in this also: 'he emptied himself and took the form of a servant.'[174] For he had already desired and intended a long time ago to find some fitting occasion to lay down his pastoral burden and have more perfect leisure to taste how sweet the Lord is, and to see the God of gods in Zion.[175] So, using his opportune illness as a pretext, he went to the venerable John, bishop of Cambrai, whom I mentioned earlier in this second volume.[176] Alleging his constant sickness and the frailty of his aged body, he begged with urgent prayers and tears to be released from pastoral responsibilities. The bishop was persuaded by this argument, albeit unwillingly, and released him from the duties of an abbot, though not from the title or the honour: he would always be called abbot and rightly honoured as master in the mouths of all. Hence the memorable Master Peter of Corbeil, then pastor of Cambrai but later Archbishop of Sens,[177] is reported to have said once, when the venerable John had come to visit him with his successor, Dom Matthew, 'Well, well! My lords have come as two substances in one person', as if to say, 'You are two men substantially, but you are named and honoured as one person in the role of pastor and abbot'. Peter is the man, full of knowledge and marvellous in faith, of whom the following tale is told. After he had breathed his last, his body was laid out in church and on the same day his funeral mass was celebrated. As the celebrant was elevating the consecrated host according to ecclesiastical custom, the dead man suddenly bowed his head on his bier, adoring the sacrament of the Lord's body.[178]

---

[174] Philippians 2. 7; cf. VMO-S IV.25, p. 162. The necrology of Cantimpré for 30 January reads 'hic autem, ut perfectius Dei filium sequeretur […] exinanivit semetipsum' ('but, so that he might follow the Son of God more perfectly, […] he emptied himself': Archives du Nord, 37 H 29).

[175] Psalm 33. 9, 83. 8; cf. BUA I.9.1, p. 36.

[176] Jean II d'Antoing. Cf. VJC II.2, p. 80 and n. 80 above.

[177] Peter II of Corbeil, bishop of Cambrai in 1199, archbishop of Sens in 1200, died on 3 June 1222. See Conrad Eubel, *Hierarchia catholica medii aevi* (Regensburg: Monasterii, 1913), p. 447.

[178] Thomas seems to be the only one to tell this story. In the words *secundum morem ecclesiasticum*, we can hear an echo of the famous synodal statute of Odo of Sully (1196–1208), prescribing that the host not be elevated until after the words of consecration. Cf. Peter Browe, 'Die Elevation in der Messe', *Jahrbuch für Liturgiewissenschaft*, 9 (1929), 20–66 (p. 22). A marginal note reads 'Miraculum in Petro de Corbolio defuncto Senonensium Archiepiscopo'

It is difficult to express the sorrow and fear that filled John's subordinates after Christ's blessed servant was released from the office of abbot. But he comforted them as best he could, promising faithfully that he would still be available to offer them Christ's counsel and that, with fewer cares, he would be all the more prompt to console them. This most vigilant shepherd of the Lord's flock governed the church of Cantimpré for ten years in accord with the ten commandments,[179] mindful of them all and preserving them inviolate so that he would not oppress any of his subjects with his power, provoke anyone to anger if he could help it, or depress anyone with undue austerity. He loved them all not only as a father, but more than a mother, and like a hen who clucks to summon her chicks,[180] he revived the weak and infirm. But since I have extended the second part of this book so long with many useful matters, as I think, I will pause for breath now to pass on more pleasantly to the rest.[181]

('a miracle concerning Peter of Corbeil, the late archbishop of Sens').

[179] John would thus have served as abbot from about 1183 to about 1193.

[180] Matthew 23. 37.

[181] Cf. VLA II.43. A marginal note reads, 'Explicit liber secundus. Incipit liber tertius in uita beati Ioannis abbatis Cantipratensis.' ('Here ends the second book. Here begins the third book in the Life of Blessed John, Abbot of Cantimpré.')

Book III

Of the election of his successor, Dom Matthew

1. After John, that shrewd investor of the Lord's talents, had retired as archimandrite,[182] the time came for the church of Cantimpré to elect a new abbot. The brothers assembled and chose the venerable Robert, whom I listed third among the first six. But John, with his prudent insight into God's dispensation, selected instead Dom Matthew, who was prior at that time — not because the man the community had chosen did not fully deserve a position even greater than this, but because John foresaw in his mind's eye, by a secret and lofty counsel, that Matthew was more suitable. So it happened as he wished and the community consented. On the night before Dom Matthew was chosen for pastoral care, which would be entrusted to him against his will, the venerable man had the following vision. He dreamed that a shaggy bed full of stinging goads had been prepared for him, and he was laid in it trembling and horribly afraid. Nor did the outcome seem far from the vision after he was entangled in pastoral responsibilities. What man who is free of such cares could easily imagine all the goading worries that sting the honour of prelates? Bad leaders find themselves less troubled by the pricks of conscience, inasmuch as they are less solicitous to discern what they should correct in their subordinates or what useful goals they should achieve in business. But as for the good ones, the better they are the more fearful they are, so the more frequently they are stung by cares. Thus Dom Matthew, elected and blessed as abbot,[183] accepted due responsibility

---

[182] An Eastern Orthodox term for abbot, relatively rare in Latin texts. Cf. VJC I.4 above. Thomas may have learned Eastern usages from his mentor, James of Vitry. [BN]

[183] Cf. VJC I.15 and n. 55 above.

for all his brethren, and diligently and devoutly set about to increase and multiply their property. Just as the blessed John had promised, he became a model of virtues to everyone near and far.

How Dom John was strengthened by the blessed Virgin to continue his preaching

2. Those who suffer from dropsy cannot survive very long unless they are sustained by a special gift of God, or by the help of extremely skilful medicine. So not long afterward, the Christlike John, weighed down by the swelling of his illness, became sicker than usual and drew near to death. Fortified by the sacraments of the Church and constrained by the disease, he lost the power of speech. Since his breathing had grown weak, he was laid on a haircloth on the ground amid great lamentation by all. He remained there all night and the following day. But in the middle of the second night, his brothers perceived from a little warmth spreading through his chest that he would survive awhile longer, so they lifted the father's body from the floor and placed him back in bed in a sitting position, supported by pillows on all sides. Then the venerable Iueta, the prioress I mentioned at the beginning of Book II, persuaded all the brothers to get some sleep on account of the long vigils they had spent watching over their father. Exhausted by these vigils, they agreed, so the prioress was left alone with the blessed man.

As the night was waning and the sun had already begun to rise, the man who had been supposed dead suddenly opened his eyes, lifted his head and hands, and began to shout, 'Where are you going, sweet lady? Where are you going?' After repeating these words many times for a long while, he finally reclined his head as before and rested with his eyes closed, as if he had fallen asleep. Gazing intently, the handmaid of Christ marvelled at these words and awaited the outcome with amazement. No long interval passed before he returned to himself and heaved a great sigh from the bottom of his chest. Then he opened his eyes, looked around, and asked who was there. The prioress at once answered, 'I am, my lord'. Throwing herself at his feet with tears, she asked him in the name of God to reveal what had happened. Since he was modest in such matters, he held back for a while, but she asked insistently and at last, growing warm as he remembered, he explained what he had seen in these words: 'I was lying here, as you saw, with scarcely enough vital heat to survive much longer. When I was already drawing near to death and my soul was frightened, behold! our venerable patroness, the Virgin Mary, mother of God, stood before me with a man of marvellous beauty. Looking on my sickness with her merciful eyes, she asked how or where I felt pain. As soon as I had indicated the place, she stretched forth a vial that she carried in her hands, full of holy medicine, and drew it from side to side across my belly. At her touch came healing, which at once consigned me both to death and to life — to death, because I will not be restored to full strength with the deadly swelling of this dropsy; but also to life, because she renewed my strength enough that I can continue preaching the word. Uplifted in spirit, therefore, I asked our glorious Lady who was the saint that accompanied her, and the blessed Virgin said, "This is my companion, the apostle Andrew".[184] I added, "O, sweetest Lady, I have a great desire to see St Martin, the confessor of Christ". She replied, "And you shall see him" — and the blessed Martin arrived with a thurible, vested as a bishop. Circling my bed, he censed it with an odour like balsam and cinnamon.[185] As I was rejoicing in exultation over the vision and the visitation of such great saints, suddenly the glorious mother of Christ and her companions departed through this window. Now then, my daughter, do not presume to reveal these things to anyone as long as you remain amid the perils of this life.' Hearing this, the prioress glorified the Lord, for she knew this was the reason he had cried out when he saw the blessed Virgin departing.

Now, brothers, lest anyone doubt this miracle because of its greatness, I take Christ as my witness that I heard the gist of the story from her own mouth. I also have Dom Matthew and Dom Thomas,[186] Abbot John's successors, and several of the brothers as witnesses of the same miracle. Indeed, it became known to many before the blessed man died — partly through certain clear signs given afterward, partly through the boldness of the prioress, who — true to the proverb about women — could not remain silent.[187]

[184] Andrew was also present at the death of Mary of Oignies (*quasi insensibilem reddebat ei dolorem*; 'he rendered her almost insensible to pain'). She cherished a particular devotion to this apostle. Cf. VMO II.97, in *Mary of Oignies*, p. 118; II.12.103, in *Mary of Oignies*, p. 122. These passages could have influenced the present chapter of Thomas.

[185] Ecclesiasticus 24. 20. Another apparition of St Martin in the same attire is related in BUA II.25.9, p. 250.

[186] Thomas, third abbot of Cantimpré (who has sometimes been confused with our author).

[187] Cf. VLA III.19.

How he advised the Countess Marie of Flanders at Valenciennes

3. Restored and strengthened and, as he said, preserved from dropsy, John began to tour the castles and towns once more as he had done in the early days of his fervour, evangelizing the people[188] and rescuing souls that the devil was trying to snatch. It was at this time that the most noble prince Baldwin, the young count of Flanders, married the equally noble Marie, daughter of the count of Champagne.[189] Now Marie, learning of the blessed John's saintliness, summoned him to Valenciennes with many entreaties to receive his salutary advice. During a brief period after he began to visit her, he led her to such sublime perfection that she would often rise from her bed before dawn, content with only a single maid, to visit poor sick people in the neighbouring villages, walking barefoot to distribute alms; and she humbly and devoutly performed many other works of mercy.[190]

Therefore, because she loved Dom John above all others with a special intimacy, she entreated him urgently and raised many large donations from the nobles so she could construct a suitable dwelling for him near Valenciennes, and have him always present to guide her actions. But John, the unshakable foe of all avarice and greed, would not accept the gift of a single garment, blanket, or horse, not even from her. For he used to preach aptly, according to the philosopher's maxim, that if he accepted any gift he would lose his freedom to reproach sin in the rigour of justice.[191] So when she proposed to build the

---

[188] Luke 9. 6.

[189] Marie's father was Count Henry I of Champagne. Her mother, also called Marie of Champagne, was the daughter of Louis VII of France and Eleanor of Aquitaine. [BN] Marie was twelve years old when she married Baldwin IX of Flanders on 13 January 1186. But it was only in 1194 that he succeeded his father in Flanders, and 1195 in Hainaut. See Luykx, *Johanna van Constantinopel*, p. 47. We can assume that Marie's meeting with John of Cantimpré took place after that date and not, as Thomas affirms, at the time of the two adolescents' marriage, inasmuch as he mentions it in Book III — thus after John had resigned from the abbatial office. Moreover, the reported events — the birth of Jeanne of Constantinople and the Fourth Crusade — situate us in the later period. We will see that our author is chronologically less well informed in this section.

[190] Cf. the testimony of Gislebert de Mons, *Chronicon Hanoniense*, 123, in *La Chronique*, p. 192.

[191] Cf. Publilius Syrus, *Sententiae* B 5, ed. by Eduard von Wölfflin (Leipzig: Teubner, 1869), p. 3, and BUA II.33.5, p. 372. For Thomas the 'philosopher' is always Seneca, abundantly cited in the BUA. Colvénère makes the same observation in the glossary that concludes his edition (p. 173). The present quotation can be explained when we recall that the *Sentences* of Publilius

brothers a place to rest — commonly called a dormitory — and the countess herself wanted to send a huge sum of money she had collected for its construction, the servant of God told her with a stern expression, 'Do not do this, lady! Do not do it, my daughter. I am not moved by these gifts of yours, but if I accept them from you, I will no longer come to you untroubled. Rather, my impulsive spirit, which now sustains me freely in admonition and reproach, will be thwarted by deference, and I will be held back by a kind of mental laziness from pursuing your salvation. Cease then to offer such gifts. I am rich, and our house is rich, as long as Christ is in our midst. I do not believe he will forsake us in the provision of temporal things as long as we seek his kingdom with pious zeal. But if our love of Christ and religion begins to cool (which God forbid!), it will not matter very much if we lack these things. For not even these created goods are fit for the wicked to have, even though a merciful God offers them to the ungrateful.'

Then the countess, terrified by the blessed man's words, was especially afraid that he would be held back from her salvation by her gifts, as he had said. So she restrained herself, albeit unwillingly, from offering him donations. As she used to say, she was deeply ashamed to repay the blessed man and his companions nothing for his labour or his love, especially since she knew she owed him temporal goods in return for the spiritual ones she received. So, when she needed the holy man's advice in his absence and she burned to send a vehicle to fetch him, she used to say anxiously to her confidants, 'I am profoundly shamed that the devout servant of Christ is fatigued by such toil — while I, who am counted worthy in his sight, do not pay him even the least reward for his labours'. Acknowledging this, the holy man established certain times when she was allowed to send a vehicle for him. To carry him more gently, the countess would send the holy man the carriage in which she herself travelled, and once he had come, she did not let him stay anywhere except her own private bedroom, while she herself stayed in a more remote chamber. Words cannot do justice to the great honour with which all the knights and courtiers welcomed him. Even the illustrious count revered him with marvellous affection and eagerly desired to receive wholesome advice from his lips.

Syrus were commonly attributed to Seneca in the Middle Ages. It is more surprising that Colvénère maintains this attribution in the BUA (cf. for example II.33.5, p. 372), given that Erasmus had already rejected it in favour of Publilius Syrus.

How the Countess Marie bore her daughter Jeanne with the help of John's prayers

4. Now the countess, who had long remained barren and childless, conceived at last by the grace of Christ and stayed at Valenciennes during her pregnancy. As the birth approached, she began to experience unbearable pains in her womb. After she had laboured anxiously for nine days in this pain, she summoned Christ's servant, sending for him with all haste. When Dom John arrived the countess said, 'Have mercy, father! Have mercy, and intercede with the Lord in compassion for my agony.' As she beseeched him with tears, Father John, himself also weeping, mercifully entered his oratory and lifted suppliant hands and eyes to the Lord, saying, 'O God, you who in your wondrous judgement saw fit to punish the disobedience of our first-created parents in the reproduction of the human race, so that the woman who initiated the transgression might bear children in pain and the man who hearkened to her might eat his daily bread in the sweat of his brow:[192] attend now to our prayers and graciously show mercy to this woman, who has already suffered sufficient pains and trusts, through my unworthy mediation, in your goodness, that she may be delivered from her labour pangs and bring forth a healthy heir to rule your people.' He had scarcely finished such words of prayer when, all of a sudden, the girls who had been assisting the countess came running to the door with immense joy and exultation,[193] announcing that their lady had given birth to a girl. Without delay, the noble matrons came out of the palace and offered the little infant to God's saint, since she had been delivered from the womb as if by his prayer. He received her with thanksgiving and gave her his holy blessing. Later, when she was reborn in the sacred font of baptism, at her parents' request she received the name of Jeanne, even though none of her relatives was called by that name.[194]

This is the same Jeanne who later married Frederick, son of the king of Portugal, and to this day she rules the counties of Flanders and Hainaut with wise government.[195] I have heard recently that — by the merits of the holy father John, as we might well believe — she and her husband and her entire household

---

[192] Genesis 3. 16, 19.

[193] Psalm 44. 16.

[194] Luke 1. 61.

[195] A marginal note reads 'De Joanna filia Regis Portugallie' ('concerning Jeanne, daughter of the King of Portugal'). Jeanne was born in January 1200 or in the last months of 1199. She married Ferrand of Portugal in 1212. See Luykx, *Johanna van Constantinopel*, pp. 51, 93.

have converted to a stricter way of life, following the advice of the holy Dominicans in Lille, who are truly servants of Christ.[196] Recently, too, she founded a monastery near the same town and endowed it with great gifts in honour of the glorious Virgin Mary.[197] But now, to finish the story of her most noble mother, I must hasten on and say no more about the daughter, whom I have fittingly remembered here.

Of the Emperor Baldwin and his death in the Holy Land

5. After the birth of her daughter, Countess Marie of Flanders was pregnant again[198] when her husband, the most noble Baldwin, made a pilgrimage to Constantinople for the defence of the faith and the honour of Christ. There he was elected and consecrated emperor and received the whole kingdom of Greece to govern.[199] At once, with supreme worldly ambition,[200] he sent messengers from Constantinople with letters commanding the countess to come to him in that city, leaving her land and daughters in the care of prudent and discreet men. On hearing such tidings, the countess summoned her noble vassals and barons and asked what she should do — remain in the land or obey her husband? It is little wonder that they almost all agreed: the countess would remain safer in custody of her own land and daughters, ignoring her husband's command. Indeed, many foresaw the great dangers that could arise from the countess's departure. But God's servant John steadfastly resisted the advice of all, saying instead that the countess should heed her husband's advice and finally obey his commands. This made sense, for no one could doubt that the young emperor's mind was frequently swayed by competing impulses. As soon as she had heard the holy man's advice, the countess at once entrusted her daughters to King Philip of

---

[196] The Dominican convent of Lille was founded 'at the end of 1224 or the beginning of 1225': J. Marseille, 'Le Couvent des dominicains de Lille de sa fondation au milieu du XVe siècle', *Archivum Fratrum Praedicatorum*, 40 (1970), 73–95 (p. 75).

[197] The Cistercian abbey of Marquette (Monasterium de Reclinatorio Beatae Mariae), founded in 1227 and richly endowed by Jeanne and Ferrand in 1228. See Luykx, *Johanna van Constantinopel*, p. 314.

[198] Her daughter Marguerite was born in 1202: Luykx, *Johanna van Constantinopel*, p. 53.

[199] A marginal note reads 'Balduinus eligitur imperator Constantinop[olis]' ('Baldwin is elected emperor of Constantinople'). He was crowned at Hagia Sophia on 16 May 1204.

[200] Cf. 1 John 2. 16 (Vetus Latina).

France,[201] left her land in the hands of certain noblemen, and set forth in haste to obey her husband's bidding. Crossing by sea to the Holy Land, she arrived at Jerusalem with amazing and unexpected speed — and a few days later she received the wretched tidings of her husband's death, to the detriment of all Christendom.[202] But I have said enough of these affairs to let the reader infer how much weight the holy man's counsel had in those days.

Of Dom John's death and burial

6. As his death approached, he lost his appetite almost completely. But when his brothers asked if he wanted anything special, he said, 'Yes, if I could have a little partridge meat.' At once they ran to the city and tried everywhere to buy a partridge, but they found none. By chance, however, one of his friends, leaving the city to tend the crops, unexpectedly found a partridge as if prepared for the holy man's hunger. He captured it alive, offered it to the blessed man, and satisfied his desire.

7. Henceforth I will take pen in hand to write of the holy man's death, omitting many things for the sake of brevity.[203] When the brothers had gathered in the sisters' house at Prémy,[204] where the saint was gladly awaiting his end, they became fearful of his death and asked him, with many tears, not to spurn the growth of his tender new plantation by hastening toward death. He answered them weeping and said, 'I believe it would not be fruitful or desirable for my life to last any longer, tossed as it is by so many pains and agonies. The prayers of my pious sons in the Lord are too harsh if they compel me to linger in such deadly suffering. Cease then, my beloved brothers! I beg you, do not hinder my passing, but let my weary spirit behold the long-desired face of Christ.' With these words, he asked for communion in the Lord's body and blood and anointing with the

---

[201] We know that Marie departed to rejoin her husband, but it seems difficult to affirm that she entrusted her daughters to Philip Augustus. Although we do not know with certainty where they stayed between 1202 and 1205, it is only in 1208 that the King of France took the two princesses under his protection. See Luykx, *Johanna van Constantinopel*, pp. 55, 68, 75–78.

[202] Here again Thomas is not well informed. It was Marie who died first, not at Jerusalem but at Acre [in August 1204]. Baldwin thus learned of her death before being taken prisoner by the Bulgars in April 1205. See Luykx, *Johanna van Constantinopel*, p. 55.

[203] This introduction marks a resumption of the narrative; it is this chapter that Thomas composed at the end of his life at the request of Anselm, abbot of Cantimpré (cf. Prologue).

[204] A marginal note reads 'Il meurt à Praemiacus' ('he dies at Prémy').

medicine of extreme unction. After this, when he could scarcely form words with his voice, being near his last breath, he saw the enemy of mankind standing on his left, as if laying a snare at his heel[205] and awaiting his end. At once he raised his head and gestured indignantly with his hand, saying, 'What do you seek, most wicked enemy of mankind? You will find no scruple of sin or iniquity in me, for with many labours in my lifetime and many afflictions before death, I have purified whatever was owing to the human stain.' As he said this, he raised himself to a sitting position in bed and spoke to the Lord with open eyes: 'O true Father and most gracious Brother of all, Christ in the substance of divinity, our brother in the form of humanity: I bless you and glorify you, for you have granted me to come to this hour with confidence in your mercy. Hear my prayer, O Lord, I beseech you: guard in all piety and peace those whom you have deigned to gather through my ministry; and receive my last breath, which I now pour out, in the hands of the holy angels.' Saying this, he breathed forth his spirit.[206]

Who could express or imagine the mourning and weeping, the crying and sighing among the brothers and sisters, especially in Cambrai and the villages and towns around it? Dom John was buried before the altar in the church of Prémy,[207] for he could not be buried in his own monastery because the city was under interdict.[208] I should note that he appeared to many friends at his death and afterward and revealed the glory of his reward. But I omit these events and many more because I too am caught in the grip of sickness.

[205] Cf. Genesis 3. 15; VMO II.108, in *Mary of Oignies*, p. 126; VLA II.15 and III.11.

[206] The necrologies of Cantimpré and Saint-Victor in Paris mention John of Cantimpré on the date of 30 January (Archives du Nord, 37 H 29); Molinier and Longnon, *Obituaires de la Province de Sens*, I.1, p. 539.

[207] When their second church was demolished in 1762, the canonesses of Prémy rediscovered John's tomb in its foundations. On the funerary slab, an inscription in Gothic characters bore the words *Corpus Domini Iohannis primi abbatis et fundatoris Cantipratensis* ('the body of Dom John, first abbot and founder of Cantimpré'). The Archives du Nord preserve a record of the inquest concerning this discovery by 'Albert, bishop of Amycle, vicar general of Cambrai' (Archives du Nord, 50 H 4).

[208] This interdict (1205–10) was Bishop John of Béthune's response to the re-establishment of the privileges of the commune by the emperor. See Wilhelm Reinecke, *Geschichte der Stadt Cambrai bis zur Erteilung der Lex Godefridi (1227)* (Marburg: Elwert, 1896), pp. 155–57. It provides our most precise touchstone for dating John's death.

THE LIFE OF CHRISTINA THE ASTONISHING

Translated by Margot H. King and Barbara Newman

CHRONOLOGY

THE LIFE OF CHRISTINA THE ASTONISHING

(*c.* 1150–1224)

PROLOGUE

Here begins the prologue to the life of blessed Christina of the town of Sint-Truiden

1. When I was planning to write the life of the unforgettable virgin Christina, I first decided to put at the beginning of my discourse what James, the revered bishop of Acre (he who later became a cardinal in the Roman Curia),[1] related about her in *The Life of the Blessed Mary of Oignies*:

I saw another [understand that he means Christina] in whom God worked so wondrously that after she had lain dead for a long time — but before her body was buried in the ground — her soul returned to her body and she lived again. She obtained from the Lord that she would endure purgatory, living in this world in her body. It was for this reason that she was afflicted for a long time by the Lord, so that sometimes she rolled herself in the fire, and sometimes in the winter she remained for lengthy periods in icy water and at other times she was driven to enter the tombs of the dead. But after she had performed penance

---

[1] James of Vitry (*c.* 1160/70–1240) was ordained a priest in 1210 after receiving his Master's degree and licence to teach at Paris. From 1211–16, he was active in the diocese of Liège. It was during this period that he became an Augustinian canon and entered the monastery of Saint Nicholas at Oignies, where he became involved in the exuberant lay spiritual movement of which Mary of Oignies was an outstanding representative. In his *Supplement* to James's life of Mary, Thomas of Cantimpré says that it was Mary who was responsible for James's ordination, transferral to Oignies, and entrance into the canonical state. In 1213 he was commissioned by the papal legate to preach the crusade against the Albigensians and shortly thereafter he preached a crusade for the Holy Land. Towards the end of 1215 he was elected to the see of Acre in Palestine, where he served until 1227. After a short period back in the diocese of Liège, he was named cardinal bishop of Tusculum in 1229, a post he held until his death in 1240.

in so many ways, she lived in peace and merited grace from the Lord and many times, rapt in spirit, she led the souls of the dead as far as purgatory, or through purgatory as far as the kingdom of heaven, without any harm to herself.[2]

2. These words are, as I have said, those that the revered Bishop James of Vitry related about her. Therefore I, an unworthy friar of the Order of Preachers, have described these things, although in unpolished language, for the edification of readers and especially for the praise of Christ. I am quite certain of the account that has been reported to me. I do not say 'certain' without cause, for I have as many witnesses to most of the events I have described as there were rational persons living at that time in the town of Sint-Truiden. These things were not done in narrow corners[3] but openly among the people. Nor has so much time elapsed that oblivion has swallowed up and buried these occurrences, for I wrote this *Life* not more than eight years after her death. I personally heard other things that no one could have known except Christina herself from people who swore they learned them from her own mouth.

3. Whoever reads these things should bear in mind that I have believed them on the testimony of witnesses who would by no means deviate from the truth even at the risk of losing their heads. I admit — and it is true — that my account surpasses all human understanding, inasmuch as these things could by no means have occurred according to the course of nature, yet they are possible to the Creator. Furthermore, I would never have presumed to have written this if the revered Bishop James had not previously testified to most of these events. For this reason, then, let me fulfil the task by approaching it in this way: first of all I will describe how she was nourished, then how she was educated, and finally

---

[2]   VMO Prologue 8, in *Mary of Oignies*, pp. 48–49.

[3]   Acts 26. 26.

I will describe her deeds,[4] just as I have learned from most truthful and indisputable accounts.

Birth of the saint; how, after her death and her vision of purgatory, she was led back to life so that she might aid those souls who were detained there; and how harshly she suffered for them, but remained unharmed in body

Here begins the life of the holy Christina, called the Astonishing

4. Christina, the unforgettable virgin of Christ, was born of respectable parents in the town of Sint-Truiden in Hesbaye. After her parents had died, she was left with two older sisters. Desiring to order their life in the manner of religious life, they arranged that the oldest sister would occupy herself in prayer, the middle one take care of the house, and the youngest — that is, Christina — watch the herds as they went to pasture.[5] Without delay Christ did not fail as consoler to the girl allotted the lower and more humble office, but rather he gave her the grace of an inward sweetness and very often visited her with heavenly secrets. Nevertheless she remained unknown to all and the more hidden she was,

---

[4] This passage is, I believe, very important for an understanding of the structure of the *vita* and clarifies some of the more bizarre details of Christina's behaviour. In William of Saint-Thierry's *Exposition on the Song of Songs* [*Expositio super Cantica canticorum*], we find an examination of the gifts God gives the soul in each of its stages of mystical growth: the animal, rational, and spiritual levels; nourishment in the animal stage, education in the rational, and freedom in the spiritual. In this context, I would interpret the terms *nutrita*, *educata*, and *gesta* as 1) the divine nutrition necessary for beginners; 2) the charismatic education given those who are labouring towards perfection; and 3) the working of God in and through his creatures and, by extension, that freedom which comes with the life of the spirit. See especially Louis M. Savary, *Psychological Themes in The Golden Epistle of William of Saint Thierry* (Salzburg: Analecta Cartusiana, 1973), and E. Rozanne Elder, 'The Way of Ascent: The Meaning of Love in the Thought of William of St Thierry', in *Studies in Medieval Culture*, ed. by John R. Sommerfeldt (Kalamazoo: Western Michigan University, 1964), pp. 39–47. Bernard McGinn disagrees with my interpretation that the tripartite structure of the *vita* is related to William's three stages of the spiritual life, but he gives no reason for his disagreement: *The Flowering of Mysticism*, pp. 399–400, n. 32.

[5] Note the correspondence of this threefold division of labour to that found in the monastic life: 1) prayer (choir nuns); 2) housework (lay sisters); and 3) farm labourers. Just as Christina would operate outside society after she returned from the dead, so now she is relegated to a position outside her monastically oriented home. According to local legend, Christina lived in Brustem and her two sisters in Ordingen and Zefferen, now all suburbs of Sint-Truiden.

the more she was known to God alone. This is why she gloried with Isaiah, saying 'My secret to myself, my secret to myself'.[6] For God is a modest lover.

How she died

5. It happened that after these events she grew sick in body through the exercise of inward contemplation and died. Her lifeless body was laid out by her friends and sisters, and they wept copiously over it. The next day it was borne to the church, and while her Requiem Mass was being said, suddenly the body stirred in the coffin and rose up and, like a bird, immediately ascended to the rafters of the church. All those present fled and only her older sister remained behind fearfully. Christina was immovable until mass was finished; then, kept in check by the priest with the sacrament of the Church, she was forced to descend.[7] Some say that the subtlety of her spirit was revolted by the smell of human bodies.[8] She soon returned home with her sisters and was reinvigorated by food. Her spiritual friends then hastened to her, asking what she had seen and wanting her to explain what had happened.[9] She said to them:

---

[6] Isaiah 24. 16.

[7] This language strongly suggests exorcism. Christina's 'resurrection' would most likely have been interpreted at the time as the reanimation of her corpse by a demon. Cf. BUA II.49.6 and II.57.8, pp. 367–68, 452, and Nancy Caciola, 'Wraiths, Revenants and Ritual in Medieval Culture', *Past & Present*, 152 (1996), 3–45 (pp. 10–15). [BN]

[8] On the face of it, Thomas's explanation for Christina's revulsion with human smells is theologically suspect. If it was occasioned by the contrast between the stench of mortality and the sweet smells of heaven, this surely undermines not only the full dignity of humanity, but of the human Christ as well. However, if she was possessed, her diabolical powers could have been restrained by the sacraments, especially the eucharist. See Wolfgang Riehle, *The Middle English Mystics* (London: Routledge & Kegan Paul, 1981), p. 116, and Ernest Becker, *Medieval Visions of Heaven and Hell* (Baltimore: Murphy, 1899), p. 61. Most of Christina's apparently antisocial activities are, in fact, an acting-out of the purgatorial torments.

[9] The 'spiritual friends' of this passage, informed of Christina's divine mission, should be distinguished from the hostile 'friends' (probably members of her extended family) who persecute her later on. [BN]

How she was led forth from the body and how she lived again after she had been brought back to the body

6. 'As soon as I died, angels of God, the ministers of light, received my soul and led me into a dark and terrible spot which was filled with the souls of men. The torments that I saw in that place were so many and so cruel that no tongue is adequate to tell of them. There I saw many dead men whom I had previously known in the flesh. Having not a little compassion on those wretched souls, I asked them what place this was. I thought it was hell, but my guides said to me, "This place is purgatory and it is here that repentant sinners atone for the sins they committed while they were alive". They then led me to the torments of hell and there also I recognized some people whom I had known while I was alive.'

7. 'After these events, I was carried into paradise, to the throne of the Divine Majesty. When I saw that the Lord was well pleased with me and wished me joy, I rejoiced above all measure, thinking that I would remain with the Lord forever after. At once the Lord answered my desire and said, "Certainly, my dearest, you will be with me here, but I now offer you two choices, either to remain with me now or to return to the body and undergo there the punishment of an immortal soul in a mortal body without damage to it, and by these your sufferings to deliver all those souls on whom you had compassion in that place of purgatory, and by the example of your suffering and your way of life to convert living men to me and make them turn aside from their sins, and after you have done all these things to return to me, having accumulated for yourself a reward of such great profit". I answered without hesitation that I wished to return under the terms that had been offered to me.'

8. 'The Lord immediately wished me joy in his response and commanded my soul to be led back to the body. And see how quick the angels were to obey the bidding of the Lord! At the same time that the Agnus Dei was being said for the first time while mass was being celebrated for me, my soul was standing before the throne of Divine Majesty, but by the time they said the Agnus Dei for the third time, I had been restored to the body by those swift angels. Thus was the manner of my returning and my departing, and I have been given back to life for the improvement of men. Now therefore do not let the things you are going to see in me trouble you, because the tasks with which God will charge me are above understanding. Indeed, such things have not been seen among mortals.' On hearing this, her friends marvelled and waited in amazement to see what would happen.

How she was captured by her friends and freed by the Lord and how she was nourished from her own virginal breasts

9. Then Christina fled the presence of men with wondrous horror into deserted places, to trees, or the tops of castle or church towers, or any lofty structure.[10] Thinking her to be filled with demons,[11] the people finally managed to capture her with great effort and to bind her with iron chains, and although she endured much suffering and privation, yet she suffered even more from the stench of men. One night, with the help of God, her chains and fetters fell off and she escaped and fled into remote, deserted forests and there lived in trees after the manner of birds. Even when she needed food (for despite the extreme subtlety of her body, she could not live without food), and she was tortured by a most grievous hunger, by no means did she wish to return home, but she desired to remain alone with God in her hiding place in the desert. Therefore, pouring forth a prayer to the Lord, she humbly begged that he gaze on her anguish with the eyes of his mercy.

When she turned her eyes to herself, she immediately saw that the dry paps of her virginal breasts were dripping sweet milk against the very law of nature.[12]

---

[10] Like the ancient stylites and dendrites (saints who preferred the unstable environment of trees to the relative security of pillars), Christina attempted to effect a complete material separation from the world. It would seem that she is also acting within the tradition of the 'fools for Christ' whose real or feigned madness acted as a running commentary on the folly of worldly concerns. See John Saward, *Perfect Fools: Folly for Christ's Sake in Catholic and Orthodox Spirituality* (Oxford: Oxford University Press, 1980); Nora Chadwick, *The Age of the Saints in the Early Celtic Church* (London: Oxford University Press, 1963), pp. 109–11; Hippolyte Delehaye, *Les Saints stylites, Subsidia hagiographica* (Paris: Picard, 1923; repr. Brussels: Société des Bollandistes, 1962); King, 'The Sacramental Witness', pp. 145–64.

[11] On the demoniac's flight from human society see Newman, 'Possessed by the Spirit', p. 738, and André Sigal, *L'Homme et le miracle dans la France médiévale (XIe–XIIe siècle)* (Paris: Cerf, 1985), pp. 236–39.

[12] This is the first stage of Christina's spiritual development, her nutrition. In his life of Lutgard, Thomas refers to 'the milk of Christ's humanity' (VLA I.13), and one is irresistibly reminded of the image of the milk of the Bridegroom's breasts found in many of the Cistercian mystical writers, notably William of Saint-Thierry. The milk that must be sucked for nourishment in the animal stage, he says, is 'the milk of all the mysteries (*sacramenta*) accomplished in time for our eternal salvation, in order to attain to the food which is the Word of God, God with God. For Christ, in his humility, is our milk; God, equal with God, he is our food. Milk nourishes, and food brings about growth' (*Exposition on the Song of Songs*, I.46, trans. by Columba Hart (Spencer, MA: Cistercian Publications, 1970), p. 36). See also Bernard of Clairvaux, *On the Song of Songs I*, Sermon 9.6, trans. by Kilian Walsh (Kalamazoo: Cistercian

Wondrous thing! Unheard of in all the centuries since the incomparable Virgin Mother of Christ![13] Using the dripping liquid as food, she was nourished for nine weeks with the milk from her own virginal breasts. In the meantime, she was being sought by her own family and was found, captured, and bound as before with iron chains — but in vain.

How she walked into the waters

10. After she had been freed by the Lord, she came to the city of Liège. Hungering for the most holy flesh of the spotless Paschal Lamb, she begged the priest of St Christopher's to strengthen her with Holy Communion against the anguish she was suffering from so many things. And when the priest promised he would do so, but said that he could not give her communion right then because he was busy, she was impatient at any delay, and went to a priest at another church and asked him for the Body of Christ. He immediately gave in to the prayers of the supplicant and gave her communion. With no delay, she was seized by a sudden impulse and fled the city. The priest wondered greatly at her flight and ran to the other priest at St Christopher's, and they both followed her as far as the rapidly flowing Meuse. When they reached the river's edge, they rejoiced because they thought they could seize her. But, stupefied, they observed the woman in front of them (in a real body) enter the deep streams of the water like a phantasm and come out untouched on the other side.[14]

How she was tormented in fire

11. Then Christina began to do those things for which she had been sent back by the Lord. She crept into fiery ovens where bread was baking and was tormented by fires — just like any of us mortals — so that her howls were

Publications, 1976), pp. 57-58; and Caroline Walker Bynum, *Jesus as Mother: Studies in the Spirituality of the High Middle Ages* (Berkeley: University of California Press, 1982), especially Ch. 4: 'Jesus as Mother and Abbot as Mother: Some Themes in Twelfth-Century Cistercian Writings'.

[13] Thomas alludes to the miraculous lactation of the Virgin. Her milk, credited with healing powers, was venerated as a relic at Chartres, Walsingham, and other shrines. [BN]

[14] Cf. Matthew 14. 25–27. Since she is endowed with a 'resurrection body', Christina is able to walk on the waters as Christ did. [BN]

terrible to hear. Nevertheless, when she emerged, no mutilation of any sort appeared in her body. When no oven was at hand, she would throw herself into roaring fires which she found in people's houses, or else she at least thrust her feet and hands into flames and held them there for so long that they would have been reduced to ashes had it not been a divine miracle. At other times she jumped into cauldrons of boiling water and stood there immersed either up to the breast or the waist, depending on the size of the cauldron, and poured scalding water over those parts of her body that were untouched. Although she howled as if she were suffering the pangs of childbirth,[15] when she climbed out again she was quite unharmed.

How she was tormented in the waters

12. Often in cold weather she would remain for a long time under the waters of the Meuse; indeed, frequently she stayed there for six or more days at a time.[16] But the priest who took care of her came and stood on the river bank and adjured her by the name of Christ, and thus she was forced to come out.[17] In the winter she would stand upright beneath the wheel of a water-mill so that the water flowing through it ran over her head and limbs. Sometimes she would swim with the current and let the water carry her over the turning wheel, yet no hurt appeared on her body.

[15] This expression was proverbial, but Thomas's frequent use of it (cf. Chs 24, 29, 37) emphasizes Christina's role as a spiritual mother. For other examples of maternal language see Ch. 9 (miraculous lactation) and 41 (Count Louis as Christina's spiritual son). [BN]

[16] In the *Visio Lazari*, immersion in icy waters is the punishment for the sin of envy: 'Secondly, said Lazarus, I have seen in hell a flood frozen as ice, wherein the envious men and women were plunged unto the navel, and then suddenly came over them a right cold and a great wind, that grieved and pained them right sore. And when they would avoid and eschew the wonderful blasts of the said wind, they plunged into the water with great shouts and cries lamentable to hear': *The Kalendar & Compost of Shepherds: From the Original Edition published by Guy Marchant in Paris in the year 1493*; and translated into English *c.* 1518, ed. by G. C. Heseltine (London: Davies, 1930), pp. 58–67. For another contemporary account of the torments of purgatory, see the Vision of the Monk of Eynsham (dated 1196) in Matthew Paris, *Chronica Majora*, ed. by H. R. Luard, 7 vols (London: Longman, 1872-83), II, pp. 423-37.

[17] An exorcism, again suggesting that Christina was thought to be possessed. The priest assigned to her *cura* could have been either her parish priest and confessor, or a custodian for someone deemed mentally incompetent. [BN]

How she was tormented on wheels and gibbets

13. She also stretched her arms and legs on the rack, that instrument on which brigands are customarily tormented, acting the part of her own torturer.[18] Yet when she descended, no fracture appeared in her limbs. She would also go to the gallows and suspend herself between the thieves who were hanging there and would so hang for one or two days.[19] Often, too, she would enter the graves of dead men and there make lamentation for the sins of men.

Marvels concerning the subtlety and form of her body; and of how her shin-bone was healed; of her liberation from captivity; of the oil which flowed from her breasts; her more ordinary manner of living; the fruits of sacred communal prayer; a commendation of begging; prophecy

How she was tormented in thorn bushes and brambles and how she was attacked by dogs

14. On another occasion she rose up in the middle of the night and, provoking the dogs of the whole city of Sint-Truiden to bark, ran before them like a fleeing beast. The dogs pursued her and chased her through woods so thick with thorns that her whole body was covered in bloody wounds. Nevertheless, when she had washed off the blood, no trace of the wounds remained.

She used to torment herself in the same way with thorns and brambles so it seemed that her whole body was entirely covered in blood.[20] The many people

---

[18] In the *Visio Lazari*, the prideful are tormented on rotating wheels: 'I have seen in hell wheels right high set on an hill, the which was to look on in manner like mills incessantly turning about by great impetuosity, roaring and whirling as it were thunder. And the wheels were fixed full of hooks and crampons of iron and steel, and on them were hanged and turned the proud men and women for their pride, with their prince, captain, and master Lucifer': *Kalendar & Compost of Shepherds*, p. 60. For this torment, see also the *Tractatus de Purgatorio Sancti Patricii*, in *St Patrick's Purgatory*, ed. by Robert Easting, Early English Text Society, 298 (Oxford: New York, 1991), pp. 131-33.

[19] A reminiscence of Christ on the cross; cf. Matthew 27. 38. [BN]

[20] The punishment meted out to the wrathful in the *Visio Lazari* bears a certain similarity to Christina's self–mutilation: 'I have seen in hell a great cave, tenebrous and obscure, full of tables like to butchers' stalls, or a great butchery, where as ireful men and women were through-pierced with trenching knives and sharp glaves and with long spears pierced their bodies, wherewith the most horrible and fearful butchers of hell hewed and detrenched them with their

who had frequently seen this happen were astonished that there could be so much blood in a single body. In addition to this bloodletting, on many occasions she bled a great quantity of blood from one of her veins.

The subtlety of her body

15. Her body was so subtle and light that she walked on dizzy heights and, like a sparrow, hung suspended from the most slender branches of trees.[21]

How she behaved when she prayed

16. When she wanted to pray, she had to flee to treetops or towers or any lofty spot so that, remote from everyone, she might find rest for her spirit. And again when she prayed and the divine grace of contemplation descended upon her, all her limbs were gathered together into a ball as if they were hot wax, and all that could be perceived of her was a round mass. After her spiritual inebriation was finished and her active physical senses had restored her limbs to their proper place, like a hedgehog her rolled-up body returned to its proper shape and the limbs that had been bent formlessly were once again spread out. Many times she would stand erect on fence palings and in that position chant the appointed Psalms,[22] for it was very painful for her to touch the ground while she was praying.

glaves and knives impiteously without ceasing. [...] The wrathful man is semblable and like unto a demoniacle, the which hath the devil within him, causing him to torment and strive with himself, foaming at the mouth and gnashing with his teeth for the intolerable pain the which the enemy doth to him': *Kalendar & Compost of Shepherds*, pp. 62–63.

[21] In scholastic theology, subtlety was one of the four 'dowries' or divine gifts, along with impassibility, clarity, and agility, promised to the glorified body after the resurrection. See Bynum, *The Resurrection of the Body*, pp. 100, 131–32. [BN]

[22] *Psalmorum decantabat cursum.* This is evidence for Christina's Latinity, since a layman would normally have used only simple prayers such as the Our Father and Hail Mary. [BN]

How her shin-bone was broken and how she was captured and freed by the Lord

17. Her sisters and friends were greatly embarrassed because of these and similar things, for people thought she was possessed by demons. They made an agreement with a most wicked man who was very strong, whom they bribed to follow and capture her and to bind her with iron chains. Although this worthless man pursued her through the wilderness, he could not capture her with his hands, but he did finally catch up with her and broke her leg with a cudgel. She was then brought home and her sisters hired a physician who took care of her broken shin-bone. It was for this reason that she was carried to Liège in a cart.[23]

18. The physician knew her strength, so he bound her firmly to a pillar[24] in a cellar where chains hung on all the walls, and locked the doors securely. He then attended to her broken shin-bone and bound it with medicated bandages. After the physician had left, she drew off the bandages, since she thought it shameful to have any doctor for her wounds but our Saviour Jesus Christ — and the Almighty did not fail her. For one night when the divine Spirit came upon her, the chains with which she was bound were loosed and, healed from all hurt, she walked around the cellar and danced, praising and blessing him for whom alone she had chosen to live and die.[25] Her spirit then felt itself to be shut up in a narrow dungeon, and she took a stone from the floor and in her impassioned spirit she threw it with such force that she made a hole in the wall. To use an analogy, just as an arrow is the more forcefully released the more strongly the bow is bent, so Christina's spirit, which had been restrained more than was just, flew through the empty air like a bird, carrying with it the fleshy weight of her body. For 'where the Spirit of the Lord is, there is liberty'.[26]

---

[23] Criminals were normally carried to execution in a cart, so this mode of transport was considered extremely shameful. In Chrétien de Troyes's romance of *Lancelot, or The Knight of the Cart* (contemporary with Christina's adventure), the hero is in such haste to rescue Guenevere that he rides in a cart after his horse is slain, knowing that the shame will destroy his reputation. [BN]

[24] A reminiscence of Christ's scourging at the pillar, one of the torments of his Passion. [BN]

[25] Cf. the miraculous prison breaks of Peter (Acts 12. 6–11) and Paul (Acts 16. 25–28). [BN]

[26] II Corinthians 3. 17.

How oil dripped from her breasts and how, in this way, she was freed and released by her friends

19. Nevertheless her sisters and friends never stopped their persecution, for after she had returned to a place where they could seize her, they bound her fast with a heavy wooden yoke and fed her like a dog with only a little bread and water. Christ allowed her to be overcome and to endure tribulation for a time in order to show in her the remarkable miracle of his strength.[27] The hardness of the wooden yoke crushed her shoulders and caused festering wounds, and she was so wasted by these pains that she could not eat her bread. No one there had compassion on her wretchedness, but the Lord marvellously had pity on her and wrought in her that great miracle, unheard of in all previous centuries. Her virginal breasts began to flow with a liquid of the clearest oil,[28] and she took that liquid and used it as a flavouring for her dry bread and ate it as food, and smeared it on the wounds of her festering limbs as an ointment.[29] When her sisters and friends saw this, they began to weep and struggled no more against the divine will in Christina's miracles. They released her from her chains and knelt down, begging pardon for the injury, and let her go.

---

[27] Cf. II Corinthians 12. 9: 'My strength is made perfect in weakness'. [BN]

[28] Cf. the mystical lactation of Ch. 9. On miraculous bodily exudings as a theme in the *vitae* of holy women, see Bynum, *Holy Feast and Holy Fast*, pp. 122–23, 211, 273–74. [BN]

[29] This portion of Christina's life can be considered the period in which she received her 'education' and hence can be called, to use William's terminology, the rational stage. Fed by the nourishing milk of Christ and the solid food of the eucharist which had promoted her spiritual growth, she now receives 'the unction of the Holy Spirit teaching the soul concerning all things' (*Exposition on the Song of Songs* I.43, p. 33). The oil which flowed from her breasts recalls, as Pinius pointed out (AASS, 24 July, V, p. 654, e7), the oil which dripped from the fingers of Lutgard as a sign of spiritual consolation (VLA I.16). It is, of course, also a reference to Song of Songs 5. 5: 'My hands dropped with myrrh, and my fingers were full of the choicest myrrh', and one cannot help but wonder if the oil which dripped from Christina's breasts might be an allusion to the 'bundle of myrrh' in Song of Songs 1. 12: 'A bundle of myrrh is my beloved to me: he shall abide between my breasts.' Whatever the reference, however, this oil certainly can be considered a sacramental sign, a symbol of the overflowing grace which God effects in the human. By means of this miracle, Christina was not only gladdened and consoled in spirit, but healed of her wounds as well, and her symbolic baptism effected her final healing with regard to society. Now, finally, she ministered to society in the way God had intended. She has been taught a salutary lesson: for the first time she shows an awareness of the potential scandal her actions might create and, in fact, did create when her sisters had thought her possessed.

How public prayers were said for Christina by religious people

20. Then, using her liberty as she pleased,[30] she suffered pains for people's sins as I mentioned above. Many people from far and near, even from the furthest regions, clustered around her every day to see the wonders God had wrought in Christina. When such crowds assembled, the religious men and women of Sint-Truiden were terrified that these supremely amazing marvels might exceed human reason, and that the beastly minds of men might convert these divine deeds into demonic activity — especially because Christina, fleeing the presence of humans, would ascend into lofty places like a bird and linger long in the waters like a fish. So they besought the Lord with earnest prayers that he moderate his miracles in Christina in accordance with the usual human state. Nor did the merciful God disdain the prayers of those who were weeping.

How her life was moderated with regard to humans

21. It happened one day that, violently stirred by a spirit,[31] she took refuge in a church in the village of Wellen and, coming upon an uncovered baptismal font, completely immersed herself in it. It is said that after she had done this, her manner of life was more moderate with regard to society, and she behaved more calmly and was more able to endure the smell of men and to live among them.

How she was driven by the Spirit to live by begging

22. She frequently partook of the sacrament of the Lord's body and blood with holy devotion, especially on Sundays, and said that she received bodily

---

[30] Having thus been taught by 'the oil of gladness and the unction of the Holy Spirit' (*Exposition on the Song of Songs*, I. 86, p. 70), Christina now finds that freedom which, according to William, 'accompanies illuminating grace [and which] comes when we are no longer under a tutor', because 'where the Spirit of the Lord is, there is liberty' (II Corinthians 3. 17). Before the miracle of the dripping oil, Christina's freedom had been limited by her 'animal' understanding. Once she received the gift of illuminating grace, however, her liberated spirit found its pleasure in a vicarious and redemptive suffering for sinners.

[31] *agitata a spiritu vehementissime.* The spirit in question is ambiguous; it could refer either to a demon possessing Christina or to the Holy Spirit, prompting her to self-exorcism through immersion in the sacred font. [BN]

strength and the greatest spiritual joy from it.[32] Consequently she, who had nothing of her own and no inheritance to renounce for Christ's sake, abstained as she could in food and drink. She used to beg from door to door every day for common alms so that she might bear the sins of those people from whose alms she was fed. Indeed, she said that she was driven by the Spirit of God to beg the alms of sinners because they might thereby be called to a horror of their sins and a penitent life. Furthermore, she said that nothing might bend God to mercy for sinners more than when sinners are moved by mercy towards their neighbours. For as the wise man says, mercy and pity can never result in anything but good at the last day. And to clarify these things by an example, I will confirm what I have said with a certain deed of Christina's.

Of the man from whom she accepted a drink

23. It happened one day that, as she was stirred by God with an intolerable thirst, she ran to the table of a most wicked man who was feasting sumptuously and asked for something to drink.[33] Moved by an unaccustomed pity, he gave her a little wine and let her drink. Contradicting the opinion of everyone who knew this man, Christina said that at his death he would be called to the grace of repentance and contrition.

How alms given to her by unjust persons tormented her; her food and clothing; her sense of those who would be damned and saved; her ability to look into hearts; various predictions; ecstasies, etc.

What happened when she ate the food which she had begged from evildoers and what her food and clothing were like

24. This is why, as I have said, she was driven to beg for alms from publicans. But when she ate anything given to her as alms which had been wrongly acquired, it seemed to her that she was swallowing the bowels of frogs and toads

---

[32] Frequent communion was rare at this time. These events occurred before the Fourth Lateran Council in 1215 mandated annual communion for all believers, and even afterwards, few laymen or women would have communicated more than four times a year without special permission. Cf. VLA II.14. [BN]

[33] Cf. the story of the rich man and Lazarus, Luke 16. 19–21. [BN]

or the intestines of snakes.[34] When she ate such things, she would cry out as if in childbirth: 'O Christ! What are you doing with me? Why do you torment me in this way?' She would beat her breast and her body and say: 'O miserable soul! What do you want? Why do you desire these foul things? Why do you eat this filth?' Thus it was torture for her to eat any unjust plunder.[35] Yet her tortures were no less painful if a guilty man denied her what she had requested. Once it happened that she snatched away with force something that a wicked man had denied her and said: 'Although now you do not wish it, yet later you will not grieve that it has been taken away. What does not profit you now will profit then.'

25. When a sleeve was missing from her gown or when her scapular lacked a hood, she would beg for it from anyone she met because she had been inwardly counselled in her spirit to receive it from that person. If it was given to her, she gave thanks. But if not, if the person were unwilling and refused her, she took it anyway and sewed it on her own garment. She was not ashamed if the sleeves of her gown did not match or were of different colours.[36] She wore a white tunic and a white scapular which covered her whole body down to her feet. Her garment was frequently sewn with thread made from the inner bark of the linden tree, or with willow twigs or little wooden spikes. She did not have shoes but walked with bare feet in all kinds of weather. The food she ate was vile and loathsome. She boiled in water bits of food that had been scraped from dirty dishes, fit only for the garbage. With this she ate bran bread so hard that it had to be first softened with water. She ate these things only after she had first fasted for two or three days at a time.

---

[34] In the *Visio Lazari*, Lazarus reports, 'I have seen in a vale a flood foul and stinking, at the brim of the which was a table with towels right dishonestly, whereat Gluttons been fed with toads and other venomous beasts and had to drink of the water of the same said flood [...] And they that nourisheth well the flesh prepareth meat for worms, and so the glutton is cook of worms. A man of worship would be ashamed for to be a cook of a great lord. More ashamed should he be to be a cook for worms': *Kalendar & Compost of Shepherds*, pp. 65–66.

[35] The rejection of profits from usury is a common theme in *vitae* from Thomas's milieu. See the extensive discussion in VJC II.14–18 and in Hugh of Floreffe, *The Life of Yvette of Huy*, IX.25-32, trans. by Jo Ann McNamara (Toronto: Peregrina, 2000), pp. 53-60. [BN]

[36] The sleeves of medieval garments were detachable and normally basted on with thread at the time of dressing. [BN]

Of her sorrow and lamentation for those who would be damned, and her joy for those who would be saved

26. She fled recognition and praise most energetically, saying it was for this especially that those to whom Christ had given knowledge of his truth in their lives were the most tormented in hell and purgatory. She always walked about as if she were dying or grieving, for God daily revealed to her whether those who were near death merited salvation or destruction. When one of the townspeople died whom she knew in spirit to be damned for his sins, she wept and twisted herself and bent herself backwards and bent and re-bent her arms and fingers as if they were pliable and had no bones. All who saw her found her sorrow so intolerable that even the hardest-hearted could not endure it without the greatest contrition and compassion. But for those who died and were destined to be saved, she danced so joyfully that it was a great marvel to see her so happy. From behaviour like this, people who knew the power of her spirit could easily mark by her joy or sorrow what would happen to the dying in the city.

27. She assisted the dying most willingly and gladly and exhorted them to a confession of their sins, to the fruit of penance, to a hope of everlasting joy, and to a fear of the destroying fire.[37] She showed solicitude and wondrous compassion not only to dying Christians, but also to Jews, of whom there was a very large company in the town. She said that Christ the Lord was full of mercy to those who wished to be converted to him, and so unwilling to take vengeance for sin that he was saddened whenever he was forced by people's sins to do so. Rather, he lovingly seeks opportunities by which he might grant salvation to sufferers. When she spoke in this way of Christ the Lord, she was filled with wondrous grace of speech.

28. She also said that there was a place near hell that was ordained by God for the purgation of those who were stained by great sins, but who had nevertheless repented at the end. This place, she said, was so fearsome because of its torments that there was no difference between these punishments and the pains of hell, except that there those who were suffering these pains sighed in the hope of pardon. Demons, she said, presided over those in torment, but those who were handed over to the demons to be tortured knew that the more cruelly they were afflicted by them, the shorter their torments would be.

---

[37] Hospice work, as we would now call it, was among the most common ministries of beguines. [BN]

How she was renowned for the spirit of prophecy

29. She was illumined with the spirit of prophecy in many things, admonished many to their salvation, and privately reprimanded many for their secret and hidden sins and recalled them to penance.

How she foretold a slaughter

At the time of that calamitous battle in October 1213 between the duke of Brabant and his enemies, when so many hundreds of men were killed in the place called Steppes,[38] on that very day this blessed woman cried out as if in childbirth, 'Alas! Alas! I see the air full of swords and blood! Hurry, sisters, hurry! Pray to the Lord! Shed tears lest he restrain his mercy in his wrath!' And she said to a nun at the monastery of St Catherine's in Sint-Truiden, 'Run, daughter, quickly run to prayer! Beg the Lord for your father because he is now in the greatest danger!'

How she foretold a nun's apostasy

30. When a nun at the same monastery was thinking of leaving, Christina said about her, 'O empty vessel! This will cause a very great scandal to the monastery.' Indeed, just as Christina had said, it soon happened that she apostasized from the order and caused great scandal to the monastery through her unrestrained behaviour. When the nun repented of her actions, the monastic community found it difficult to take her back and reinstate her. But Christina reproached them and said, 'Although you consider her damnation to be a minor thing, yet Christ did not pay so little for her soul. Rather, he poured out his blood for her and considered her worthy to die for.' Christina did not cease repeating these words until the repentant nun was reinstated.

---

[38] At this battle Duke Henry I of Brabant was defeated by the allied forces of Hugh of Pierrepont, prince-bishop of Liège, and Count Louis II of Loon, Christina's patron. [BN]

How, by her prayers, she protected a certain nobleman who was on pilgrimage

31. When a nobleman wanted to go on pilgrimage to the Lord's tomb, his wife begged and pleaded with Christina to bring him back safe and sound by her prayer. Christina took her plea seriously and offered many prayers, labours and vows to the Lord for the knight that he bring him back safely. But she said as if angrily to his wife, 'Behold, I have brought your husband back safely because of your insistent pleading, but know now that you will not long rejoice in his presence'. The truth of these words soon became clear, for a few days later the nobleman died and left his wife and children in grief and desolation.

How she foretold the taking of Jerusalem and announced the day when it was captured

32. On another occasion, she foretold long before the event that Jerusalem in the Holy Land would be taken by the ungodly Saracens. On the day that Jerusalem was captured by Saladin, king of the Persians,[39] along with the Lord's tomb and the cross of Christ, she was in the castle of Loon and knew the event in the spirit. She exulted with great passion over this deed and those who were present asked her why she exulted so much. 'Rightly', she said, 'I exult, because today Christ the Lord rejoices with the angels, and he exults because he has given so many men the occasion by which they might be saved'.

33. When the bystanders asked what this occasion might be, she said, 'Know that today the Holy Land has been given into the hands of the ungodly, and through this event a great opportunity for salvation has been given.[40] For Christ has seen fit, because of the shame he has suffered, to let the land consecrated by his passion fall into disgrace. Although it shall perish with the world at the end of time, yet by its recovery immortal souls redeemed by his blood shall be turned to the path of justice from the path of ungodliness. Men shall shed their blood in this affair of the Holy Land and they, in turn, shall repay the death of Christ with great devotion.'[41] All who were there marvelled. Some of them noted the

[39] This took place in 1187. Saladin was actually the sultan of Egypt. [BN]

[40] Cf. the account of Christ's betrayal in Matthew 26. 45. [BN]

[41] A prediction of the Third Crusade in 1189. [BN]

time and found that on the same day — that is, after the time required for the journey — the news could have reached those across the sea.

How she foretold the coming great famine

34. She also predicted a great famine, which took place around 1170, a long time before it occurred.⁴² Christina prophesied many other things as well that have now been fulfilled, and others that we believe will be fulfilled in the future.

Of how she was rapt in spirit and of her wondrous song at the aforesaid monastery

35. Now she was very familiar with the nuns of St Catherine's outside the town of Sint-Truiden.⁴³ Sometimes while she was sitting with them, she would speak of Christ and suddenly and unexpectedly she would be ravished in the spirit and her body would whirl around like a hoop in a children's game. She whirled around with such extreme violence that the individual limbs of her body could not be distinguished. When she had whirled around for a long time in this manner, it seemed as if she became weakened by the violence of the rolling and all her limbs grew quiet. Then there sounded between her throat and her breast a wondrous harmony that no mortal man could understand, nor could it be imitated by any artificial instrument.⁴⁴ That song of hers had only the pliancy and the tones of music. But the words of the melody, so to speak — if they could even be called words — sounded together incomprehensibly. No sound

---

⁴² This date must be erroneous, as Christina would have been only twenty years old in 1170 and her public ministry did not begin until 1182. [BN]

⁴³ Lutgard of Aywières was a Benedictine nun at this convent from 1194–1206; some time after 1200 she became prioress. In 1206 Christina encouraged her to move to the Cistercian monastery of Aywières. See VLA I.22. In 1231 the convent was moved to Mielen (Nonnemielen), a move that occasioned the translation of Christina's grave. See Ch. 54 below, and J. Grauwels, 'Abbaye de Mielen à Saint Trond', MB 6, Province de Limbourg (1976), pp. 89–90.

⁴⁴ On music as an expression of mystical ecstasy, see Carolyn Muessig, 'Prophecy and Song: Teaching and Preaching by Medieval Women', in *Women Preachers and Prophets through Two Millennia of Christianity*, ed. by Beverly Mayne Kienzle and Pamela Walker (Berkeley: University of California Press, 1998), pp. 146–58, and Wiethaus, 'The Death Song of Marie d'Oignies', pp. 153–79. [BN]

or breath came out of her mouth or nose during this time, but a harmony of the angelic voice resounded only from between her breast and throat.[45]

36. While all this was happening, all her limbs were quiet and her eyes were closed as if she were sleeping. Then after a while, restored to herself somewhat, she rose up like one who was drunk — indeed she was drunk — and cried aloud, 'Bring the nuns to me that together we might praise Jesus for the great liberality of his miracles'. Shortly thereafter the nuns of the convent came running from all sides (for they greatly rejoiced in Christina's solace) and she began to sing the *Te Deum laudamus*. All the convent joined in as she finished her song. Afterwards, when she was fully restored to herself and learned from the others what she had done and how she had invited the community to praise Christ, she fled for shame and embarrassment, and if anyone forcibly detained her, she languished with a great sorrow and declared herself stupid and foolish.

How she reproached those who did not recognize their Creator

37. At other times when she had returned to herself from the state I have just described, she would say in great bitterness of heart, 'O wretched and miserable world that does not recognize its Maker! Why do you not serve him? Why do you not consider the forbearance of his patience? If you could see his goodness

---

[45] In the first stage of Christina's ascent to God — that is to say, in the animal stage — she had been nourished with the food of Christ's body and did penance. In the second stage (the rational) she had been taught by the unction of the Holy Spirit that dripped from her breasts. In this stage, the spiritual, her body is entirely taken over by God, and in her worship her song is united with the music of the spheres, an expression of the identification of the sacramental universe with its Creator. Thus does Christina's material and spiritual life mirror the eternal cosmic harmony which obeys those 'laws of equality, unity and order' found in music: just as God unites all things in the universe, so too does number or proportion, the basis of music. Thus should human action reflect the cosmic order of 'the hymn of the universe' which obeys 'the laws of equality and unity and order': Augustine, *De musica liber VI*, 11:29, ed. and trans. by Martin Jacobsson (Stockholm: Almqvist & Wiksell, 2002), p. 67. See Kathi Meyer-Baer, *Music of the Spheres and the Dance of Death: Studies in Musical Iconology* (Princeton: Princeton University Press, 1970), and 'Psychologic and Ontologic Ideas in Augustine's *De Musica*', *Journal of Aesthetics & Art Criticism*, 11 (1953), 224–30. The thorax (*pectus*) was considered to be the place where the ark of the heart was placed: the point of the intersection of the arms of the cross, the centre, the origin of the world. Thus was the heart of Christ lanced and it is to this location that Thomas refers in his life of Lutgard (VLA I.2). Christina's song is thus a sign of her complete identification with the cosmic order. See M.-M. Davy, *Initiation à la symbolique romane (XII* *siècle)* (Paris: Flammarion, 1977), p. 177.

even from another, you could not be turned away from loving him, even if the world opposed you. But you, O wretched world, have turned aside. You have closed your eyes and do not wish to understand.' When she said these things, she cried out with great lamentations as if in childbirth and twisted her limbs and rolled around on the ground and, redoubling her cries, asked why the world did not recognize its Creator.

How the saint withdrew to Jutta the recluse; her singing and knowledge of Scripture; the esteem she rightly deserved from the Count of Loon in his lifetime, and after his death, her participation in his purgatorial punishments; her love of solitude

How she left her own home and came to Loon

38. After these events, she left her own home and kin[46] and went to a castle on the border of Germany called Loon. There she stayed for nine years with a recluse called Jutta, who led a very religious life, and the Lord wrought wonders through her. It was from this recluse that I received many of the revelations I have written concerning Christina. Indeed, this was the reason I came to her from the far parts of Gaul.[47]

How she understood Scripture by divine inspiration

39. While she was in that place Christina went to the vigils of matins every night. Then, after everyone had left the church and the doors were locked, she would walk around the church floor and utter a song so sweet that it seemed to be angelic rather than human singing. This song was so marvellous to hear that it surpassed the music of all instruments and the voices of all mortals. Nevertheless, this song was less sweet and much unequal to the jubilant harmony[48] which, during her ecstasies, resounded incomparably from between

---

[46] Like Abraham; cf. Genesis 12. 1. [BN]

[47] 'Germany' and 'Gaul' refer to Dutch-speaking and French-speaking regions, rather than ancient or medieval political entities. [BN]

[48] *Jubilus*, originally a wordless chant following the Alleluia at mass, had by the thirteenth century become a quasi-technical term for ecstatic, mystical song. [BN]

her throat and breast. The song [that she sang in church] was in Latin and wondrously adorned with harmonious phrases.[49]

40. Although she had been completely illiterate from birth, yet she understood all Latin and fully knew the meaning of Holy Scripture. When she was asked very obscure questions by certain spiritual friends, she would explain them very openly. But she did this most unwillingly and rarely, for she said that to expound Holy Scriptures belonged to the clergy and not to the ministry of such as her.[50] Because of her very great love of Christ, she wondrously venerated the clergy and especially priests, even though for her part she had suffered many injuries from them.[51] She would gently admonish sinning priests or clerics lest they blaspheme the good name of Christ through their public excesses, but she did so in great secrecy and with a wondrous reverence as if they were her own fathers.

How greatly she was venerated by Count Louis

41. When Louis, count of Loon and a most noble man,[52] learned of her famous sanctity through hearsay, he began to love her in his heart and to follow sincerely her counsels and advice. Wherever he saw her, he would rise and run to her and call her 'mother'. When he had done anything against justice or against the Church of Christ or its ministers, she would weep for him like a mother weeping for her son. She would go to him in his palace and reprimand him with a mother's confidence, and obtain from him whatever was owing for the satisfaction of justice.

What stirring words she possessed

42. One day when Count Louis was reclining in the churchyard, surrounded by many soldiers, she arrived unexpectedly and came close to the count's head. She raised her eyes and hands and began to say with a wondrous grace of speech,

[49] *mirisque consonantium clausulis*; the reference could be either musical or rhetorical. [BN]

[50] This pious sentiment was probably added by Thomas to give Christina respectability in the eyes of the hierarchy.

[51] An indication that not all priests shared James of Vitry's and Thomas of Cantimpré's view of Christina as a holy woman. [BN]

[52] Louis II, count of Loon (1197–1218), and victor in the battle of Steppes (Ch. 29). [BN]

'O Lord, how beautiful you are!' When the knights heard this, they said to the count, 'Do you not hear, Lord Count, how this holy woman praises you?' The count, however, said, 'I know who it is that she is praising. I am not he. She praises her heavenly Lord who is the creator of all beauty and the most beautiful of all.' She then said, 'You have spoken truly. Why therefore do you not love him?'

How she foretold treachery to the same count

43. One summer afternoon the count was staying in his palace at Loon (which is now destroyed), talking with the Duke of Limburg and another count as they sat on a quilt. Christina ran unwaveringly to them and cried out to Count Louis, 'O most wretched one! Who are you talking to? Behold, he who is acting like a friend to you is no friend; the hand he is stretching forth is the hand of a traitor!' Fearing the woman's voice, the traitor immediately fell silent for a time and dissimulated the truth by his words, but the outcome proved the truth of the prophecy.

How she behaved at the death of the aforesaid count

44. When Count Louis was near death, he had Christina called to him and most persistently begged her to stay with him until the hour of death. She very obligingly granted this, and the count commanded all who were with him to leave the bedchamber and kept Christina alone with him in the chamber. Without delay, the count pulled himself up with all the strength he could summon and lay fully prostrate before Christina's feet and, with much weeping, recited to her all his sins from his eleventh year right up to that very day. He did this not for absolution, which she had no power to give,[53] but rather that she might be moved by this atonement to pray for him. After this the count called

---

[53] This famous passage indicates Christina's assumption of what later would be seen to be the sole prerogative of priests. Official absolution seems not to have been the point; what was at issue was that the laity (and women at that!) heard confessions. This obviously distressed Thomas. See Jean Leclercq, 'Medieval Feminine Monasticism: Reality Versus Romantic Images', in *Benedictus: Studies in Honour of St Benedict of Nursia*, ed. by E. Rozanne Elder (Kalamazoo: Cistercian Publications, 1981), pp. 53–70 (p. 61): 'If the 1228 General Chapter of the Cistercian Order, and then, in the early fourteenth century Boniface XIII, forbade abbesses to hear confessions, it is because they were hearing them'.

his whole household into the bedchamber and disposed of his goods, following Christina's advice, and then he died. She saw his soul being carried to purgatory to be tormented with the most bitter punishments.

How she shared the punishments of purgatory with the soul of the count

45. The merciful woman was not a little compassionate towards him and obtained from the Lord that she might share with him the punishments to be exacted in purgatory. When therefore he appeared to her after his death and asked for help, Christina said to him, 'Well then, go hence and fulfil the punishments due your sins according to the divine judgement. As for me, I will accept in my own body a half part of your purgatorial torments which must be exacted.' Having taken on these burdens, for a long time afterwards you might have seen Christina in the middle of the night being tormented with burning smoke and at other times with freezing cold. Indeed she suffered torments in turn according to what the soul of the count was suffering.[54] She also watered with inconsolable tears the places where the count had been accustomed to sin, and she grieved in the places where he had rejoiced in empty pleasures.

How she behaved in the last year of her life

46. In the last year of her life, solitude and the wilderness were frequently her home. She returned, although most rarely, when she was driven by the spirit, either for the salvation of men or for the partaking of food. No mortal man could, at that time, restrain her when she wanted to go into the desert. When she returned no one dared greet her, no one dared ask her anything. Once she returned at vespers and passed above the ground right through the middle of a house like a spirit. People could scarcely tell whether a spirit or a material body had passed by, since she barely seemed to touch the ground. Indeed in the last year of her life, the spirit so controlled almost all the parts of her corporeal body that scarcely could human minds or eyes look at the shadow her body cast without horror and a trembling of the spirit. She then returned to the town of Sint-Truiden and more frequently dwelt in the monastery of St Catherine's.

---

[54] These purgatorial torments, suffered in the spirit, echo the literal and bodily torments of fire and water that Christina undergoes earlier. [BN]

The quality of her life before her death; her sickness; her second and third death; her burial and translation; exhortation by the author; the removal of her corpse; a miracle

The narrative about her by Thomas, Abbot of Sint-Truiden

47. A venerable man whom I remember, Thomas, now abbot of Sint-Truiden[55] but then a priest in that city, told me a very edifying story about Christina. One day at dawn he was returning home from matins with a companion when, all of a sudden, he saw her impulsively entering a church. They followed her surreptitiously and observed her secretly from behind a pillar of the church to see what she would do or how she would pray.[56] Immediately, she threw herself before the altar as if she were a sack filled with dry bones. Then, wailing bitterly, she began to beat her breast and her body most often and said, 'O miserable and wretched body! How long will you torment me, miserable as I am? What are you doing with me? Why do you keep my wretched soul in you for so long? Why do you delay me from seeing the face of Christ? When will you abandon me so that my soul can return freely to its Creator? Woe to you, most miserable one! And woe to me who am united to you!'

48. As she said these and similar things, she would beat her body. But then, taking the part of the body, she would say, as if to the spirit, 'O miserable soul! Why are you tormenting me in this way? What is keeping you in me and what is it that you love in me? Why do you not allow me to return to the earth from whence I was taken, and rest until I am restored to you on the last day of judgement? Why do you not go to your rest, so that you might enjoy more desirable things in heaven?'

As she said this, she would sigh and gasp and weep. She then rested a little in silence and, burning most purely with a holy thought directed toward God, she dissolved into a most sweet smile. Then, taking her feet with both hands, she kissed the soles of her feet with the greatest affection and said, 'O most beloved

---

[55] Thomas was abbot of Sint-Truiden from 1239–48.

[56] Christina here acts out a debate between body and soul, a popular literary genre. For some Middle English examples see *Middle English Debate Poetry*, ed. by John Conlee (East Lansing: Colleagues Press, 1991), pp. 7–49. On the performative character of beguine spirituality see Walter Simons, 'Reading a Saint's Body: Rapture and Bodily Movement in the *Vitae* of Thirteenth-Century Beguines', in *Framing Medieval Bodies*, ed. by Sarah Kay and Miri Rubin (Manchester: Manchester University Press, 1994), pp. 10–23, and *Performance and Transformation*, ed. by Suydam and Ziegler. [BN]

body! Why have I beaten you? Why have I reviled you? Did you not obey me in every good deed I undertook to do with God's help? You have most generously and patiently endured the torments and hardships the spirit imposed on you.'

49. Then doubling her kisses, she said, 'Now, O best and sweetest body, endure patiently. The end of your labour is at hand. Now you will rest in the dust and sleep for a little and then, at last, when the trumpet blows, you will rise again, purified of all corruptibility, and be joined in eternal happiness with the soul you have had as a companion in the present sadness.' After gentling her body with such words and kisses for an hour, she uttered that wondrous, jubilant sound I have already described and was inwardly filled with such joy that one would have believed her exterior body would burst. Truly God is wonderful in his saints,[57] and in this one, if I may say so, his wonders pass all admiration.

Her manner of life before her death

50. At the end of her life, she ate little and very rarely. No longer did she wish to sit and talk with the sisters and nuns as she used to do, but would eat only a scrap of food and sleep only a little before midnight and then go into the wilderness. In those days, no one ever saw a smile on her lips: she was like one who has gone mad from excessive sorrow. She would wander around praying, weeping, and mourning and, for this reason, some people believed that the Lord had shown her even more than usual about the condition and malice of the world. The one thing for which she mourned most frequently with wondrous outcries was that almost all mankind was corrupted by an explosion of licentiousness.[58] It was because of this that the anger and vengeance of God would swiftly threaten all Christendom.

Of her sickness before her death

51. When the time approached for her to be gripped by the sickness of death, she was overtaken by such an unbroken grace of contemplation that she found it very difficult to direct the attention of her mind anywhere else. At the very end, untroubled by anything, she gently asked Beatrice, a nun at St Catherine's, to prepare a bed for her secretly in one of the rooms because her final sickness

---

[57] Psalm 67. 36.

[58] *in effusionibus seminum*; the reference could also be to original sin. [BN]

was at hand. Beatrice quickly did what she was asked, and Christina lay down and was overcome by an increasingly serious illness. After three days of this sickness, she asked for the communion of the body of the Lord and anointing with holy oil. When this was done, the Beatrice of whom I have spoken fell down on her knees and begged her to make certain things known before she died. When Christina did not answer, Beatrice thought that her attention was on other things and, postponing her question, left the room to do something else and left her alone for a time.

Of her second death and of how she once again lived, and of how she died a third time

52. Some people say that, while she was alive, Christina often prayed to the Lord that he not honour her in death by any miracles, but allow her to die the common death of men. In this also, the Lord heard her, for before Beatrice could return, Christina gave up her spirit at the call of Christ. As soon as Beatrice returned with a certain sister, she found her lifeless body stretched out on the ground after the manner of corpses — truly, I believe, laid out by angels. Beatrice was fearsomely impatient at this and fell upon the body of the dead woman and began to wail violently. She often interrupted her shouts by asking the dead woman why she had gone to the Lord without permission and without leave of the sisters. Nevertheless, in the vehemence of her spirit, she took confidence and, gazing fixedly on the face of the dead woman, said: 'O Christina! You were ever obedient to me in life! I now therefore beseech you and admonish you earnestly through the Lord Jesus Christ, whom you loved with ardent desire while you lived, that you obey me even now. For you are powerfully able, through him to whom you are now joined, to do whatever you want.[59] So return to life and tell me what I begged you to reveal to me with great desire while you were alive.'

53. Wondrous event! As soon as Beatrice had cried these words into the ears of the dead woman, Christina returned to her body and, heaving a great sigh, opened her haggard eyes. Turning her grief-stricken face to the one who had called her back, she said, 'O Beatrice! Why have you disturbed me? Why have you called me back? Just now I was being led to the face of Christ! But now, my

---

[59] See Elizabeth Petroff's article on the power which emanated from medieval women mystics and which so impressed those around them: 'Medieval Women Visionaries: Seven Stages to Power', *Frontiers*, 3 (1978), 34–45.

sister, quickly ask me what you want and then, I beg you, allow me to return to the Lord for whom I have longed so eagerly.' Then Beatrice asked Christina her question and received a reply from her. In the meantime the sisters of the monastery gathered together from all sides and Christina blessed them with a word and with the sign of the cross. In this way, she who had experienced death three times and died three times, passed to the immortal age of ages.

Of the burial of blessed Christina and of the translation of her body

54. She lived for forty-two years after she had first risen from the dead and died around the year 1224. She was buried in the monastery of St Catherine's just outside the town of Sint-Truiden, and there she rested for seven years until they transferred the whole monastic complex to a more fitting place that was close at hand. Then all the citizens, together with the clerics and nuns of the convent, gathered together at the grave of the holy and revered Christina. When they opened the lid and laid it on the side, a grace of such sweetness seized everyone both collectively and individually that they all cried out together with one mind and one voice, 'Christina! You were marvellous in life and now after death you are no less glorious!' No one doubts the grace of healing bestowed on those who had come to her tomb with due faith. We cannot, however, pursue these matters.

The conclusion of the book

55. See then, reader, to how many people we ourselves may be indebted, having seen Christina suffer so many torments and punishments not for herself, but for her neighbours. And yet we fear to do penance even for ourselves and our own transgressions! A day will surely come — it will come and not delay — when we would gladly try to do even greater things than these[60] if an occasion for penance were given to those who asked, and it were permitted to make up for lost time. Woe to those who want to buy the oil of mercy after the time of trading has passed! With empty lamps they will beat on the door and will not be allowed to enter. Rather, the bridegroom will say to them, 'Amen, I say to you, I know you not. Watch therefore, because you know not the day nor the hour.'[61]

---

[60] John 14. 12.
[61] Matthew 25. 12–13.

56. Necessarily, therefore, the sleepers are locked out, because, neglecting the day and the hour, they were not willing to keep vigil with a lamp filled with the oil of good works, bearing fruits worthy of penance.[62] Watch therefore, because you know not the day nor the hour when your Lord will come. What else did Christina cry out during her entire life except to do penance and be ready at every hour? This she taught with many words, with tears, with lamentations and boundless cries, and with the example[63] of her life. This, indeed, she taught more insistently and shouted louder than anyone we have heard of before or since, whether through writings or by report, to the praise and glory of Christ who, with the Father and the Holy Spirit, lives and reigns as God forever and ever. Amen.[64]

---

[62] Cf. Matthew 25. 1–12.

[63] 'Example' is a weak translation of *exemplum*. The medieval use of the *exemplum* has been examined by Claude Bremond, Jacques Le Goff, and Jean-Claude Schmitt in *L'Exemplum*, Typologie des sources du Moyen Âge occidental, 40 (Turnhout: Brepols, 1982) and defined as 'a brief tale presented as truth and destined to be included in a discourse (usually a sermon) to edify the audience by the utilization of a salutary lesson' (pp. 37–38). They break down the *exemplum* into nine elements: 1) its narrative character; 2) its brevity when delivered orally, although they add that in written form, it frequently manifests 'une certaine longueur'; 3) its historicity; 4) its subordination to a broader theme; 5) its frequent utilization in a sermon; 6) its persuasive tone and its relation to the rhetorical arts; 7) the relationship between speaker and a particular audience whom the speaker 8) teaches (the *exemplum* derives from pedagogical rhetoric and is therefore didactic); and 9) its eschatological perspective. Its end is neither good behaviour nor entertainment nor even the earthly well-being of the listener. Rather, the *exemplum* is characterized by its emphasis on the last things and by a preoccupation with eternal salvation. Unquestionably, the VCM is eschatological in nature. In my article 'Sacramental Witness', I applied the phrase 'living sermon' to describe it, a phrase I only later discovered that Jo Ann McNamara had already applied to medieval religious women who 'speak their messages of peace by this living witness, or by being living sermons of the gospel message': *Distant Echoes*, ed. by John A. Nichols and Lillian Thomas Shank (Kalamazoo: Cistercian Publications, 1984), p. viii.

[64] Thomas's *vita* ends at Ch. 56 in the AASS, but three more paragraphs were appended at the end by an unknown hand. Although this later ending seems to follow logically upon Christina's inability to remain dead, it does not compare with the artistry of Thomas's original ending.

About the second translation of her body

57. Afterwards it happened one day, in the year of the Lord 1249, that just as the day had dawned, one who seemed like an aged woman dressed in white knocked at the door. Once she was admitted, she asked for the monastic priest and, when she had been led to him, she said, 'I have been sent by divine revelation to make known to you that, inasmuch as the body of a most holy woman named Christina lies neglected, you must translate it from its location. If you do, this house will obtain grace and glory through her merits and prayers. But if you are negligent, you will incur the displeasure of the divine power.' And when the monk asked her if she should not rather be telling this to the prioress of the convent, she refrained from speaking.

The first miracle; the events after the exhumation of the holy body

58. At once the monk ran to bring the prioress and the community, but when he returned, he did not find the aforesaid person. He therefore dashed through many streets and inquired, but he did not find anyone who had seen her either departing or remaining. Yet many people testified that they had seen her going in through the door. This was not inappropriate, for the angel Raphael did not see fit to reveal heavenly secrets to the multitude, but only to [Tobit] and his son,[65] and we judge that it fell out the same way in this affair. When the convent heard this report, they were afraid lest, as stated above, they incur the displeasure of the divine power. So they hastened with joy to remove the sacred bones from the grave, diligently washed and dried them, and set them beside the altar in an honoured place.

59. Immediately after the body of Christina the Astonishing was raised from the grave, a woman in the vicinity of the monastery, who had been sick for a long time, was lying with her limbs so completely wasted that even had her house been on fire, she would not have been able to rise from her bed. Roused to greater confidence by the rumour of this grand event, she begged her husband to carry her to the monastery. Moved by his wife's tears, he placed her in a vehicle which in the vernacular is called a grass cart and brought her there. After she had been led by the hand to the grave, she rose up completely healed in all

---

[65] Cf. Tobit 12. 11–20. The text reads 'Tobias' (the son) for 'Tobit' (his father).

her limbs and, blessing God and his bride Christina, she walked back home by her own strength.

THE LIFE OF MARGARET OF YPRES

Translated by Margot H. King and Barbara Newman

CHRONOLOGY
THE LIFE OF MARGARET OF YPRES
(1216–37)

1216	Birth of Margaret of Ypres
1220	Death of Margaret's father; she is sent to a nunnery for early education, then goes to live with her mother, sisters, and maiden aunt at the home of a clerical uncle
1224	Founding of Dominican friary in Lille
1228	Early Dominican constitutions forbid 'the pastoral care of nuns or any other women'
1233	Countess Jeanne founds the first beguinage in Flanders (Ghent) and entrusts its direction to the Dominicans
1234	Death of Margaret's uncle; brief romantic fling; meeting with Friar Zeger of Lille leads to her conversion
1234–36	Years of intense asceticism at home; Friar Zeger introduces Margaret of Ypres to Marguerite, sister of Countess Jeanne
1236	Margaret becomes an invalid but continues to receive visits from her spiritual friends
1237	Death of Margaret; miracles reported at her burial
1240	Thomas of Cantimpré meets Friar Zeger at Ypres and learns of Margaret's life
1240–43	*The Life of Margaret of Ypres* written
1244	Marguerite of Flanders succeeds her sister as countess
1272	Countess Marguerite founds first Dominican nunnery in Flanders (Lille)

PROLOGUE

Here begins the Prologue to the life of the illustrious virgin Margaret of Ypres

To my friend and beloved brother in Christ, Friar Zeger, an active member of the Order of Preachers in Lille, I, a brother of the same Order whose name need not be mentioned at present, send greetings and, with your permission, this work which pertains to you. My interest in you was often aroused by your fame, my friend, and for a long time I had been eager to meet you. Then last August as I was returning from Paris, it happened that I came to Ypres and saw you, an encounter which I hope was not without fruit. When you told me of the reputation of that illustrious young woman named Margaret, I was amazed, struck by such wonderful news, and though I say so myself, aroused to better things. Thus, early one morning at your request, I filled two small sheets of parchment with some memorable facts about her life as you recounted them. But alas, I was in a great hurry, compelled by the business of the friar who was with me, for he had to sail to Denmark before the feast of All Saints. On the same day that I took leave of you, we were toiling on our weary way before the hour of none when suddenly the whole sky became dark, and we feared there would be a heavy downpour. We were all the more anxious because we were a great distance from the town. As I was still glowing from the memory of the recent talk I had had with you about the spouse of Christ, I said to the brother, 'Let us ask the Lord to protect us from the impending rain through the merits of that woman about whom we have heard so much'. So we prayed and were heard because of the reverence we showed her; and you may believe, as Christ is my witness, that suddenly the clouds scattered, the sky was bright again, cloudless sunlight returned, and we completed the rest of our journey in great cheerfulness and joy. These were the first fruits of the goodness of Christ's bride, which I, unworthy as I am, have experienced. Indeed, this leisure that I have enjoyed I attribute wholly to her merits, for never since I entered the Order of Preachers have I been able to have as much uninterrupted free time as since I set my hand to write this work.

Therefore, dearest friend, accept this work, which is outstanding as far as its subject is concerned. But if the work has to be corrected anywhere, then correct it yourself, or if you do not have the time, send it back to me for corrections. For it is more fitting for me to be soiled by my own dirt and wash it myself than to let another be stained by my dirt. Go and, as you have promised, pray for me.

Greet for me Friar Jacques de Halle[1] and whomever else you wish of the other friars, but especially the mother of Margaret of holy memory, her sisters, and those who welcome our brothers, that is, her maternal aunt and her husband. I commend all of them together to the divine mercy.

Here ends the Prologue.

Here begins the Life of the illustrious Margaret of Ypres.

The town in which she was born

1. In a town of Flanders called Ypres, there was a certain girl named Margaret, born of respectable parents. From her youth and even from the cradle, she so served Christ the Lord that, according to Friar Zeger of the Order of Preachers, from whom I learned all her doings, she never relaxed the vigilance of her mind to commit any mortal sin.[2] Indeed, from the time Margaret was placed in a certain monastery at the age of four to be educated by the nuns, she was prepared as a dwelling-place of the Holy Spirit for the attainment of a nun-like purity,[3] and this was revealed by an obvious miracle.

---

[1] Jacques de Halle, prior of the Dominican convent in the parish of Saint-Étienne in Lille and confessor of the Countess Jeanne, who manifested her esteem for him by bequeathing to the convent her ivory madonna. Although his death date is unknown, it is recorded that he founded the convent of Valenciennes in 1233 and was still alive in 1240. See Meersseman, 'Jeanne de Constantinople', pp. 122–68.

[2] Friar Zeger's testimony must be invoked because only Margaret's confessor would be able to make such a judgement. [BN]

[3] *Divini spiritus habitaculum habilitabatur ad sanctimonie puritatem*: Thomas is presumably attempting to legitimize Margaret in the eyes of the hierarchy by emphasizing her similarity to 'real' nuns. Note also his use of the word *habitaculum* (a little dwelling), underlining the fact that her cloister was a spiritual cloister and that she, as much as cloistered nuns, was 'alone with

How she received the Body of Christ when she was five

2. When she had not yet completed her fifth year, she happened to be present when the community received the sacrament of the Lord's body, and smelled a wonderful odour. She therefore directed her attention towards it and, although she did not yet know God,[4] yet by the interior working and manifestation of divine power she realized that Jesus, our health and salvation, had come upon the altar.

At once she ran to the abbess of the monastery and prayed and begged with tears to be allowed to receive communion with the others. The abbess was astonished beyond belief at the insistence of the little girl, and asked her with tears what it was that she so persistently demanded. 'I know', she said to her, 'I know that it is the body of Christ which the priest consecrates at the altar and is now giving to the nuns. This is what I ask for, most beloved lady. Do not deprive me, I beseech you, of that which I cannot be without.' When the abbess with the other nuns saw this, she ordered that the Lord's body be given to the girl.[5]

O truly blessed and totally omnipotent God, you 'call into being things that are not, as if they were', to empty of power those things that are![6] Indeed, Father, because it was pleasing in your sight, 'you have hidden these things from the wise and revealed them to little ones'.[7] And behold the result: ever afterwards — that is, from the age of five — Margaret received the sacrament of the Lord's body three times a year.[8] From that time, too, she despised all childish things and began to embrace Christ and cling to him by holy deeds.

God'. Later he compares her heart to a chapel (Ch. 28). See Gerhard Bauer, *Claustrum animae: Untersuchungen zur Geschichte der Metapher vom Herzen als Kloster* (Munich: Fink, 1973).

[4] I Samuel 3. 7. Compare Thomas's description of the young Lutgard in VLA I.1. Thomas always seems to use the verb *cognosco* in the sense of direct knowledge.

[5] This early first communion, received in 1220 or 1221, was a special privilege granted to Margaret in violation of the Fourth Lateran Council's decree a few years earlier, denying communion to children under the age of twelve: Meersseman, 'Les Frères Prêcheurs', p. 77. [BN]

[6] Romans 4. 17, I Corinthians 1. 28; VJC II.9; VLA I.1.

[7] Matthew 11. 25.

[8] In accordance with the early rule of the Dominican Penitents, adopted in 1221. [BN]

Her penance and fasting at the age of seven

3. Even before she had reached the age of seven and 'put her hand to difficult things',⁹ she used to press nettles and the stinging barbs of flax seeds into the flesh of her bosom, purposefully recalling the wounds of Christ. When she was nine, she fasted the entire forty days before Easter. She fasted no less every Friday and on vigils of the Annunciation of the Blessed Virgin Mary, so that she could abstain from all food except bread and water twice a week during the whole year.¹⁰ She omitted no fast of the Church nor the vigil of any saint. She avoided eating all the things that usually arouse the appetite, such as garlic, pepper, and the like. At about the same age, she arose from her bed one night and a maidservant who was awake found her prostrate upon the ground in prayer. Who ever heard or saw such things? Everything completely blossomed before the harvest!

How, at the age of ten, she scourged herself with thorns out of compassion for Christ crucified

4. Later, at the age of ten, she noticed the crucifix in the church and said, 'O Jesus, our true salvation, up to this time I have done nothing to repay you'. Saying this, she wept plentifully and at once went alone into the forest where, stripping naked, she scourged herself with yew branches and thorns even to the shedding of blood. She did this not just once or twice but very often, whenever she tearfully recalled the wounds of Christ. Once when her guardians noticed this and asked, 'Why do you afflict yourself when you are only a tender child?' she replied, 'I am now prepared to suffer any kind of torment for Christ if the time or the place presents itself'.

⁹ Proverbs 31. 19.

¹⁰ The sentence makes little sense as it stands. Since the Little Office of the Virgin is said every Saturday, Thomas could mean that Margaret fasted on Fridays and Saturdays throughout the year. In Ch. 17, however, he says more plausibly that she fasted on Wednesdays and Fridays. [BN]

How, at the age of eighteen, she entangled herself in the world by falling in love with a young man

5. Having passed through the natural stages of childhood[11] for eleven years, though she had never mingled with playmates,[12] she began to cling to virtue through ascetic practices with a mighty spirit.[13] This fervour lasted until she was eighteen years old. Having an uncle who was a priest, a religious and righteous man in all things, she remained with him from childhood and lived a most religious life. The following event occurred after he died. For no mortal — except that man and his mother who alone among the dead are free[14] — can ever say 'I am clean',[15] even though he may be a day-old infant. Neither was she free, although — as I have said — she was most holy. Even though she was without the venom of mortal sin, she had to endure in a cruel way the snares of the pursuing enemy. For, glancing incautiously at a very attractive young man, she fell in love with him with a most burning love for a while, although without the filth of lustful desire. Even though she sat and talked with him alone very often,[16] she was never defiled either in will or in inclination.[17] For Christ, the lover of chastity, was pleasing to her above all things. She had loved him from her youth and sought to take him as her spouse, and he became the lover of her beauty.[18]

---

[11] *Quasi legitime*: *Oxford Latin Dictionary* (Oxford: Clarendon Press, 1968-) defines *legitimus* as 'prescribed by natural law'.

[12] A hagiographic commonplace; cf. VLA I.1.

[13] Cf. Acts 2. 2.

[14] That is, Jesus and Mary: Psalm 87. 6.

[15] Compare Job 25. 4, 33. 9, and Leo the Great, Sermo 21, *In Nativitate Domini* (PL 54: 191b): *nemo mundus a sorde*, cited in Blaise, *Vocabulaire*, p. 367.

[16] Margaret's short experience of human love is, in many ways, similar to that of Lutgard, except that Christ appeared to the latter and offered himself as her betrothed while she was in the midst of a conversation with the young man (VLA I.2).

[17] *Animo*: Thomas frequently uses the word in this sense in VLA I.2, 4 and others. Thomas, no less than William of Saint-Thierry, was heir to the patristic tradition of the three faculties of the human soul. See Savary, *Psychological Themes*, p. 45: 'Animus is the principle that thinks, reasons, decides on courses of action, and gives human existence its personal and responsible character. Broadly speaking, it is the conscious part of an individual.'

[18] *Et amator factus est forme illius*. Cf. Wisdom 8. 2. Note that Thomas uses the same word (*forma*) for Margaret's attraction to the young man and Christ's attraction to her. In the VLA, Thomas emphasizes the active agency of Christ while here, it is Margaret's passive readiness for the mystic marriage that is emphasized.

If the topic was ever broached that she take a husband — whether another man or even that youth whom she loved so much — she immediately became feverish with extreme horror, as was often noticed. For the zeal of the eternal Lover of human souls[19] had espoused her by a hidden calling and did not permit her to be carried off by another lover.[20] Yet she was dressed at that time in most prideful clothing. So at once he extracted the foot that she had set lightly, not firmly, on the threshold of the world.[21]

How she was converted to the religious state by Friar Zeger

6. At this time Friar Zeger of the Order of Preachers in Lille had come to Ypres and, after his sermon, he was sitting in the church to hear the confessions of the repentant people. By chance he cast his eyes on Margaret, who was dressed in secular clothing among other women, and saw with a kind of divine instinct — for he had never seen her before — that she would be apt to receive God's grace and become a chosen vessel,[22] as Christ revealed to him.

When he had called her and admonished her to reject all secular things, like Saul she said without reluctance, 'Lord, what do you want me to do?'[23] Without

---

[19] *Sacramentarium Leonianum* 24, ed. by C. L. Felto (Cambridge: Cambridge University Press, 1896), p. 139: *incorruptarum Deus amator animarum* ('God is the lover of uncorrupted souls').

[20] Cf. VLA I.2–3. There are echoes here of the words put into the mouth of St Agnes and repeated by Lutgard: 'I have been overtaken by another lover': Pseudo-Ambrose, *Vita S. Agnetis* I.I, in AASS, 21 January, I, p. 715; *Epistolae ex Ambrosianarum numero egregatae*, I (PL 17: 735–42). St Agnes was, of course, the exemplar for all those women who spurned carnal marriage in favour of their heavenly Bridegroom. Cf. Ch. 55 below.

[21] Although she loves Christ, Margaret still suffers from the wound of concupiscence. See Charles S. Singleton, *The Divine Comedy: Inferno, Volume 2: Commentary* (Princeton: Princeton University Press, 1970), pp. 9–10: 'A long tradition applied the metaphor of feet to the faculties of the soul. As this metaphor merged with Aristotle's dictum that all motion originates from the right, it was said that the first step is taken by the right foot while the left remains stationary. The left foot was seen as the *pes firmior*, the firmer or less agile [...] In Adam's sin, wherein all men sinned, it was the intellect or right "foot" that suffered the wound of ignorance, while left "foot", the *affectus* or will — the *pes firmior* — suffered the wound of concupiscence'. See also John Freccero, 'Dante's Firm Foot and the Journey without a Guide', *Harvard Theological Review*, 52 (1959), 245–81, and VLA I.10.

[22] Acts 9. 15.

[23] Acts 22. 10.

delay she was as changed from her former state as heaven is distant from earth. At once she abandoned the world completely, and she was joined to Christ all the more ardently, the more she feared that she had distanced herself from him.

After awhile she came to her mother — and her mother, seeing her suddenly so changed, asked, 'What is it, daughter?' She added, 'If you embark on a religious life today, tomorrow you will return to the world'. Margaret replied, 'That speech is worthless, mother, for I have accepted another speech that I will never relinquish'.[24] From that day forth she always venerated even the eastward-facing place[25] where she had sat when she was converted and accepted the grace of the one who admonished her. It was there that she sensed the dawning light of the sun of justice[26] flowing into her for a lasting affective knowledge.[27]

How once, feeling a passion, she manfully ended it

7. A day or two after her conversion, she met that young man whom she had loved so much and felt faint stirrings of that affection[28] she had so recently withdrawn from him creeping seductively back into her mind. Perceiving at once why she was falling back, she was very angry with herself and ran in haste to the church. Extending her arms in the form of a cross before the crucifix, she said with tears, 'O Christ Jesus, yesterday I was converted to you, and am I now falling back into a relapse? No, Lord, not even if my heart should burst! But now, O Lord, to strengthen myself and to implore the grace of your mercy, I am making a vow of chastity of mind and body.' As soon as she did this, God saw the virgin's perfection of heart and granted her this great favour: for the rest of her life, never would she feel even the first stirrings of temptation in her flesh.[29]

---

[24] Thomas plays on the two senses of *sermo*, 'saying' and 'sermon'. [BN]

[25] Just as the sun rises in the east, so too do churches face the east and it is not surprising that the place of Margaret's conversion looked east, towards the rising Sun of Justice.

[26] Malachi 4. 2.

[27] *Cognicionis affectum*: knowledge with an admixture of feeling.

[28] *Levi motu animi affectum suum.*

[29] Lutgard was also immune to all carnal temptations after she and Christ had exchanged hearts: VLA I.12.

How she made a vow of chastity and how Christ appeared with three crowns

8. As soon as she made the vow, she remembered with immense gladness of heart that she was now espoused to Christ and had escaped the nuptials of the world. Absorbed in ecstasy, her head fell upon the Psalter that she held in her hands. When she returned to herself, she came to the Friar Preacher who, as I have said, had called her from the world. 'I have dreamed', she said, 'but I do not know whether it ought to be called a dream, for even when I was living a worldly life, I never fell asleep during a sermon or in church'. She said this because she did not yet have direct knowledge of the Lord, for he had never been revealed to her.[30]

Her spiritual father laughed and replied, 'What did you dream, daughter?' 'I saw', she said, 'as if in a dream,[31] but that which I saw I know[32] with utmost certainty and even more plainly. I say that I saw my Lord Jesus Christ standing before me with three golden crowns and, placing one on my head, he said, "I confer this on you, daughter, for the vow of chastity you made to me.[33] The other two I promise to your sisters if they will persevere with you."'[34]

When her spiritual father heard this, he rejoiced in the Lord with his whole being, observing and seeing that God had visited the young woman with his grace. Already she had received fruit in her body, and already he had watered the young plant with his efficacious words.

---

[30] 1 Samuel 3. 7; cf. Ch. 2 and VLA I.1. Up to this point, she had not known the Lord directly because she had not seen him. Note the use of the passive: it is the Lord who reveals himself. Thus does Margaret become a visionary.

[31] According to Macrobius's *Commentary on the Dream of Scipio*, a widely read guide on the interpretation of dreams, what Margaret experiences is an oracular dream. Cf. DNR II.13, p. 94: 'An oracle is a dream in which a parent or some holy and solemn person, a priest, or even God announces plainly what will or will not happen, what should be done or avoided. A vision is a dream in which someone sees a thing that will happen in the same way it appeared. An [ordinary] dream is concealed in figures and cannot be understood without interpretation'.

[32] Note that here the word is *scio* — to know, in the sense of an intellectual activity — whereas Thomas has just used the word *cognosco*, i.e. to know directly.

[33] Lutgard was also crowned with a golden crown as a sign of her consecrated virginity: VLA I.17.

[34] In fact, one sister subsequently married and bore a child (Ch. 27). [BN]

Her constancy and how she was healed by Christ

9. About the same time, the devil wickedly launched a false and pernicious rumour that each of her sisters had borne a child, although they were utterly unsullied in every respect and very well known for their good character. Although this rumour distressed many people in their family, Margaret remained as firm as a pillar,[35] knowing without a doubt that the Lord would preserve his innocent ones free from harm.[36] And so it happened. She was struck with a most serious illness, and the doctor who was called in said that unless she took a husband, she could not be cured.[37] She replied, 'May the Lord's will be done in me!'[38] I am the more fully espoused to Christ because of this.' Behold a worthy miracle; for, contrary to nature and the doctor's judgement, God soon cured her.

How it seemed to her that Christ was offended

10. After this the blessed young girl worked to bring forth good fruit in others, first by calling her sisters back from their worldly ways. About the same time she carelessly broke a wooden goblet and sent it to be repaired by that young man whom she had loved in the world. When she decided to do this, the simple dove[39] was conscious of no evil in herself. For she was afraid of offending her mother because she had shattered the goblet and, having nothing of her own

---

[35] Thomas uses the image of the pillar to emphasize Margaret's rootedness in the solid ground of the spirit and her indifference to external events. Cf. Psalm 74. 4, Galatians 2. 9, and VLA II.18.

[36] Cf. the hymn sung on Sunday at prime: 'Iam lucis orto sidere / Deum precemur supplices, / Ut in diurnis actibus / Nos servet a nocentibus' ('Now that the daystar has risen, let us humbly pray God to keep us in this day's actions from what is harmful').

[37] Marriage might be prescribed as a cure for various ailments, including lovesickness, 'hysteria', and other gynecological conditions. See Mary Wack, *Lovesickness in the Middle Ages: The 'Viaticum' and Its Commentaries* (Philadelphia: University of Pennsylvania Press, 1990), pp. 66, 175–76. [BN]

[38] Cf. Matthew 6. 10, Luke 1. 38. The echoes of Mary at the Annunciation are surely not accidental. In the previous chapter, Margaret's vow of virginity is immediately followed by the visit of God and she receives fruit (*acceptus fructus*) from her discourse with him (*efficaci sermone*). Here she is paraphrasing the Lord's Prayer with overtones of Mary's response to Gabriel.

[39] The dove was considered to be the 'type' of simplicity. Thomas also calls Lutgard 'a simple dove': VLA I.3 and III.17.

(for she had given everything back to her mother), she wanted it to be repaired the more secretly. The youth happily did as the virgin requested and sent back the repaired goblet without delay.

As soon as Margaret had come to church for her customary prayers, she found very little of her usual peace of heart and sensed that the Lord had distanced himself from her by her own fault. So she came at once to her spiritual father in tears and bewailed that she had lost Christ because of her faults. Then he asked her if she knew why he had turned away. 'I am conscious of nothing in myself', she said, 'unless perhaps the cause might be that I sent a goblet for repairs to that young man. But I take the offended Christ as my witness that I did not do this from any affection I now have or might wish to have for him, but only because there was no one else around who could fix it more quickly and discreetly'.

Then Friar Zeger said, 'This is the reason you sensed that the Lord had abandoned you. Although you might have perceived no harm in this mutual contact, yet the young man has taken occasion from it to believe that you are clinging to his affections, and he will be tempted with good reason'. When the modest virgin perceived this, she blushed profusely and, weeping and mourning over what she had done, did penance. Having thus learned of the serpent's cunning and avoiding similar incidents from then on, she took care never again to encounter or see that young man.

How the Blessed Virgin Mary appeared to her and told her that her sins had been forgiven

11. Although she was, as I have said, of a most innocent life, yet she remained in tears and mortifications and always accounted herself the worst and most wicked sinner, as if she had committed an infinite number of mortal sins. Thus it happened that she lamented her sins continuously for three whole days and nights. And behold, while she was still prostrate in grief and tears, the most blessed Virgin Mary appeared to her and, as it seemed to her in spirit, the venerable Lady placed a hand on Margaret's breast and asked if this was the place of the sorrow and evil by which she was burdened. She replied, 'Yes, my Lady'. And the blessed Virgin asked, 'What is the cause of such languor and grief?' She answered, 'because I have offended you and your Son by so many disgraceful sins'. Without delay the Blessed Mother approached at once, drawing near as if to a fellow sufferer, and drew her hand through her entire heart and breast, saying these exact words which I shall write: 'I heal you in soul and body. Know that all your sins have been forgiven you by my Son.' Truly blessed and most worthy is she whom the glorious Virgin Mary has deigned to visit and heal from all sorrow![40]

And see the fruit. From that time on, she did not feel any labour whatsoever from penance, but was always effortless in prayer, always fasting, and always ready to endure bodily mortifications. Previously she would have suffered and become weak from excessive hardship, but now she found this remedy for her defect: every fortnight she received the sacrament of the body of Christ, and afterwards, fully recovered, she rose up in good health. From that time on, she kept the custom of receiving communion every fortnight.[41]

Concerning her bearing and outward disposition and how she feared the faces of men

12. What shall I say of your[42] bearing and exterior disposition, O worthy girl? Indeed, 'how beautiful are your steps in sandals, O daughter of Christ the prince!'[43] I say 'in sandals' because you have ordered your outward appearance after the example of all the blessed ones.[44] Her eyes were downcast, her head bent, her bearing subdued, her gait light and moderate. Her countenance was so reverent that angelic grace and a hint of majesty glimmered in her face.

Scarcely was anyone so perverse and stubborn that the sight of her countenance and disciplined bearing would not influence him for the better. Wherefore a certain thing happened as I shall tell. There was in the remoter parts of Flanders a man who, having heard the rumour of her sanctity, decided to see her. This man had been lax and remiss in his actions all the days of his life. Without delay, when he saw her countenance and heard her words — which he

---

[40] Thus did Mary console Lutgard: VLA I.8.

[41] On frequent communion cf. VCM 22 and VLA II.14. [BN]

[42] MSS *suo*: her.

[43] Song of Songs 7. 1.

[44] That is, the model ('exemplum') of the saints is a protection to their followers in the same way as shoes protect the exposed feet. James of Vitry uses a variation of the same theme: 'so that the feet might be protected, as it were, with shoes by means of the various examples of the saints' (VMO Prologue 1, in *Mary of Oignies*, p. 40).

did not understand[45] — he was attracted by the wonderful grace in her. Visibly struck by remorse in his heart, he received an improvement of life quite unexpectedly. Afterwards he could not remember her face without at once receiving an increase in spiritual health.

Because this blessed woman was unable to bear the sight of men, she frequently passed through town in such a way that she saw neither man nor woman. There was a boy in her mother's house, perhaps twelve years old, who used to wash the dishes. She begged her mother that he be removed from the house because he was male, for her spirit shrank from the presence of men so much that she quivered with alarm whenever she saw one. And where did this come from? Certainly from her jealous Spouse, Jesus, who in former times had spoken through the prophet Isaiah: 'The bed is so narrow that the other must fall out: and a short blanket cannot cover both.'[46]

There was no levity in her appearance, no word in her mouth, no levity in her bearing. If she happened to hear anything about God, she covered her face and raised her eyes to heaven, and as Solomon advised, she shattered harsh and bitter words with mild speech.[47] So simple and chaste was her bearing that you could hardly ever see her without believing that she was thinking about heavenly things. Such was her external appearance.

Her silence

13. According to Isaiah, 'silence is the cultivation of righteousness'.[48] This virtue in Margaret was so praiseworthy that she surpassed even many cloistered monks and nuns, who could not be compared to her. When her mother complained to her spiritual father that she hardly spoke to her whole family, he ordered her, for their consolation, to talk to her mother and sisters every day

---

[45] This could mean either that he did not understand the dialect Margaret was speaking, or that she was speaking too obscurely, or 'in tongues'. In VLA II.40 Lutgard, a Flemish-speaker, is able to communicate with French-speakers despite the language barrier. In a private communication, Walter Simons pointed out that in a later period, French was used in the Ypres communal administration, but the 'townspeople were certainly Flemish-speaking. Margaret's visitor probably also spoke Flemish, since Thomas says he came from the "*remocioribus partibus Flandrie*"'.

[46] Isaiah 28. 20.

[47] Cf. Proverbs 15. 1.

[48] Isaiah 32. 17.

after eating for as long as it took to recite the Seven Psalms.[49] Obedient to her father in all things, she spoke as she had been directed, but of absolutely nothing except God. If they discussed anything else in her presence, any ordinary subject or gossip, at once she turned away and fell asleep. Whenever her mother compelled her to sit and talk longer than the appointed time, she obeyed her by sitting there, but promptly slumped down against the wall, and her face and hands would turn livid.

There was no one she loved so much that their words did not burden her — no matter how few — with the sole exception of her spiritual father, through whom she had attained salvation. She used to sit hanging on his words, and her soul internalized[50] his conversation as the body incorporates the food by which it lives. For the sake of peace, she would briefly answer questions, but if they lasted more than a minute, this was a torture to her and she could not hold back her tears. For the same reason she sometimes fell into trance. Although she had great grace in speech, what seemed greater to her was the fruit of meditation, prayer, and contemplation in the presence of Almighty God.

How she preserved peace with her neighbours

14. Following the apostle, she kept the peace with everyone,[51] nor could she easily suffer anyone to be harmed by her words or deeds. For the sake of peace she patiently endured serious tribulation of heart and body. Although her soul thirsted with an open heart[52] for the words of her spiritual father, she would never speak with him as long as anyone was waiting for him or he was needed elsewhere; and she did this for the sake of peace with her neighbour.

O how far from such perfect harmony are those who always seek their own good, not that of others, and imagine that their own peace is shared by everyone. If what they want suffices them, they think that it should be satisfying to everyone!

Once when this blessed woman was suffering grievously from an illness, her spiritual father sat with her and concealed the fact that commands had come

---

[49] The Seven Penitential Psalms (6, 31, 37, 50, 101, 129, and 142 in the Vulgate), a common devotion in books of hours. [BN]

[50] *Incorporabat sibi.*

[51] Romans 12. 18.

[52] *Hianti corde sitiret*, referring to the mouth of the heart. Cf. Ch. 44 below.

from the venerable and worthy man of God, Master Guiard, bishop of
Cambrai,[53] as well as the countess of Flanders.[54] With averted eyes, she protested
and said, 'My father, it will not be so! Who am I — a most miserable woman —
that even the least honour owing to Christ should be relinquished for my sake?
Go quickly where you are summoned by such as these, and do not worry about
me in any way. Hurry now, and when you return you will find me in better
health.'

O truly modest lamb of Christ, patient and discerning,[55] who did not seek her
own,[56] but the things of Jesus Christ! Her word brought about its effect, and
when her spiritual father returned he found her improved.

Whenever her mother reproached her for always having time for prayer, but
none for working with her sisters, to keep the peace she would snatch up a distaff
or some such thing to work — and then fall into ecstasy. Her mother, seeing
that this happened frequently, gave Christ's beloved fawn her freedom[57] and did
not disturb her nor awaken her until she pleased.[58] In nothing did the blessed

---

[53] Guiard de Laon (1170–1248) was a canon of Notre Dame in Paris at the time of this
incident. He became Chancellor of the University in 1237 and was elected Bishop of Cambrai
in 1238. See P. C. Boeren, *La Vie et les oeuvres de Guiard de Laon, 1170 env.–1248* (The Hague:
Nijhoff, 1956). Thomas mentions him in the VLA in a story concerning Lutgard's miraculous
gift of tongues: VLA II.40.

[54] Jeanne, countess of Flanders (1202–44), a noted patron of the beguines and of the new
mendicant orders, had especially close ties with the Dominicans who acted as her spiritual
advisers, including Zeger and his prior, Jacques de Halle. Her birth is mentioned in VJC III.4.
See Meersseman, 'Jeanne de Constantinople'.

[55] *Discreta*: Thomas aligns this virtue with patience, perhaps a reference to Proverbs 14. 29.
According to Thomas Aquinas, *discretio* is 'a form of prudence, queen and mistress of the moral
virtues' (*Summa theologiae*, ed. by Blackfriars, 61 vols (New York: McGraw-Hill, 1964-81), II–II
q. 47). Dom Paul Delatte describes it as 'the virtue which, conscious of the end to be obtained
and of the means at its disposal, ordains all acts to this desired end, sets itself to proportion all
things and exceed in none, to measure the difficulty of a task both by its character and by the
capacity of the individual': *The Rule of St Benedict: A Commentary*, trans. by Justin McCann
(London: Burns, Oates & Co., 1921; repr. Latrobe: Archabbey Press, 1950), pp. 453–54. See also
Purity of Heart in Early Ascetic and Monastic Literature: Essays in Honour of Juana Raasch, O.S.B.,
ed. by Harriet Luckman and Linda Kulzer (Collegeville, MN: Liturgical Press, 1999), and Regis
Appel, 'Cassian's *Discretio*: A Timeless Virtue', *American Benedictine Review*, 17 (1960), 20–29.

[56] I Corinthians 13. 5.

[57] *Dilectam hynnulam Christi tribuit libertati*: Song of Songs 2. 9 and others. Thomas uses
this metaphor for Lutgard in the same context and with the same conclusion: VLA II.1.

[58] Song of Songs 2. 7. This idea of freedom from external restraint also occurs in VCM 18.

young woman censure herself so much as in this, that she disturbed her companions by her long vigils and fasts. With this sole exception, she never said anything after her conversion that might disquiet anyone, nor could anyone say anything that could cause her distress insofar as it involved physical discomfort.[59]

How discarded and broken eggs were found intact because of her prayer

15. Hear this most wondrous miracle, recognized as true by many people, which is said to have happened because of her holy simplicity. As the handmaid of Christ was returning from church intoxicated[60] with heavenly delights, she entered the house and found a bowl full of raw eggs on a bench. Thinking they were eggshells, she emptied the bowl and threw them out of the house — so it would look as if she had done something useful and constructive on a day she had devoted to prayer[61] while others worked.

As soon as her mother looked around for the eggs to put them on the fire to cook, she found them thrown outside the house, broken and scattered. Then the mother, blaming no one except her daughter for such a deed, shouted at her, 'What have you done, you right fool and most foolish of all girls! Why did you throw out the eggs which were all we had left to eat today?' Margaret was grieved by her mother's words — for she greatly respected her — and did not answer at once, but knelt for a little time and prayed with great intensity. Then she rose and said, 'Forgive me, sweetest mother, for I thought they were only eggshells. But go back now to the place where the eggs were thrown and see if anything is left unbroken'.

Behold a truly great and stupendous miracle, not heard of in ages past! The mother quickly proceeded to put her daughter's word to the test and found the eggs completely intact. There was not even a scratch to show that they had ever been broken! Then the mother, amazed at the miracle which was beyond belief, blessed the Lord, collected and cooked the eggs and, after saying grace, ate them

---

[59] *Et hoc quantum ad molestiam corporalem.*

[60] Spiritual inebriation is a mystical phenomenon with its roots in the monastic fathers and is everywhere found in the Lives of the Flemish holy women: VMO I.20, I.22, II.87, in *Mary of Oignies*, pp. 59–60, 110; VLA I.16; VCM 16, 36, and others. In Thomas's *Lives*, the enraptured woman is always overcome by embarrassment after 'she returns to herself' and Thomas always remarks on the 'folly' which pertains to this state.

[61] 1 Corinthians 7. 5.

and distributed them to her family to be eaten.[62] But Christ's handmaid, not a little embarrassed, hid[63] in her bedroom and went all day without food.[64]

The austerity of her penance

16. I have heard such great things about her austere penance that it is proper to praise it, since it was found so worthy before God that the fingers of her discerning deeds were 'full of the choicest myrrh'.[65] She very frequently scourged herself even to the shedding of blood. A child of three could barely have lived on the food she ate while she dwelt in the flesh. If any table companion urged her to take a morsel, she seemed quite unaware of the food, and when her mother rebuked her and asked why she paid no attention to it, she would sigh and say, 'I have many things to think about which distract my mind elsewhere'. Often she fasted continually for two or three days, eating nothing, and she scarcely ever had anything to drink. She abstained completely from wine and meat and delicate foods.

Her vigils and sleep

17. What shall I say of her vigils and sleep? After she had perfectly renounced the world, she scarcely ever slept at night for as long as it takes to walk one league,[66] yet she was often unaware of whether she was really sleeping. For she said she behaved the same way asleep as she did when awake: she remembered

---

[62] The ritual language suggests something more like the distribution of communion than an ordinary family supper. [BN]

[63] *Inclusa*: lit. 'enclosed', commonly used in reference to recluses.

[64] Christina suffered from the same kind of embarrassment: see VCM 36. By the time Thomas wrote the VLA, his treatment of this kind of holy folly had become a little more subtle. See Yochanan Lewy, *Sobria Ebrietas: Untersuchungen zur Geschichte der antiken Mystik* (Giessen: Töpelmann, 1929), and Saward, *Perfect Fools*.

[65] Song of Songs 5. 5. This metaphor is reported as fact in VLA where Lutgard's fingers are seen to drip oil (VLA I.16), and in VCM 19 where Christina's breasts drip a kind of oil. This would seem to be 'the oil of gladness' (Psalm 44. 8), which William of Saint-Thierry called the 'unction of the Holy Spirit which teaches, the taste of divine sweetness, the perfume of eternity, the powerful experience of the spiritual senses': *Exposition on the Song of Songs*, 3.47, p. 138.

[66] A league, though variable from one region to another, was about three miles, so Thomas suggests that Margaret scarcely slept for more than an hour a night. [BN]

God at all times, both sleeping and waking.[67] She lay in bed fully dressed in her clothes and shoes, yet by divine favour she never got a headache. Very frequently she spent entire nights without sleep.

Let the contemplatives of our time blush for shame! If they weep just once out of devotion, mindful of Christ, or keep just one vigil longer than usual, or fast beyond the appointed hour, they quickly cry like the boy in Elisha's story (and truly he was just a boy): 'My head hurts! My head hurts!'[68] For if they had really attained a man's virtue in true strength of spirit,[69] they would never be so quickly rendered effeminate.

I remember that most blessed woman Mary of Oignies, whose reply the venerable James of Vitry commemorated in his biography of her. She said, 'These tears are my refreshment [...] They do not afflict the head, but nourish the mind; they twist without pain, but refresh the soul with a kind of serenity; they do not empty the brain, but fill the soul to the full.'[70] On the contrary, people nowadays say, 'Tears exhaust the brain; vigils disturb the lungs; fasting weakens the limbs. And since no one can serve God by so depriving the body, let us use perfumes to restore the head, sleep to relieve the lungs, and whatever meat or fish the earth and the sea produce to refresh the deteriorating body.'

Woe to those who without cause (or only slight cause) turn the words and deeds of the Fathers upside down! Of these people Paul himself — who is spiritual and greater than they — speaks most plainly: 'I chastise my body and bring it into subjection', and then this, which clearly opposes them: 'When I am weak, then I am strong and powerful.'[71] Apart from the maxims of the saints, which I hold to be firmer than everything,[72] I find the most manifest sign in this tender young woman of whom I speak. For she proves that the human body can do and endure many great things without harm to itself, far beyond what carnal people believe, but especially when love endures them all.[73] Wherefore

---

[67] I Thessalonians 5. 10.

[68] IV Kings 4. 19.

[69] *Si enim vere virtutem viri in veris anime viribus attigissent.* Thomas plays on the etymologically related words *vir* (man), *vires* (strength), and *virtus* (virtue), using the example of a weak woman's strength to shame effeminate men (cf. I Corinthians 1. 27–28). [BN]

[70] VMO I.18, in *Mary of Oignies*, p. 58.

[71] I Corinthians 9. 27; II Corinthians 12. 10.

[72] Cf. II Peter 1. 19.

[73] Cf. I Corinthians 13. 7.

Augustine, the greatest of exegetes, says, 'One who loves does not labour'.[74] 'Do you wish not to experience labour? Think of the reward.'[75]

Now then, see what was accomplished in Margaret. Already at the age of seven, as I have said, she was piercing herself with stings and nettles. When she was nine years old she fasted on bread and water on Wednesdays and Fridays, vigils and fasts of the Church, and without a break during the whole of Lent.

What are you doing, woman, powerful among all others? And what of you, strong and bearded man? Your love indeed is tepid, and therefore there is no man who bears the burden. But see this woman, rejoicing in hope! Because of the greatness of her love, none of the things she did seemed like anything to her, and therefore she endured them all without self-destruction. Behold the sign!

How she spent Christmas Eve without knowing it

18. On the night of the Lord's Nativity, her spiritual father ordered her to sleep for a few hours. When she did not sleep, she was censured and bitterly upbraided by her sisters in his presence, but she answered with this plainly wondrous utterance: 'Sweetest father, I disposed myself in prayer for a little while, and when I wished to withdraw from prayer so that I might sleep, I saw that day was already breaking in the east'. At this response — it is no wonder! — he laughed loudly and exclaimed, 'O foolish woman, you say you prayed for just a little while, but the longest night of the year passed by in the meantime!' Yet was not the night brief and short indeed, if measured by the length and breadth of divine love? Let us therefore contemplate in Margaret a wondrous marvel of virtue. Although she was most hard on herself, yet she could not peacefully bear for anyone else to struggle in abstinence, even within the limits of their power. And although she accused herself harshly for the smallest things, she judged no one at all, excusing the grave sins of her neighbours as best she could.

---

[74] Augustine, *In Johannis Evangelium Tractatus*, 48.1.10, in CCSL 36, p. 413.

[75] Augustine, *Enarrationes in Psalmos*, 36, 12.16.5, ed. by Dekkers and Fraipont, in CCSL 38, p. 357.

The insistency of her prayer

19. Who could explain the power of her unceasing prayer? I do not believe anyone could do this easily, least of all myself. I confess I have scarcely heard of such insistency of prayer by anyone in our time. It is said that in her whole life after conversion, she did nothing else but pray. If she seemed to be doing something else — eating, speaking, working, or other things like that, which was very rare — even then she was always meditating, praying, and thinking how she might please the divine gaze.[76] For this reason it can be said that 'in the heaven of her heart there was silence as if for half an hour'.[77] This silence was placed there not for its own sake but to show an analogy. For just as the divine spirits in heaven never cease from praising Almighty God for even half an hour, so here on earth, neither was Margaret silent in praising God. If she seemed to be silent as though for half an hour when, in outward semblance, she showed anything different (though not alien) from prayer, yet inwardly she prayed without ceasing[78] or losing the warmth of her love. There indeed was her delight, there her holy conversations with Christ, and all other occupation was miserable torment to her.

She believed she could never enter a church early enough or leave it late enough. She wore only a single fold in her headdress, lest making too many folds detain her from her prayers. And when her mother rebuked her for this, she said, 'Good mother, do not be concerned: for in the time I would have spent covering my head so carefully, I could have said a Hail Mary.' Just as anyone would grieve deeply at being separated from a most beloved friend, so did she when she was separated from prayer. If it was necessary for her to rise or if she were called elsewhere to speak with people, she wept, but she went because, for the sake of peace, she did not dare send them away.

She had a secret place in an upper room where she rested in prayer and meditation at midday.[79] When she had to walk upstairs after the midday meal,

---

[76] The term *divinus aspectus* was commonly used for the Beatific Vision, but here it clearly has the meaning found in Thomas's *De natura rerum*: 'The eye of the soul is the mind purified from all bodily stain; the gaze of the mind (*mentis aspectus*) is reason; the intellect is vision. [...] Indeed, the vision of God itself, which is the end of gazing, follows from a right gaze (*aspectum*)' (DNR II.7, p. 86).

[77] Apocalypse 8. 1.

[78] 1 Thessalonians 1. 2, 5. 17.

[79] Cf. Song of Songs 1. 6.

on the first step she would pause to rest, as if weak and gasping for breath. Her sisters thought this was because of her frailty, and when they berated her for it to her spiritual father, she said, 'Dearest father, you may be certain of my secret: by no means is this due to my frailty. But when I remember that I should be free from those demands that detain me downstairs and unite myself with Christ in meditation in my room upstairs, I feel so much inner joy that I cannot stand on my feet for awhile.'

What was it, then, to cling to the Lord so closely in the secret of her heart when, in the hope of future joy, she was filled with such jubilation?[80] Without doubt her 'soul melted as her Beloved spoke'.[81] She would therefore say her prayers so devoutly that, if you had heard but not seen her, you would have thought she was speaking to Christ in person. In this way she roused many to tears and devotion. On the subject of prayer, she made a remark worth remembering to her spiritual father: 'Oh, father, what a great loss it is that people who understand the divine Scriptures, even in the words they pray, send their required prayers to the ears of Almighty God in such a hurry and with so little charm.' How well and worthily she spoke![82]

[80] Cf. VCM 35–36 and VLA I.16. The *tripudium*, translated by Du Cange as 'jubilation', means that dance to which many of the beguines were driven as a result of a mystic experience, the physical equivalent to the mystical prayer also called a *jubilus*: 'The mystical "jubilus" denotes the state of exultation, the experience of an extreme and most intensive feeling of joy [...] During the twelfth and thirteenth centuries, the concept of "jubilus" came to signify the high point of an ineffable mystical experience and of ecstasy': Gertrud Jaron Lewis, 'The Mystical Jubilus: An Example from Gertrud of Helfta', *Vox Benedictina*, 1 (1984), 237–47. See also E. Louis Backman, *Religious Dances in the Christian Church and in Popular Medicine* (London: Allen & Unwin, 1952), p. 45. Here it is clearly the 'feet of the heart' which are dancing. The 'tripudium', however, can have more ominous overtones as when, in VMO 56, in *Mary of Oignies*, p. 90, the demons danced when holy women were led astray by their wiles.

[81] Song of Songs 5. 6.

[82] Here as in Ch. 17, Thomas uses the example of a pious laywoman to reproach professed religious. If Margaret — who perhaps could pronounce the Latin in her prayer book without fully understanding it — could pray with such fervour, should not the fully literate clergy and monastics display even greater devotion? [BN]

How she was wondrously afraid because she once omitted to say the hours

20. Once her spiritual father told her to observe the canonical hours at the proper times of the day.[83] It happened one day, however, that she did not say the hours at their appointed times because she had been rapt in ecstasy. Not a little frightened by this negligence, she came weeping and wailing to her instructor. When he saw her grieving so bitterly, he assumed she must be weeping because of something serious. Suddenly he grew pale, sat down beside her and urged her to tell him what the matter was. When, with copious tears, she confessed what had happened, her father was moved to indignant gratitude: 'Leave!' he said, 'Get out of my sight, O most miserable woman! You have left me trembling and almost senseless from anguish.'

How two angels palpably raised her when she was weary in prayer

21. Every day she would say four hundred Our Fathers and four hundred Hail Marys with the same number of genuflections, as well as fifty psalms.[84] Above and beyond these devotions, she would lie prostrate in prayer for a very long time. Indeed, because she was ravished every day by an ardent desire for contemplation, sometimes she could rise only with difficulty, because of stress and bodily weakness, to stand for the psalms and complete her usual prayers. At such times she could palpably feel the touch of two angels, one on her right side and one on her left, lifting her by the elbows.[85] After she had greeted the blessed Mary ten times in this way, she would become so alert and energetic that she found no difficulty whatsoever in performing her other prayers. Thus she was as strong at the end of her prayers as she had been at the beginning, sometimes much stronger.

Moreover, her body became so hot while she was praying that even in the bitterest winter cold she was content with one tunic, for just as a pot belches

---

[83] This monastic exercise reflects Margaret's early training at a nunnery (Chs 1–2). [BN]

[84] *de psalterio quinquagenam.* Since the liturgical psalter was included in the canonical hours (Ch. 20), Meersseman argues that these additional 'psalms' represented the so-called Marian Psalter, i.e. fifty Ave Marias interspersed with devotional verses to the Virgin. Thus Margaret combined the canonical hours of monastics with the numbered devotions of lay penitents, in addition to long hours of mental or contemplative prayer. It is no wonder that Thomas says she prayed without ceasing. Meersseman, 'Les Frères Prêcheurs', pp. 75–76. [BN]

[85] Cf. VLA II.39.

forth steam while it is bubbling on the fire, so did she burn while she remained steadfast in prayer. Do not wonder at this, for she was one of those mountains of which David joyfully exclaimed, 'Touch the mountains and they will smoke'.[86]

Her wretched clothing and her almsgiving

22. She used to wear wretched and humble clothing. When she refused new clothes she would always say, 'Old and second-hand clothes are good enough for a poor little woman like me', for she was assiduously mindful of the poverty of Christ.[87] Sometimes she fled from her mother and aunts to go begging, but she was compelled by her spiritual father's repeated command to go home and remain with her mother.[88]

She fled idle curiosity with the greatest energy, and although she had been considered wise and wondrously judicious when she was in the world, she had forgotten all that after she was converted to Christ.

When lepers sat in the middle of the road to beg and asked Margaret for something as she passed by, she replied with tears, 'I would gladly give you something if I had anything to give. But I will beg on your behalf to see if I can receive anything.' Then the humble handmaid of Christ would promptly kneel on the ground before passers-by and beg for a small coin. It would have been a very hard and merciless person indeed who could have refused such a poor little woman! Whatever she received as an offering, she gave to the lepers. For this reason the priest of the church had the habit of sometimes giving Margaret a small coin. In this way he satisfied both the beggars and his conscience.

---

[86] Psalm 103. 32. Cf. VJC II.8b on John of Montmirail. [BN]

[87] Cf. VMO II.45, in *Mary of Oignies*, pp. 81–82, on Mary of Oignies's love of poverty. The term *paupercula Christi* is a common epithet in these *Lives* for women who went out to beg. James calls Mary 'a poor little woman' (VMO II.45–46, in *Mary of Oignies*, p. 82), Beatrice of Nazareth is called 'the poor little woman of Christ' (I.37), and Ida of Leuven is labelled 'the poor little woman of Christ who is worthy of veneration' [*venerabilis*] (Ch. 7). Thomas does not use the term for Christina although she did, in fact, beg (VCM 22), nor does he call the nun Lutgard a *paupercula*. The term is, however, used in VLA II.33 in reference to a needy woman.

[88] In the same way Mary was forced to return because of the entreaties of her spiritual friends (VMO II.45, in *Mary of Oignies*, p. 82).

The love which she had for Christ

23. Who could ever show forth in words the burning fire of her love for Christ? It cannot be described except to say how very sweet it was.[89] But when the poor begged for bread at the door in the name of God, she instructed them to ask in the name of the sweetest Lord Jesus Christ. Hence the custom prevailed among many beggars in the town of Ypres that they begged in the name of the sweetest Lord Jesus Christ.

As for religious women, when they came to her as their custom was so she could tell them something about Christ, she replied with troubled indignation, 'What can I say about "Christ" as if he were your serf? Can you not call him "the sweetest Lord Jesus Christ", as is fitting?' Truly she spoke worthily! For the Lord most worthily commended the custom to his apostles, saying, 'You call me Master and Lord. And you say well, for so I am.'[90] And the blessed Thomas said, 'You are my Lord and my God'.[91] How then should we, who are most unworthy, call him simply Christ, when he was called Lord and Master by the most worthy apostles?

Once when a very religious lady was speaking with her, she made this prediction as if in jest. 'Daughter', she said, 'you will not always be thus, forever resting in the embrace of Christ your Spouse with whom you are united in meditation. Later you will have to suffer those inconveniences you have left behind you.' On hearing this she was suddenly frightened and cried out in lamentation. When she could not be restrained by anyone, her spiritual father said to her, 'Is it true then, my daughter, that you now fear harmful adversities?' 'No, father', she said. 'I am not afraid to suffer adversities, but I cannot bear to be separated from my most sweet Lord Jesus Christ for even a little while.'

How she received Christ's body from Christ himself

24. Sometimes if she needed instruction, correction, or solace, it seemed that her spiritual father was present to her in spirit, and then she was filled with a

---

[89] *Dulcissimum.* See Rachel Fulton, '"Taste and See that the Lord is Sweet" (Ps. 33. 9): The Flavor of God in the Monastic West', *Journal of Religion*, 86 (2006), 169–204. [BN]

[90] John 13. 13.

[91] John 20. 28.

certain interior knowledge[92] that sufficed her for the time. But it happened one morning that when she arose, she did not feel the grace of the Lord as was her wont, nor could she sense the reason for this. Since her spiritual father was not present in any way, nor was she filled with her usual inward knowledge, she ran weeping to a man of religion in the town, but he lacked discernment in such matters and, laughing, he looked down on her and drove her off. Turning away at once in confusion, she entered a church, turned to Christ, and said in tears, 'I do not have the presence of my spiritual father, nor do I find consolation from your friends. What then, most merciful Lord, am I to do in my misery?' At once she fell into ecstasy and the Lord appeared to her, saying, 'Do not weep, my daughter! Today you will receive consolation from your Beloved.' Because of this response, she more eagerly awaited the Lord with sure expectation. Nor was she disappointed. The Lord gave her a share in his own body under the species of bread, and afterward she revealed to her spiritual father this certain proof: what she received outwardly in her mouth, she chewed with her teeth and tasted for as long as its material form remained.[93] This grace stayed with her for fifteen days. This, however, was not the only proof, for what is even greater is the grace she drank in with this favour from the Lord. Afterwards she could not bear to see or hear anything trivial or secular. And if she were sometimes compelled to hear such things to avoid scandalizing her neighbours, her understanding was estranged from them at once, or else, as if tired out from her vigils, she fell asleep out of boredom.

How she feared to love her spiritual father more than anyone else

25. Now she loved her spiritual father more than anybody or anything she had in the world, because it was he who had called her back from the world. From her simplicity of heart, however, she began to fear that this was against the Lord in some way, and she said to him in prayer: 'Most merciful Lord Jesus Christ, as you know, I love you above all things and, for your sake, I love that man who made me recognize you and taught me to love you. But since mutual love and frequent conversation between a man and a woman seem suspicious to

---

[92] *Cognicione*: a direct knowledge.

[93] See Bynum, *Holy Feast and Holy Fast*, pp. 228–33, for similar miracles. [BN]

our superiors,[94] I ask you through your matchless humility that you mercifully show me, your handmaid, whether I will incur any loss of your love by loving and conversing with your servant. I solemnly promise that if I find anything against your love, I will never speak to him again. God forbid! For I would not want your love towards me to diminish — no, not for everything in heaven and earth.' Scarcely had she finished these words than the Lord replied to her in spirit: 'Do not fear to trust him in my stead. Nothing he commands will harm you in flesh or in spirit.' God is truthful; indeed, he himself is the very truth. See therefore what occurred.

How she fasted four days before Easter without suffering any harm

26. Although her spiritual father knew the Lord's reply, he wanted to experience a proof of its truth. Now, after Margaret had fasted continually with no food or drink from the Wednesday after Palm Sunday until Easter Eve, she was still zealous in spirit, but weakened in body by four days of fasting. So he said to her in the hearing of many, as she was still fasting after the midday meal on Easter, 'I am planning to preach a sermon this evening about a league away. As for you, get up without breaking your fast and follow me.' Marvel at the miracle! At his words, she at once rose up strengthened and, without difficulty, fulfilled her father's command. What is more, it seemed to her that she was being carried like a bird in the air.

The Lord's revelations to her: first, how the blessed Mary appeared to her and revealed that her sister would be healed

27. Here follow the revelations which the Lord made to her. Indeed, they are so many and so excellent and great that I am afraid to bring them to the notice of carnal men, who never 'perceive those things that belong to the spirit of God'.[95] But then, should the good name of Christ, which is 'the fragrance of life

---

[94] Meersseman suggests that these 'superiors' were probably Margaret's parish priest (in effect, her superior, since she was a laywoman) and Zeger's prior in Lille: 'Les Frères Prêcheurs', p. 73.

[95] I Corinthians 2. 14.

unto life', not be communicated to all lest it become 'the odour of death unto death' for the wicked?[96] By no means! Therefore let me speak.

Christ's handmaid received many revelations from the Lord, but she wished to reveal certain things to no one except her spiritual father. For this indeed she must be highly praised, for many religious women in our day follow the pernicious conduct of the hen: as soon as they produce an egg, they begin to cackle.[97]

Once when her blood sister was almost at the point of death in childbirth and all had despaired of her life, Margaret's mother reproved her, asking why she did not attend her dying sister. For her part, however, she was prostrate in prayer beseeching the Lord for her sister, for she believed this would help her more. Without delay, the blessed Virgin Mary appeared to her as she prayed and said, 'Go and tell your sister, "You will be healed at once, and the baby will be born safe and sound"'. Going quickly to her sister, who was still clinging to life with her last breath, Margaret announced that she would be delivered at once. Wonder to behold! Not a second passed between the words of Christ's handmaid and the moment her sister was delivered of a living boy.

How, when she was afraid, Christ showed her the condition of her heart as she received his body

28. At about the same time, she was gravely tormented by scruples and, considering herself a sinner, she did not dare to receive the body of Christ as had been her wont.[98] Because her spiritual father who usually comforted her in such matters was not present, she asked the Lord to show her the condition of her heart in some way. At once she was rapt in ecstasy and the Lord inwardly showed her her own heart in the likeness of a small, beautifully decorated

---

[96] II Corinthians 2. 16.

[97] The comparison was proverbial. Cf. the Middle English *Ancrene Wisse*, Part II (*c.* 1225): 'The hen, when she has laid, can only cackle — and what happens on account of it? The crow comes right away and steals her eggs from her, and eats what should bring forth living birds. In just the same way the devil-crow carries off and swallows all the good which cackling anchoresses have given birth to': *Anchoritic Spirituality*, ed. and trans. by Anne Savage and Nicholas Watson (New York: Paulist, 1991), p. 73. [BN]

[98] Lutgard also suffered from scruples: cf. VLA II.5, II.17. [BN]

chapel.[99] He said to her, 'Do not fear, daughter, to approach me, your spouse, because in such a place and such a manner, I have prepared for myself a dwelling in your heart'.[100] Paul indeed spoke the truth when he said, 'God's temple is holy, and that temple you are'.[101]

How she reproved an illustrious lady with a reply from the Lord

29. Once when she was seriously ill, her spiritual father visited the sick woman along with a noble lady from the ruling family.[102] He said to her, 'Look, my daughter, here is the lady whom I have so frequently commended to you. I have brought her to you now that you may more solicitously intercede with the Lord for her.' But she turned her eyes away from the lady and said, 'Truly, I have often interceded with the Lord for her, just as now and so often you have asked me as a friend to pray for this lady. But now, at this very hour, the Lord revealed this to me about her. He said, "I will by no means listen to the prayers you pour out for her because her hands are filled with blood: every day she plunders my poor by her taxes."'[103]

The lady was horrified beyond belief to hear this and, recognizing herself, she cried out. Margaret's spiritual father also wondered not a little and adjured her in the name of Christ to say whether the Lord had expressly used the word 'taxes'. 'It is not necessary, holy father', she said, 'to make me take any oath, for I hope you will simply take my word on faith. However, so that the lady herself may believe more surely, I swear to you in the name of Christ our Lord that never in my life until today have I heard the word "taxes" in divine revelation. Therefore, let her trust the Lord's words — if she wishes — that unless she

---

[99] This image has its origin in the temple of Solomon (III Kings 6). See Davy, *Initiation à la symbolique romane*, pp. 175–89.

[100] Compare the communion prayer 'Mundi quoque eidem Christo cordis hospitium praeparemus': *Le Liber mozarabicus sacramentorum et les manuscrits mozarabes*, ed. by Marius Ferotin (Paris: Firmin-Didot, 1912), p. 703; quoted in Blaise, *Vocabulaire*, p. 279.

[101] I Corinthians 3. 16–17; cf. II Corinthians 6. 16.

[102] *cum illustri quadam e principalibus domina.* Meersseman identifies this lady as Marguerite II (1202–78), sister of Countess Jeanne of Flanders, herself countess from 1244 to 1278: 'Les Frères Prêcheurs', p. 78. Thomas mentions her birth in VJC III.5. For Marguerite's posthumous devotion to Margaret of Ypres see Ch. 54. [BN]

[103] *tallias.* See C. Stephenson, 'The Origin and Nature of the Taille', *Revue belge de philologie et d'histoire*, 5 (1926), 801–70.

shows concern for the poor whom she has plundered, she will feel the Lord's unmistakable retribution.' As a result of these words, the lady changed many of her policies for the better. Not only did she lighten the burden of her taxes, but she restored many things to those whom she had ravaged.[104]

How the Lord revealed to her that her spiritual father would pray for her and told her the day and the hour

30. One day when she entered the church, she was suddenly filled with a wonderful joy. She said afterwards that never had she conceived such joy except when her spirit was rapt[105] in contemplation. When she asked the Lord why she was so suddenly filled with consolation, she sensed by the Lord's revelation that her spiritual father was about to celebrate mass for her. Not long afterward, she went into ecstasy as he was coming to her for consolation, and she told him the day, the hour, the place, and the mass he had celebrated on her behalf, adding that she never heard him say mass without receiving some special grace from the Lord. Do not marvel, for if a mother's curse renders a son wretched,[106] how much more is a daughter comforted by a father's blessing?

How she could think only of Christ, and how the blessed Mary appeared to her on the feast of the Annunciation

31. She so clung to the Lord Jesus Christ in the very depths of her heart[107] that she could think only a little of his glorious mother, and then only in relation to her Son. Hence it happened that on the feast of the Annunciation, the blessed and venerable Virgin Mary appeared to her in a great and glorious light, saying, 'It is fitting today, most beloved daughter, that you offer your heart wholly to me and meditate in your thoughts on nothing except my dignity'. She replied to her, 'O sweetest Lady, if I use this day solely for you, tomorrow let me cling once again to your beloved Son'. Blessed Mary said, 'My Son gives himself

---

[104] For dramatic scenes of restitution cf. VJC II.8b, II.12, and II.13. [BN]

[105] *Excessisset*: the same root as *excessus [mentis]*, or ecstasy.

[106] Cf. Ecclesiasticus 3. 11.

[107] *Precordiis*: the intimacy of the soul. In medieval writings, the term refers to the lower chest in front of the heart, the region over the diaphragm, the upper abdomen below the ribs where the soul was thought to reside. In VCM and VLA, Thomas uses the word *pectus*.

totally to you, and me with him — and along with us, he will give you whatever paradise contains'. What a truly great and blessed promise!

Therefore whoever has the Son has also the Mother; whoever has the Mother with the Son has also eternal life,[108] which consists in full enjoyment of the knowledge[109] of our Lord Jesus Christ.

How she and another holy woman saw an angel standing near a certain preacher

32. Once when a certain friar of the Order of Preachers was preaching, while she sat at his feet with another most religious lady, they both saw with their bodily eyes an angel of the Lord surrounding the preacher's face with wondrous brightness and whispering in his ear what he should preach to the people.[110] In this vision the blessed women, worthy of God, 'bore witness to the truth'.[111] By this you may understand that the legal maxim, 'every word shall be confirmed by the mouth of two witnesses', pertains not only to men as in civil law, but also to women as in ecclesiastical and divine law.[112]

How a golden hand appeared above her and a certain Friar Preacher

33. A Dominican friar from Lille who was about to give a sermon in Ypres came to her that morning, bitterly complaining that since he had been busy elsewhere, he had given no thought beforehand to what or how he should speak to the people. At once a golden hand appeared above both of them — and unlike Jacob, who blessed Joseph's sons Ephraim and Manasseh with separated hands,[113] it gave them a common blessing as its own children.

---

[108] Cf. I John 2. 23, II John 9, John 6. 40. The passage commends Margaret for properly subordinating Mary to Christ and simultaneously lifts the Mother to parity with the Father through the quotations from John. [BN]

[109] *Cognitionis fruicione*: i.e. the Beatific Vision.

[110] This story and the next presumably refer to Zeger himself. [BN]

[111] John 18. 37.

[112] Cf. Deuteronomy 9. 15, Matthew 18. 16, John 8. 17, II Corinthians 13. 1, I Timothy 5. 19; and VLA I.9, I.17, and III.5. This is a significant defence of women's canonical rights. [BN]

[113] Genesis 48.

See how great a result followed this blessing! The friar preached and the divine mercy bestowed so much grace on his sermon that all the people wept profusely, as if thrown into confusion by a sudden sound, and they cried aloud and wailed prodigiously from fervour of spirit. The friar himself was filled inwardly with such sweetness of spirit that all day long he seemed to be strolling among the delights of paradise.

For her part, Christ's handmaid was not cheated of her share in the blessing. When the friar had lifted his eyes to heaven at the end of his sermon and exclaimed with the Bride, 'Draw me after you; we will run in the fragrance of your ointments',[114] she seemed at once to see herself drawn up to heaven and ravished in a sudden ecstasy. What she saw there, we can only guess but cannot say.

The amazing miracle by which she saw her spiritual father in Lille with her bodily eyes

34. I will now relate something that is difficult to understand, but it constrains my spirit to refrain any longer from speaking of it. Once when her spiritual father was occupied elsewhere, he was delayed longer than expected in the friary with his brothers in Lille, so he could not console the handmaid of Christ. Burning with desire, she was not a little distressed because her soul depended on his, so to speak, as she was often tormented by scruples of conscience. One day, therefore, she rose and lifted her eyes towards Lille, a distance of five leagues away — and saw with her bodily eyes the one she had imagined in the fervour of her spirit, yet with incomparably greater clarity.[115] She received full consolation from her vision of him.

Here it might be asked how the human eye could see anything distinctly across such a great distance, perhaps with many objects blocking the way. It is clear that if she saw with her bodily eyes, she saw whatever she saw in some

---

[114] Song of Songs 1. 3.

[115] Thomas has no trouble crediting spiritual visions. Because this incident involves bodily vision, however, it seems to him an incomparably greater miracle, yet still requires a scientific explanation which he now attempts to provide. He reverses the traditional Augustinian hierarchy which held spiritual vision to be higher than corporeal (*De Genesi ad litteram libri duodecim*, ed. by Joseph Zycha, in CSEL 28, 1, Book 12). [BN]

place.[116] If, therefore, she saw in space, her act of seeing was uninterrupted and contiguous with the thing seen.[117] It is obvious, however, that this act of seeing was not uninterrupted because its terminus was not the same, nor was it contiguous because a medium of the same kind fell between the eye and the object of vision.

What therefore shall I say? Would it be right to believe that so perfect a bride of Christ had lied? By no means! For I do not believe that, even if her life were at stake, she would have deliberately and knowingly told a lie, especially not about this.

---

[116] Thomas's excursus into optics has caused this translator enormous difficulties and I am grateful for the help given me by Fr Simon Tugwell OP and Professor Judith Neaman in a series of private letters. [On optical theory see David Lindberg, *Theories of Vision from al-Kindi to Kepler* (Chicago: University of Chicago Press, 1976); idem, *Studies in the History of Medieval Optics* (London: Variorum, 1983); and Suzanne Conklin Akbari, *Seeing through the Veil: Optical Theory and Medieval Allegory* (Toronto: University of Toronto Press, 2004), Ch. 2. BN]. On this passage cf. Aristotle: 'it is not true that the one sees, and the other is seen, just because the two are in a certain relation, e.g., that of equality; for in that case there would be no need for each of them to be in some particular place; for when things are equal it makes no difference whether they are near to or far from one another': Aristotle, *Parva naturalia: On Sense and Sensible Objects*, VI, in *On the Soul, Parva naturalia, On Breath*, trans. by W. S. Hett (Cambridge, MA: Harvard University Press, 1975), p. 267. Neaman comments, 'There is confusion here between a reference to physical space and Aristotle's intended reference to the mode of seeing partly by means of or with the necessary aid of a medium (air, light, water) that extends from the eye to the object and from the object to the eye.' For a further explanation of Aristotle's views on physical vision, see Lindberg, *Theories*, p. 7.

[117] *Ergo visus continuus et contiguus fuit ad rem visam.* According to Neaman, 'this link [between the eye and its object] is the medium'. In *On the Soul*, II.7, Aristotle says: 'For vision occurs when the sensitive faculty is acted upon; as it cannot be acted upon by the actual colour which is seen, there only remains the medium to act on it, so that some medium must exist; in fact, if the intervening space were void, not merely would accurate vision be impossible, but nothing would be seen at all'. (trans. by Hett, p. 107) Aristotle's argument was that a continuous medium was necessary to sight and that, in the presence of light and a medium that extended from eye to object and object to eye, the seer would become one with the thing seen. He seems to have sometimes and sometimes not rejected the Platonic idea of sight. That is, that sight occurs when an emanation of ocular fire from the eye (extramission) is fused by light with the eidola or physical images streaming off the object toward the eye (intromission), carrying the image of the object to the eye. (For a fuller explanation of Plato's theory of vision, see Lindberg, *Theories*, Ch. 5.) Aristotle maintained that there could be no vision if the object was directly in contact with the eye, for, without the presence of a medium (transparence or translucence) between the eye and the object, no fusion between seer and seen could take place. This may be one of Thomas's intentions in raising the issue of continuity and contiguity'.

What then shall I say? If, as *The Book of the Nature of Things* says, nature has given the lynx the ability to penetrate solid and opaque bodies with the light of its eyes (contrary to the normal condition of animals, yet without any miracle),[118] why then couldn't Christ, who is said to be wonderful in his saints,[119] have been willing and able to let Margaret see for awhile, to comfort her, the man in whose absence she could have no peace in her heart — and to see him even from a great distance? But you will perhaps respond, 'I do not believe that such a miracle occurred in this girl, nor do I believe that the lynx's vision can penetrate solid and opaque bodies'. To this I reply: 'It is not necessary to prove that a divine miracle occurred in the girl because Christ, who wished to do this, was able to do it; and that is reason enough.'[120] But I do wish to prove that nature is operating in the lynx according to its own law.

According to the Philosopher, it is agreed that the eye is situated in the 'wet' category.[121] There are three properties in water: moisture, translucence, and transparency.[122] Water shares the last of these properties with the celestial substance, and in the nature of light, this is the ultimate stage of purification from matter.[123] For these two reasons — because light is the most penetrating

---

[118] DNR IV.58, p. 143: 'As Pliny and James and the Lapidary say, the lynx is an animal which has such piercing eyes that with its keenness of vision it can see through solid bodies'; cf. Pliny the Elder, *Naturalis historia* 28.32, ed. and trans. by H. Rackham and W. H. S. Jones, 10 vols (London: Heinemann, 1938–63), VIII, pp. 86–87; James of Vitry, *Historia orientalis*, 86, ed. by Claude Buridant (Paris: Klincksieck, 1986), p. 140. See also Gudrun Schleusener-Eichholz, *Das Auge im Mittelalter*, 2 vols (Munich: Fink, 1985), I, pp. 278–81.

[119] Psalm 67. 36; cf. VCM 49. Christina, Lutgard and Margaret are all 'living sermons' (VCM 56; VLA Prologue). See Jo Ann McNamara, 'Living Sermons: Consecrated Women and the Conversion of Gaul', in *Peace Weavers*, ed. by Shank and Nichols, pp. 19–37.

[120] Thomas echoes Anselm's famous principle formulated with regard to the Immaculate Conception: *potuit, decuit, ergo fecit* (God could do it, it was fitting, therefore he did it). [BN]

[121] 'It is true that the eye consists of water, but it has the power of vision not because it is water, but because it is transparent; an attribute it shares with air': Aristotle, *On Sense and Sensible Objects*, II, trans. by Hett, p. 225.

[122] *Tria autem in aqua sunt: aquea humiditas, diaphaneitas et perspicuitas lucis.* This whole paragraph is found verbatim in DNR IV.58, p. 143. [Where the VMY reads *perspicuitas* (transparency), Boese's edition of DNR reads *perspicacitas* (visual acuity). The reading *perspicuitas* makes better sense in this context. BN]

[123] *ultima depuracio a materia in natura lucis.* Cf. Aristotle, *On the Soul*, II.7: 'It is not *qua* water or air that water or air is transparent, but because the same nature belongs to these two as to the everlasting upper firmament. Now light is the activity of this transparent substance *qua* transparent' (trans. by Hett, p. 105).

force in nature, and because it attains the ultimate stage of transparency in the body to which it is directed — let us then posit in the eye of the lynx a watery substance in its highest degree of purification with respect to transparency. It follows then that the light of the lynx's eye can penetrate a solid and opaque body.

But this could not have happened in the girl unless her eyesight had been miraculously improved for a time. Such an improvement is naturally present in the eagle, which discerns its prey from a great distance.[124] What then if God should immediately grant to his bride, by his personal intervention, that which he has given to the eagle and many other birds of prey by means of nature? It is evident that this would be more appropriate for his bride.

How on Good Friday she saw Christ as if crucified

35. On Good Friday when the Passion of the Lord according to John is read, she plainly saw Christ crucified on the wood of the cross. When the lector said the words 'he bowed his head and gave up his spirit',[125] she saw the spirit of the Lord borne up above herself and the celebrating priest. In this act her heart immediately felt itself dying with Christ in his Passion, as it were, and on the day of the Lord's Resurrection when she received the body of Christ, it was as if she returned joyfully to life. From this it is clear that Paul spoke truly when he said, 'If we have shared in his sufferings, so shall we also share in his consolations'.[126]

How she frequently saw the spiritual condition of people

36. The Lord frequently revealed to her many things about the condition of other people. Some she recalled from evil with merciful admonitions, or if she saw some in a good state, she would urge them to do even better. Yet, as I have

---

[124] Isidore of Seville, *Etymologiae* 12.7.10: 'The eagle is so called from the sharpness of its eyes, for it is said to have such wonderful eyesight that, when it is poised above the seas on motionless plume — not even visible to the human gaze — yet from such a height he can see the little fishes swimming and, coming down like a thunderbolt, he can carry off his captured prey to the shore, on the wing': *The Bestiary*, trans. by T. H. White (London: Cape, 1954; repr. New York: Putnam, 1960), p. 105.

[125] John 19. 30.

[126] II Corinthians 1. 7.

said, she never revealed anything of what she saw in others to anyone except her spiritual father alone. And in this Christ rendered her cautious: he who led her inwardly by revelation preserved her reputation outwardly by prudence.

How it seemed to her that she was rapt to heaven, and of the things she saw there

37. Frequently it seemed to her as she was rapt in spirit that she lay at Christ's feet with Mary Magdalene. Sometimes — indeed frequently, even daily — she seemed to lie prostrate on the threshold of paradise, half in and half out, and there she would receive consolation by directing her attention to one of the saints. Often she was conveyed upwards among the very choirs of angels and virgins, as though she were walking with the Lord in the afternoon breeze in a paradise of angelic pleasure,[127] where every order rejoiced with her in great glory. Sometimes, too, it seemed to her spirit that the Mother of Christ came to meet her and led her to a goodly and pleasant place[128] full of wondrous grace. The same was done for her by the blessed Mary Magdalene, whom she venerated with wondrous affection.[129] And this was wonderful indeed in her, that she inwardly discerned the feast of every saint, and received an increase of grace and great consolation in each one.[130]

How a star appeared on her shoulder

38. Once she was sitting with her mother and her maternal aunt and they were talking about God. Quite suddenly the light of a most brilliant star appeared on Margaret's shoulder. When her astonished mother exclaimed, 'What is this, daughter?' she replied, 'Do not be afraid, mother, for the Lord is

---

[127] Genesis 3. 8.

[128] *loca mire amenitatis*: *locus amenus* is a topos for paradise.

[129] Mary Magdalene, the patron saint of penitents and contemplatives, was much venerated by the Netherlandish *mulieres sanctae*. See Susan Haskins, *Mary Magdalen: Myth and Metaphor* (New York: Riverhead Books, 1993), Ch. 5. [BN]

[130] Mary of Oignies could also distinguish feast days of individual saints. 'She was able to distinguish one angel or saint from the other as well as she could distinguish one neighbour from another': VMO II.89, in *Mary of Oignies*, p. 111. See also VLA III.13.

in our midst'. This was in keeping with what he said long ago: 'Where two or three are gathered in my name, there I am in the midst of them.'[131]

How St Catherine appeared to her

39. She piously venerated the most blessed virgin Catherine with a special love, and it happened on her feast day that the blessed Catherine appeared to her in a marvelous royal robe with a golden border.[132] Seeing that she had acquired her favour, Margaret asked St Catherine to approach the Lord and entreat him on her behalf. When the blessed virgin assented, Margaret saw her lie down at the feet of Christ in earnest supplication for her. Without delay, the saint returned to the girl with a revelation from Christ and said, 'Let not your soul grow weary of its life, my daughter, and do not tire yourself any longer, because the time is fast approaching when you will obtain your desire from your bridegroom'.

Her death; how she first became ill

40. Here follows the blessed death of the handmaid of Christ, a death the more glorious as her life was more worthy. For a whole year before she died, she felt hardly any sensation in her body, and she could no longer discern the taste of foods with her palate. Almost daily she felt some new torment in her limbs. After she received the body of Christ on Sundays, however, she felt no pain at all, in accord with what the blessed doctor Augustine said: 'Strengthen yourself with the body of Christ: it is a medicine to counteract sicknesses and a food to heal weaknesses.'[133] After Sunday, though, on Monday her sickness returned and she was once again racked with her accustomed pains. Observing this, those around her concluded most certainly that she had completed her purgation in this life and would fly straight to heaven, free as a bird.

---

[131] Matthew 18. 20.

[132] Cf. VLA I.9.

[133] Augustine, *Sermo* 57:7, in PL 38:389; *Sermo* 132:1, in PL 38:1099.

How she predicted her death; how a serious haemorrhage was sometimes restrained by her prayer; and of the fragrant smell that surrounded her

41. One evening when her aunt was sitting with her, she indirectly predicted her death in these words: 'See, my dearest, I will lead an alien life no longer.' As soon as morning came, a very high fever seized her. Every day thereafter she was bathed in sweat, and the foul stench of her sweat was so intolerable that neither her mother nor her sisters could bear it. On the sixth day her spiritual father came and gave her communion in the body of Christ, and at once she sensed a kind of relief in her body. But this was not yet the crisis.

Then she was stricken by a severe internal haemorrhage. When her aunt, who especially loved her, had anxiously fretted over her for days and nights and could not rest at all, Margaret had compassion on her aunt and said, 'Go now, dearest lady, and rest peacefully all night, for my illness will be relieved for awhile so you can get some sleep!' Although the aunt marvelled, nevertheless she trusted the words of Christ's handmaid and went to sleep. But Margaret said to the Lord, 'I do not ask, Lord, to be wholly freed from this sickness, but while my aunt is sleeping, may I be shaken in the meantime by some other, even more cruel infirmity!'

And it happened just as she had predicted in hope before she prayed to the Lord. The next morning when her aunt returned after her sleep, Margaret's massive haemorrhage was even worse. Yet there was in this flux from her internal organs something contrary to all nature, astonishing and wondrous: the whole place in which the girl lay suffering was filled with an aromatic fragrance as if from the most precious spices. We truly believe this happened because her prayers and worthy merits deserved it, so that the friends who came to visit her would not be horrified by her frightful illness.

Now she suffered constantly from this haemorrhage, but when the Preaching Friars sat with her, she was not troubled by any attack and remained free of discomfort. As soon as they departed, the haemorrhage at once resumed. The friars tested this phenomenon very often by staying for long periods, and thus proved it to be the greatest miracle.

How Christ appeared to her with a crystal vessel and refreshed her with a drop flowing from the vessel

42. Now her spiritual father ordered her not to afflict herself during her illness in any other way she might desire. Since she was obedient to her father in all things, she lay for three days and nights, not daring to occupy herself even with many thoughts about God. When this time had passed, Christ appeared to her plainly in visible form with a most beautiful crystal vessel in which there were many little golden crowns, decorated with most delicate ornamentation. Inclining his hand towards her with the vessel, Christ gave her something like a tiny drop with which to moisten her lips.[134] By displaying the crowns, he indicated the many rewards he was about to lavish on her for the manifold grace of her virtues. As soon as she had drained the tiny drop from the vessel in the Lord's hand, she was fully refreshed, although she had tasted nothing for three days previously.

The mystical words which she said to her mother about her death

43. She was quite distressed to be tended with such solicitous care because her death was thereby delayed. But when her mother rebuked her for her simplicity in this, even though it arose from her desire to see the Lord, she replied, 'My death resembles the death of Christ in one respect, and for this I am especially glad: all my members except my tongue are so bound that I cannot move even a hand or a foot. If my Lord Jesus Christ wished it, I would gladly remain in this state until Judgement Day.' And when her mother marvelled greatly at these words, she said, 'I would reckon it best of all to be in hell with Christ's good pleasure, and there to do something worthy of Christ.[135] How much more should I endure this sickness, which is very little in comparison to hell.'

How she was rapt in ecstasy when she saw green grass and remembered paradise

44. In her mortal sickness she always kept the divine presence and the loveliness of paradise before her mind's eye. As a bird shut up in a cage always thinks about escape, so the handmaid of Christ sought to capture the hour of

---

[134] *Sorbendam*: literally 'to suck on'.

[135] This statement recalls Christina's remark to Lutgard: 'I would rather be in hell with God than in heaven with the angels without God' (VLA I.22). [For similar attitudes among other holy women, see Newman, 'On the Threshold of the Dead', pp. 108–36. BN]

death in the panting mouth of her mind,[136] so that she might fly back to the free air of heaven.

Once when a basin with grass in it was placed before her face to catch the spittle from her mouth, she was suddenly drawn into contemplation by the greenness of the grass and fell into ecstasy, remembering that eternally green paradise. In ecstasy the soul, already refreshed by certain first-fruits of heaven, is more willingly released from the body to which it is joined with marvellous love.

The wondrous torment of her illness and what she said about it

45. Three days before her death, she began to be tormented in all her members beyond all imagination. Her bones, indescribably shaken by this torment, made such a loud noise that the sound of their clattering could be clearly heard outside the house. She experienced such violent, burning pain as if she felt the torments of fire in every limb. If anyone touched any part of her body, she cried out as though in labour. The blood in her hair gave proof of her advanced disease and even her fingernails and toenails were shifted from their proper places. When she no longer had the ability to move a single member and only her tongue was free, she said, 'Lord Jesus, scourge this most miserable body and multiply your vengeance on that which for so long undertook so many wicked offences against you!'

Although she kept repeating these and many similar things, her face was never changed by any of her torments but, always gazing at the face of her dear Christ, her countenance appeared happy and smiling. Indeed, once when her spiritual father was exhorting her more urgently to patience, she reproached him with an anxious face, saying, 'Never have you wounded me in speech, father, except in this, that you command me to be patient as if you lacked confidence in me. Not only is this the least I can suffer, but I am prepared to endure all the torments which have been devised by the will of Christ my Lord since the beginning of the world.' At these words he recognized the girl's constancy and, rejoicing with her, praised the name of the Lord.

---

[136] *Hianti mentis ore*: Although this concept has an odd ring in English, it is a commonplace in medieval mystical treatises and carries with it the idea of the mind gasping with an almost sensuous desire for the waters of life. Cf. Ch. 14 above.

How she predicted that her mother would not grieve, but rather rejoice at her death

46. After all this Margaret said to her mother, 'You should be very happy, mother, for the Lord Christ hastens my death with all these torments'. Her mother said, 'I am not happy, daughter! I will sooner die with you from sorrow.' 'Far be it from the merciful Creator of all, mother, to leave you desolate', she said. 'For I know that in my death he will comfort you, so that you too may be glad that I have departed this world.' How this prophecy of Christ's handmaid was fulfilled I will explain later in its proper place.

How she received the body of Christ without harm, although she could eat nothing else

47. On the same day that she migrated from this flesh to Christ, she asked a priest if she might receive communion. As she had been so weakened for a long time that she could not take even a drop of water, the priest is said to have responded well and fittingly. 'If it had been anyone else', he said, 'I would in no way consider it. But since the Lord has now done so many good things for you, I cannot believe that he will not show his miraculous power still further on this occasion.' So the body of Christ was brought, and she adored and consumed it so easily that there seemed to be no obstructions in her throat at all as she received it.

How Christ appeared to her before the hour of her death and told her that she had totally completed her purgatory and should die at once

48. As soon as evening came, all her pain completely vanished, so that it seemed there was nothing wrong with her except weakness — to such a degree that some of her attendants withdrew, expecting her soon to arise restored to health. Not much more than an hour later, the Lord again appeared to her and comforted her with wondrous grace of speech as his most beloved bride and daughter, saying that she had totally completed her purgatory and would immediately pass away to live with him.

Her wonderful praise at the hour of death, and the light that shone around her face

49. After a little time had passed, she looked at her hands and smiled. Contrary to the opinion of all who believed she would be healed, she said, 'For I am even now ready to be sacrificed, and the time of my dissolution is at hand'.[137] To her mother she said, 'See, now my earthly flesh is prepared for my mother the earth'. Then, as everyone in the house came running to help, she said, 'Raise me up'. When they all refused, terrified by the weakness of her body, she compelled them to do it and was lifted to a sitting position in her bed. Then she ordered them to hold her hands and arms up high, and she said to them all with great joy of heart and countenance, 'Help me to praise my Lord Jesus Christ'. Then she said, 'To you be praise, to you be glory, to you be thanksgiving for all the countless good things you have deigned to do for me, a poor and most unworthy little woman'. When she had repeated this three times in honour of the Holy Trinity, she spoke again with great vehemence of spirit, and even her voice became much louder and stronger:

'Praise to you, O Christ, good Lord, best and sweetest Jesus, to you be praise, praise through all things and all people. May this house be filled with your praise. May this whole world and the vault of the sky itself be heaped high with your praise. May every creature on earth praise you; may your angels and saints in heaven praise you; and may your praise be fulfilled on my account, unworthy as I am. Amen.'

When her mother and those who stood around her heard this, they gazed into her face and saw it so wondrously bright that it seemed beyond human nature; and truly, so it was.

How, when she was dying, she said she saw nothing except Christ and his mother, and how she departed from the body

50. After a little while her mother, sighing in extreme wonder, asked, 'Do you see us, daughter?' With a weak voice she replied, 'No, mother, I do not see you, I can only hear. I see only the Lord Jesus and his most gracious Mother.' As she said this she raised her arms by her own strength and lay in silence for a long time. After awhile, when she had let her arms fall, much of the brightness (but

---

[137] II Timothy 4. 6.

not all of it) faded, and she said, 'Now I no longer see the Lord Jesus Christ'. As she said this her face became ashen, her eyes drooped, and, after a short while, she smiled faintly and gave up her spirit. After her death the smile remained on her mouth, showing by her bodily attitude that the wise and faithful servant had entered into the joy of her Lord,[138] in the year 1237 after Christ's Incarnation, in the twenty-first year of her age.

The ladder that appeared at her death

51. One of Margaret's spiritual friends said that at the hour of her death, he had seen a silver ladder reaching up from the house where Christ's handmaid lay to the heights of heaven. At its summit stood Mary, the glorious Mother of God, with countless virgins, awaiting the imminent release of her soul. Then, sending two virgins from her company, Mary ordered them to carry the departed woman up quickly by means of the ladder. He saw that this was done — and Margaret was led upwards in the greatest glory to be presented to the sight of God.

O truly blessed and happy soul, whom the Christ-bearing Virgin Mary deigned to welcome as you passed from the body, and to join with the sacred virgins in her company!

How her word was fulfilled that her mother would be consoled at her death; of the joy that was poured into the hearts of all; and how she was buried

52. As soon as her blessed soul had departed from the body, by no means did her friends weep for her according to the custom of worldly people. Rather, such joy was poured into the hearts of all as many of them had never experienced before — and this absolute joy lasted until she was buried. Thus was fulfilled the word of Christ's handmaid who, as I said, had predicted that her mother would be consoled at the time of her death. Her consolation was so great, in fact, that when Margaret's spiritual father wished to comfort her, he saw her filled with so much happiness that her face appeared rosy with joy. In the morning people from all parts flocked together in a great crowd. After the sacrifice of the Lord's body had been offered with the greatest solemnity, her body was given over for burial.

[138] Matthew 25. 21.

The first miracle: how a woman's arm was healed at her burial

53. As her spiritual father was sitting near her grave, a woman came up to him with her arm swollen from the shoulder to the hand. As the custom is in such matters, she asked his advice about how she might receive healing. Rejoicing in spirit and trusting in the merits of the newly buried woman, he said, 'Go and tell my daughter that, now that she is dead, she should obey me as she did when alive, and that she should ask the Lord to cure you'. At the friar's word, the woman quickly approached the tomb and said, 'Through me, Friar Zeger asks you in these words that, even though you are dead, you obey him as you did when alive, and ask the Lord to heal my arm'. See how great was the power of the friar's word and the obedience of the newly departed! For at that very moment, before many witnesses, the woman's arm was restored to health.

How, after nine weeks, her headdress was found buried in the earth, shining brightly, redolent with an aromatic fragrance and without corruption

54. Friar Zeger had often begged Margaret's mother before her death to preserve all her possessions for him, such as her headdress, shoelaces, and similar things. After her death, he asked for each item under a seal. Everything was quickly brought before him and only her linen headdress was missing. Then he asked her mother, 'Where is the headdress?' She replied, 'Her headdress was putrefied, for she had a horrible wound, and when the dressing was removed, it was so foully infected with putrid matter that I was afraid to wash it, so I buried it in the ground outside the house. It must have long since disintegrated, for it has been there more than nine weeks.'[139] As if offended, he objected and said, 'I must have that headdress even if it has putrefied'. Wonder to behold! When they dug up the earth where the headdress had lain, it was found to be completely intact, shining white, and with no stain of putrid matter; and this was seen by many astonished witnesses. And the greatest miracle in that headdress was that, instead of a stench from the bloody filth with which it had been spattered, you would have thought it had lain among aromatic spices. On account of this miracle, Friar Zeger embraced the headdress with such veneration that he regularly refused to give it to the most illustrious and devout matron, Lady

---

[139] This miracle echoes both the raising of Lazarus, whose body was expected to stink because he had been dead four days (John 11. 39), and the finding of Christ's uncorrupted grave clothes (John 20. 5–7). [BN]

Marguerite, sister of the Countess of Flanders.[140] I understand from the same friar that healings have been performed through this headdress.

How one of her friends saw her as if with a crystalline body and a rose-coloured breast

55. Not long after her death, one of her spiritual friends saw her in a vision with a transparent, crystalline body and a rosy colour in her breast. She smiled at the one to whom she appeared and spoke to him, using the words of the most blessed Agnes: 'Behold, what I have desired, I now see; what I hoped for, I now possess. I am united in heaven with him whom I loved with total devotion on earth.'[141] And see, brother, how suitably these two are joined: when the diaphanous red of roses is pleasantly mixed with the translucent whiteness of lilies, virginity is signified by the whiteness and her charity denoted by the red.

The three places that a certain person saw in paradise, and the one allotted to Margaret

56. During the lifetime of Christ's handmaid, one of her spiritual friends saw in a vision three different places in paradise. Of these, one place was reserved for Margaret and the others for two other people. After her death, he saw that Margaret had been allotted her place, but the two remaining ones were still vacant. We confidently hope that they will be filled by those destined to sit in them.

How she was seen standing near a certain preacher with an open book and showing him what he ought to say

57. When one of our brothers in the Order of Preachers rose to preach to the people, Margaret was plainly seen standing before him in the hall with an open

---

[140] This is probably the same lady whom Margaret had rebuked for her excessive taxes in Ch. 29. [BN] Marguerite, like her sister Jeanne whom she succeeded as Countess of Flanders in December 1244, continued to support and protect the Flemish beguines until her death. See McDonnell, *The Beguines and Beghards in Medieval Culture*, pp. 208–17.

[141] Pseudo-Ambrose, *Vita S. Agnetis*, 11: 'ecce jam quod credidi, video; quod speravi, jam teneo; quod concupivi, complector': AASS, 21 January, I, p. 717.

book, as if to show the preacher what he should say. After the friar had preached, she seemed to close the book and suddenly disappeared, penetrating into the heights of heaven.

Here ends the life and book of the illustrious young woman Margaret of Ypres. May those who read this book pray for me, therefore, that I may experience in myself the power[142] of the one whose virtues I have faithfully described, to the praise and glory of Christ who, with God the Father and the Holy Spirit, lives and reigns as God forever and ever. Amen.

---

[142] *virtutem:* Thomas plays on the double sense of the word as 'power' and 'virtue'. [BN]

THE LIFE OF LUTGARD OF AYWIÈRES

Translated by Margot H. King and Barbara Newman

CHRONOLOGY

THE LIFE OF LUTGARD OF AYWIÈRES

(1182–1246)

1182	Birth of Lutgard at Tongeren
1194	Joins beguine community of St Catherine's, Sint-Truiden
c. 1200–05	Receives consecration of virgins from bishop of Liège; the women of St Catherine's formally become nuns and adopt the Benedictine Rule; Lutgard is elected prioress
1206	Transfers to a small group of devout women at Les Awirs near Liège; the community petitions to join the Cistercian order
1210	Women of Les Awirs officially received by Cistercian General Chapter
1211	Community moves to Lillois in the duchy of Brabant, under patronage of Iwan de Raive; Marie de Raive becomes first abbess
c. 1212–15	Community moves again to Aywières under patronage of Godfrey, castellan of Brussels
1213 (23 June)	Death of Mary of Oignies
1215	Fourth Lateran Council
c. 1215	Death of John of Liroux, Lutgard's spiritual father
1216	Dominicans take over Albigensian Crusade preaching; Virgin Mary asks Lutgard to intercede
1216 (16 July)	Death of Pope Innocent III
c. 1216–23?	First seven-year fast on bread and beer
c. 1223–30?	Second seven-year fast on bread and vegetables

1224	Death of Mary, duchess of Brabant
c. 1228–30	Thomas of Cantimpré's first meeting with Lutgard
1229	Death of Simon of Aulne, saintly lay brother
c. 1230	Hadewijch becomes abbess of Aywières
1232	Thomas joins Dominican order
1235	Lutgard goes blind
1235 (26 May)	Canonization of Elizabeth of Hungary
1237 (12 Feb.)	Death of Jordan of Saxony, Dominican Master General
1238	Guiard de Laon elected bishop of Cambrai
1239–46	Final seven-year fast
1240 (1 May)	Death of Cardinal James of Vitry
1241	Tartars invade Bohemia; Lutgard prophesies that they will not reach Germany
1242	Death of Baldwin de Barbençon, prior of Oignies
1246 (16 June)	Death of Lutgard
1246–48	*The Life of Lutgard of Aywières* written
before 1274	*The Life of Lutgard* translated into Middle Dutch verse
1616	Solemn elevation of Lutgard's relics
1656	Cistercian Order grants Lutgard a major feast day

PROLOGUE

To Hadewijch,[1] a lady reverenced and much loved in Christ, abbess of Aywières[2] by divine permission, and to all the most holy community with her, a brother, subprior by office but least of the Friars Preachers, sends greetings and good wishes as he would for himself.

Instead of a proper name, I have put the author's office and his order in this salutation so that the office and the order might commend the authority of the work that follows, rather than making it worthless by the intrusion of my personal name.

Since it was not only your charity which incited me, but also that of many monasteries, as well as the most burning love I had for this most special personage, I have described in writing the life of the gracious Lutgard.[3] I have divided the whole work into three books according to the three states of the soul: the state of beginners, of those who are progressing, and of the perfect.[4] The first

---

[1] Hadewijch (Hawide) was abbess of Aywières from about 1230 until her death in 1248.

[2] Aywières=Euvvier=Aquiria: A convent established *c.* 1195 in the village of Les Awirs between Huy and Liège which, in 1211, was transferred to Lillois in Brabant and found its final site in 1215 at Couture-Saint-Germain, northeast of Nivelles. It was incorporated into the Cistercian Order in 1210 under the spiritual direction of the Abbot of Aulne. For a discussion of Lutgard's relationship to the convent, see Simone Roisin, 'Sainte Lutgarde d'Aywières dans son ordre et dans son temps', *Collectanea O.C.R.*, 8 (1946), 161–72.

[3] *Pia Lutgardis*. Thomas uses *pia* 131 times in this *vita*. It is his standard epithet for Lutgard and has a wide range of meanings: gracious, saintly, compassionate, righteous, devout, and so forth. I have generally translated it as 'gracious' but have often omitted the adjective. [BN]

[4] This structural division parallels that found in the VJC and VCM and echoes the terminology used by William of Saint-Thierry to describe the stages of the mystic ascent of the soul: 1) the animal [novices]; 2) the rational [progressants]; and 3) the spiritual [the perfect]. See

book will tell how she began her conversion as a nun in the order of St Benedict; the second, how she progressed when she crossed over to the Cistercian order;[5] and the third book will contain the stage of perfection, as it were, and tell what the Lord deigned to accomplish through her in the eleven years before her death, in her death, and after death.

Not for many years, I believe, has there been written the life of any person so filled with remarkable virtues and so privileged by marvels and miracles. If you ask how I am to convince readers of the truth of all these things, I briefly say (and may Christ himself be my witness and judge) that I received many of them from Lutgard's own mouth as one of her closest friends. In these matters no one, I believe, would be so bold as to contradict her testimonies. I acknowledge that I collected the rest from people of a kind who would never stray from the path of truth. There were many things — splendid ones in fact — which I have not consented to write, either because they would not make sense to the uncultivated or because I did not find suitable witnesses. But since 'charity believes all things, bears with all things',[6] I entreat those into whom God has poured the spirit of his charity that, in these matters, they believe 'such things as are holy, such things as are useful',[7] such things as are consonant with truth, and at the same time patiently bear with such things as I might have put down in a less rhetorically pleasing or discerning style. Nevertheless, they ought not to be rejected by the wicked on that account, for, as the most glorious Augustine says, 'it is a mark of good and distinguished minds to love the truth within words and not the words'.[8] Gold is no less precious for being taken from the earth, nor wine

---

William of Saint-Thierry, *Exposition on the Song of Songs*, Praef. 13–23, and Elder, 'The Way of Ascent', pp. 39–47.

[5] I doubt that Thomas was naïve enough to consider that Benedictines were spiritually inferior to Cistercians, although his use of the words *transeundo* and *profecit* seem to indicate this. He almost always uses the former ('passing to the other side') to indicate the passage of the soul to paradise or a turning away from worldly entanglements. Thomas's interpretation of Lutgard's decision to leave the Benedictines, triggered as it was by her election as prioress, was probably less an indication of sectarianism than of his preference for the spirituality espoused by the new orders, with their emphasis on solitude, poverty, and manual labour.

[6] 1 Corinthians 13. 7.

[7] Cf. Philippians 4. 8.

[8] Augustine, *De doctrina christiana*, IV.11.26, in *On Christian Doctrine*, trans. by Robertson Jr, p. 136. Conversely, when Thomas speaks in II.16 of Lutgard's inability to understand the Psalter, he says that power resides less in our understanding of the words than in the words themselves.

the less tasty for being pressed out of worthless wood. Therefore not only you, but the virgins of all the monasteries of Brabant should receive this life of the gracious Lutgard so that she, whose reputation for virtue was known to all, should become even more widely known by the publication of this little book. May it increase virtue and merit in its readers, to whom it will provide a lesson and example of virtue.[9] May your holy and genuine kindness prosper, and may God in his mercy guard all of you unharmed, remembering me in your prayers. Amen.

[9] On the concept of the *exemplum* see VCM 56, p. 155, n. 63.

BOOK I

1. Concerning her birth and infancy

The gracious virgin Lutgard took her origin from that once famous city of Tongeren,[10] her mother a noble and her father a burgher.[11] Since her father tenderly loved[12] his daughter and was eager that she prosper according to the pride of the world, he entrusted twenty silver marks to a merchant while she was still an infant, so that while the little one was growing up, the wealth might multiply and increase for her dowry when the daughter would marry.[13]

As the girl grew and became aware of what was in store for her, she yearned for marriage insofar as someone of her age could wish for it. But the merciful

---

[10] Tongeren (Tongres), situated between Sint-Truiden and Liège in the province of Limburg, was part of the diocese of Liège until 1967.

[11] *cive*: the Middle Dutch Life of Lutgard makes her father a porter of the city [poirter vander stadt]. See D. A. Stracke, 'Proza Fragmente van S. Lutgart's Leven', *Ons Geestelijk Erf*, 11 (1937), 281–99 (p. 284).

[12] *diligens*: note the different terms Thomas uses for love. In this case, *diligo* is that human love which can turn sour and becomes muddled with concerns for Lutgard's earthly welfare. Cf. 1 John 2. 15: 'If anyone loves (*diligit*) the world, the love (*caritas*) of the Father is not in him'.

[13] *Multiplicatis [...] augerentur*: terms normally used in the context of God's command to Adam and Eve, but here set in the context of usury, which underlines the 'unnaturalness' of natural love when seen in the light of divine love. Thomas Aquinas, quoting Aristotle, says: 'to make money by usury is exceedingly unnatural' (*Summa theologiae*, II–II, q. 78). See also his *Commentary on Aristotle's Politics* (*In libros Politicos expositio*), Book I, Ch. 8, trans. by Richard Regan (Indianapolis: Hackett, 2007), p. 60: 'there is a kind of generation when money increases from money. And so also such acquisition of money is the most contrary to nature, since it is according to nature that money is acquired from natural things, not from money [itself]'.

Lord, provident of the future, he who 'calls upon things that are not as upon things that are',[14] frustrated the father's resolution and disposed otherwise for Lutgard so that she might be espoused to himself.

The man who had received Lutgard's money in the hopes of increasing it through trade frequently crossed to England but, coming to grief through various misfortunes, completely squandered the twenty marks until only one mark was left.

These events, however, would not have recalled the father's intention nor the daughter's shameless effrontery from their scheme, had not the pious mother's urgent insistence overruled her daughter's mind, sometimes with threats, sometimes with caresses. The mother would frequently say and impress this on her daughter: 'If you are willing to wed Christ, I shall arrange for you a most respectable monastery[15] wherever you wish. If, however, you choose a mortal husband, you shall have no one but a cowherd.' With these and similar words, this excellent woman changed[16] both her husband's desire and her daughter's will to a plan for a better condition.

As long as she stayed in her father's house, Lutgard was attired in splendid clothing, but she would have nothing to do with indecent jokes, love talk, or girlish silliness. In a wondrous way, although she did not yet know the Lord (for he had not yet been revealed to her in any way),[17] yet when she was alone, she

---

[14] Romans 4. 17.

[15] *monasterium honestissimum*: this threat is also recorded in the Dutch version: 'een eerbair cloester stichten' ('a noble monastery'). It would seem that the mother, despite her spiritual acumen is, like her husband, still attached to material concerns. The literal alternative she gives Lutgard — to marry her off to a cowherd — is unlikely but could underline this reading. Life as an abbess or prioress in a wealthy convent in charge of humans is preferable to a life where an absorption in carnal affairs could be compared to authority over beasts. In the event, St Catherine's was soon to become a *monasterium honestissimum*: at the time of writing it only accepted women from the nobility.

[16] *inclinavit*: Thomas uses this verb throughout the *vita* to refer to the will, which is most operative in the early stages of the soul's progress.

[17] 1 Samuel 3. 7; cf. VMY 2. *Cognosceret* is to 'know' in the sense of direct knowledge. The progression seems to be from natural parental love to awareness to unformed will to direct knowledge. In Lutgard's case, however, this is only the beginning. These early chapters concentrate on love (the will) and knowledge (*mens/spiritus*) which, if animated by infused grace, are in turn transformed into *caritas* (love of God and one's neighbour) and prophetic contemplation.

sensed[18] in her heart I know not what divine presence. And in fact, from that time on, the Lord was preparing for himself within Lutgard a temple most worthy to be his dwelling place.[19]

Thus, with divine grace, the mother's right prevailed in the daughter and, reaching the age of a little more than twelve years, she was committed to the divine service among the nuns of the order of St Benedict in the monastery of St Catherine,[20] adjoining the town of Sint-Truiden in Hesbaye.

2. How she was wooed by a certain youth and, through a vision of Christ, she was completely converted and suddenly liberated

A young man, potent in wealth and breeding, had been wooing her and after a time he began to bend her mind gently towards his words. Since the youth was on the alert for the right time and place, one night he secretly attempted to approach the house where the virgin was lying. As soon as he came near, however, he was gripped by sudden fear and ran away. Thus in wondrous ways,

---

[18] Still in the earliest stages of her development (what William of Saint-Thierry calls the 'animal' stage), Lutgard does not yet 'know' but relies on knowledge derived from the senses (*sentiebat*).

[19] Cf. II Maccabees 14. 35. Note the contrast between the mother's preparation of an *honestissimum monasterium* and the Lord's preparation of a *dignissimum templum*. The image of the temple focuses our attention once again on love. In the Augustinian Rule, we read, '"You are all to live together, therefore, one in mind and one in heart" (cf. Acts 4. 32), and honour God in one another, because "each of you has become his temple"' (II Corinthians 6. 16).

[20] The Benedictine convent of St Catherine's at Sint-Truiden was originally founded in the ninth century and situated near the Stapelpoort, where the railway station now stands. In 1231 the nuns abandoned the convent to settle at Mielen (Nonnemielen) near Melveren, a fief of Loon. Like many convents of the time, St Catherine's only accepted women from the nobility, presumably one of its attractions for Lutgard's mother. That it enjoyed the favour of the bourgeois inhabitants of Sint-Truiden is attested to by their numerous donations, but such endowments, combined with lax rules regarding recruitment, frequently led to a weakening of the monastic ideal, especially with regard to the vow of poverty. See J. L. Charles, *La Ville de Saint-Trond au moyen âge: Des origines à la fin du XIVᵉ siècle* (Paris: Société d'édition 'Les Belles Lettres', 1965), p. 280; M. J. Wolters, *Notice historique sur l'ancienne abbaye noble de Milen près de Saint-Trond* (Ghent: Gyselynk, 1853); G. Heynen, 'De Benedictinessen te Sint-Truiden en te Nonnemielen', in *Christina de Wonderbare: Gedenkboek 1150–1950*, ed. by P. Clerinx (Leuven: Bibliotheca Alfonsiana, 1950), pp. 25–30; and J. Grauwels, 'Abbaye de Mielen à Saint-Trond', in MB 6, Province de Limbourg (1976), pp. 89–101.

the devil zealously urged that she bend her mind to girlish consent — but in vain, for the Almighty did not permit it.

Thus once when the simple[21] girl was sitting in conversation with the young man, Christ appeared to her in that human form[22] in which he had once lived among mortals. Drawing back from his breast the garment in which he seemed to be covered, he showed the wound in his side, bleeding as if recently opened, and said, 'Do not seek any longer the caresses of unseemly love. Here you may perpetually contemplate what you should love[23] and why you should love it. Here I pledge[24] that you shall attain the delights of total purity.'[25]

[21] *simplicitas*: this is a monastic commonplace but its use here is interesting. See William of Saint-Thierry, *Golden Epistle*, I, xiii, 49, in *The Golden Epistle: A Letter to the Brethren at Mont Dieu*, trans. by Theodore Berkeley (Kalamazoo: Cistercian Publications, 1976), p. 28: 'However, turned to God this animal state becomes holy simplicity, that is, the will always the same in its attachment to the same object [...] For properly speaking simplicity is a will that is wholly turned toward God, seeking one thing from the Lord with all earnestness, without any desire to disperse its energies in the world.' See Chrysogonus Waddell, 'Simplicity and Ordinariness: The Climate of Early Cistercian Hagiography', in *Simplicity and Ordinariness*, ed. by John Sommerfeldt (Kalamazoo: Cistercian Publications, 1980), pp. 1–47.

[22] *in ipsa forma humanitatis*: Reypens considered that, by the use of the term *forma*, Thomas is here indicating that Lutgard's vision was a sensory one: L. Reypens, 'Sint Lutgarts mystieke opgang', *Ons Geestelijk Erf*, 20 (1946), 7–49 (pp. 17–18).

[23] *diligas*: in keeping with Lutgard's spiritual immaturity, Christ is speaking here of human, natural love and, for this reason, his first appearance to her is in human form.

[24] Thomas's use of the term *spondeo* resonates with overtones of what was later called the mystical marriage. The whole *vita*, and the first book in particular, revolves around love and these early chapters contrast carnal love (parental and sexual) with divine love.

[25] See William of Saint-Thierry, *Exposition on the Song of Songs*, IV.60, p. 48: 'The Bride who eagerly strives to see God desires a pure heart, a pure conscience, pure senses, pure understanding — complete purity'. Cf. VMY 7 where Christ promises Margaret that she will be free of carnal temptations.

3. How a devout and noble matron prophesied that she would be like another Agnes

Alarmed by such an oracle,[26] Lutgard therefore immediately held fast with the eyes of her heart[27] to what she had seen. Like a dove meditating at a window at the entrance of the sunlight,[28] she keenly observed the crystalline opening of the Ark,[29] the typological Body of Christ.[30] At once her fleshly bloom was consumed away and, like every lover, her countenance paled. Inwardly brightened by a supernal brilliance, she sensed that what she had lost was the darkness of total vanity.

One day a noble and devout matron saw her and, in the spirit of prophecy, uttered the following words. 'You, as I see', she said, 'are a good lamb. Yes, truly, you will be a second Agnes.'[31] Immediately thereafter her young suitor came and began to talk about what they had proposed to discuss. With open mouth, she replied like the most blessed Agnes of old, 'Depart from me, fodder of death, nourishment of villainy, for I have been overtaken by another lover'.[32]

---

[26] Thomas, drawing on Macrobius, *In somnio Scipionis*, I, 3, defines an oracle as 'a dream in which a parent or some holy and solemn person, a priest, or even God announces plainly what will or will not happen, what should be done or avoided' (DNR II.13, p. 94).

[27] *oculis cordis*: a common image taken from Ephesians 1. 18.

[28] Isaiah 38. 14. The dove is a common image of simplicity and Caesarius of Heisterbach uses it in the same context as Thomas: 'The windows of the doves are the eyes of the simple-minded monks. [...] Their dove-like appearance is the simplicity of their attention. Both eyes of the religious ought to be simple, both the outward and the inward; the eye of the body so that suspicion may be far from it; the eye of the heart so that its intention may be pure': Caesarius of Heisterbach, *The Dialogue on Miracles*, VI.I, trans. by H. von E. Scott and C. C. Swinton Bland (London: Routledge, 1929), I, p. 391.

[29] See William of Saint-Thierry, *On Contemplating God*, 3, trans. by Sister Penelope (Kalamazoo: Cistercian Publications, 1977), p. 38: 'Like Thomas, that man of desires, I want to see and touch the whole of him and — what is more — to approach the most holy wound in his side, the portal of the ark that is there made, and that not only to put my finger or my whole hand into it, but wholly enter into Jesus' very heart'.

[30] For the ark as Christ, see Gregory the Great, *Homiliae in evangelia*, I.19.I (PL 76:1154).

[31] This is not only a reference to the virginity of Agnes and Lutgard but an obvious pun on their sacrificial vocation and the fact that they both went to their martyrdom of their own free will, the one to a red martyrdom and the other to a white. Cf. VMY 55.

[32] These words were put into the mouth of Agnes herself: Pseudo-Ambrose, *Vita S. Agnetis*, I.I, in AASS, 21 January, I, p. 715, and *Epistolae ex Ambrosianarum numero segregatae*, Epistola I (PL 17:735–42). [Cf. Jacobus de Voragine, *The Golden Legend*, I, p. 102. The passage was also

4. How a certain knight wooed her and she manfully repulsed and confounded him

Another youth, a knight vigorous in arms, loved Lutgard deeply, even more now that she was clinging so genuinely to God. He had already wooed her for many years despite her reluctance. At first she had refused him politely but afterwards she turned away in earnest. When however she saw that the knight was stubborn in his folly, she finally repulsed him with abusive speech.

5. How the same knight wanted to seize her violently and she miraculously escaped

Grieved to find himself thus despised, the knight thought carefully what he could do. It happened that Lutgard was to undertake a journey,[33] having been summoned by messengers from her sister, and the young man encountered her on the way with a crowd of attendants and attempted to seize her.[34] The girl quickly leapt off her horse and violently wrenched herself from the young man's hands. All through the night she fled through unknown woods, led by an angel, until at dawn she reached the cottage of her nurse.[35] As soon as she saw her, the nurse suspected rape and said, 'Did the young man oppress you by violence last night?' 'No', she replied. It was little wonder that the nurse suspected this, as I said, for Lutgard's servants had fled the night before as soon as they had seen the young man coming against her with force. As the custom is in such matters, they had set up a hue and cry against the youth as a rapist. Alarmed by this outcry,

used as an antiphon for matins on the feast of St Agnes: *The Hours of the Divine Office in English and Latin*, I, p. 1701. BN]

[33] Note the subtle way in which Thomas introduces the idea of motion. It is still not the motion of the soul, but this kind of journey frequently marks the beginning of the monastic flight from the world and, inwardly, of the soul's journey to God.

[34] *rapere*: the word means 'to seize' in Latin, but with overtones of its contemporary cognate. It is clear that rape is what the knight has in mind. This incident continues the motif of natural vis-à-vis divine love.

[35] Lutgard's flight through the woods greatly resembles the many Desert Mothers who through the centuries fled rape and/or marriage and carnal love. See Margot King, *The Desert Mothers: A Survey of the Feminine Anchoretic Tradition in Western Europe* (Toronto: Peregrina, 1989).

he ceased his pursuit of the virgin and ran away. It was on account of this uproar and his flight that the innocent girl had become an object of suspicion.

6. How she predicted a grave misfortune to a follower of the knight who attacked her

In the aftermath of this event, something happened that should by no means be passed over in silence. As the knight dismounted to seize Lutgard, one of his followers offered the friendly service of holding his horse. While the virgin Lutgard was thwarting the knight's power, she looked at the stubborn man and cried out, more as a prophecy than a curse, 'With the same hand by which you hold the reins of this hostile knight's horse, you will soon perform deeds that will bring you to ruin in this world'. Now see, reader, how quickly and truly this prediction was fulfilled. For, upon returning home, with the very hand that had held the bridle he killed his own wife, and for this he was banished from his country and deprived of all his goods.

7. How, on her return to Sint-Truiden, she did not yield to shame when the people confronted her

Not long afterwards, she returned from her sister's house to the town of Sint-Truiden, coming on horseback with her servants. A crowd of people bursting with curiosity gathered around her and she began to be wearied by an immense weight of shame, but she immediately called Christ to mind and bravely brought herself under control. Quickly laying her hand to her face, she lifted her veil while saying to Christ, 'For us, O Lord, most innocent of all, for us O most beautiful one, you were despoiled of your garments, bound to a column, and clothed in a purple tunic for the mockery of the raging populace. You were crowned with a wreath of thorns and hung naked on a gibbet. Since I cannot find anything with which to repay you, I offer up to you my modesty, spurned as it has been for your sake.'[36] Wondrous thing! Scarcely had she completed these

---

[36] A neat twist which has a double edge: her modesty had been threatened by the attempted rape and she now throws the same modesty back to the curious crowd, while at the same time offering it to her betrothed, Christ. Note her conscious decision to be a sacrificial victim (*agnes/agnus*). The false charge of rape underlines the contrast between pure and selfless love and the perverse and violent selfishness of rape. Lutgard's conscious acceptance of white martyrdom

words than the throng of people moved away, disturbed by the unveiling of her face.

Upon returning to her monastery, she exulted from that day forth in her progress[37] towards the Lord with even more powerful gifts.

She herself fully revealed all these secrets of her heart to Friar Bernard,[38] a friar of the Order of Preachers and penitentiary to the lord Pope,[39] as well as to me, although he is worthier than I and spiritually more capable of grasping them. I believe, however, that she told me no less fully, even if I am less worthy, as I myself agree — that long before, she had asked the Lord at some time to send her a disgrace through which she might imitate the disgrace of the Lord's Passion as a present experience.

8. How the blessed Virgin comforted her when she was frightened by certain words of the nuns

Set apart for this reason[40] from almost all human speech and consolation, she yearned with all her being for heavenly things.[41] When some jealous nuns slandered her stricter way of life — which they could not imitate — they would say, 'Leave her alone now while her fervour is in full flood. Afterwards, when it has cooled down, you will see her go back with shame to what she now

---

recalls and anticipates the identification with Agnes when she suffers a haemorrhage (I.3 and II.21).

[37] *proficiens*: Lutgard has, through this trial, entered the second stage of her mystic ascent and her soul is finally 'on the move'.

[38] The Bollandist Henschen thinks that Friar Bernard added some texts to Thomas's *vita* after the death in 1254 of Pope Innocent IV (AASS, 16 June, III, p. 187). Private revelations of this kind have always required some kind of external verification by learned critics, and Bernard would have been an impeccable witness in his official role as papal penitentiary.

[39] Innocent IV (1243–54).

[40] *segregata*: this is the first time in the *vita* that the spiritual condition of solitude has been mentioned. Hitherto Lutgard has been surrounded and influenced by other people: her family, her suitors, her sister, her nurse, the nuns, and the hostile crowd. Now, having moved into the second stage, she truly begins her monastic vocation.

[41] *inhiabat*: the yearning desire of the soul for the goal of its pilgrimage. Lutgard now yearns for heavenly things just as she had previously yearned for marriage (I.1).

foolishly[42] condemns.' When Lutgard, in her humility,[43] heard these things, she began to fear for herself[44] lest perhaps those things which the older nuns said about her might happen; and she sighed in her terror. Then the blessed Virgin Mary appeared to her with a joyous countenance and said, 'No, most beloved daughter, it shall not be as you fear. Do not worry about a relapse. With my solicitude protecting you, you will be made firm in salvation. Neither active virtue[45] nor grace will be lessened in you, but both will always daily accumulate and be added to your crown.' O excellent and ineffably embracing promise! While she was sweetly joined to the Lord in prayer or contemplation and any urgent business called her away, she would speak to the Lord with great simplicity and purity of heart as if she spoke familiarly[46] to a friend: 'Lord Jesus, wait for me here, for I shall quickly come back to you.' O what wondrous simplicity in soft persuasion! O the wondrous clemency of the Redeemer towards her! For he demonstrated that he was ready for her 'in every place of his dominion'[47] and in every occupation.

9. How St Catherine appeared to her

About the same time, the most blessed Catherine, protectress and patroness of her monastery, appeared to her in the greatest, most dazzling glory as she wept

---

[42] *stulta*: this is the foolishness of those holy fools who isolate themselves from worldly delights and serve God with a disconcerting literalness. See Saward, *Perfect Fools*, and King, 'The Sacramental Witness'.

[43] This is the first time that Lutgard has been credited with this basic spiritual quality, which the monastic aspirant must have 'if we desire to attain speedily that exaltation in heaven to which we climb by the humility of this present life' (RB 7. 5).

[44] 'The first step of humility, then, is that a man keeps the "fear of God" always "before his eyes" (Psalm 35. 2) and never forgets it' (RB 7. 10).

[45] This has a scholastic ring to it. See Thomas Aquinas: 'sicut peccatum consistit in hoc quod homo contempto Deo, commutabilibus bonis inhaeret, ita meritum virtuosi actus consistit e contrario in hoc quod homo contemptis bonis creatis, Deo inhaeret sicut fini' (*Summa theologiae*, II–II, q. 104).

[46] 'The familiar conversation of Bridegroom and Bride is both the witness and the devotion of a well disposed conscience': William of Saint-Thierry, *Exposition on the Song of Songs*, I.34, p. 28. Thus Thomas introduces the idea of friendship which is so central to this life: a friendship with all, having its origin in the friendship of Bridegroom and Bride.

[47] Psalm 102. 22.

and prayed. Most frightened,[48] she beseeched her to entreat the Lord for her, but St Catherine replied, 'Have confidence, daughter,[49] that the Almighty will always increase his grace in you until, at the summit of your life, you will acquire the most powerful merit among virgins'.

She herself told me these things and many others before her death when I compelled her to it by sacred oath.[50] But, that the word of truth might be confirmed by the mouth of two witnesses,[51] St Catherine appeared to a certain blessed woman and said, 'Seek out Lutgard as a mediator and as your mother, for she will obtain from the Almighty Lord a merit and a place in heaven equal to mine'.

O you nuns of Aywières, see how many merits this woman possessed who lived among you for forty years! Assess how far you have progressed because of her. Consider diligently whether all of you have paid her the reverence she deserves. For I am certain that she will plead for a reward for those who honour her, and pardon for those who have neglected her if they sorrow for it.

10. How she was seen suspended in the air by the whole community

So that even greater things than these[52] may be believed and proven of her, I shall recount in detail a most glorious miracle vouchsafed to several persons. On the holy day of Pentecost, when the nuns were chanting 'Veni Creator Spiritus' in choir, they manifestly saw Lutgard elevated two cubits from the earth into the air.[53] It is no wonder if her body was thus raised from the earth towards heaven, for her soul had already become more exalted than the world and gained possession of heaven, according to the Lord's promise: 'Every place your foot has

---

[48] In this beginning stage, Lutgard alternates between 'grief for the absence of the Bridegroom and joy at his presence'. This is a grief experienced by those 'who, being now converted to the Lord, walk in newness of life': William of Saint-Thierry, *Exposition on the Song of Songs*, I.32, p.26.

[49] Matthew 9. 22.

[50] *Sacramentum* could mean either 'a sacred oath' or the sacrament of penance.

[51] Cf. Deuteronomy 9. 15, VLA I.17 and III.5 below, and VMY 32. [BN]

[52] John 14. 12.

[53] Thus begins a series of mystical phenomena (here, levitation) which Thomas, following hagiographical tradition, uses to give external proof of the promise of the Virgin Mary.

trodden shall become your own.'[54] For with the foot of her affection,[55] she had trodden so far in heaven (which has neither space nor place) that it was given to her to manifest even through the disposition of her body — insofar as it was able — the land wherein she walked in her chaste mind. That is why Lutgard, whose body and soul exulted in the living God,[56] was blessed through so great a miracle.

11. How the brightness of the sun was seen to descend on her during the night

I will add another no less solemn miracle. As the Mother of the Lord had promised, she gave herself more perfectly to the Lord from day to day as a willing sacrifice,[57] afflicting her body with fasts without relaxing her spirit from prayer. But lest the slightest suspicion remain in the hearts of her sisters, who seemed to envy her a little, Christ embellished his bride with a miracle in this wondrous way. It happened one night, while Lutgard had been keeping vigil without interruption, that the nuns saw a heavenly radiance above her, more brilliant than the sun, lasting for a great part of the night.[58] This light, poured inwardly not only into her but also into those who saw it, increased the grace of their spiritual life.

12. How the Lord gave her the grace of healing because she had compassion on the sick, and afterwards the grace of understanding the Psalter; and how still later, having lost these gifts, she begged for the grace of God as long as she lived

Lutgard was so wondrously moved by a spirit of pity for the sick and the weak that, when she was with the afflicted, she was more tormented in spirit

---

[54] Deuteronomy 11. 24; Joshua 1. 3.

[55] The 'foot of the mind' is a patristic commonplace. See, inter alia, Gregory the Great, *Moralia in Iob*, 14, 14, 16, ed. by Marcus Adriaen, in CCSL 143a, p. 707: 'so when gain [with sin] is sought after by one with a covetous view, it is as if the trap which is not seen laid hold of the foot of the mind'. The two feet of the soul are the right foot of the intellect (*apprehensivus*) and the left foot of the will (*affectus*). Cf. VMY 5, p. 168, n. 21.

[56] Psalm 83. 3.

[57] II Kings 24. 24.

[58] Luminosity follows levitation in this list of mystical phenomena, a common occurrence in the lives of ecstatics.

than they were. Therefore God gave her a grace of healing so universal that if there were a spot in anyone's eye or any ailment in the hand, the foot, or other parts of the body, they would at once be cured by contact[59] with her spit or her hand. But when she was overwhelmed by crowds of people who, because of this grace, very often hindered her in her prayers, she said to the Lord, 'Of what use to me is this grace, through which I am so often hindered from dallying with you?[60] Take it away from me, but in such a way that the grace is changed into something better for me.'

The Lord replied, 'What do you want to be given to you in exchange for this grace?' Lutgard said, 'I wish that I might understand the Psalter through which I pray, so that I might be more devout'. And thus it happened, for it has been proven that in that period she understood the Psalter more lucidly since she had been illumined by a more radiant light. Later, however, she discovered that she had not yet made as much progress in this grace as she had expected — for the reverence of a veiled mystery is the mother of devotion, what is hidden is the more avidly sought, and what is concealed is looked upon with more veneration.[61] So she said to the Lord, 'What use is it to me to know the secrets of Scripture — I, an unlettered, uncultivated, and uneducated nun?'[62]

[59] *contractum*: I here follow the reading in the VA, *contactum*.

[60] William of Saint-Thierry says that charitable activity is to be preferred to the consolations of contemplation only when these graces are withdrawn: 'The Bride is forced to awake when she is disturbed in the slumber of contemplation. Sometimes she is pleased to awake from the quiet of her slumber, and sometimes she is not pleased, because in the slumber of contemplation it is given to her to taste solely the charity of truth. This is why she has no wish to be stirred up and called away except when the truth of charity itself calls her away from the contemplation of the loved truth; and then she never refuses the needy work of service' (*Exposition on the Song of Songs*, Finale, p. 139). See also ibid. IV.59. This would explain Lutgard's apparently strange lack of compassion and charity to her neighbours.

[61] See Augustine on that useful and healthful obscurity which 'exercis[es] and sharpen[s], as it were, the minds of the readers [...] and stimulat[es] the desire to learn, concealing their intention in such a way that the minds of the impious are either converted to piety or excluded from the mysteries of the faith' (*On Christian Doctrine*, IV, 8, 22, p. 132).

[62] *idiotae et rusticae et laicae moniali*: Henschen notes that this term does not mean 'lay nun' but rather is used to draw a contrast between 'lettered' nuns like Sibylle de Gages (see II.8 and II.10) and those who, like Lutgard, allegedly could not read. Lutgard was not occupied with domestic chores like lay sisters; she sang in choir (I.19) and was elected prioress (I.20). Thomas emphasizes her illiteracy in II.16 and II.20.

Then the Lord said to her, 'What do you want?' 'I want your heart.' 'No, rather it is I who want your heart',[63] replied the Lord. 'So be it, Lord, on condition that you temper your heart's love to my heart and that I may possess my heart in you. Indeed, with you as my shield, my heart will be secure for all time.'

And so a communion of hearts occurred from that time on, or rather, the union of an uncreated with a created spirit[64] through a surplus of grace.[65] It was this of which the Apostle says: she 'who clings to God is made one spirit with him'.[66]

Pay attention, reader, for I am about to speak marvels. From that day forth, just as a nurse[67] watches over an infant in its cradle with a fan lest the importunate flies disquiet it,[68] so did Christ stand guard at the entrance of her heart so that no temptation of the flesh nor the smallest unclean thought might

---

[63] It is in the VLA that we have the first mention of 'the exchange of hearts', although there is no reference to the formal veneration of the Sacred Heart. The mystical experiences of Mechthild of Hackeborn and Gertrud of Helfta a generation later are, as is well known, remarkably similar to those of Lutgard.

[64] This is the 'unity of spirit' described by Bernard of Clairvaux and William: Bernard, *On the Song of Songs*, Sermon 71, 7-8, trans. by Kilian Walsh and Irene M. Edmonds, 4 vols (Kalamazoo: Cistercian Publications, 1971–80), IV, pp. 53-54; William, *The Golden Epistle*, 2, 10, 235, and 2, 15, 256, trans. by Berkeley, pp. 88, 94.

[65] *excellentiam*: 'excess, surplus, the opposite of *defectus*': *Lexicon of St Thomas Aquinas*, ed. by Roy Deferrari and Sister M. I. Barry, 5 vols (Washington: Catholic University of America Press, 1949), II, p. 387.

[66] I Corinthians 6. 17.

[67] Thus does Christ replace the childhood nurse who, before Lutgard's real conversion, represented security at the end of her flight through the woods. See above, I.5.

[68] See *The Nine Ways of Prayer of St Dominic*, trans. by Simon Tugwell (Dublin: Dominican Publications, 1978), p. 46: 'A curious thing about [the ninth way of prayer] was that he seemed to be brushing away ashes and flies from before his face, and because of this he often defended himself with the sign of the cross'. Tugwell comments: 'This very curious detail seems to refer to some kind of demonic molestation, in view of the explicit connexion between the gesture of brushing away flies and Dominic's making the sign of the cross. The Middle Ages certainly knew about Beelzebub as "the Lord of the Flies", but they do not seem to have taken the flies to be anything more than ordinary flies attracted by the bloody sacrifices associated with the horrible cult of Beelzebub.' See also William of Saint-Thierry, *Meditations*, 3, in *On Contemplating God*, p. 146: 'Idle and troublesome thoughts I drive away like a swarm of unmannerly flies'; and VMO II.50, in *Mary of Oignies*, p. 86: Mary 'set herself against the unclean spirits, not only fighting against them with her prayers but even driving them away with her mantle as though they were flies'.

discompose her mind even for a moment. What is so surprising about this? What is new? For he is the same who said long ago: 'He who touches you touches the apple of my eye.'[69] We are accustomed to take more care of the eyes than the other members of the body. What therefore is new if Christ cared for the soul of the gracious Lutgard, whom he compared[70] to the apple of his eye? I have said less than I ought. Every faithful soul has more worth than the eye of Christ's body, which was darkened in death when, in the Redemption, he offered up his whole body as a sin-offering for the soul.

13. How, when she was troubled by anything, she would be rapt in spirit and suck a wondrous sweetness from the side of the Lord

About the same time, while Lutgard was still most tender in body and age,[71] it happened one night around the time of matins that an intense natural sweat overcame her.[72] She therefore planned in her heart to rest during matins so that afterwards she might be stronger in the service of God, since she presumed that the sweat was helpful for her body. Suddenly a voice cried out to her in this manner: 'Get up quickly! Why are you lying down? You must now do penance for sinners who are lying in their own filth! You must not indulge yourself by sweating in this way!' Alarmed by this voice, she quickly arose and hurried to the church although matins had already begun. There was no delay. Christ came to meet her at the very entrance to the church, all bloody and nailed to the Cross. Lowering his arm which was attached to the Cross, he embraced her who was standing opposite and pressed her mouth against the wound in his right side.[73] There she drank in so much sweetness that, from that time forward, she was always stronger and quicker in the service of God. Those to whom she revealed this event have reported and certified that then and for a long time afterwards the saliva in her mouth tasted mellower than the sweetest honey. What is there

---

[69] Zechariah 2. 8.

[70] *comparavit*: 'compared', but the alternative sense of 'purchased' is suggested by the sentence that follows. [BN]

[71] This might be Thomas's subtle way of saying that Lutgard had not yet reached puberty.

[72] This is the mystical phenomenon called the *incendium amoris* (fire of love).

[73] As noted by Alcantara Mens, *L'Ombrie italienne et l'Ombrie brabançonne: Deux courants religieux parallèles d'inspiration commune* (Paris: Études Franciscaines, 1968), p. 19, n. 30, a very similar vision is reported in the life of St Bernard: *Vita Prima*, 1.7.10 (PL 185:420a)

to wonder in this? 'Your lips, my bride, are a dripping honeycomb.'[74] Thus did her heart inwardly ruminate[75] on the honey of Christ's divinity and the milk of his humanity even when her tongue was silent.

14. How Christ appeared to her nailed to the Cross, and she kissed his wound*

Whenever she was burdened by any disquiet of heart or body, she would stand before an image of the Crucified One. After she had looked at the image with a steady gaze for a long time, her eyes would close, her limbs would sink to the ground, and she would faint like Daniel 'the man of desires',[76] no longer able to stand on her feet.[77] Then, completely rapt in spirit,[78] she would see Christ with the bloody wound in his side and, pressing the mouth of her heart against it, she would suck such sweetness that nothing at all could distress her. Whence it sometimes happened that when she was suffering from an acute fever, as soon as it had reached its critical point she would rise from her bed with no difficulty and enter the community and the choir for chanting.

15. How John the Evangelist appeared to her in the form of an eagle, and what was shown to her by that eagle

Now let us recall that eagle of keenest vision, namely John the Evangelist, 'who drank the streams of the Gospel from the sacred fountain of the Lord's

---

[74] Song of Songs 4. 11.

[75] *ruminatio*: a monastic term for complete physical absorption of the *lectio divina*.

* This chapter heading and that for Ch. 15 are transposed in the AASS edition.

[76] Daniel 9. 23. The emphasis here is on the result of Lutgard's experiential union with Christ and her rumination: her total absorption in him and her consequent understanding. This kind of understanding is utterly unlike what she had expected to receive from an exegetical reading of Scripture.

[77] The Bride 'faints after God's salvation' (William of Saint-Thierry, *Exposition on the Song of Songs*, I.35, p. 28). In the first stage, the Bride 'strives to do more than she can and endeavours to accomplish, as if by one single exertion of love, whatever God wills. But fainting after God's salvation, she languishes until, after additional progress and blessed advance, the King sets in order charity in her' (ibid. I.130, p. 103).

[78] This is the first time that the word *rapio* has been used in this sense, the meaning no longer ambiguous as it was in I.5.

breast'.[79] An eagle[80] appeared to her in the spirit, his wings brightly shining with such lustre that all the universe could have been enlightened by the dazzling clarity of its rays. She was so astonished at this vision — with a wonderment exceeding any words to describe it — that she had to wait until the Lord tempered the glory of so great a spectacle to the capacity of her weak sight.[81] And so it happened. When the mode of the vision had been moderated, she saw in contemplation that the eagle was placing its beak in her mouth and filling her soul with flashes of such ineffable light that no secrets of divinity lay hidden from her insofar as it is possible for mortals to know them,[82] for as it was said to Moses, 'No human shall see me and live'.[83] For the more abundantly she drank from the torrent of pleasure in the house of God,[84] the more magnificently the eagle found the capacity of her heart increased by her desire.

Concerning this matter I have unerring testimony to her, as I hope in all conscience. Although she seemed and indeed was rather uncultivated and very simple in common speech, yet in private spiritual conversations, never from anyone's lips have I heard more genuine, more ardent, or more decisive words in accord with the spirit of truth — to such an extent that I often accounted myself to be quite uncultivated and dull in my understanding of her speech. I still remember the place and time when, I confess, I was so astonished by the subtlety of her words that, had that sweet and ineffable wonderment held me any

[79] Gregorian Sacramentary, Feast of St John the Evangelist, Preface (PL 80:34), 27 December, matins, first nocturn, second responsory: 'Fluenta evangelii de ipso sacro Dominici pectoris fonte potavit'; cf. the Octave of the Feast of St John, second nocturn, I.5. Hendrix refers to the *Breviarium Cisterciense*, In festo S. Joannis Apost. et Evang., Lectio XI (Guido Hendrix, 'Primitive Versions of Thomas of Cantimpré's *Vita Lutgardis*', *Cîteaux*, 29 (1978), 153–206 (p. 180).

[80] The traditional symbol of St John and of contemplation. Cf. VMO II.81, in *Mary of Oignies*, p. 106: 'her soul chose suspension [from all worldliness] because it often flew higher for whole days at a time and she gazed on the sun of justice like an eagle, not cast back down below by the rays of the sun'.

[81] *secundum capacitatem debilis acie [...] temperet*: a reference to the fact that she is still a progressant in the ascent to perfection. In I.2 she was able to see Christ (*in ipsa forma humanitatis*) with no difficulty; in III.9 Christ has become too dazzling for her sight. She is here in the middle stage.

[82] Here Thomas draws an implicit contrast between infused understanding and understanding acquired through formal study; cf. I.12 and II.16.

[83] Exodus 33. 20.

[84] Psalm 35. 9.

longer, it would either have rendered me mad or utterly destroyed me. Yet this did not happen at the time about which I am writing, but about sixteen years before her death.

16. How it seemed to her that her hands dripped oil

There is in Haspengauw[85] a town called Loon. Next to the church of this town lived a recluse[86] serving God, a very close friend of the gracious Lutgard because of the merit of her life. Once when she had been staying with this woman for a fortnight, it happened that after contemplative prayer, she was so filled with spiritual sweetness that she called the recluse and showed her the fingers of her hand. Squeezing them, she said, 'Look, sister, how the Almighty deals with me! I am so filled up inwardly by his superabundant grace that now even my fingers are outwardly dripping a kind of oil as a manifestation of grace.'[87] Saying this as if she were drunk[88] — and indeed she was drunk — she danced around the reclusorium with wondrous gestures.[89] What is so marvellous about this? Invited by the bridegroom, she had been 'led into the wine-cellar'.[90]

---

[85] Hesbaye, Haspengauw: a province of Brabant, now in Limburg.

[86] This recluse was probably Jutta of Borgloon, whom Thomas knew and with whom Christina lived for nine years (VCM 38).

[87] A clear reference to Song of Songs 5. 5: 'Manus meae stillaverunt myrrham et digiti mei pleni myrrha probatissima' ('My hands dropped with myrrh, and my fingers were full of the choicest myrrh'). This visible sign of an invisible grace is paralleled in the VCM when Christina's breasts drip a kind of oil (VCM 19). This would seem to be 'the oil of gladness' (Psalm 44. 8), 'the unction of the Holy Spirit which teaches, the taste of divine sweetness, the perfume of eternity, the powerful experience of the spiritual senses' (William of Saint-Thierry, *Exposition on the Song of Songs*, III.47, p. 138).

[88] Spiritual inebriation is another mystical phenomenon with its roots in the monastic fathers and is found everywhere in the vitae of the Flemish mothers: VMO I.20; I.22; II.87, in *Mary of Oignies*, pp. 59–60, 110 ; VCM 16, 36.

[89] *tripudium*, translated by DuCange as 'jubilation', is that dance to which many of the beguines were driven as a result of a mystic experience, the physical equivalent to the mystical song called a *jubilus*: 'The mystical jubilus denotes the state of exultation, the experience of an extreme and most intensive feeling of joy [...]. During the twelfth and thirteenth centuries, the concept of jubilus came to signify the high point of an ineffable mystical experience and of ecstasy' (Lewis, 'The Mystical Jubilus', pp. 237–47. Cf. VCM 35).

[90] Song of Songs 2. 3. See William of Saint-Thierry, *Exposition on the Song of Songs* I, 37; I, 130; I, 120, p. 96: 'The Bride therefore is led into the house of wine, into the joy of her Lord and

After she had eaten the bread of penance with toil, like one beloved, and drunk the abundance of his grace, like one more beloved, at last she became drunk, like one most beloved.[91] And thus, exceeding the measure of fools, she rejoiced ineffably in the spirit.

17. How she was consecrated, and how it seemed to two witnesses that a golden crown was placed on her head

Then she began to yearn[92] to be more perfectly joined to her only husband,[93] Christ the Lord, through the ceremony of consecration at the hands of a bishop. An occasion was granted when Lord Huard, the bishop of Liège,[94] decided to consecrate a great number of nuns who had gathered there. Lutgard was therefore led to the assembly of virgins for her consecration. While the aforesaid bishop was fastening the wreath[95] made out of linen on their heads in token of a golden crown, he reached Lutgard in due turn. A certain holy and simple man who was standing nearby saw the bishop quite clearly place a huge golden crown on Lutgard's head, honouring her uniquely above the rest. Assuming that this had been seen by everyone, he asked the assisting priest why the bishop had placed the golden crown on Lady Lutgard alone. Knowing nothing of this, the priest jeered and said, 'Are your eyes inside out that you call it a golden crown, when everyone here can see that it is linen?' The blessed man fell silent but smiled, for he knew of Lutgard's unparalleled merit. In fact there are two witnesses to the truth of this event, for a nun who had been consecrated saw this as well. Still greater wonders followed upon these wonders!

Bridegroom; but at the first experiences of this blessing, impatient of measure and reason, from an abundance of wine she abandons order and yields to the inebriation of exceeding fervour and the languor of human weakness, fainting after God's salvation'.

[91] Here Thomas is referring to the three steps of mystical perfection: (1) beginning *ut cara*; (2) progressing *ut carior*; (3) perfect *ut carissima*.

[92] *anhelare*: the sense is of panting for something ('to draw the breath with great difficulty').

[93] This is the first explicit reference to the mystical marriage which, however, has been foreshadowed by the early references to betrothal.

[94] An error for Hugh of Pierrepont, who was bishop of Liège from 1200–27 and archbishop from 1227–29.

[95] *sertum*: the feminine equivalent to a tonsure. The same word is used for Christ's crown of thorns when Lutgard offers herself as a sacrificial victim before the jeering crowd (I.7).

18. How perfectly she followed Christ the Lamb

Thereafter, clinging more perfectly to her Bridegroom, she 'followed the Lamb wherever he went'.[96] If I were preaching about the humble way of Christ, then you would see it followed by the humble Lutgard, whom pride never provoked.[97] If I were contemplating the way of poverty, then you would understand that Lutgard was so poor she never thought about her daily bread, yet daily toiled with her hands. If I considered the way of Christ in mercy and pity, I have never seen anyone more merciful than Lutgard in this life. If I proclaimed the way of Christ in tribulation, then you should think of Lutgard wearing herself out in fasts and afflictions, which I will show that she practised throughout her life more thoroughly than all the men and women of our age. If I were to venerate Christ's path to glory, I should extol Lutgard beyond compare, for her 'homeland was in heaven',[98] as will be seen in what follows. In all these things, both Peter and Mary Magdalene followed the Lamb most perfectly, but not 'wherever he went'.[99] Lutgard, on the other hand, with the company of virgin disciples, followed the Lamb on that way of incorruption that he was the first to travel.

19. How Christ appeared to her in the form of a lamb and applauded her while she was singing

Since I have said that Lutgard followed the Lamb everywhere, now you will see how the Lamb repaid her. It is the custom of the bridegroom to repay his bride in his turn, but see in what measure he made recompense. In the monastery of St Catherine, every Friday the first vespers of the following Saturday was fittingly set aside for the veneration of the most blessed Virgin Mary. When the verse for the responsory was chanted (a verse that Lutgard

---

[96] Revelation 14. 4.

[97] Thomas states that it was he who preached these virtues; the VA simply speaks of 'the way of humility and poverty, mercy and graciousness, tribulation and incorruption'.

[98] Philippians 3. 20.

[99] Revelation 14. 4. Thomas's unfavourable comparison between Lutgard and Peter is explained in II.42. Peter, unlike Lutgard, had betrayed Christ when put to a public test. Mary Magdalene, of course, had been a habitual public sinner whose sins of the flesh contrasted with Lutgard's determination to preserve her virginal innocence in the face of great trial.

usually sang solo for the sake of devotion),[100] it sometimes seemed to her as she was singing that Christ, in the form of a lamb, positioned himself on her breast so that one foot was on her right shoulder and the other on her left. He would place his mouth on hers and by thus sucking, drew out from her breast a melody of wondrous mellowness. Nor could anyone doubt that a divine miracle took place in this chanting, for in that verse alone her voice was heard to be infinitely more gracious than usual, and by it the hearts of all who heard her were marvellously stirred to devotion.[101]

20. How she was made prioress in the monastery of St Catherine

Then, since it was not fitting for such a lamp to be concealed under a bushel, she was placed upon a lampstand[102] so that the resplendence of her grace might appear to all. She was therefore unanimously elected superior, that is prioress, of the handmaids of God in the monastery of St Catherine, for they were not accustomed to have an abbess. But since she considered that a most grave injury had been done to her by this action, from that moment on she determined to change her location and her profession.

21. How Christ placed his hand between her and a certain abbot when she suffered the violence of his kiss, and how religious women should flee far from the kisses of men

It was during this time that the abbot of Sint-Truiden, who was the spiritual father of St Catherine's monastery,[103] returned from the General Lateran Council

---

[100] The verse is 'Diffusa est gratia in labiis tuis', followed by the response 'Propterea benedixit te Deus in aeternum' ('Grace is poured out on your lips'. — 'Therefore God has blessed you forever'.) [BN]

[101] Most of the *mulieres sanctae* sang in some wondrous manner. See, for instance, Mary who sang ceaselessly before her death (VMO II.98–99, in *Mary of Oignies*, pp. 119–20) and Christina (VCM 34–36).

[102] Matthew 5. 15.

[103] Christianus (Chrétien de Stapel) was elected abbot of the Benedictine abbey at Sint-Truiden in 1193. He took part in the Lateran Council in 1215 and died in 1222. As J.-B. Lefèvre notes, this anecdote is historically impossible, since Lutgard had left St Catherine's in 1206, nine years before Fourth Lateran: 'Sainte Lutgarde', p. 305. According to the Bollandists, Christianus was himself the subject of a hagiographic *vita*, and his body was

and was welcomed by the nuns in procession. After he had said his prayers in the church, he summoned the whole community to chapter and, as is the less cautious habit among the simple, he gave a kiss to each. When he came to the prioress Lutgard that she might give the abbot a kiss, she firmly refused. But since everyone was joking about this and pushing her forward with their hands, she suffered and bore with the violence. The most courteous[104] Jesus, however, placed the hand of his mercy between them so that she did not feel the taint of even the first carnal stirring in the man's kiss.

Alas! May that contemporary devotion, more disgraceful than blind, blush for shame whereby men 'who have the outward appearance of piety'[105] think they can kiss women and virgins with impunity, without offending divine grace and law. They take as defence for their error a saying of the blessed apostle Paul where, writing to the Corinthians, he said, 'Greet one another with a holy kiss'.[106] But, to be sure, these words should not be taken to mean that men should kiss women. According to Augustine, in the kiss of holy peace men may kiss men and women may kiss women. Otherwise, this most circumspect preacher of chastity would have given a most manifest occasion for unchastity. Therefore he said in another place, 'Abstain from the outward appearance of every kind of evil'.[107]

Is it not the outward appearance of evil when corruption of souls follows through the contact of bodies? And is it the corruption of minds alone or of bodies as well? I am sure that if this becomes habitual, bodies too will be corrupted. If in his Rule for canons, Augustine, the greatest doctor of the Church, forbids anyone to look fixedly at another and instructs that for this reason a person can be expelled from the monastic community[108] (for one can be corrupted in mind this way, even though he be far removed from a woman), what kind of punishment would Augustine have decreed for those who conceive

---

found to be incorrupt in 1557. [BN]

[104] *summae benignitatis.*

[105] II Timothy 3. 5.

[106] II Corinthians 13. 12.

[107] I Thessalonians 5. 22.

[108] *Rule of St Augustine*, IV.4: 'When you see a woman, do not keep provocatively looking at her. […] For it is not only by affectionate embraces that desire between man and woman is awakened, but also by looks': *The Rule of St Augustine: Masculine and Feminine Versions*, intro. and commentary by T. J. Van Bavel, trans. by Raymond Canning (London: Darton, Longman & Todd, 1984), p. 16. See IV.9 on dismissal as the penalty for disobedience.

the incentive of filth through the kisses of women, in which there is an actual contact of bodies? In his book *On the Nature of Things*, Pliny says that the fish who sees defectively[109] bites into baited fish-hooks by mistake. This example designates those who shun the act of fornication itself as the fish-hook, but snatch at the soft touch of pleasure as the bait.[110] While they despise the filth of adultery as though they were lovers of chastity, yet they fall into something even graver through kisses and illicit touchings. Wherefore Paul says of such people, 'God delivered them up to a reprobate sense to do things which are not fitting'.[111] Thus by a true judgement I consider such people more shameful than fornicators. By this they blaspheme against the Holy Spirit[112] in that they pretend to love chastity when they are, in fact, enemies of chastity.

Do you then, virgin, whether you are a bride of Christ or any woman who loves chastity, flee such things as Lutgard did. Abhor debasement! If anyone wishes to solicit you as it were to a holy kiss, if anyone tries to put his hand on your breast, your bosom, or any other part of your body, give him spittle instead of a kiss and let your fist meet his groping hand. Nor should you defer to any cleric or person of rank in such matters, because it is just as lawful to protect the chastity of the mind as the life of the body, even with a beating. Look upon such a one not as a servant of Christ, but of Satan; not spiritual but animal; not a follower of modesty, but indeed the vilest lickspittle.

22. How she moved from the Order of St Benedict to the Cistercian Order

The excellent Lutgard was a nun in the convent of St Catherine for about twelve years. At that time there was in the diocese of Liège a master called John of Liroux,[113] a man distinguished in every kind of holiness. Knowing of this

---

[109] reading *glaucius* for *claucius*.

[110] Pliny the Elder, *Naturalis historia*, IX, 23, 56, ed. and trans. by Rackham and Jones, III, pp. 200–01, which Thomas reproduces again in his DNR VII.20, pp. 257–58: 'Clautius qui glanis vocatur, sicut dicit Plinius, aversus mordet inescatos hamos nec devorat eos, sed despoliando grassatur. Hic piscis signat eos, qui et si aperte fornicationis vitium fugiunt, ne forte proventure prolis indicio capiantur, tamen ipsis circumstantiis fornicationum, sicut sunt oscula, confabulationes illicite et sceleratissime contrectationes, impudentissime polluuntur.'

[111] Romans 1. 28.

[112] Mark 3. 29.

[113] Roisin (*L'Hagiographie cistercienne*, p. 51, n. 1), following Albertus van Roy, *Lutgardis van Tongeren* (Brugge: De Kinkhoren, 1946), considers that the native city of this John was Lierre

blessed woman's most perfect plan, he advised her to leave behind both her house and the office of prioress and to pass over[114] to the Cistercian monastery of Aywières. When she excused herself on the ground that the French nuns there spoke a different language, saying she would prefer to enter another monastery of the same order — Herkenrode,[115] where Flemish is spoken — the Lord said to her, 'I wish you to go to Aywières in the end, and unless you do, I shall desert you'.

Moreover, a most blessed virgin called Christina,[116] whom the venerable James of Vitry mentioned in his *Life of Mary of Oignies* and whose life I also wrote, came to her divinely compelled in the spirit[117] and exclaimed: 'Why do you hesitate to fulfil what a divine instinct commands you to do?' When, as I said before, Lutgard objected on the ground of language difference — reasonably enough, from a human point of view — the inspired Christina at once replied, 'I would rather be in hell with God than in heaven with the angels without God'. To be sure, she replied beautifully and worthily. For wherever Christ is, there is paradise — since Truth, who could not lie, said to the thief on the cross, 'Today you will be with me in paradise'.[118] It is established that on that day the soul of Christ by no means ascended either to the empyrean or to the earthly paradise, but descended to hell with his divinity, and with him went the soul of the thief, who he had foretold would be with him. Thereby he proved, by a

(Liroux) and that he was the preacher mentioned by James of Vitry in his *Historia orientalis et occidentalis*, II.9, ed. by Franciscus Moschus (Douai: [n. pub], 1597), pp. 288–90. See also Alfred Deboutte, 'Sint Lutgart en Magister Johannes de Liro', *Sinte Lutgart Schutsvrouwe van Vlaanderen*, 18 (1976), 46–53.

[114] *transiret*: to pass over in the sense of passing over to paradise.

[115] Herkenrode is situated in the territory of the commune of Kuringen (province of Limburg and canton of Hasselt) and, according to tradition, was founded in 1182 by Gerard, Count of Loon. In 1217 it was officially incorporated into the Cistercian Order and was the first Cistercian convent in Belgium. Like St Catherine's and Moustier-sur-Sambre, it only accepted aristocratic women and displayed this class consciousness by wearing a habit different from that imposed by the Cistercian Order. See *Abbayes de Belgique: Guide*, ed. by Léon Dewincklear (Brussels: Services interbancaires, 1973), pp. 445–57, and C. Opsomer, 'Abbaye de Herkenrode à Curange' in MB 6, Province de Limburg (1976), pp. 1316–59.

[116] Note that Christina is called *beatissima*, not just *beata*. Her *Life*, of course, is the VCM and James mentions her in the VMO Prologue, 8, in *Mary of Oignies*, pp. 48–49.

[117] *spiritu compulsa divinitus*: Thomas here uses the same ambiguous language for Christina's 'spirit possession' as in the VCM. [BN]

[118] Luke 23. 43.

necessary a priori argument,[119] that paradise is wherever he himself is. For the presence of Christ renders every place, no matter how hateful, supremely delightful and remarkably desirable. Granted that hell cannot simply be equated with paradise, Christina's reply must nevertheless be approved. For it is far preferable to be in any place whatsoever with the supreme and uncreated Good than to be in a place, no matter how good — even the earthly or heavenly paradise — with any created good.[120]

Confirmed by Christina's words, therefore, the gracious Lutgard worthily offered herself, prepared for whatever might come. Nor was it difficult to persuade her to do anything that might suggest a more holy and perfect life. Therefore, obeying the advice of the aforementioned Master John, she passed over to the Cistercian monastery of Aywières in the duchy of Brabant, in all tranquility of mind.

Hearing of this, the nuns of St Catherine's grieved inconsolably, but when Lutgard discovered their sorrow, she showed compassion on their tribulations. While she was supplicating the Lord for their peace, the glorious Virgin Mary, the most sweet consoler, appeared to her. She congratulated her on having entered a house and an order especially dedicated to her, but promised that with her prayers, she would advance the spiritual and temporal well-being of the house for which Lutgard was pleading. Without doubt we see this up to the present day in the house of St Catherine, for while almost everywhere else the discipline of that order has grown tepid, that monastery has flourished in virtue and increased in temporal goods more richly than ever before. Yet I counsel you, O nuns of St Catherine's, that you still importune your mother on your behalf, that she may continue to do for you in heaven what she once did here on earth.

Here let the first book on the gracious Lutgard's deeds in the Order of St Benedict come to an end, that we may proceed more expeditiously to the second book.

---

[119] In Thomas Aquinas, *locus* is a synonym for *argumentum*, a quotation adduced for the sake of proof, and the term *locus a causa* means a proof deduced from the cause or an a priori proof: *Lexicon of St Thomas Aquinas*, ed. by Deferrari and Barry, III, pp. 644–45.

[120] Thus does Thomas try to extricate the Flemish-speaking Lutgard from the impolite equation of Flanders with paradise and France with hell!

1. How the blessed Virgin Mary appeared to her when she feared that she might be chosen abbess, and how she was miraculously unable to learn French

Thus the fame of the blessed Lutgard's virtues expanded everywhere. During this period new monasteries were beginning to be built in the French-speaking districts, and several of them longed to have Lutgard as abbess had she learned even a little French. When the gracious Lutgard learned of this, she was horrified and, turning to the glorious Virgin Mary, tearfully entreated her to avert this from her. The blessed Mother appeared to her and said, 'Do not worry at all about this because I will set the shield of my protection before you'. See, O reader, how this fate was averted, and you will see the pure truth of the one who replied. Lutgard was barely twenty-four years old when she entered Aywières and yet, in the forty years she lived among French-speaking companions, she could barely learn more French than she needed to ask for bread correctly when she was hungry. Since this was known by everyone, the beloved fawn of Christ was permitted to rest in the sleep of contemplation.[121] No one aroused her, no one awakened her for pastoral cares unless she herself wished it,[122] and it never happened that she so wished.

[121] Song of Songs 2. 9; 2. 17; 4. 5; 8. 14. Cf. VMY 14.
[122] Song of Songs 2. 7; 3. 5; 8. 4.

2. How the blessed Virgin bewailed the cruelty of the Albigensians, and on this account she was commanded to fast on bread and beer for seven years without respite to propitiate the Lord for his people

When the most grievous plague of the Albigensian heretics was threatening, the blessed Virgin Mary appeared to her with a dispirited countenance and a gloomy face.[123] Lutgard was filled with compassion for her in this vision and asked her, with a mighty howl of her heart and voice, 'What is the matter, most gracious lady, that your face, full of all graciousness, has become so frowzy[124]and wan?' And the blessed Virgin said, 'Behold, once again my Son is being crucified by heretics and bad Christians; once again he is spat upon. You then must take up a lament and fast continuously for seven years to appease the anger of my Son, which is now threatening everywhere on the face of the earth.'

Therefore from that time onward for seven years, Lutgard continuously fasted on bread and beer alone. And see the magnitude of the miracle! She was often compelled by obedience and tried to take some food into her mouth, yet nothing even as small as a bean could pass through her throat. Although she constantly toiled in this wondrous and incredible abstinence, nevertheless she rejoiced when the community had some better kind of food.[125] In this regard, she used to say that she felt better for a whole month when the community had an abundance of alms. For she knew that what the divine goodness had bestowed upon her as an individual gift for the remedy of many, and as a token of grace, could not be shared in common with all. I say this against those 'who make toil into a precept',[126] ordaining that what they themselves have been able to observe without harm — either by the help of grace or by natural disposition — must be observed in common by all. As for Lutgard, the longer she continued her fast, the stronger she was in body and heart.

---

[123] The Albigensian Crusade (1209–29) was a protracted war launched by the papacy and, eventually, the French monarchy against the Cathars (or Albigensians) of Languedoc. James of Vitry preached the crusade in 1210–11. In 1216 the Dominicans took over anti-Cathar conversion efforts from the Cistercians, and it may have been at this time that Lutgard was asked to intercede. [BN]

[124] *squalleat.*

[125] On the conjunction of extreme fasting, eucharistic feasting, and charitable feeding in women's piety see Bynum, *Holy Feast and Holy Fast.* [BN]

[126] Psalm 93. 20.

3. How she delivered Master James of Vitry from a certain very grave temptation

When Master James of Vitry[127] had received the grace of preaching through the prayers of the venerable Mary of Oignies, as he himself recounts in the book of her life, it happened that he loved a certain religious woman who was languishing in bed, not lustfully but with an all too human love. Keenly intent on consoling this woman, he became indolent and laid aside his office of preaching. So Lutgard, sensing in her spirit the fetters of his heart and the deceit of the devil, approached the Lord with many tears to intercede for him. When she did not make progress in her praying, she accused the Lord of cruelty, but the Lord replied, 'The man for whom you entreat is striving against your prayers'. Saying this, the Lord deferred the fulfillment of what she asked. When Lutgard saw this, she grew impatient and cried out to the Lord with a mighty voice, 'What are you doing, O most just and courteous Lord? Either separate me from yourself or liberate that man for whom I pray, even if he is not willing.' Wondrous event! There was no delay between her plea and its result. Utterly and immediately set free, he blessed his divine Liberator and his handmaid. For only after his deliverance did he sense with open eyes the danger he had been unable to see before, blinded as he was by human love. Not long afterward, the venerable James was elected to the bishopric of Acre over the sea.[128]

4. How she delivered a certain Simon, Abbot of Foigny, from purgatory by praying to God with great violence

At about the same time a certain Simon, a nobleman born in Germany[129] and very highly qualified in letters, entered the Cistercian Order and later was made

---

[127] James of Vitry (1160/70–1240), born into a noble family at Reims, studied in Paris and was drawn to the diocese of Liège by the fame of Mary of Oignies (VMO-S 1–2, pp. 140–41). It was Mary who, in a sense, converted him from an institutional Christian into one who burned with apostolic zeal. After a brief return to Paris to finish his studies, he was ordained in 1210 and celebrated his first mass in the church of St Nicholas at Oignies. In letters he wrote to Lutgard and to the convent of Aywières which are still extant, he calls Lutgard his 'most spiritual friend' (*amice sue spiritualissime*): *Lettres de Jacques de Vitry*, p. 79.

[128] James was elected bishop of Acre in Palestine in 1216 and made a cardinal in 1229.

[129] *Teutonia*. The Old French version has *un noble et docte homme flamang:* 'a noble and learned Flemish man'.

Abbot of Foigny.[130] Although he was fervent in desire, he was driven by a bitter zeal towards his subjects and was overtaken by a premature death. He had greatly loved the gracious Lutgard because of the holiness of her life and left her grievously disturbed by his death. At once performing mortifications and fasts for him, she pleaded with the Lord that he liberate the soul of the dead man. After she had insisted with many prayers, the Lord replied to her, 'Be consoled because, on account of the favour in which I hold you, I will be good to him for whom you pray'. Yet she insisted the more importunately and received a reply for the second time that the man would soon be set free. And she said, 'Whatever comfort you are willing to give me, grant to his soul in purgatory'. And she added, 'By no means will I desist from sobbing, Lord, nor will I ever be consoled by your promises, unless I see that the one for whom I pray has been liberated'. The Lord did not suffer her to be disturbed any longer and appeared to her in person, leading with him the soul which had been liberated from purgatory and saying, 'Be consoled, beloved, for behold, here is the soul for whom you pray'. No sooner had he said this than Lutgard prostrated herself and blessed the Lord for the liberation of that soul. And the soul, exulting and praising God,[131] rendered thanks to Lutgard and, passing over to a better state, penetrated the heights of heaven with great glory.

Simon frequently appeared to the gracious Lutgard afterwards and, among other things, told her that he would have spent forty years in purgatory had not her prayer helped him before the merciful Lord.[132]

---

[130] Simon was prior of Foigny, the Cistercian abbey at Thiérache, and later abbot. He was a German nobleman and the brother of Otto, Bishop of Osnabrück.

[131] Cf. Isaiah 35. 2.

[132] An elaboration of the same vision can be found in Brussels, Bibliothèque Royale MS 8609–20: 'But the venerable Otto, bishop of Osnabrück and blood brother of the same Simon, told Friar Bernard the same thing: it was shown to a certain religious person in the monastery of Werslo that the above-mentioned Simon would have remained in purgatory for forty years because of his zeal for souls, had not the virgin of Christ liberated him by her insistent prayers. This wonderful truth was confirmed — as in the case of other prayers — when it was established by the testimony of two witnesses' ('Sed venerabilis Ottho Osnaburgensis episcopus uterinus frater ejusdem Symonis fratri Bernardo retulit hoc idem: cuidam religiosae personae in Werslo monasterio ostensum fuisse, quod dictus Symon propter animarum zelum quadraginta annis in purgatorio perstitisset, nisi cum virgo Christi precum instantia liberasset; et in hoc quoque sicut in aliis precibus mira veritas patuit, cum in ore duorum veritatis testimonium stetit'). See 'Supplément à l'édition de la Vita Lutgardis', *Catalogus codicum hagiographicorum Bibliothecae Regiae Bruxellensis*, 2 vols (Brussels: Polleunis, Ceuterick & Lefébure, 1886–89), II, p. 220.

5. How she wanted to be reassured about the state of her soul and, for her consolation, a splendid youth appeared in the sight of all

Lutgard was also humbly esteemed for the spirit of fear of the Lord, for she feared the Lord 'as waves swelling over her'[133] and 'she feared all her works'[134] as if they had been done in a questionable way. Therefore for a long time she wailed and implored the Lord daily, begging him to give her certainty in the present life. Having remained in this desire for a long while, one day she heard a voice saying to her quite plainly, 'Be secure now, dearest one, because your life is pleasing to the Lord'. So the gracious Lutgard was exultant for a time, but soon began to tremble with fear again. Once more the divine voice said to her, 'Do you want to have Marie de Raive[135] as a witness of your security?' And she said, 'No, she is too timid and, through her anxiety, would delay revealing to me what she had found out'. The divine voice said to her, 'In the meantime, dearest, be at rest. Soon you will be made manifestly and perfectly secure.'

Scarcely four days had passed when, behold, a man of striking appearance who was unknown to everyone entered the parlour where the nuns were sitting together. He briefly greeted them all and requested that Lutgard be quickly fetched. When she came, he greeted her and said, in the hearing of all, 'The Almighty commands you: henceforth you are to live secure, because the Lord is well pleased in you.' Saying this, the young man immediately disappeared before anyone could inquire whence he had come or who he was.

Not long afterwards a certain man of most holy life received a divine revelation, came to Aywières, and confirmed her in the aforesaid consolations.

6. How she wanted to die and the wounds of Christ appeared to her, crying out to her for sinners

As a result of this, she desired even more fervently to die and pass over to the eternal, and her eyes daily poured out tears to the Lord.[136] And behold, hastening to relieve her cries, the Lord appeared to her and displayed the wounds in his

---

[133] Job 31. 23.

[134] Job 9. 28.

[135] Marie de Raive or Roavia was the first prioress of Aywières and a sister or relative of Beatrice de Raive. See below, III.23.

[136] Job 16. 21.

hands, feet, and side. He said, 'Behold and contemplate, dearest, that my wounds are calling out to you, lest in vain I shed my blood, lest in vain I endured death'. Seeing and hearing this, Lutgard was wonderfully alarmed and, with fear and trembling, she asked what the cry of Christ's wounds might be. She was answered, 'By your toil and your weeping you will mitigate the enkindled wrath of the Father, so that he may not destroy sinners in death, but rather, through the mercy of God, "they may be converted and live"'.[137]

7. How Pope Innocent III appeared to her just after his death

About this time the lord Pope Innocent III travelled[138] from this life after the celebrated Lateran Council.[139] With no delay after his death, the same pope visibly appeared to the gracious Lutgard. When she saw that the apparition was surrounded by an enormous flame, she asked who it was and he said, 'I am Pope Innocent'. With a groan, she asked, 'How is it that you, the father of us all, are being tortured with such great pain?' He told her, 'There are three reasons why I am thus tortured, and because of them I was most worthy to be handed over to eternal torment. But through the intercession of the most gracious Virgin Mary, for whom I built a monastery, I repented at the end and escaped eternal death. Yet I will be tortured by the most atrocious punishments until the day of the Last Judgement. The Mother of mercy, however, obtained this for me from her Son, that I was able to come to you to ask for your suffrages.' When he had said this, he quickly disappeared. Lutgard told her sisters about the death and the need of the deceased so they could come to his aid. She herself had compassion on so great a punishment[140] and afflicted herself with wondrous pain for the one who appeared to her.

Note well, reader, that Lutgard revealed these three reasons to me, but I will shroud them over out of reverence for so great a pontiff.[141]

---

[137] Ezekiel 18. 23; 33. 11.

[138] *migravit*: note that Innocent III only 'migrates', whereas Lutgard wanted to 'transmigrate'; i.e. she wanted to travel across to paradise.

[139] Innocent III died on 16 July 1216, shortly after the Fourth Lateran Council ended.

[140] *piaculum*: atonement or a crime which demands ceremonial expiation and, metonymically, punishment.

[141] Knowledge of these three things presumably died with Lutgard and Thomas. Probably one of them was the role played by Innocent in the prohibition of new orders.

8. How Master John of Liroux appeared to her immediately after his death, and what Christ said to her while she was lamenting his death

A vision similar in kind but much different in consequence appeared to Lutgard about the same time. The venerable John of Liroux, who has been mentioned before,[142] had made a pact with Lutgard while he was still living that whoever departed the world first should appear after death to the survivor. Thus, as John was on his way to the Roman Curia on business involving religious women, who were being troubled throughout Brabant by the envious,[143] he died while crossing the Alps. At the very moment of his death, he visibly appeared to Lutgard, who was standing in the cloister. Believing him to be alive, she beckoned to him with her hand to enter the parlor where, according to the monastic rule, they could speak. He said to her, 'I have died and passed from this world, but I have appeared to you as a dead man to fulfil the truth of God which we agreed upon in our pact'.

She immediately prostrated herself on the ground and inquired, 'What does the triple vestment you are wearing signify, you who have obtained such great glory?' He said, 'The snow-white vestment signifies the innocence of my virginal flesh, which I kept unstained from the womb. The red colour fittingly shows forth the labours and sufferings I endured for a long time for justice and truth, through which I was brought to my death. The blue colour of my outermost garment signifies the perfection of the spiritual life.' Saying this, he vanished from her wondering eyes. She reported the vision and the death of Master John to his sister in the flesh and the other nuns.

Nevertheless, the gracious Lutgard wept that this venerable man had been taken from her, even though he had been given to God. The Lord replied to her grief with these words: 'Why are you weeping, Lutgard? And wherefore is your heart afflicted? Am I not more precious to you than ten sons?'[144] As an unlettered

---

[142] See I.22.

[143] James himself performed the same kind of worthy act on behalf of the *mulieres religiosae* and, indeed, his life is another instance of clerical efforts to establish their credentials. That they were given a hard time is confirmed by James in his prologue to the VMO: 'You have seen and marvelled at those shameless men [...] who, hostile to all religion, maliciously slandered the religious life of these women and, like mad dogs, railed against customs which were contrary to theirs' (Prologue, 4, in *Mary of Oignies*, p. 43).

[144] I Samuel I. 8. Henschen points out that these words of Elcana to his wife Anna, who had been weeping for her sterility, are fittingly placed in the mouth of Lutgard who was weeping for her spiritual son (AASS, 16 June, III, p. 199).

nun, she did not understand these words, but when she heard them translated, she no longer grieved for the deceased, but fully blessed the Lord for his death.

9. How it was revealed to her a second time that she should fast another seven years for sinners, and just as Christ daily offered himself to the Father for sinners in the sacrifice of the Eucharist, she too should offer herself to Christ

At the end of the seven years during which she fasted on bread and beer, it was again revealed to her that she should fast for sinners everywhere. She gladly accepted this and fasted seven more years, this time on bread and vegetables. Then the Lord gave her another vision and, rapt in spirit, she saw Jesus, the prince of our salvation, with his wounds blood-red as if recently opened, standing before the Father's countenance and supplicating him for sinners. Turning to Lutgard, he said, 'Do you not see how I surrender myself wholly to the Father for my sinners? So too I wish you to surrender yourself wholly to me for my sinners, and turn away the zeal kindled against them for vengeance.'[145] The Lord Jesus repeated these words to her almost every day during the sacrifice of the mass.

That the prayers, fasts, and labours of the blessed Lutgard had great power was attested by the most blessed Mary of Oignies as she was dying.[146] Mary covered and bound her head with Lutgard's veil and predicted, touched with the spirit of prophecy: 'Under heaven, the world has no more faithful or efficacious intercessor than Lady Lutgard in praying for sinners and delivering souls from purgatory. While she lives, she now performs spiritual miracles, but after her death she will work bodily ones.' Many have experienced the truth of this prophecy, both in her lifetime and after her death. As this account will later testify, she has never ceased to work miracles.

[145] This vision is modelled on the motif of the Double Intercession, whereby Christ offers his wounds to the Father in intercession for sinners and Mary in turn offers her breasts to Christ. [BN]

[146] Mary died on 23 June 1213, thirty-three years before Lutgard's death on 16 June 1246.

10. *How a demon appeared to her and said he had deceived a certain nun, and how that nun was freed*

A very religious nun was deceived by the devil with revelations that seemed as if they came from God.[147] When the gracious Lutgard prayed to the Lord for her, he replied, 'Illumine those who sit in darkness and in the shadow of death'.[148] As an unlettered nun, she did not understand these words, but she asked another nun and received understanding. So, as she even more urgently supplicated the Lord, a demon appeared to her saying, 'I am the lying spirit,[149] the one who is deceiving that nun'. She told him, 'Go to Brother Simon who lives at the monastery of Aulne[150] and tell him also, that I might have a witness to the truth'. At once the demon obeyed and Brother Simon came to Aywières. This Simon was a man filled with the spirit of God and, as the book of his life testifies, the Lord revealed many things to him. Thus Lutgard and Brother Simon agreed together according to the Lord's revelation and quickly summoned the nun.

No sooner had they done this than the nun's hands and limbs contracted with an overpowering rigidity,[151] and her mouth was closed so firmly that it could not be opened at all, not even with a knife. Seeing this, they were shaken by an appalling fear[152] and, bending their knees in prayer, they entreated the Lord for mercy for such a great torment. Then what happened? By no means would it have been right for the Lord to remain unmoved by the prayers of such great ones. As soon as the supplicants had risen from their prayer, the nun's limbs returned to their original state, and she opened her mouth and was strengthened by taking some food.[153] From that day on she was freed from the spirit of

[147] See VMO I.31–32, in *Mary of Oignies*, pp. 67–69, for a story of the same kind of demonic temptation, but James's narration, as is his wont, is more exaggerated.

[148] Luke I. 79.

[149] I Kings 22. 22; II Chronicles 18. 21.

[150] Simon (BHL, 7755, II, pp. 1122–23), a lay brother at Aulne (d. 1229), was so famous for his clairvoyance that even cardinals of the Roman Curia came to visit him, and Innocent III invited him to the Fourth Lateran Council in 1215. Caesarius of Heisterbach, *Dialogus miraculorum*, III.33, trans. in *The Dialogue on Miracles*, I, pp. 169–73. To my knowledge, his *vita* has never been adequately edited.

[151] *rigore fortissimo.*

[152] Wisdom 5. 2.

[153] Acts 9. 19.

deception. Afterwards, as I myself saw, she was granted so many special merits in her life that it could be said that she was not only illumined herself, but also illumined many others who sat in darkness by the example of her behaviour.

11. How she delivered certain nuns from indwelling demons

I myself saw a nun of the Cistercian order, troubled for many years by a demon, who on being brought to Lutgard was liberated through the great earnestness of her prayers. And I saw another who, wondrously wearied by a demonic incubus for many years, was set free and cleansed through her prayers. As the woman herself frequently testified to me, it was that pernicious demon who had vexed her and polluted her body with such filth that, had she not been restrained by the most violent prayers, she would very often have offered herself as a public prostitute. But, liberated through Lady Lutgard's prayers, she thereafter led a very peaceful life, as if the goad of demonic disturbance had never stung her.

Certainly it is by a wondrous, a most wondrous, permission of the Saviour and Redeemer that Satan should receive power over a pure body, even a virginal body — power that is not only exercised for the pollution of the flesh, but can even proceed to the corruption of the mind and the detriment of the soul. What is cleaner than a bride of Christ?[154] What is cleaner than a virgin who is 'holy in body and spirit?'[155] And yet it was to such a one that we perceived such things happening. What therefore remains but to exclaim with the Apostle, 'O the depth of the riches of the wisdom and knowledge of God! How incomprehensible are his judgements and how unsearchable his ways!'[156] Yet we believe that women are brought to this defilement through an illicit excess of temptation, by a hidden and just judgement of God. Were it not so, we do not see how else it could happen.

[154] *mundus*: a reference to the clean animals offered as sacrifice to the Lord.

[155] 1 Corinthians 7. 34.

[156] Romans 11. 33. On this incident see Newman, 'Possessed by the Spirit', pp. 743–44. [BN]

12. How the nun Yolendis, warned by Lutgard before she died, appeared to her afterwards

A certain Yolendis, a Benedictine nun at the monastery of Moustier-sur-Sambre[157] who had been devoted to the gratifications of the world, transferred to the monastery at Aywières at the encouragement of a holy woman. Yolendis was a woman of noble breeding and had a very delicate constitution. Lutgard entreated the Lord on her behalf with wondrous insistency to forgive her sins and pour into her the grace of devotion. Nor could Christ deny what she asked, but he led the woman to a holy state of life. When therefore she had served the Lord at Aywières for many years, she learned of her impending death through a revelation and ran to her holy mother, Lady Lutgard. 'Beseech the Lord most insistently for me', she said, 'since the end of my life is drawing near'. The gracious Lutgard replied, 'Wait for the Lord with confidence, for I am sure he will deal mercifully with you and quickly rescue you from the punishments you fear. But you must come back to me after death and, on returning, first say to me 'Benedicite' and then pray the Our Father and the Hail Mary from beginning to end, lest the devil — as is his wont — induce some hallucination.'

Thus, as she predicted, Yolendis died in a wondrous fervour of spirit.[158] Not thirty days had elapsed when, behold, while Lutgard was praying, the dead Yolendis appeared to her and, just as she had been asked while alive, she first said 'Benedicite' and the other prayers I mentioned. Lutgard replied 'Dominus'[159] and immediately asked, 'How is it with you?' And the dead woman said, 'The Lord did not draw back in horror at the enormity of my sins, but because of his favour to you I have obtained great mercy'. With these words she disappeared. Then Lutgard blessed the divine mercy toward sinners and wept many tears over it.

[157] Moustier-sur-Sambre had been founded in 660 by St Amand and is situated in the diocese and province of Namur. It only accepted women of the nobility (McDonnell, *The Beguines and Beghards in Medieval Culture*, p. 63). See Ursmer Berlière in MB I, p. 63; *Gallia Christiana*, III, p. 579; and Mabillon, *Analecta*, I.

[158] Henschen notes that, according to Rayssius (AASS, 16 June, III, p. 199), Yolendis was buried in the church at Aywières; he calls her blessed [*beatam*] and a penitent [*poenitentem*].

[159] A standard Benedictine greeting: when two monks or nuns meet, the junior says 'Benedicite' ('Bless me') and the senior replies 'Dominus' ('May the Lord bless you'). [BN]

13. How her dead sister appeared to her

Her sister in the flesh also passed over from the world to purgatory. Before her sister's death had been reported to Lutgard, a horrible and lamenting voice suddenly shouted to her in the air, 'Have mercy, dearest sister! Have mercy on me and graciously grant me the same mercy you have shown to other souls!' Prostrate in prayer, Lutgard understood that her sister's soul was begging for the suffrage of her prayers and quickly required the whole community to come to her aid with many disciplines and prayers.

14. How she was forbidden to approach the sacrament of the altar every Sunday

At about the same time there occurred an event that caused many to marvel. Lutgard used to receive the body of Christ every Sunday in accord with the advice of St Augustine.[160] But Lady Agnes, who was then abbess,[161] endorsed less discreet counsel and forbade her to take the sacrament every Sunday. The gracious Lutgard said to her, 'I will be obedient, dearest mother, but I have most certain foreknowledge that Christ will avenge this injury on your body'. There was no delay. In revenge for this deed, the abbess was so afflicted by an unbearable sickness that she could not enter the church, nor did her pain cease for even a moment, but kept on increasing until she acknowledged her sin of imprudence and, repentant, relaxed the prohibition on Lutgard. The other nuns who had also opposed her in this were either conspicuously taken from the light of this world or else converted to her side in a spirit of humility. Worthy is the Bridegroom's zeal against those who perversely disturb his bride!

---

[160] Although frequent communion had been the norm in the early Church, by the thirteenth century this practice was in decline. Innocent III limited reception of the Eucharist to feast days and at the moment of death. Albert the Great considered that receiving communion once a month was frequent and especially opposed daily reception by women (*In quattuor libros sententiarum*, 13, a. 27 (Basel: [n. pub], 1506). Augustine, on the other hand, attested to the practice of frequent communion: *De sermone domini in monte*, in PL 34:1280; *Sermo 112* (PL 38:645) and recommended it on condition that the recipient was without mortal sin (*Epist. 54 ad Inquisitiones Januarii*, c. 2, 3 (PL 33:200–01). See Joseph Duhr, 'Communion fréquente', DS, II.ii, cols. 1234–92 (especially cols. 1250, 1260).

[161] Agnes was third abbess of Aywières, succeeding Woaris and preceding Hadewijch.

15. How a demon appeared to her upon the death of a certain sister

Her spirit was always moved by great mercy towards the dying and so she used to visit them, admonishing and urging them to confess their sins and promising them in return sure hope for the penitent and glory once their penance was completed. So when a certain sister was labouring most grievously in her last agony, a demon appeared to insult her and said, 'Behold, I disturbed this sister, but as soon as the people had come, I had no more power over her'. He called the community 'the people': as soon as they came to commend the sister's soul, they sapped his strength by their prayers. Thus it is holy and devout to assist the dying and to aid them with prayers against the demons, who always lie in ambush at the heel of our end.[162]

16. How demons frequently appeared to her, and how they feared her

Demons frequently came to Lutgard as well to announce something calamitous or sad, but she spat on them and drove off the insistent ones with the sign of the cross. For this reason the demons feared her so much that they avoided touching even the place where she prayed as if it were burning iron. As for her, although she understood neither the psalms nor anything in the Scriptures, yet when she was ruminating on the psalm verse, 'O God, come to my assistance',[163] and certain other verses in the Psalter, she would see demons running away with wondrous horror, and they would cease their evil suggestions. Hence she understood that it was by the strength of the words, even when she did not understand them, that the demons were repulsed and their power weakened in temptations.

Friar Bernard reports that he heard her privately saying she did not fear the devil at all, nor could he prevail against her, even in part, through any kind of deception. But according to the Lord's promise, she would powerfully crush his

---

[162] *finis nostri calcaneo*: Cf. Gregory, *Moralia in Iob*, I, 54, in CCSL 143, p. 55 and Bede, *In Genesim*, I, iii, 15, 2129–34: The serpent 'will lie in wait for her heel when at the end of our present life he tries to seize us, for since the heel is the end of the body, so not without reason is the end of our life called the heel': ed. by C. W. Jones, in CCSL 118A, p. 66. See below III.11, and VJC III.7.

[163] Psalm 69. 2, 'Deus in adiutorium meum intende'. The prayers of the Hours begin with this verse. [BN]

head — that is, the first stage of his temptations — with the foot of the virtues.[164]

17. How she feared that she had not always said the prescribed Hours well and, for this reason, a certain person sent by the Lord reassured her

Because the gracious Lutgard longed for total perfection, she began trying in a wondrous way to banish every thought while saying the Hours, not just evil thoughts but even good ones, so as to occupy her mind solely with what she was saying — a feat which is impossible in this mortal life. When she could not accomplish this at all, she became troubled with great scrupulosity and took to repeating each of her Hours a second or third time, as if she had said nothing at all. Thus she mourned for this inescapable defect of living, and none of her friends could console her in this matter.[165] So they prayed to God that he would liberate her from this scruple. The Almighty did not fail them. Unexpectedly the Lord disguised himself as a shepherd following his lambs, just like the prophet Amos,[166] and the gracious Father put words of comfort in his mouth.

So an uncultivated shepherd left his sheep and came thirteen leagues to Aywières. Sending for Lutgard, he told her in the hearing of others, 'Thus says the Lord: "Do not torture yourself any longer with sorrow or scruples when you are saying the Hours. Your prayers are pleasing and graciously accepted in my sight."' When the shepherd had spoken he quickly ran away, so there was no opportunity to ask who he was or to learn anything more about him. Nevertheless, his identity was later revealed. And the Lord also told her himself, 'Fear no more, since I will make up for this defect in you'. Then Lutgard, sensing that the words in both cases came from the mouth of the Lord, rested in peace of conscience. Never again did inordinate scruples weary her over this matter.

---

[164] Genesis 3. 15. Cf. Gregory, *Moralia in Iob*, 5, 43, in CCSL 143, p. 248: 'But spiritual minds trample upon [Satan's] weakness with the foot of virtue'.

[165] The persons who could not console her are called *amicorum suorum* — her male friends — and later Thomas says that the Almighty did not fail them (*eos*).

[166] Amos 7. 15.

18. How a flame was seen to proceed from her mouth as she was chanting

It is hard to believe the alacrity of spirit with which she served the Lord in chanting the Hours. One day when she was chanting vespers in choir, a nun standing on the opposite side of the choir saw with her bodily eyes a flame of material light rising from Lutgard's mouth and piercing the upper air. The girl was so apprehensive and alarmed at this unusual sight that she almost fainted. For this reason, when vespers were over Lutgard sweetly consoled the nun. Since she was still frightened, she said, 'I do not want you to be terrified by this vision, my dearest daughter, because you should understand that in truth it was divinely sent'. Note well, reader: we read that this has happened to many people, and the material flame seen above them signifies the desire of fervid prayer. Many less spiritual people are surprised at how, with such magnificent deeds, Lutgard could trample human glory underfoot. To this I reply — as she herself told me — that she was filled inwardly with such spiritual and solid glory that no vainglory from without could disturb her. Rather, the Holy Spirit had planted her like a firm pillar.

19. How after receiving communion, she did not wish to miss lunch, but told the Lord to occupy a certain weak nun with thoughts of him; and so it happened and was proven

Augustine, the greatest of all teachers, says in his book *On the City of God* that discretion should be preeminent in us, always moderating our individual desires so that we act discerningly.[167] We know that Lutgard flourished in the greatest discretion, as I will show in this chapter.

One Sunday after she had received the saving sacrament of Christ's body and 'the remainder of her thoughts were keeping holiday'[168] for the Saviour, so that it would have been hard for her to approach the table of bodily food, she said, 'Lord Jesus, now is not the right time for me to be occupied with your delights. Go instead to Elizabeth, who cannot abstain from food for even one hour, and occupy her heart. As for me, allow me to eat and be refreshed.'

---

[167] Possibly a reference to *The City of God*, XIX.4, trans. by Marcus Dods (New York: Modern Library, 1950), p. 678: 'What shall I say of that virtue which is called prudence? Is not all its vigilance spent in the discernment of good from evil things […]?' See also *Regula S. Benedicti*, 64, 19: 'discretion is the mother of all virtues' (*RB*, pp. 282–83).

[168] Psalm 75. 11.

For there was a nun at Aywières with an illness such that she needed to eat frequently both day and night. At once Christ, obeying Lutgard's words, went suddenly to that nun and filled her heart with such sweetness that, contrary to her usual custom, she was able to abstain from bodily food without trouble for a long time. In this we can observe the gracious Lutgard's great discretion. She did not want to weaken her body, even for spiritual occupations, for she considered it more useful to keep it strong for many other labours useful for souls than to weary it in vain to the point of destruction, 'because all things have their proper time'.[169]

I tell this story against those who, having tasted a sweetness of the spirit once or twice, become enemies to themselves and reject their bodies cruelly. Although they direct themselves to God in this way with a stronger spirit, they destroy the body which was given to help the spirit. Thus they have a way of vexing the spirit too, weakened by the destruction of the body, with incredible miseries. 'For the corrupted body weighs down the soul.'[170] Paul, that most experienced teacher, speaks against these people when he says, 'No one has ever hated his own flesh, but nourishes and cherishes it'[171] — not for pleasure but for sustenance. When Abraham ascended the mount of vision, after he had offered sacrifice he returned to his ass,[172] on which Solomon says a burden should be placed, but afterwards it must be given fodder.[173] Let the reader think carefully how to behave in such matters. But for the sake of brevity, let us move on.

20. How the same nun Elizabeth was cured by her prayers

As for Elizabeth, there occurred a most unexpected miracle which I shall describe. As I have said, she had to eat almost every hour, not only during the day but sometimes even at night. Yet she was so weak that she could by no means stand on her feet, but used to lie in bed continuously. Since she recognized that the power of prayer in Lutgard shone clearer than light, she implored her with heartfelt insistence to plead with the Lord, that he might

---

[169] Ecclesiastes 3. 1.

[170] Wisdom 9. 15.

[171] Ephesians 5. 29.

[172] Cf. Genesis 22. 5, 19.

[173] Cf. Ecclesiasticus 33. 25. Thomas's thought here is remarkably similar to that of St Francis and his Brother Ass.

grant her before death the ability to rise and join the community so she could serve the Lord Jesus Christ more fully until her life's end. Lutgard agreed to pray for her, and the Lord replied in these words: 'Arise, arise, daughter of Jerusalem, and lift up the chalice of his wrath which you have drunk at the hand of the Lord'.[174] When Lutgard had reported the Lord's response and its occasion to the lettered nuns, they understood that Elizabeth was to be raised from her sickbed and resurrected to full health, in which the bonds of her neck would be loosened and her captivity shattered.[175] By this it was meant that the sick in the infirmary are subject, willingly or not, to those who minister to them, not only 'to the good and gentle but also to those who are irritable'.[176] So it happened as the Lord had told Lutgard. Elizabeth was raised from the sickbed where she had lain for many years, arose to shoulder the burden of the Order without wearying, and served Christ the Lord in perfect health for a long time afterwards.

21. How she desired to suffer martyrdom for Christ and, in that desire, a vein opposite her heart was ruptured and poured forth blood in wonderful abundance; and thus the Lord told her that henceforth she would receive the merit of Agnes in martyrdom

Lutgard thought a great deal about the One who had 'suffered such tribulation from sinners'[177] and wondrously burned to repay Christ and suffer martyrdom for him. But since the time of martyrdom had 'passed like the winter and the rains had come and gone',[178] Christ prepared for her another kind of bodily martyrdom. It happened one night as she was standing before her bed in the dormitory just after compline, occupied with her prayers. Thinking of what I have just mentioned, she began in a wondrous and ineffable way to desire to endure martyrdom for Christ like the most blessed Agnes. As she burned with such great longing that she expected to die from desire alone, one of the outer veins opposite her heart burst, and so much blood flowed from it that her tunics

[174] Isaiah 51. 17.

[175] Cf. Isaiah 52. 2.

[176] I Peter 2. 18.

[177] Hebrews 12. 3.

[178] Song of Songs 2. 11.

and cowl were copiously drenched.¹⁷⁹ She was so weakened by this that she sat down for a little while, and at once Christ appeared to her with a joyful countenance and said, 'For the most fervent yearning for martyrdom that you experienced in shedding this blood, you will receive in heaven the same reward for martyrdom that St Agnes earned when she was beheaded for her faith. By your desire you have equalled her martyrdom in blood.' This accords with what I wrote at the beginning of Book I, when a noble and devout matron was reported to have said to Lutgard while she was still a girl: 'You are a good lamb, and indeed you will be a second Agnes.'¹⁸⁰ O woman most entirely blessed,¹⁸¹ whom Christ himself embellished with the crown of martyrdom in peacetime!

Two nuns were witnesses of this glorious event, very devout women — Margaret and Lutgard, whose surname is Limmos — for they washed Lutgard's clothes after that effusion of blood. Another witness was the scar left by the ruptured vein, which remained until the day her happy soul passed from this world. Yet another witness was the termination of the nuisance with which God tamed pride in the sex of Eve, for she was only twenty-eight years old when these things are said to have happened to her.¹⁸²

22. How a certain nun, Lady Mechthild, regained her lost hearing through the imposition of Lutgard's finger

Mechthild, a noble matron born in the district of Liège, left her knightly sons as her heirs and served the Lord in Aywières. Enfeebled by old age and debility, she completely lost her hearing, as frequently happens at this time of life. One day during Solemn Vespers when the nuns were chanting loudly, a certain nun indicated this to the deaf matron by means of a sign, and understanding the sign, she wept for her deafness. The gracious Lutgard came to her and asked with a sign why she was weeping. She answered, 'Why should I not weep, I the most

---

¹⁷⁹ This incident is frequently mentioned as an early example of stigmatization, although it is clearly not. There is no indication that it in any way resembles the wounds of Christ; rather it is a new kind of martyrdom, neither 'red' nor 'white'. Fr Martinus Cawley has remarked on the fact that since Lutgard is wearing more than one tunic (*tunicae ejus*), this event probably occurred during the winter and most likely on the feast of St Agnes, 21 January.

¹⁸⁰ See I.3 above, punning on Agnes and *agna* (lamb).

¹⁸¹ This is the first time that Thomas has called Lutgard *beatissima*.

¹⁸² As a result of this haemorrhage Lutgard stopped menstruating, which probably both she and Thomas saw as another miracle because of her youth.

miserable of women, so deaf that I cannot even hear the solemn chant by which God is served?'

At once Lutgard had compassion on the weeping woman. Bowing in prayer for a little while, she arose and, moistening two of her fingers with saliva, she placed them in the ears of the deaf woman. Wondrous thing! The woman suddenly heard the obstruction inside her ears breaking with a loud noise, and now that her ears were fully opened, she could hear again. After experiencing Lutgard's power in so great a miracle, she solemnly blessed the Lord.

23. How, when she was mindful of Christ's Passion, a certain priest saw her in contemplation as if totally bedewed with blood

Whenever she was rapt in spirit, remembering the Lord's Passion, it seemed to her that her whole body, her very essence, was reddened and besprinkled with blood. When a certain monastic priest had been told of this as a great secret, he approached to observe her at an opportune time when there was no doubt that, because of the season, she would be thinking of Christ's Passion. He found her leaning against a wall in contemplation.[183] And behold, he saw her face and hands (the only exposed parts of her body) gleaming as if sprinkled with freshly shed blood, and the curls of her hair were also drenched with blood like 'drops of the night'.[184] Seeing this, he secretly cut off a bit of hair with scissors and carried it in his hand to the light, where he marvelled, astonished above all measure. When Lutgard returned from her rapture of contemplation to her outward senses, at once the hair which the astonished priest was holding also returned to its natural colour. Alarmed at such a prodigious spectacle beyond anything that can be believed, he almost fell flat on the ground. But note, reader, the reason why Lutgard seemed to become red with blood. In this life, she had a very special role among those who 'washed their robes in the blood of the Lamb',[185] for, from the intellectual consideration of her mind inwardly, her body outwardly drew its likeness.

---

[183] Exactly so did Mary of Oignies pray: 'She had in her cell a bed covered with only a scrap of straw, but she rarely rested on it since she more often used to sit in the church and, leaning her head against the wall, would refresh herself with a little sleep' (VMO I.34, in *Mary of Oignies*, p. 70).

[184] Song of Songs 5. 2.

[185] Apocalypse 7. 14.

24. *How by the most violent prayers she converted Lord Thiemer, an infamous knight, to the Lord*

A certain knight, potent in birth and riches, had a daughter who was a nun at Aywières. When her father became ensnared in scandals of various kinds, she induced him to beg the gracious Lutgard for prayers and he asked to be received as her spiritual son, for this is the custom in such matters. She agreed and started to beseech the Lord for him. And behold, Satan appeared to one of the nuns in the same monastery and said, 'Look, Lady Lutgard is trying[186] to snatch the knight Thiemer[187] out of my chains, he who served me for so many years. Let her try to do it! What she has begun is not the work of a short time. But if I can do nothing else, I will at least make his heart burn in the forge of poverty, and his soul will shrivel up like meat in the frying pan.' And see, reader, what wondrous truth there was in that liar! At that time the knight had enormous possessions and riches, but within a short time he had sunk so low that he had spent his ready money to the sum of £1500. Then, selling his possessions, he arrived at such poverty that he scarcely had bread in his utmost need. Yet through all these troubles, he is known to have had such patience that no one doubted that Lutgard's prayers had helped the knight. I myself saw him as a monk in Afflighem, the best-regulated monastery in the order,[188] and he was venerated by everyone for his wondrous way of life and his patience at such an age. In such ways the gracious Lutgard snatched many from the snares of the devil by her prayers and led them to an improved and virtuous way of life.

[186] Reading *nititur* for *mititur*.

[187] Thiemer or Thimerus de Rogenier (Rogenies) was the earliest known bailiff of Nivelles and died about 1237. The last years of his life were spent at Afflighem. See Guido Hendrix, 'Willem van Afflighems Auteurschap van het Leven van Lutgart getoetst aan het Hoofdstuk', *Ons Geestelijk Erf*, 40 (1966), 344–49, and J. Aerts, 'Ridder Thimerus van Rogenier uit de Vita S. Lutgardis', *Ons Geestelijk Erf*, 43 (1969), 316–23.

[188] The Benedictine monastery of Afflighem had been founded in 1083 by Henry III, count of Leuven, for the knights converted by Guery, a monk of St Pierre at Ghent. Both Lutgard and Thomas were especially attracted to the brothers of this monastery because of their very strict observance of the Rule. See BUA I.5.4, p. 21.

25. How she liberated a nun from temptations, and the same nun miraculously obtained what she had prayed for

A certain girl of the Cistercian Order, who was troubled by the most burdensome and annoying temptations, had many years ago seen Lutgard in her dreams, and she was told that she would be liberated by her prayers. Much later she came to Aywières and recognized her face from her earlier dreams. As I said before, she was delivered from every disquieting temptation by the great urgency of her prayers. Then, having experienced Lutgard's power in her liberation, she begged her to obtain for her from Almighty God the ability to bear the labours of her order and abstain from eating meat. For this girl had been sickly from her earliest childhood and could barely do without meat on fasting days. Although Lutgard argued that the girl was too young for such abstinence, the girl implored her insistently to fulfil her wish. At last, won over by her tears, Lutgard said, 'Begone, and from this day on, you will be able to do without meat and to keep the usages of your order, and beyond that, add whatever pleases you'.

This was truly a wondrous and breathtaking miracle! The girl returned to her monastery, and as usual, meat was brought to her in the infirmary. When she gazed at it, the food on the plate before her appeared so disgusting that at once she drew back from it in horror, and, turning her face away, she was quite unable to eat. The experiment was often repeated, but she conceived in her mind such a loathing for meat that never again, after Lutgard's words, did she eat any flesh. Moreover, she found it very easy to bear without harm not only the labours of the order, but also whatever she wished to endure beyond the rule for the mortification of her body. These things were reported to me with great modesty by the girl herself, who is now an elderly abbess ruling her monastery, because the gracious Lutgard's praise compelled her to tell the story.

26. How she predicted to a gravely tempted woman that she would die on Good Friday[*]

A religious girl named Hespelendis was in despair, tempted to excess by a measureless sadness. When she asked Lutgard for the support of her prayers, she copiously wept and prayed for her and replied as the Lord revealed to her, 'Take comfort, dearest one, because on Good Friday after the adoration of the cross,

---

[*] The anecdote that follows does not bear out this title.

when the priest lifts up the cross and says "Behold the wood of the Cross", you will be freed from every assault of temptation and attain confidence and comfort'. And so it happened, for at the predicted hour she was liberated and endowed by divine grace with confidence and comfort.

27. How at the mere sight of her, a man repented of his sins, made satisfaction, and was liberated

Once the venerable John, abbot of Afflighem, brought a certain man with him to the gracious Lutgard. At the sight of her, the man's anxiety was reflected in his face. The abbot therefore marvelled and, when he had withdrawn some distance, he asked the man, 'Did you see that holy woman?' He sighed deeply and said, 'I did, and in her gaze I was struck through and through with such a horror of sin that it was as if the Divine Majesty had been looking at me. With the help of her intercession, I am freed from my sins. May God grant that I never fall back into them!' The abbot of worthy memory recalled that it happened in just this way.

28. How she cured an epileptic

A certain woman had an epileptic son named John, for whom she had grieved anxiously for a long time. It happened that in a dream she heard these words spoken to her: 'Go to Lady Lutgard who lives at Aywières, and your son will be delivered by her'. On the next day she came to Aywières with her son and offered the boy to Lutgard. As soon as she had prayed, she put her finger in his mouth and traced a cross on his breast with her thumb, and from that day forth the boy was delivered from all the trouble of epilepsy.

29. How on the Feast of All Saints a multitude of saints appeared to her

Once on the feast of All Saints, a vast multitude of saints appeared to the gracious Lutgard in a vision, and the Holy Spirit revealed to her that she would be filled with the spirit and grace of them all. What is there to marvel at? For if gifts are in proportion to virtues, in what gift or grace should she be lacking, she who shone so brightly, filled with every virtue?

30. How, one night, a voice replied to Lady Sybille when she was troubled by her service to Lutgard

Once while Lutgard was lying ill with a bodily weakness, Lady Sybille de Gages,[189] who had been accustomed to serve her most devotedly ever since she entered the order, was wearied in heart and body and almost ready to faint from her long toil. Incited by the spirit of evil, she said in her heart just once, 'Why should I labour like this in service to Lady Lutgard? My mother never served anyone so much in her life, nor is it fitting for me to be given over to such servitude'. There was no delay. That very night she heard a voice saying to her, 'I did not come to be served, but to serve'.[190] When she heard this, she berated herself grievously, and thereafter served Lutgard with the greatest good humour and pleasure.

31. How a person in despair saw a bright light shining above her while he was speaking to her and was comforted

A man in despair over the stain of his crimes was brought to Lutgard so that he might be consoled at least by speaking with her. No sooner had he sat down beside her and begun to listen to her words than he saw above her an indescribable brightness, brighter than any lightning. On seeing this the man was exhilarated and left greatly comforted at the hope of pardon.

32. How the blessed Virgin appeared to her while she was singing the 'Te Deum laudamus'

It often happened that while she was ruminating the Psalter, the Holy Spirit revealed to her the power and meaning of the verses. Thus one night during the canticle 'Te Deum laudamus', while she was saying the verse 'When you were to become man to save mankind, you did not abhor the Virgin's womb', the

---

[189] Sybille de Gages had been a canoness at Nivelles before coming to Aywières. Henschen refers to Arnoldus de Raisse, *Hierogazophylacium Belgicum, sive thesaurus sacrarum reliquiarum Belgii* (Douai: Pinchon, 1628), p. 60, on the miraculous cures effected by a fountain near her grave, from which her bones were taken in 1611. According to the Bollandists, her feast day is 9 October: AASS, 16 June, III, pp. 187–88.

[190] Matthew 20. 28. The text is defective and reads *Non veni ministrare*.

most blessed Virgin Mary appeared to her as if rejoicing, and she understood how pleasing the blessed Virgin finds this verse, which reminds her that she received the Son of God. She herself revealed this to me as her beloved son[191] and advised me that whenever I say this verse, I should make a deep bow in praise of the glorious Virgin. I have done this for a long time and still do, and I advise all my readers to do the same thing.

33. How, when she had compassion on a poor little woman, the Lord said to her, 'My portion'

Once she noticed a poor little woman[192] in dire need, and she was instructed by a wondrous spirit of compassion to do her some good deed. At once the Lord said to her in spirit, 'In the psalm you read and say to me "O Lord, my portion, I have said I would keep your law".[193] This is how you should understand it: I am your portion, you have nothing else. So then, you should respond to the needy woman, "Gold and silver I have none, but what I have I give you".[194] If you pray for her, you will have given her what is yours. You will have kept my law.'

Enlightened inwardly in a wondrous manner by these words of God, she came to Lady Sybille de Gages and reported what the Lord had told her. When Sibylle looked up the gloss for that passage in the Psalter, 'O Lord, my portion, I have said I would keep your law', she discovered that the Lord's response to Lutgard accorded exactly with the gloss. This shows that the holy Scriptures are expounded by the same Spirit by which they were composed.

Similarly, when a monk of Afflighem was being sent to a very dissolute parish, he pleaded with Lutgard to pray to the Lord for him in such great danger. She replied, 'With expectation I have waited for the Lord, and he was

[191] Thomas here for the first time refers to himself as her son. The VA refers to this incident without mentioning Thomas by name.

[192] *paupercula*: James calls Mary of Oignies 'a poor little woman' (II.45–46, pp. 81–82) and Beatrice of Nazareth is called *Christi paupercula* (1.7.3): *The Life of Beatrice of Nazareth*, ed. by L. Reypens and trans. by Roger De Ganck (Kalamazoo: Cistercian Publications, 1991) p. 44. Ida of Leuven is oddly called *venerabilis Christi paupercula* (p. 323). Thomas does not use the term for Christina or Lutgard.

[193] Psalm 118. 57.

[194] Acts 3. 6.

attentive' to him.[195] Seeing most clearly that this was so, he had no doubt that the gracious Lutgard had replied to him from the Spirit of God.

34. How she shone with a prophetic spirit in many ways, and how she revealed the name and merit of the virgin Osanna, which had been unknown for many years

It is agreed by many, for there are many proofs, that Lutgard shone with a spirit of prophecy. A monastic priest who had come to the French monastery of Jouarre-en-Brie[196] was praying at night in a crypt where the bodies of the saints were resting. Unexpectedly he came upon the alabaster tomb of a saintly woman whose name and merit he was unable to learn. Later he asked the gracious Lutgard to pray for a revelation of her name. Accepting the man's request, she gave herself totally to prayer and at once obtained what she asked. For the saint appeared to her and said, 'I am called Osanna. I was once the virgin daughter of a king of Scotland, and through a miracle of the Lord I was brought to France where I lived a holy life. I died there and was solemnly buried, but at last the inhabitants forgot me through the neglect of time.'[197]

When Lutgard reported this to the man, she added, 'I wish the Lord would show you the same things as a witness of their truth'. But he said, 'I am not worthy that such things should be shown to me'. She replied, 'Even if you are perhaps less worthy, yet she is worthy that her rightful fame should be worthily revealed'. There was no delay. That very night as Lutgard prayed to the Lord, the virgin appeared three times to the man in his sleep and announced that she was called Osanna. 'He who saw this gave testimony and we know his testimony is true.'[198]

---

[195] Psalm 39. 2.

[196] Jouarre-en-Brie was a Benedictine monastery in the diocese of Meaux (Seine-et-Marne) near the Marne river (L. H. Cottineau, *Répertoire topo-bibliographique des abbayes et prieurés*, 2 vols (Mâcon: Protat frères, 1935), I, cols. 1489–90).

[197] Osanna, more frequently called Osmanna, probably lived in the seventh century. Escaping marriage in either Ireland or England, she fled to Brittany and lived a virginal and penitent life in the neighbourhood of Saint-Brieuc. Her *vitae* (BHL, 6354–57, II, pp. 918–19) have been edited by the Bollandists: AASS, 9 September, III, pp. 422–25.

[198] John 19. 35.

35. How she predicted the return of a certain apostate to the Order

In the monastery of Vrouwenpark[199] near Leuven, there was a devout nun[200] who mourned inconsolably for her brother in the flesh, who had for twelve years been an apostate from the Franciscans. So the gracious Lutgard was asked to pray for this apostate because his sister seemed to be going mad with sorrow. With compassion for both of them, Lutgard prayed to the Lord. After her prayer she said, 'Let that good girl be told to trust and take comfort, because this very year her brother will return to his holy order'. I learned that this did in fact happen — unexpectedly, inasmuch as he had been deeply entangled in worldly affairs.

Let it not surprise readers if some have fallen from the Friars Minor and other orders through apostasy. For none of these orders is greater, in fact they are not nearly as great, as the habitation of Christ, in which eleven good men tolerated the traitor Judas. Nor are they better than heaven itself, from which the angels fell.[201]

36. How she predicted the death of the Duchess of Brabant

It was about the same time that the illustrious Duchess of Brabant, a daughter of the late King Philip of France,[202] fell seriously ill. Since she had loved the gracious Lutgard for a long time, she sent word that she should pray to the Lord for her. After praying, Lutgard immediately sent back word that the duchess should by no means rise from her bed, but prepare herself fully through confession and wait for the Lord with a most trusting heart. There was no delay:

---

[199] Vrouwenpark or Parc-les-Dames (situated at Wesemael between Aarschot and Leuven) was originally founded for Augustinian canons and incorporated into the Cistercian Order about 1215 under the jurisdiction of Villers.

[200] The name of this nun was Beatrijs van Dendermonde. See Broeder Geraert, *Leven van Sinte Lutgardis: Een Dietsch Gedicht ten laetste van de tweede helft der XIVe eeuw*, ed. by J. H. Bormans, 2 vols (Amsterdam: [n. pub.], 1857-58), II, verses 12165–68: 'In dese abdie was hir voren / Ene uter port daerbi geboren, / Die was genamt ver Beatrijs / Van Denremonde'. See also L. Reypens, 'Een derde Beatrijs in onze dertiendeeuwse letteren? Beatrijs van Dendermonde', *Ons Geestelijk Erf*, 37 (1963), 419–22.

[201] Cf. VJC I.15.

[202] Mary, duchess of Brabant and daughter of Philip Augustus, was married in 1206 to Henry I, duke of Brabant, and died in 1224. She was buried in the church of St Peter at Leuven and her name is found in the necrology of Afflighem, probably in her role as benefactor.

just as she had predicted, the duchess died. After her death she appeared to Lutgard and revealed by unmistakable signs that through the intercession of the glorious Virgin Mary, whom she had loved in a wondrous way while she lived, she had been rescued from the pains of purgatory beyond all expectation.

I learned and have written these things at the report of Lady Margaret of Velpia, who is worthy of veneration and devoted to God. The same thing also happened with regard to a nobleman, the Lord Godfrey, son of Lord Godfrey, Constable of Brussels,[203] whose death Lutgard announced to the sisters before it was otherwise known.

37. How she predicted a hidden temptation to a certain woman and liberated her

There was a very young recluse of Court Saint-Etienne[204] who, being seriously troubled by a temptation, went to the gracious Lutgard to ask for her prayers. When she asked what the trouble was and the girl was ashamed to tell her, Lutgard said, 'See, the Lord has revealed to me what you are too embarrassed to say'. And with these words she laid bare the whole state of the girl's heart, which she had been unwilling to reveal even to a priest. Thus exhorted to confess, the girl left Lutgard for the confession of her sins[205] and the correction of her ways, so perfectly healed and consoled from every trouble that thereafter she served the Lord with the greatest joy and alacrity of spirit.

It is known that much the same kind of thing happened to Werric, a lay brother at Aywières. Why marvel at this? For Lutgard had with her in spirit the One whose 'eyes are brighter than the sun',[206] as the following will show.

---

[203] Godfrey the Elder was constable of Brussels and died in 1216/17; his son Godfrey, lord of Seneffe, died after 12 February 1234. See J. Aerts, 'De schenkingen van Godefridus, Kasteelheer van Brussel en van zijn zoon Godefridus, Heer van Seneffe aan de Abdij van Aywières', *Ons Geestelijk Erf*, 42 (1968), 298–303.

[204] Hendrix identifies Curia S. Stephani as Court Saint-Etienne near Wavre: 'Primitive Versions', p. 195, n. 47.

[205] Apparently the girl's confession to Lutgard prepared the way for her subsequent confession to a priest. In VCM 44, Thomas is at pains to emphasize that this kind of lay 'confession' was not sacramental. See Amédée Teetaert, *La Confession aux laïques dans l'église latine depuis le VIIIᵉ siècle jusqu'au XIV siècle: Étude de théologie positive* (Paris: Gabalda, 1926).

[206] Ecclesiasticus 23. 28.

A man had committed a sin in a very hidden place and was ashamed to reveal it to a priest. And behold, not long afterward a man who looked like a pilgrim asked him, for the remission of the sin he most feared, to wash the pilgrim's head. When he had just begun to do this, he discovered at the top of the pilgrim's head a luminous eye and shouted, 'What kind of man is this who, against nature, has an eye at the top of his head?' 'This', said the pilgrim, 'is the eye that saw you sinning in private, the eye from which no secrets can be hidden'. With these words he vanished from the man's wondering eyes.

38. How by her prayers she liberated a man who had been disturbed in the hearing of confessions

Often Lutgard showed an exceptional solicitude in admonishing the priests she knew, and with a wondrous grace of speech, she urged them to care solicitously for the flock entrusted to them and to deliver the souls Christ redeemed from demonic servitude.

When I was a young man and had advanced, although unworthy, to the order of priesthood (although I was not yet a member of the Order of Preachers),[207] I was compelled — without just cause and beyond my strength — to serve as the bishop's deputy in hearing confessions.[208] I began this duty with great fear in my heart, and when my ears were troubled outwardly by what I heard, I became agitated inwardly with the stirrings of temptation. Seized with the greatest fear and horror because of this, I approached the gracious Lutgard as my most special mother and, touched with sorrow, I revealed my burden to her. Moved by compassion for me, she gave herself to prayer, then returned and said with great confidence, 'Go back to your own house, my son, and expend due labour for the care of souls. Christ will be with you as protector and teacher, and when you hear confessions he will powerfully deliver you from the enemy's attacks and add a greater grace to make up for your lack of knowledge, of which you are ashamed.' Wondrous thing! Although I report this about myself with embarrassment, yet I will not keep silent about what happened for the praise of

---

[207] At this time Thomas was still an Augustinian canon at Cantimpré. He became a Dominican in 1232.

[208] In this capacity Thomas would have heard the confession of 'reserved' sins considered too grave for absolution by ordinary parish priests. As the context makes clear, many of these were of a sexual nature. [BN]

Christ and his handmaid.²⁰⁹ From that day until the present, as long as I have performed the office assigned to me (and sixteen years have passed since then), I have experienced the absolute truth of Lutgard's prophecy — even though I have often been unbearably tempted at other times, when I was not busy hearing confessions. But when I perform my office, the more unclean the things that I hear, the less they bother me and the less I am shaken by hearing them.

39. How two angels were seen leading her to the altar, and how another time before her death the blessed Virgin Mary and blessed John the Baptist were seen standing on either side of her

In order to reveal Lutgard's merit to some in Aywières who might have thought less worthily of her, this solemn miracle occurred. It was her custom to be refreshed with the sacrament of the Lord's body every Sunday.²¹⁰ When she was going up to the altar and there was no one to support her weakened body, some of the nuns — those to whom it was given to see — unmistakably saw two angels holding her between them and leading her to the altar.²¹¹ Similarly on another occasion, the most glorious Virgin Mary and the blessed John the Baptist were unmistakably seen to accompany her in this act of worship. But this took place long afterwards, when the time was approaching for her to be taken from this world.

40. How, to console a woman who was in despair, she received the knowledge of an unknown language, and how she delivered her

She strove with wondrous solicitude to comfort and strengthen those who were troubled and tempted. To be sure, God himself had conferred this wonderful grace on her, namely that no one who was tempted or troubled would depart from her without relief. Now a certain woman came to her in utter

---

²⁰⁹ This is the only time in this vita that Lutgard is called *ancilla* ('handmaid'). In II.43 Thomas says that the Bride of the Song of Songs is called 'bride' and not 'handmaid' and, with this exception, he is consistent in his avoidance of the term, which James uses constantly for Mary of Oignies.

²¹⁰ See II.14 above.

²¹¹ Thus was Mary supported by two angels when she went on pilgrimage to the church of St Mary of Heigne (VMO I.28, in *Mary of Oignies*, p. 64). See also VMY 21.

despair, lacking all hope of pardon. When she entered the parlour, the nuns pleaded with her to be consoled and set her hope in God, who 'does not wish sinners to die but to be converted and live'.[212] Their efforts were in vain, for she tried to flee, but they held her back and begged her to wait for the gracious Lutgard. Although Lutgard was Flemish and could not give her any words of consolation (for the woman spoke only French), nevertheless she could pray to the Lord for her. As soon as Lutgard was brought in, she withdrew into a far corner with the woman, for she sensed in her spirit that she was in deep distress. Everyone began to laugh and wonder how they could communicate, since neither knew the other's language. But after they had been sitting there together for a long time, the woman got up, recalled to the fullest confidence and hope. She returned to the parlour and said to the nuns, 'Why did you say that this most holy lady was Flemish? Indeed, I have found by experience that she is quite French! No one else under heaven could have recalled me to a hope of pardon with her words.'

It is no wonder that the two women could communicate for awhile without knowing each other's languages, for Lutgard was filled with the same Spirit that filled the assembled disciples with a variety of tongues.[213]

Father Bernard reports that he saw her and Master Guiard, the worthy and venerable bishop of Cambrai,[214] conversing and understanding each other — yet he was as completely ignorant of the Flemish language as she was of French. I myself once saw a woman who had knowledge of all languages from terce to vespers on Pentecost, but I do not wish to give her name because she is still alive.

41. How the Lord appeared to her after she had wept for sinners for a long time and, with his own hand, wiped the tears from her eyes

She afflicted herself for a long time in lamentation for sinners, and her face was daily bathed in water until, as the prophet Jeremiah says, 'her eyes seemed to give forth a fountain of tears'.[215] This grief and groaning were so unspeakable to those who saw her that scarcely anyone could watch without feeling heavy

---

[212] Ezekiel 33. 11.

[213] On Pentecost; see Acts 2. 1–12.

[214] Guiard de Laon (*c.* 1170–1248) was elected bishop of Cambrai in 1238 and retired to Afflighem in 1248. See Boeren, *La Vie et les oeuvres de Guiard de Laon.*

[215] Jeremiah 9. 1, 18; 13. 17; 14. 17.

sorrow at heart.[216] So, when it pleased the Lord to relieve her intense compassion in such cases, he appeared to her as she was wailing and weeping. Congratulating her that she had faithfully cared for the wretched for so long, he wiped the tears from her face with his own hand, which he had stretched out on the cross for sinners, saying, 'I wish you to be consoled in these lamentations for my sinners, nor will I allow you any longer to weary yourself in tears. Rather, you will persist in prayer with a peaceful fervour, and by this means you will worthily avert the Father's wrath just as you formerly did with tears.' This condition lasted in her without change until her dying day.

42. How for five years she was visited daily by angels and often by the Lord's Mother or the apostles, yet nothing sufficed her but God alone

Five years passed by during which — as she herself told me with great weeping — almost every day she was visited by the Mother of Christ, the apostles, or other special saints, not counting continual visits from the angels. Yet in all these she found no perfect rest for her spirit until she had found the Holy of Holies, ineffably sweeter than them all, since he is the sanctifier of all.[217] And what is wonderful about this? What is new? Lutgard's feelings were like those of the bride in the Song of Songs whose soul melts, is wounded, languishes, pants, arises, and searches among the districts of the new grace (the saints) and the streets of the Old Testament (the patriarchs).[218] She had scarcely passed them (since 'he is not far from every one of us') when she 'found him whom her soul loves', having fixed the gaze of her mind on higher things.[219] Thus did Peter pass by 'the watchmen of the city'[220] — that is, 'Elijah, Jeremiah

---

[216] The beguines seem to have been awash in tears, a gift Henrietta Leyser has described as 'the crowning glory of personal prayers': *Hermits and the New Monasticism: A Study of Religious Communities in Western Europe, 1000–1150* (London: Macmillan, 1984), p. 64. This gift of tears was so extreme in Mary of Oignies that, 'lest her tears make the ground all muddy, she caught them in the veil with which she covered her head' (VMO I.18, in *Mary of Oignies*, p. 58).

[217] With this ineffable experience, Thomas moves into his first explicit comparison of Lutgard to the Bride of the Song of Songs. If Thomas knew the *Vitis Mystica*, this use of the expression Sanctorum Sanctum might refer to the wounded heart of Christ.

[218] Song of Songs 5. 6; 4. 9; 2. 5; 5. 8; 3. 2.

[219] Acts 17. 27; Song of Songs 3.4.

[220] Song of Songs 3. 3.

or one of the prophets'[221] or even John the Baptist himself, 'the friend of the Bridegroom'[222] who clings most closely — and 'found him whom he loved', to whom he said, 'You are the Christ, the Son of the living God'.[223] The Christ Peter found was the Son of God about to die; the Christ Lutgard found has risen from the dead and will die no more.[224] Peter lost him by denying him at the Passion;[225] Lutgard found and held him reigning in heaven. I say she held him, for certainly she 'held him and would not let him go'.[226] For the more ardently she sought him, the more tightly she holds him. Happy are those who seek but happier those who hold. She held him by faith and did not let him go with any change in intent. But now let us examine the triple mode of her search.

43. How she lived in a triple state: that is, how she lay in the triple bed of the Song of Songs

The three beds in the Song of Songs distinguish three states of the soul. The first is when it is said, 'In my bed by night I sought him whom my soul loves'.[227] The second is that bed of Solomon surrounded by 'threescore valiant ones of the most valiant of Israel'.[228] The third is that of which it is said, 'Our bed is flowery'.[229] The first bed is compared to the state of penance, which is that of beginners; the second to the state of battle, which is for those who are progressing; the third is the contemplative life, the state of the perfect.[230] In the first, the soul lies wounded; in the second, wearied; and in the third, delighted.

Thus in the first bed, that of penance, the gracious Lutgard perfectly sought the Beloved when, like the Psalmist, she wept every night for every sin of her

---

[221] Matthew 16. 14.

[222] John 3. 29.

[223] Matthew 16. 16.

[224] Romans 6. 9.

[225] See above, I.18: 'Peter and Mary Magdalene followed the Lamb most perfectly, but not "wherever he went"'.

[226] Song of Songs 3. 4.

[227] Song of Songs 3. 1.

[228] Song of Songs 3. 7.

[229] Song of Songs 1. 15.

[230] Here again Thomas follows William of Saint-Thierry in the triple classification of the soul's progress.

ignorance (even though she had never been wounded by the bruise of any mortal sin) and washed the bed of her conscience most diligently, and bathed her cot with the wondrous abundance of her tears.[231]

In the second bed, that of battle, she sought the Beloved when, fighting against the flesh, she subjugated it with wondrous abstinence and labour; conquered the world with her extreme poverty and humility; and cast down the devil with remedial tears and prayer. 'Threescore valiant ones of the most valiant of Israel' surrounded this bed when, as I have already written, not only the angels but the very Mother of Christ protected her, with hosts of other saints.

In the third bed, that of rest, Lutgard sought the Beloved perfectly when she did not lean on the angels or the saints, but rested sweetly in contemplation on the couch of the Bridegroom alone. Hence she could say with Isaiah, 'the bed is so narrow that one or another must fall out' and 'a short covering cannot cover both'.[232] This bed is called 'flowery' because it is sprinkled with a variety of virtues like spring flowers, and redolent with the sweetness of high esteem. It is called 'ours' because it is shared by the Bridegroom and the Bride alone. As it is said, 'My beloved is mine and I am his, who feeds among the lilies',[233] and again, 'I am my beloved's and his turning is towards me'.[234] What is marvelous about that?

> Love knows no lord; to no lordship it cedes.
> Though lofty the lover, an equal he needs.[235]

If this were not so, she would have been called handmaid rather than bride.[236] Indeed there is a prefiguration of this mystery in the first parents: Eve was taken from Adam's side, not his foot.[237]

---

[231] Cf. Psalm 6. 7.

[232] Isaiah 28. 20.

[233] Song of Songs 2. 16.

[234] Song of Songs 7. 10.

[235] 'Nescit amor dominum, non novit amor dominari; / Quamlibet altus amet, non amat absque pari'.

[236] This explains why Thomas has only once (probably by mistake) called Lutgard 'the handmaid of Christ' (II.38). By emphasizing her bridal role in contrast to James's characterization of Mary and by his allusions to Mary's prophecy about Lutgard's power as mediator (II.9; III.8), Thomas is implying that Lutgard took pride of place in spiritual matters.

[237] Cf. Hugh of St-Victor, *De sacramentis*, I, 6, 35, in *On the Sacraments of the Christian Faith*, trans. by Roy Deferrari (Cambridge, MA: Medieval Academy of America, 1951), p. 117. The idea is ultimately rabbinic.

So Lutgard's spirit was absorbed in God and, like the Queen of Sheba, fainting in admiration, she 'no longer had any spirit in her'.[238] Now she was wholly translated into God, like a drop of water in a cask of wine, and mingled with him as one spirit.[239] And this indeed is what Christ asked at his Passion as he hastened from his Father for the sake of those who would believe: 'Father, even as you are in me and I in you, so may they also be one in us.'[240]

Because we have extended this second book at great length with many matters — useful ones, as I think — let us now catch our breath with a short pause so that we may more agreeably pass on to the story of her precious death.

---

[238] 1 Kings 10. 5.

[239] 1 Corinthians 6. 17. Cf. I.12 above, and Bernard of Clairvaux's famous image in *De diligendo Deo*, 10, 28, trans. by Robert Walton in *On Loving God* (Kalamazoo: Cistercian Publications, 1973, repr. 1980), p. 120: 'As a drop of water seems to disappear completely in a big quantity of wine, even assuming the wine's taste and colour [...] so it is necessary for the saints that all human feelings melt in a mysterious way and flow into the will of God. Otherwise, how will God be all in all if something human survives in man?'

[240] John 17. 21.

1. How she went blind eleven years before she died, hence she attained a more radiant inner light

Now then, having faithfully completed the second book, let us begin the third which concerns her death. About eleven years before she travelled from this life, she received a sort of prelude to a most quiet life[241] and a happy death. Like the patriarchs Isaac and Jacob, she was deprived of both her eyes[242] and attained more perfectly than before to the resplendence of the heavenly light. For it was unworthy for her mind, inwardly adorned with a most radiant light, to be darkened outwardly in any way by the shadows of this earthly light. Who can doubt that the highest spiritual ability of the mind is dulled by the images of corporeal things,[243] which are known to flow into it through the eyes? Blinded outwardly, therefore, inwardly Lutgard was borne along in light with her whole mind. In her blindness she wept for only one thing: never again would she see her spiritual friends in this life. Christ in his mercy, however, quickly took from her this very natural feeling, and she prayed only to see them in heaven. In this

---

[241] *quietissima vita*: clearly this refers to the state of resting in the Lord.

[242] Genesis 27. 1; 48. 10.

[243] See DNR II.3, p. 84: The *animus* 'sees itself through itself, through itself it sees its very self. It does not seek the help of the bodily eyes; indeed it rather withdraws itself to itself from all corporeal senses as if they were impediments and noisy distractions so that it might see itself in itself […] and when it wishes to know God, it raises itself above the highest ability [*aciem*] of the mind.'

regard,[244] Friar Bernard added that he had heard from her own mouth what the Lord had replied to her: 'Patiently accept this blindness into which I have plunged you, for I promise that I will take you from your body without purgatory. As for the friends you say you will never see again in this life, I will preserve them for you to see in the eternal homeland.'

2. How Jordan of holy memory, Master General of the Dominicans, appeared to her and said he was among the choirs of the apostles and prophets

About the same time but a little later, Jordan of blessed memory, the Master General of the Order of Preachers,[245] who had long desired to visit the Holy Land, was returning by sea when, by a hidden judgement of God, he was drowned along with a great multitude of men, including two other Dominicans. Immediately a great column of light, divinely kindled, shone brightly through the night from the highest peak of heaven down to the ship where he lay drowned, for the space of five hours. When his sacred body was tossed ashore, a heavenly torch flashed over him three times and a fourth time over his companion, Brother Gerald, and then the torch withdrew and was received into a cloud. The witnesses to these events were Catholic Christians, Greek schismatics, and Gentiles. One of our brothers described them plainly in a prose sequence containing his gesta:[246]

> He went to the Holy Land to visit his brothers there,
> But as he was returning by sea,
> Drowning, he began to chant psalms

[244] literally 'in this chapter' (*capitulo*). This revelation is cited in the VA with no such attribution.

[245] Jordan of Saxony (1190–1237), the second Master General of the Dominican Order, was elected only six years after its foundation. He is famous for enthusiastically promoting the cause of the Friar Preachers by increasing their manpower and by founding four new provinces, as well as twice obtaining a chair at the University of Paris and helping to found the University of Toulouse. It was he who established the custom of singing the Salve Regina after compline each night. He died suddenly in the shipwreck described here. That Thomas knew and admired him immensely cannot be doubted, since he had studied at Cologne from *c.* 1232 and in Paris from 1238–1239/40. See *Early Dominicans: Selected Writings*, ed. by Simon Tugwell (New York: Paulist, 1982), and M.-H. Vicaire, *Saint Thomas and His Times*, trans. by Kathleen Pond (London: Darton, Longman & Todd, 1964).

[246] See the Letter of Godfrey and Reginald announcing the death of Jordan: Gérard de Frachet, *Vitae fratrum Ordinis Praedicatorum* (Leuven: Charpentier & Schoonjans, 1896), p. 129.

And to bless Christ,
And so he immediately went up to heaven,
As we are given to believe by signs.
No delay! At once there glowed
A great column of light
Which twinkled from heaven,
Shining on his most holy limbs,
And where his soul had travelled
He wanted the witnesses to know
In a most manifest way.
The lamp of heaven shone above
His sacred body, tossed on shore,
Glinted over his corpse three times,
Shone again a fourth time
Upon his companion,
And thus in a swift return,
Caught into a cloud, was seen no more.
The body, with wondrous fragrance,
Was tended by the faithful.
Praises to Christ with tears
Are offered in unison by the Greeks,
The Latins, and the Gentiles.
And thus the truth is magnificently
Revealed by three witnesses.

We heard these things from brothers at our German house who were counted worthy to see them with their own eyes. But we have also read an account of them in a letter from the Dominican prior in Venice.

3. How Master Jordan appeared to her on Christmas Eve of the same year and said that her death was imminent[*]

On Christmas Eve of the same year, while the blessed Lutgard was praying from prime until sext, she felt a kind of darkness in her spirit and became so weary that she burst out with these words: 'Lord, what is it I feel? What is it I suffer? Certainly if I had any friend in heaven or earth to pray for me, I would not feel such hardness in my heart!' When she had tearfully spoken, behold, suddenly there appeared before the eyes of her mind a spirit so lightsome and glorious that she did not recognize it because of the dazzling radiance. She asked,

[*] The headings of Chs 3–6 are given in the wrong order in the AASS edition.

'Lord, who are you?' He replied, 'I am Friar Jordan, once called Master of the Order of Friars Preachers. I have passed from this world into glory, and I have been exalted to shine among the choirs of apostles and prophets. Behold, I have been sent to console you on this most gracious feast. Be confident now of your reward because you will soon be crowned by the Lord. Until the end of your life, diligently continue to say the Psalm "May God have mercy upon us",[247] along with the Collect of the Holy Spirit which, while I was living and at my request, you promised to say for our order.' When Lutgard asked him about a certain brother of the order, he replied, 'God will favour him very soon because of the obedience he showed me and the love he showed you'. With these words he disappeared and left her in as much consolation as she had ever had.

After his death, the worthy father revealed almost the same things to a brother of the order, though in a different way, and showed by his honourable habit that in heaven he was placed in the order of sublime prelates.

Lutgard had an amazing love for this venerable man in life, and he confided in her above all women, making her the mother and nourisher of the whole Order of Preachers. We saw how devoted and diligent she was toward the friars above all other orders, so that every day she offered God diligent service especially for them.

4. How she completed a third seven-year fast

After she had completed her second seven-year fast, during which she fasted on bread and vegetables alone, it was again revealed to her that she should take on a third votive fast by which God might avert an evil that was looming from a certain enemy of Christ's Church, as it was feared with good reason.[248] From

---

[247] Psalm 66. 2.

[248] In the context of the Tartar invasions mentioned in III.7, this was probably Frederick II. Cardinal Rainer, whose see of Viterbo had been laid waste by Frederick in 1245, composed numerous 'unbridled and hate-ridden' pamphlets in which he set out to prove that Frederick was the forerunner of the Antichrist, in comparison to which Gregory IX's bull of excommunication was mild. See Ernst Kantorowicz, *Frederick the Second, 1194–1250*, trans. by E. O. Lorimer (London: Constable, 1931), pp. 592–95. Matthew Paris reported rumours current in 1241 and 1247 that Frederick II was the Antichrist and that he had allied himself with the Tartars for the downfall of the Christian faith, as noted by Maurice Powicke, *The Thirteenth Century, 1216–1307* (Oxford: Clarendon Press, 1953), p. 110, n. 1. See also Richard Vaughan, *Matthew Paris* (Cambridge: Cambridge University Press, 1958), pp. 147–48. If this event took place the year before Lutgard died, it must have been in 1245 or, conceivably, 1244. Frederick

that time, therefore, until the end of her life she continued her fast without interruption, not omitting to fast for a single day — not even the most solemn day of Easter. She died, as I will later explain more fully, in the seventh year of this saving fast. Nor were her fasts without fruit, as I now most certainly hope. For she told me when I was grievously fearing the aforesaid danger (in the year before she departed this life), 'You can be consoled, dearest, as I trust that he who is called a secret traitor to the Church will either be humbled by the prayers of the faithful or else he will soon die and leave the Church in peace, which it was thought he would overturn'. We have not yet seen the things she predicted, but we are truly confident that they will be accomplished. For of all the future events she predicted, we have not seen even one 'fall to the ground'[249] and come to naught, inasmuch as she drew her words in abundance from the Spirit of God.

5. How Cardinal James appeared to her as she was rapt into heaven on the fourth day after he died in Rome, and said he had been delivered from purgatory

About the same time James, venerable and worthy before God, once bishop of Acre and then cardinal of the Roman Curia, whom I have already mentioned,[250] passed from this world in Rome on the Vigil of Saints Philip and James.[251] On the fourth day of his funeral — that is, on the Feast of the Cross — the gracious Lutgard, who knew nothing of this because she lived in Brabant, a thirty days' journey from Rome, was rapt in ecstasy into heaven and saw the bishop's soul brought into paradise at that very hour. Lutgard's spirit, rejoicing with him in heaven, said, 'O most reverend father, I did not know you had died! When did you leave your body?' And he answered, 'It is now the fourth day, for I have already completed three nights and two days in purgatory'. At once she asked with wonderment, 'Why did you not tell me immediately after your death, so that your punishment could be remitted by our sisters' prayers?' 'The Lord', he said, 'did not want you to be grieved by my punishment, but rather

died in 1250, not long after Thomas completed this *vita*.

[249] I Samuel 3. 19.

[250] See II.3 above.

[251] James died in Rome on 1 May 1240 and, after a year, his body was exhumed and carried to Oignies, where he was buried close to his beloved Mary.

comforted by my deliverance and glorification once my purgatory was
completed. As for you, you will soon follow me.' With these words Lutgard
returned to herself and announced to her sisters the day of his death, his
purgatory, and his glorification with the most exuberant joy.[252]

This truth had two witnesses, for the Lord revealed what I have said about
the bishop's purgatory and glorification on the fourth day after his death to a
friar of the Dominican house in Rome, where he had first been buried.
Furthermore, Friar Bernard learned from Lutgard that she had experienced the
same kind of revelation on the deaths of many close friends. What could be
more obvious? What Jew or Gentile, through their unbelief, could invalidate a
truth so evident? Scarcely had James died in Rome than she knew of it on the
fourth day in Brabant. May that vile slanderer blush for shame — he who said
and wrote that people who record the fantastic visions of insignificant women
should be considered profane![253] By such slander he wanted to point his finger
at the venerable James, who wrote the most blessed life of Mary of Oignies in an
elegant style.

6. How she predicted the day of her death five years in advance

In the fifth year before her death, on the third Sunday after Pentecost, the
Gospel 'a certain man made a great banquet'[254] was being read in church.
Inwardly touched by the spirit of prophecy, Lutgard said to Lady Sybille de
Gages, to whom she had been committed in everything since she was a more
lettered nun,[255] 'You should know, dearest, that on the Sunday when this Gospel
is read, I shall have been carried to the Lamb's wedding feast,[256] newly dead'.
After she had said this, Sybille remembered and awaited this Sunday with the

---

[252] *Tripudium.* See I.16, p. 232, n. 89.

[253] James reports similar slanders in the VMO Prologue, 10, in *Mary of Oignies*, p. 50: 'There
are many animal men who do not have the Spirit of God, although they are considered to be
prudent among themselves. They do not want to see what they cannot understand by human
reasoning [...] [T]hey despise prophecies because they scorn spiritual people, thinking them to
be either insane or idiots, and they consider prophecies and the revelations of the saints to be
fantasies or illusions of sleep.'

[254] Luke 14. 16.

[255] Presumably Sybille, more 'lettered' in Scripture and exegetical matters, had been given
this charge so that Lutgard's visions could be interpreted.

[256] Apocalypse 19. 9.

greatest expectation as the future date of Lutgard's passing. When that day came a year later and she had not died, Sybille thought the prophetic vision had been a fantasy and forgot it for awhile. But when the fifth year had passed and Lutgard's dead body lay on the bier on the same Sunday she had predicted, the Gospel of which I spoke was being read in church at the community's morning mass. As she heard it, Sybille was astonished, remembering what I have mentioned. To the wonderment of all, she reported how Lutgard had predicted this five years ago with a prophetic spirit.

7. How, four years before her death, when the Tartars were attacking many kingdoms and it was feared that they would conquer all Germany, she predicted that they would not come so far, but be driven back

In the fourth year before her death, the exceedingly cruel race of the Tartars poured out of their own lands and destroyed Greater Hungary in the east and Lesser Hungary in the west, together with the greater part of Turkey and Greece, Bulgaria and Russia, as well as killing the powerful Duke of Poland and laying waste his lands and people.[257] When they began to invade part of the Teutonic region, namely Bohemia, there was terrible fear throughout France and Germany that they would invade and devastate those lands as they had done elsewhere. Therefore Friar Bernard, a friar of the Order of Preachers and confessor to the lord Pope, crushed by the fearful rumour, came and begged Lutgard to pray urgently that the Lord would avert the Tartar scourge from the borders of Germany. She said, 'I have not yet begun to pray to the Lord about this, but I am already certain that the Tartars will not now proceed to these lands'.[258] He accepted this as if it had been divinely proclaimed from heaven.

---

[257] Reports from Poland, Hungary, and elsewhere of the Mongol invasion of 1241–42 caused great anxiety in Western Europe. The Mongol leader Batu Khan overran Kiev in December 1240 and, on 9 April 1241, defeated a joint force of German and Polish Teutonic Knights at Liegnitz under Duke Henry II of Poland.

[258] In the event, Lutgard was right. The great khan Ogadai died on 11 December 1241, and in the confusion arising from his death, the Mongols were diverted from their invasion of Western Europe.

8. How Dom Baldwin de Barbençon, Prior of Oignies, was shown to her after his death

About the same time Baldwin, surnamed de Barbençon, prior of Oignies,[259] formerly chaplain at Aywières for many years and a most solemn preacher of God's Word, became involved in worldly affairs in a less than worthy fashion, against the advice of his friends. He was chastised with a serious illness and, on the day before he died, he ordered that the finger of the blessed Mary of Oignies be shown to him.[260] When he had it before him, he said, 'O lady worthy of veneration, while you were still living, you promised to help me at the hour of death. Help me now then, lady! Help, for the time is at hand!' So Baldwin died there and was buried with worthy veneration in Oignies. Our Friar Bernard assisted at his funeral services and, as soon as the body had been buried, he came to Aywières. No sooner did he arrive than Lutgard greeted him and said, 'Has Dom Baldwin died?' Friar Bernard, wondering at such a sudden and unexpected question, said, 'He has died and is just buried. Why do you ask?' She replied, 'Because just now my lady Mary of Oignies appeared to me, saying, "Rise up, rise quickly, dearest, hurry and pray to the Lord, because at this hour the soul of our friend Dom Baldwin is being brought before divine judgement to give an account of the deeds he has committed and omitted"'.

Behold, how truthful in testimony, how faithful in your promise you have been, venerable Mary, for you wished to approach the gracious Lutgard for the suffrage of her prayers before any other mortal. Not only did you testify while still alive that she was most powerful in liberating souls from purgatory,[261] but after you had been raised into heavenly joys, you sought her help for a dead

---

[259] Baldwin de Barbençon (d. 1242), prior of the Augustinian canons at Oignies. Although he had been highly respected for a long time, he became negligent in his role as prior and allowed discipline to slacken. At the behest of Bishop Robert of Thourotte, two Dominicans were called in to restore order and new customs were codified for the priory. See McDonnell, *The Beguines and Beghards in Medieval Culture*, pp. 15–16.

[260] Cf. III.19 below. The reliquary for this finger, made by Hugo of Oignies with the inscription, 'Hic est iuncturae beate Marie de Oignies', can still be seen at the Musées Royaux d'Art et d'Histoire in Brussels. See the exhibition catalogue *Autour de Hugo d'Oignies*, ed. by Robert Didier and Jacques Toussaint, Musée des Arts anciens du Namurois, 25 (Namur: Société archéologique de Namur, 2003), especially the article by Suzanne Vandecan, 'L'histoire du Trésor d'Oignies', pp. 47–57.

[261] See II.9 above.

friend. Blessed therefore in all things be God, who wished to declare the holiness and merits of his bride with such evident testimony.

Now see, reader, with what severe judgement those men are tried who, according to Isaiah, beat the sword of God's Word into the plowshares of worldly labour,[262] and instead of attacking sins with their spears, they are already hurrying to reap the fruit of a transitory peace so that they might have leisure for delights.

9. How she contemplated the face of Christ in accord with the verse of the Song of Songs, 'My soul melted when my beloved spoke', etc

When she was asked by one of her intimate spiritual friends how she was accustomed to see the face of Christ in contemplation, she replied, 'An indescribable brilliance appears to me in an instant, and I see the ineffable beauty of his glorified being[263] like a flash of lightning. Were this vision not to pass quickly from the gaze of my contemplation, I would not be able to endure it and remain alive.[264] After this flash, there remains an intellectual brilliance, and when in that brilliance I seek the one I had seen for an instant, I cannot find him.'

Note well, reader, that this is what is described in the Song of Songs: 'My soul melted when my beloved spoke; I sought him and found him not; I called and he did not answer me.'[265] What else is it for Christ to speak in the soul except to make present to it[266] the riches of his goodness, wisdom, and beauty? From these riches let the soul measure how good, how deliciously wise,[267] and how beautifully adorned with virtues one must be to deserve his love in perpetual charity.[268] When the soul hears his voice, it melts with desire and

---

[262] Isaiah 2. 4.

[263] Thomas Merton makes the point that the term *glorificationem* refers to Christ's glorified body: *What Are These Wounds?*, pp. 103–04.

[264] Note the difference between this apprehension of Christ and that in her first vision (I.2) when she had seen him *in ipsa forma humanitatis*. Then she 'saw' him as a man; now she is blinded by his brightness.

[265] Song of Songs 5. 6.

[266] *repraesentare*: Thomas often uses forms of the verb *praesum* (*praesentialiter*, etc.) to refer to an intermediate state between immediate presence and a more distant communication.

[267] *sapide sapientem*: playing on the derivation of *sapientia* (wisdom) from *sapor* (taste). [BN]

[268] See Augustine, *The City of God*, XV, 23: 'But if the Creator is truly loved, that is, if He Himself is loved and not another thing in His stead, He cannot be evilly loved; for love itself

strives to obtain what it has glimpsed, but since the time of perfect vision has not yet come, it suddenly loses him whom it held as if he were present. Thus the more diligently the soul seeks him, the more ardently it loves him, and the more thoroughly the mind prepares itself to possess him, the more frequently it is renewed to seek him. That is why Lutgard said the eyes of Christ flashed with such a radiant light that, if it were possible for that light to be poured over the sun in its splendour, it would darken the sun's rays just as the sun darkens the stars, and infinitely more so.

This is what a certain monastic priest was shown when he desired to know what these words mean: 'His eyes are more beautiful than wine.'[269] One day while he was celebrating the Divine Mysteries, the face of Christ appeared to him in the holy chalice. His eyes sent forth radiant beams of light so splendid that they could illumine the whole world, even in the dead of night, more than a thousand suns.

Taught by the Spirit of truth, a preacher who was deeply experienced in the spiritual life[270] said that he had never known anyone in the world who so perfectly travelled through faith into understanding and affection as the gracious Lutgard.[271] I too can make that claim, as I gather in part from the writings and accounts of spiritual people — even though I am a wretched little man,[272] inexperienced in such light. It is not easy to believe how intensely Lutgard burned with desire to see Christ. I myself once saw her in such a flood of tears that one could scarcely bear it without weeping oneself.

Two years before she travelled from the world, it happened that our Friar Bernard came to Aywières and found that she had been sick for a month and was already prepared for the sacrament of anointing, as if she expected to die any

---

is to be ordinately loved, because we do well to love that which, when we love it, makes us live well and virtuously. So that it seems to me that it is a brief but true definition of virtue to say, it is the order of love; and on this account, in the Song of Songs, the bride of Christ, the city of God, sings, "Order love within me"': *The City of God*, trans. by Marcus Dods (New York: Modern Library, 1950), p. 511.

[269] Genesis 49. 12.

[270] Presumably James of Vitry.

[271] *ita perfecte per fidem migrantem in intellectum et affectum.* Cf. Étienne Gilson, *The Christian Philosophy of Saint Augustine* (New York: Random House, 1960), pp. 30–31: 'What does it mean, then, to believe in God? It means that you love Him while believing Him; it means that in believing Him you cherish Him, enter into Him through love and become incorporated with His members'.

[272] *homuncio.*

day. From her ardent yearning to see Christ, she had developed a fixed idea that she should pass over to the Lord at that time. When the friar discovered no sign of imminent death in her, although she was suspended in such great desire, he said, 'It does not seem to me, dearest, that you are going to pass from this world now'. She answered him with an anxious expression, 'O may it not be as you say, my dearest, for I long to contemplate Christ the Lord with unveiled face'.[273] Smiling, he said, 'No, dearest mother, this will not happen now'. She raised her eyes to heaven and said, 'If it will not happen now, may his will be done tomorrow. Then I will rise from bed and receive his body as a consolation.'

10. How, in the hearing of another nun, a voice came to her saying, 'My delights are to be with the children of men'

One day when Lutgard's soul was inclined to piety and sincerely united with Christ in contemplation, a voice came upon her in the hearing of a most devout nun, saying, 'My delights are to be with the children of men'.[274] What is there to marvel at? What is new? Augustine, the greatest of contemplatives, called the faithful and devout soul 'the paradise of paradises',[275] and rightly so. For in the creation of heaven and earth, God merely spoke the word and they were created. But in the recreation of the soul, fallen through Adam's sin, who can imagine the toil Christ endured for thirty-three years before his ignominious death? I do not doubt that he who suffered thus was God and true man, but what value should be set on the one for whom Christ endured such great and terrible things? No one will ever be able to marvel enough at this — especially one who, repaying him as far as possible, does not cease to 'fulfil in her own flesh those

---

[273] II Corinthians 3. 18.

[274] Proverbs 8. 31.

[275] Augustine, *De Genesi ad Litteram*, XII, 34, 67, in *La Genèse au sens littéral en douze livres*, trans. by Paul Agaësse and A. Solignac, 2 vols (Paris: de Brouwer, 1972), II, p. 450: 'The third heaven is that which the intellectual soul contemplates as soon as it is separated, removed and cut off from the carnal senses and so cleansed that it can see and hear in an ineffable way those things which are in heaven and even the very substance of God as well as the Word of God through Whom everything was made and through charity [see and hear] the Holy Spirit. Thus we think that it is not unreasonable that this was that paradise into which the apostle was rapt and that perhaps the paradise which is better than all others was there, the paradise of paradises; for if a good soul which delights in good things finds its joy in all created things, how much more excellent is the joy which it finds in the Word of God through Whom everything has been made?'

things that are lacking in the passion of Christ'.[276] That Lutgard did this supremely, no one doubts who knew her; no one argues who has read these pages. According to the foregoing account, then, what in our times could have been more delightful to Christ, the Son of God, than Lutgard? If there is anything, I do not know; God knows.[277] One thing I do know: I believed, therefore I have spoken.[278] I do not recall ever having read or heard of another woman such as this.

11. How, a year before her death, Christ required only three things of her

A little more than a year before her death, the Lord Jesus Christ appeared to her, applauding her with a joyful countenance, and said, 'Now the end of your labour is at hand. I do not wish you to be separated from me much longer. This year I require only three things of you. First, I would have you render thanks to me for the benefits you have already attained, and in this you will require the intercessions of the blessed. The second is that you pour yourself out entirely in prayers to the Father for my sinners. The third is that you long with a yearning desire[279] to come to me, with no other cares.' Ponder then, reader, how much merit she had before God, who occupied her mind with only these three concerns at a time when the ancient serpent should have been lying in wait at her heel.[280]

12. How, during the Easter season before her death, the Lord Christ and his mother Mary appeared to her and predicted her death

During the Easter season shortly before her death, the Lord Jesus Christ appeared to her in immensely dazzling clarity with his glorious Mother. While the gracious Lutgard was lamenting the exile of the present life and her desire for the supernal homeland, as she almost always did, they said, 'There is no need, dearest, for you to be wearied any longer by this present time, for even now the

---

[276] Colossians 1. 24.

[277] II Corinthians 12. 2.

[278] John 9. 25; Psalm 115. 1.

[279] *hianti desiderio concupiscas:* a 'carnal' image transferred to the transcendental plane. Cf. Lutgard's yearning for carnal marriage in I.1 and her yearning for heavenly things in I.8.

[280] Genesis 3. 15. See above, II.15.

remedy of perpetual peace is being prepared as your crown. We do not wish you to wait much longer.' As soon as Lutgard had received this revelation from the Lord, with the greatest fear and exultation she told it to Sybille de Gages, whom I have often mentioned, for she had no dearer or more intimate friend in all respects. And rightly so, for in accord with the venerable James of Vitry's command, she was governed in all things by Sybille's counsel, since she was more lettered.

13. How, fifteen days before she died, the blessed Virgin Mary, John the Baptist, and some of her special friends who had already died appeared to her and predicted her death; and her glorious reply as to how she could recognize and distinguish particular saints who appeared to her in a multitude

Fifteen days before her death, the glorious Virgin Mary and the most blessed John the Baptist (whom she loved with a very special love) appeared to her and said, 'Now your consummation is at hand; there remains to you the crown of justice.[281] We do not wish you to remain here any longer, for all the citizens of heaven await you.'

The saints frequently appeared to her that year in a great multitude and predicted her departure, which she was soon to accomplish.[282] In addition, some of her close friends who had predeceased her appeared, telling her how splendidly they rejoiced that she would soon make her passage and be united with them.

When she told these things to some of her friends, they asked how she could distinguish among the saints. She replied, 'From Christ himself, the Holy of Holies, there proceeds a radiance that illumines the soul, and in it I can perfectly recognize each saint who appears to me'.

Note, reader, that by this radiance I understand nothing else than the mirror of the Trinity or of eternity. For as the book of Wisdom says in the seventh chapter, 'She is the brightness of the eternal light, the unspotted mirror of God's majesty, and the image of his goodness. Although she is one, she can do all, and

---

[281] II Timothy 4. 8.

[282] Luke 9. 31. The word *excessus* is used for both 'ecstasy' and departure in the sense of death.

in herself unchanging, she makes all things new. Among the nations she enters into holy souls and makes them friends of God and prophets.'[283]

When the saints appeared to Lutgard, she unfailingly asked them to thank God for her and for the benefits she had received from him.

14. How she reproved the sisters in the infirmary and predicted that the Lord would chastise them after her death, and how this came to pass

She frequently reproved her sisters, the nuns in the infirmary, because they were not very attentive in offering to God the divinely appointed canonical hours. Half a year before her death, when she did not see among the other nuns the full correction that was owing to the divine reverence, she said, 'I know that after my death, the Lord's hand will avenge this defect in the sisters. Then, remembering my words and my lashing reproach, they will be humbly corrected, and soon the Lord will withdraw the hand he had stretched out in vengeance.'[284] No one doubts the truth of this prophecy. For just after the gracious Lutgard's blessed death, a grievous plague raged in the convent, and within a short time fourteen of the most proven nuns had died. I myself came there at the time to celebrate mass for two sisters (in the flesh as well as the spirit) who had died in the same instant, and I buried them in a single grave. Immediately afterward, when the sick nuns in the infirmary had thoroughly corrected themselves by saying the Hours punctiliously, the Lord mercifully withdrew his hand, just as Lutgard had predicted, and the plague soon ceased.

I therefore beg you, ladies and sisters of Aywières, to observe all of Lutgard's precepts as best you can and to follow in her footsteps. And I hope that, by her prayers, you will achieve the palm of victory and take to heart the exemplary tale I now add.

15. How a secular friend of hers gravely sinned and earned pardon by her prayers, and not he alone, but for her sake the Lord would be gracious to all whom she loved, and all who loved her and hoped in her

A certain worldly man, one of her close friends, fell into serious sin. He therefore made his confession and did penance for the sin, but he did not deserve

---

[283] Wisdom 7. 26–27.

[284] II Samuel 24. 16.

to feel any consolation or forgiveness in his prayers. For this reason, he almost fell into the abyss of despair, and coming to Lutgard as if to his own mother, he bewailed with deep sorrow what he had done and what he was enduring for his offense. Once, twice, and yet again a third time, Lutgard poured out her prayers for the sinner, but she did not receive her accustomed response from the Lord, nor did he feel that he was any the better for it. Seeing this, Lutgard wrestled with the Lord in prayer with wondrous urgency of spirit. At last, when she could not vanquish the Lord, who was holding back his mercy in his anger,[285] she said, 'Either erase me from the book of life[286] or else remit this offense of his'. No sooner had she said this than the Lord inclined to mercy and said, 'Behold, I have dismissed his offense because he trusted in you; and for your sake I will be gracious not only to him, but to all who have set their hope in you and whom you love.' At these words of God, the man swiftly and perfectly received the hope of pardon and attained a more gracious state than he had before his lapse, because the Lord had been appeased.

16. How she died and what she did on her deathbed, and how she said there was a heavenly host in the cloister when death entered

And so the day came which, for her, was a day of exultation and praise. But for us and all who lived by the comfort of her patronage, it was a day of mourning, a day of groans and lamentation — a day that I, unhappiest of all, could neither anticipate by my own death (as I had often begged her) nor follow soon afterward. So I was abandoned, more wretched than any orphan.

Thus the day came, the vigil of the octave of the holy and undivided Trinity, and she, who had been an undivided venerator of the Triune God, lay in bed with a fever that was now quite serious, but slow. As the sickness grew worse she was troubled. On the following Monday William, a lay brother from Afflighem, came to visit her, for she especially loved the brothers of that monastery because of their religious observance.[287] Among other things, he said, 'If only our lord abbot[288] knew how gravely ill you are!' And she answered, 'Tomorrow my dearest

---

[285] Psalm 76. 10.

[286] Cf. Exodus 32. 32.

[287] See above, II.24.

[288] John I, eleventh Benedictine abbot of Afflighem (1242–62).

one will come and see me'. Not expecting this reply, he fell silent in astonishment.

The next morning, the venerable abbot was passing nearby, about two leagues away. Though he was totally unaware that the gracious Lutgard was ill, he said to his companions, 'Let us go see Lady Lutgard, for it is a long time since I have seen her'. So he came to Aywières and, when he had entered, she was delighted to see him and sat up, raised from her bed. Taking his hand she said, 'Now, dearest one, I am going away, and I leave nothing under heaven dearer than you. You know that I have been consoled by the Lord concerning you!'

After she had said this the abbot left, distracted by other things, and she remained in very cheerful spirits until Thursday. But on Thursday when she heard the voice of Sybille de Gages coming in, she said, 'Sit down here next to my heart. Look, the monastery is filled with the heavenly hosts! The souls of the blessed are here, with many of our sisters who have passed from this world.' With these words she fell silent. From that time throughout Friday she remained rapt in spirit, contemplating God alone with a most grace-filled expression. But on Saturday, as the hour of her death drew near, she opened her eyes to the heavens and, fortified with the holy sacraments, her happy soul flew up to the supernal heights, exulting in the open air, amid young girls with their timbrels mingled with the princes of the heavenly host, all chanting psalms.[289]

It was the year of the Lord's Incarnation 1246, on the sixteenth of June, in the fourth indiction, in the sixty-fourth year of her life, at about the hour of vespers, under the reign of our Lord Jesus Christ, to whom be honour and glory with the Father and the Holy Spirit through immortal ages of ages. Amen.

17. How she did not close her open eyes before her death, and what some nuns felt as she died, and how her face looked in and after death

When the gracious Lutgard breathed her last breath, a few of the nuns to whom God granted this superlative gift were filled with such sweetness and alacrity of spirit that they could not contain themselves for wonder. They knew with perfect certainty that Jesus himself, the prince of our salvation, had come in person, amid the measureless exultation of the saints, to call her soul to the delights of paradise. Moreover, although it is a natural property of the dying to

---

[289] Psalm 67. 26. *Tympanistriarum*: thus is Mary described in her last hours (VMO II.99, in *Mary of Oignies*, pp. 119–20).

be darkened in the blue-grey pallor of death, yet Lutgard's face shone with the lustre of a lily as a sign of her virginal innocence. At the very instant of her death she had, as I have said, opened her eyes to heaven, though they had previously been closed for a long time. Afterwards they could not be shut, neither in death nor after death, for the direction her eyes had taken showed the path her spirit had travelled. The skin of her whole body was found to be so soft to the touch that it felt like linen beneath the hand, lustrous and utterly soft. Certainly this simple dove without guile had eyes bathed in the milk of purity, she who dwelt in contemplation beside plentiful streams.[290]

18. How a sister's shrivelled hand was cured by touching her body when it was being washed

There was a certain sister who for many years had completely lost the use of her hand. When Lutgard's sacred, lifeless corpse was being washed, this sister accidentally touched the body with her paralyzed hand while she was washing it, and suddenly the hand was restored to health, fully functional for all tasks. See how suddenly and plainly the prophetic word of the venerable Mary of Oignies was fulfilled! As I said above, when Mary was dying she had predicted concerning Lutgard, 'While she lives, she now performs spiritual miracles; after death she will work bodily ones'.[291] It was worthy — indeed, most worthy — that God himself, whom the living Lutgard preached as wonderful among his saints,[292] should show by conspicuous signs that she too was wonderful after death.

---

[290] Cf. Song of Songs 5. 12 and I.3 above. The dove is noted in contemporary bestiaries for its lack of gall (or acrimony) and its habit of sitting by streams 'so that on seeing a hawk it can dive in and escape'. See Pseudo-Hugh of St-Victor, *De bestiis et aliis rebus*, I.3, in PL 157:16: 'Columba est quaelibet fidelis et simplex anima'; Florence McCulloch, *Mediaeval Latin and French Bestiaries* (Chapel Hill: University of North Carolina Press, 1962), pp. 111–12; *The Bestiary: A Book of Beasts, Being a Translation from a Latin Bestiary of the Twelfth Century*, trans. by T. H. White (London: Cape, 1954; repr. New York: Putnam, 1960), p. 144.

[291] See II.9 above.

[292] Psalm 67. 36.

19. How she had predicted many years ago, when I had desired to have her hand after her death, that her little finger should be enough for me; and how this was miraculously fulfilled

Many years before her death, I had urgently pleaded with several nuns and lay brothers that if it happened (as alas, it did) that I should be absent when the gracious Mother Lutgard died, they were to cut off her hand and keep it for me as a sacred memorial of her; and I had obtained permission from the venerable Hadewijch, abbess of the monastery. But since it is women's nature to be unable to keep secrets (as the vernacular proverb says, 'be quiet, woman — if you can'),[293] the nuns told Lutgard how I had ordered her hand to be cut off. Not long afterward, I came to Aywières and when I had just begun a conversation with her, she said with a serious expression, 'I have heard, dearest son, that you are already planning to cut off my hand after I die. I cannot imagine what you plan to do with my hand!' Blushing, I said, 'I believe your hand would be good for my soul and body if I manage to get it, as I intend'. Then, serenely smiling, she laid the little finger of her right hand on the windowsill where we were speaking and said, 'It will be enough for you if you are able to have this finger after my death'. More confidently, I returned to the charge: 'No part of your body could be enough for me, mother, unless I had your hand or head to comfort me when I am bereft of your whole self.' With this we moved on to other topics. Saying nothing to anyone about this, I thought no more of it.

Now after she died, while her body was still in the infirmary and had not yet been brought into the church, two lay brothers — a devout youth named Guido and one of his companions — thought of cutting off Lutgard's hand, but they did not dare go so far, so they amputated the very finger of the right hand that she had said would be enough for me, and extracted sixteen teeth from her mouth. When I learned of her death and heard about the amputated finger, but did not know which one it was, I said, 'Now I shall see plainly whether Lutgard is proven to be a prophet, for she predicted years ago that the little finger of her right hand would be enough for me'. So I came to Aywières and found, as she had predicted, that very finger amputated. I nervously thought that it would indeed be enough for me and I would be happy if I could get it.

So I went to the abbess and begged her with tears for the relic, but much to my sorrow, I soon found that the abbess — and she alone — was inexorable. I believe, though, that this took place by the dispensation of God's counsel, for

---

[293] Cf. VJC III.2.

the Almighty had arranged a test so that I might obtain Lutgard's finger according to her promise — the finger that my ignorant simplicity had once refused. Once again I came to Aywières and, promising to write Lutgard's life, I received with immense and heartfelt joy the gift I desired more than gold and silver.[294]

Let no envious person snap at me or judge me accusingly if I embrace Lutgard's finger with such love, even though she is not yet canonized. For the most blessed Natalia cut off the martyr Adrian's arm just minutes after he was killed.[295] And James of pious memory, the former bishop of Acre and later cardinal of the Roman Curia, cut off the venerable Mary of Oignies's finger when she died, though she was not yet canonized.[296] He gave it as an especially valuable gift to Pope Gregory IX of solemn memory, who wore it suspended around his neck for many years against the spirit of blasphemy, by which he was atrociously tempted.[297] In our own time as well, the thumb and index finger of

---

[294] Cf. Proverbs 22. 1. We owe the present text to the abbess's prudent negotiations. [BN]

[295] Natalia (whose feast is celebrated on 1 December) was the young wife of Adrian (8 September; BHL, 3744–45, I, pp. 558 and II, p. 880), martyred in Nicomedia under Maximianus (c. 304).

[296] See above, III.8.

[297] 'The bishop of Ostia [Ugolino of Segni, later Gregory IX] said to the bishop of Acre [...] "A spirit of blasphemy troubles my soul and submerges it with waves of temptations" [...] The bishop of Acre, a prudent and experienced man, knew that in such cases it often happens that a mind overwhelmed by precisely this kind of temptation does not grasp such reasoning easily unless it is buttressed with the most telling examples. So he immediately added the following story. "In Lorraine, before I was a bishop, I had a most dear friend of God who by the prerogative of her sanctity and merit, which were without equal in her time, had obtained from God a special grace of expelling blasphemous spirits. In the book of her life, which I wrote, there are many examples of this. This grace was not just for those who invoked her while she was dwelling in this life; she also kept it after her death. So take the book about her way of life with you and read it. With all my heart and with confidence in the mercy of God and the holiness of His handmaid, I anticipate that shortly you will sense that you have been relieved of the temptation which keeps you in turmoil." The cardinal of Ostia received these words with a joyful heart. He said to the bishop of Acre, "Dearest brother, I have heard many wondrous things about this woman. If you have any relics of her, I ask that you lend them to me so that, because of my veneration of them, I will be all the more pleased to invoke that holy woman just as if she were present." Then the bishop of Acre smiled happily at his request, saying, "There is a finger of hers enclosed in a silver case which is constantly hanging from my neck. It has always kept me safe in various dangers and during crises at sea. Take it with you if you insist." After the bishop of Ostia had gratefully received the items offered him, he first devoted himself to a vigilant reading of the *Life* of the handmaid of Christ. He found in it wondrous hope and

the blessed Elizabeth, countess of Thuringia, were cut off immediately after she died.[298] Given the precedent set by St Natalia, the memorable Cardinal James, the Roman pontiff Gregory, and many other trustworthy people of great authority, no one will judge my action foolish or impious unless he is unmistakably foolish and impious himself.

20. How her body was buried

While her sacred body was lying on its bier awaiting burial, the question arose as to where such great and solemn relics should be laid to rest. It happened, by divine providence, that the venerable Abbot of Aulne,[299] the Father Visitor of the monastery according to the Rule, had been present for three days before Lutgard's burial and eagerly awaited the outcome. So when he was asked where it would be fitting to inter such a precious treasure, the abbot replied, 'Where else but in the church, where she can be worthily visited by everyone?' This was a sensible, providential, and worthy answer in full accord with what she herself

peace for himself. From the relic which remained with him he derived great mental confidence. Shortly afterwards he was praying alone before an altar which he had in a secret place. The lethargy of his familiar temptation began to flood his mind. He immediately rose from the ground and grasped the finger of the handmaid of Christ in his devout hands. Clasping it tightly to his breast, he suppliantly invoked the handmaid of God and her prayers. Instantly the spirit of blasphemy and his mental torpor were completely dispelled and he was illumined with the heavenly light of interior grace. With the palate of his heart he tasted how sweet is the Lord.' See VMO-S 15–17, pp. 153–55.

[298] Elizabeth of Thuringia or Hungary (BHL, 2488–2514, I, pp. 373–77) was canonized on 26 May (Pentecost) 1235 by Pope Gregory IX and news of the event was first published in Erfurt, where a festival of ten days was proclaimed. Her relics were translated to Mainz on 1 May 1236, and the bishops and people of Germany were invited to attend the solemn ceremony. According to contemporary historians, 'When the tomb was first opened, her body was seen to be incorrupt and emitting a delightful perfume. Her remains were laid in a lead coffin and when on the following day it was opened for public veneration, they found it full of a pure and delicate oil which gave forth a perfume like to that of the most precious spikenard': Count de Montalambert, *The Life of Saint Elizabeth of Hungary, Duchess of Thuringia*, trans. by Mary Hackett (New York: Sadlier, 1886), p. 374. Before her burial, her body was laid in a chapel and 'very many people, stimulated by devotion, cut off not only pieces of the cloth but also her fingernails. One woman even lopped off her ears and some men cut off the nipples of her breasts': *Dicta IV ancillarum S. Elisabeth Thuringiae*, quoted by E. Horn, *Sainte Elisabeth de Hongrie* (Montreal: Revue du Tiers-Ordre et de la Terre Saint, 1914), p. 227.

[299] Joannes Onkelin, tenth abbot of Aulne (1231–66).

had predicted in life. For when some of the nuns at Aywières who were closest to her had asked what they should do when she died and they were deprived of the support of her prayers, she replied, 'Flee to my tomb. There I will be as present to you in death as I was in life.' Anyone who has confidently invoked her help no doubt knows how truly and prophetically she spoke. But where else could this more fittingly happen than in her accustomed place, where she used to cling to God in prayer and contemplation? So the abbot's words won the consent of all, and she was buried in a solemn and honourable place on the right side of the choir, next to the wall where she used to pray. Sybille de Gages composed her epitaph in verse:

> Leading a life without offence, Lutgardis shone:
> She lives with Christ who lies beneath this stone.
> In hunger and thirst for heaven, she mourned;
> Now let the Bridegroom's face, pure light of morn,
> Illumine her. Mirror of life, her convent's flower,
> She glowed with mercy and bright virtue's power.[300]

21. How she appeared to a certain nun and told her that she had passed over without purgatory and liberated many souls from it; and she predicted the death of another nun, who died immediately afterward

As soon as she had been buried, Lutgard appeared to Elizabeth de Wans,[301] a nun at Aywières who had once been abbess at St Desiderius near Nogent-sur-Seine.[302] She asked the apparition, which was clothed in great glory, 'O sweetest lady, did you never endure any time in purgatory?' She replied, 'Not only did I

---

[300] 'Lutgardis luxit; vitam sine crimine duxit; / Cum Christo degit, quam lapis iste tegit. / Esuriens haec et sitiens coelestia, luxit; / Mera dies, sponsi facies, illi modo lux sit. / Haec speculum vitae, flos claustri, gemma sororum, / Fulsit in hac pietas, compassio, gloria morum'. The epitaph puns on *luxit*, which is the past tense of both *luceo* (to shine) and *lugeo* (to mourn). In line 4, the VA reading *lux sit* is superior to the AASS *luxit*. [BN]

[301] The Bollandists have put Elizabeth de Wans (d. 1250) among the *Praetermissi* for 1 July and transfer her feast (as well as that of Sibylle de Gages) to 9 October. Agnes Dunbar notes that Elizabeth, Lutgard and Sibylle are invoked in a prayer of the nuns of Aywières: 'Vos Domina S. Lutgardis, Domina S. Sybilla, Domina S. Elizabeth de Wans meae honoratissimae majores et carissimae consorores estote benedictae in saecula' ('Blessed be you for ever, Saints Lutgard, Sybille, and Elizabeth de Wans, my most esteemed predecessors and dearest sisters'): *A Dictionary of Saintly Women*, 2 vols (London: George Bell, 1904–05), I, p. 264.

[302] A Benedictine monastery in Champagne: *Gallia Christiana*, IV, p. 329.

pass to my rest without purgatory, but as I was passing in front of purgatory, I had compassion on those who were afflicted there and blessed them. And I brought many souls with me to the loveliness of paradise, exempted from punishment by divine favour.' When she had said this, it seemed to Elizabeth that Lutgard spoke to a young nun called Mechthild, who was still alive, and said, 'Follow me'. From this Elizabeth understood that the young nun would follow Lutgard in death, and she offered to follow as well, saying, 'Let me also follow you, sweetest mother!' But Lutgard said, 'You cannot follow me now, daughter, but later you will follow me as your mother'. This vision took effect at once, for the young nun whom Lutgard invited to follow her died within nine days. As for Elizabeth, who had offered to follow but this was not granted her, she is still alive.

22. How she seemed in the vision of a certain nun to allay a plague that had come among them, just as she had prophesied

Furthermore, when according to Lutgard's prophecy a dire and fatal plague attacked the nuns of Aywières, one of the nuns saw in a vision that a crowd was insolently attacking the monastery church. When no one could restrain their insolence, she saw the gracious Lutgard rise from her tomb and drive them all from the church with the greatest violence. At once the blessed vision took effect, and the monastery of Aywières was delivered from the assault of the contagious plague.

23. How the noble girl Beatrice was cured by means of her veil

Each of the nuns hastily snatched whatever they could of Lutgard's belts, robes, veils, and other goods as relics, and indeed, the very greatest relics. A young nun, Beatrice de Raive,[303] came of very noble stock and had most generously relieved the poverty of Aywières with her inheritance. She had an ulcer on her neck which the doctors diagnosed as a carbuncle. When she placed a veil from Lutgard's head around her neck, the pernicious swelling visibly disappeared at once. O gracious Lutgard, you acted altogether justly and

---

[303] Beatrice de Raive [Roavia] was a sister or close relative of the prioress Marie de Raive and the patron of Aywières, Iwan de Raive. See above, II.5.

worthily, so that she whose temporal goods you received in this life might reap your spiritual ones after you died.

24. How the chaplain Dom Alard was cured

Dom Alard, who had been chaplain at Aywières for many years, suffered great distress from a swollen thumb. Binding Lutgard's relics to his thumb, he quickly and sensibly experienced relief of the pain and swelling.

25. How the subprioress Oda was cured

When Oda, subprioress of Aywières, was suffering grievously with a swollen hand, she tied some of Lutgard's relics around it and at once sensed the restoration of perfect health.

26. How a nun experienced her power by means of the lilies on her tomb

A nun, a blood relative of mine who was also called Oda, born in the town of Braine,[304] had long been troubled by a weakness of the head and could not bear the scent of lilies. When lilies were placed on Lutgard's tomb, she was horrified at the very sight of them, but nevertheless decided to give it a try. Poking her head alone into the doorway, she suffered no distress. Then, more confidently, she entered, lingered on the spot, approached the tomb, and touched the lilies to her nose, feeling absolutely no pain in her head.

One night, when the same nun went to prostrate herself at Lutgard's tomb in the dark for prayer, she stabbed her eye on the iron spike of a candelabrum. Thinking that her eyeball had been ripped out of its socket, she quickly put her hand to her eye and held it there lest the eye fall out entirely. Stricken with intolerable pain, she said, 'Holy mother Lutgard, what has happened to me? Prostrating myself to venerate you, I have lost an eye, which you ought to have guarded, and I have left with injury where I looked for healing.' So saying, she arose — and in the short space of an hour, she was fully restored to health and retained absolutely no weakness or pain.

---

[304] Brania-Comitis; OF Braine.

27. How Marie d'Andenne was suddenly cured of a terrible headache by her veil

Once Marie d'Andenne, a nun of Aywières, was in torment with such a terrible headache that she could find no rest in any part of her body for even a moment and began to roll impatiently on the ground. Everyone was struck with astonishment and thought she had suddenly lost her senses, but she was so quickly and visibly cured by Lutgard's veil that no pain at all remained in her.

28. How a matron who had been labouring in dangerous childbirth was delivered by her belt; and many other women experienced the same thing

When a certain noble matron had been labouring for a very long time in childbirth and was in great danger, someone brought her a belt made of horse hair, which Lutgard had been wont to wear against her skin for the laceration of her body. Placing it on her womb, the mother was painlessly and safely delivered of a healthy child, to the astonishment of all. The same remedy has been proven efficacious in diverse places and by diverse persons.

SELECT BIBLIOGRAPHY

Texts, Translations, and Reference Works

Abbayes de Belgique: Guide, ed. by Léon Dewincklear (Brussels: Services interbancaires, 1973)

Achard de Saint-Victor, *Sermons inédits*, ed. by Jean Châtillon (Paris: Vrin, 1970)

Anchoritic Spirituality, ed. and trans. by Anne Savage and Nicholas Watson (New York: Paulist, 1991)

Archives historiques et littéraires du Nord de la France et du Midi de la Belgique (Archives du Nord), ed. by A. M. Dinaux, A. J. G. Le Glay, and A. N. Leroy, 16 vols (Valenciennes: Bureau des Archives, 1829–57)

Aristotle, *Parva naturalia: On Sense and Sensible Objects*, in *On the Soul, Parva naturalia, On Breath*, trans. by W. S. Hett (Cambridge, MA: Harvard University Press, 1975)

Arnoldus de Raisse, *Ad Natales Sanctorum Belgii Ioannis Molani Auctarium* (Douai: Avroy, 1626)

——. *Hierogazophylacium Belgicum, sive thesaurus sacrarum reliquiarum Belgii* (Douai: Pinchon, 1628)

Augustine, *Adnotationum in Iob liber I*, ed. by Joseph Zycha, in CSEL 28–2

——. *Confessiones*, ed. by Martin Skutella (Stuttgart: Teubner, 1969)

——. *De civitate Dei*, ed. by Bernard Dombart and Alphonsus Kalb, in CCSL 47–48

——. *The City of God*, trans. by Marcus Dods (New York: Modern Library, 1950)

——. *De disciplina christiana*, ed. by R. vander Plaetse, in CCSL 46

——. *De doctrina christiana*, ed. by William Green, in CCSL 80

——. *On Christian Doctrine*, trans. by D. W. Robertson Jr (New York: Macmillan, 1958)

——. *De Genesi ad litteram libri duodecim*, ed. by Joseph Zycha, in CSEL 28–1

——. *La Genèse au sens littéral en douze livres*, trans. by Paul Agaësse and A. Solignac, 2 vols (Paris: de Brouwer, 1972)

——. *De musica liber VI*, ed. and trans. by Martin Jacobsson (Stockholm: Almqvist & Wiksell, 2002)

————. *De peccatorum meritis et remissione*, ed. by Carolus Urba and Joseph Zycha, in CSEL 60

————. *Enarrationes in Psalmos*, ed. by Eligius Dekkers and Iohannes Fraipont, in CCSL 38–40

————. *In Epistolas Ioannis ad Parthos*, in PL 35, cols 1977–2062

————. *In Iohannis Evangelium Tractatus*, ed. by D. Radbodus Willems, in CCSL 36

————. *Sermones*, in PL 38–39

Bede, *In Genesim*, ed. by C. W. Jones, in CCSL 118A

Bernard of Clairvaux, *Sancti Bernardi Opera*, ed. by Jean Leclercq, Henri Rochais, and C. H. Talbot, 5 vols (Rome: Editiones Cistercienses, 1957–77)

————. *On the Song of Songs*, trans. by Kilian Walsh and Irene M. Edmonds, 4 vols (Kalamazoo: Cistercian Publications, 1971–80)

————. *Treatises II: The Steps of Humility and Pride*, trans. by M. Ambrose Conway, and *On Loving God*, trans. by Robert Walton (Kalamazoo: Cistercian Publications, 1973; repr. 1980)

The Bestiary: A Book of Beasts, Being a Translation from a Latin Bestiary of the Twelfth Century, trans. by T. H. White (New York: Putnam, 1954)

Bibliotheca hagiographica latina antiquae et mediae aetatis, 2 vols (Brussels: Société des Bollandistes, 1949)

Blaise, Albert, *Vocabulaire latin des principaux thèmes liturgiques*, rev. by Antoine Dumas (Turnhout: Brepols, 1966)

Caesarius of Heisterbach, *Dialogus miraculorum*, ed. by Joseph Strange, 2 vols (Cologne: Heberle, 1851)

————. *The Dialogue on Miracles*, trans. by H. von E. Scott and C. C. Swinton Bland, 2 vols (London: Routledge, 1929)

Catalogus codicum hagiographicorum Bibliothecae Regiae Bruxellensis, 2 vols (Brussels: Polleunis, Ceuterick & Lefébure, 1886–89)

Conciliorum oecumenicorum decreta, 3rd edn (Bologna: Istituto per le scienze religiose, 1973)

Corpus antiphonalium officii, ed. by R.-J. Hesbert, in *Rerum ecclesiasticarum documenta, Series maior, Fontes 7–12* (Rome: Herder, 1963–79)

Cottineau, L. H., *Répertoire topo-bibliographique des abbayes et prieurés*, 2 vols (Mâcon: Protat frères, 1935)

Du Cange, Charles Du Fresne, *Glossarium mediae et infimae latinitatis*, 10 vols (Niort: Favre, 1883–87)

Early Dominicans: Selected Writings, ed. by Simon Tugwell (New York: Paulist, 1982)

Étienne de Bourbon [Stephen of Bourbon], *Tractatus de diversis materiis praedicabilibus*, abridged trans. by A. Lecoy de La Marche, in *Anecdotes historiques, légendes et apologues, tirés du recueil inédit d'Étienne de Bourbon* (Paris: Librairie Renouard, 1877)

Eubel, Conrad, *Hierarchia catholica medii aevi* (Regensburg: Monasterium, 1913)

Gallia christiana, in provincias ecclesiasticas distributa, 16 vols (Paris: Coignard, 1715–1865; repr. Farnborough: Gregg International, 1970)

Geraert, Broeder, *Leven van Sinte Lutgardis: Een Dietsch Gedicht ten laetste van de tweede helft der XIVe eeuw*, ed. by J. H. Bormans, 2 vols (Amsterdam: [n. pub.], 1857-58)

Gérard de Frachet, *Vitae fratrum Ordinis Praedicatorum* (Leuven: Charpentier & Schoonjans, 1896)

———. *Lives of the Brethren of the Order of Preachers, 1206–1259*, trans. by Placid Conway (London: Blackfriars, 1955)

Gislebert de Mons, *La Chronique de Gislebert de Mons, Recueil de textes pour servir à l'histoire de Belgique*, ed. by Léon Vanderkindere (Brussels: Kiessling, 1904)

Gregory the Great, *Homiliae in evangelia*, in PL 76

———. *Moralia in Iob*, ed. by Marcus Adriaen, in CCSL 143–43b

The Hours of the Divine Office in English and Latin, 3 vols (Collegeville, MN: Liturgical Press, 1963)

Hugh of Floreffe, *The Life of Yvette of Huy*, trans. by Jo Ann McNamara (Toronto: Peregrina, 2000)

Hugh of Saint-Victor, *On the Sacraments of the Christian Faith*, trans. by Roy Deferrari (Cambridge, MA: Medieval Academy of America, 1951)

Isidore of Seville, *The Bestiary*, trans. by T. H. White (London: Cape, 1954; repr. New York: Putnam, 1960)

Jacobus de Voragine, *The Golden Legend: Readings on the Saints*, trans. by William Granger Ryan, 2 vols (Princeton: Princeton University Press, 1993)

James of Vitry, *Historia orientalis*, ed. by Claude Buridant (Paris: Klincksieck, 1986)

———. *Historia orientalis et occidentalis*, ed. by Franciscus Moschus (Douai: [n. pub], 1597)

———. *Lettres de Jacques de Vitry, 1160/1170–1240*, ed. by R. B. C. Huygens (Leiden: Brill, 1960)

———. *Vita Mariae Oigniacensis*, ed. by D. Papebroeck, in AASS, 23 June, V, pp. 542–72

Kalendar & Compost of Shepherds: From the Original Edition published by Guy Marchant in Paris in the year 1493; and translated into English *c*. 1518, ed. by G. C. Heseltine (London: Davies, 1930)

Le Glay, André, *Glossaire topographique de l'ancien Cambrésis, suivi d'un recueil de chartes et diplomes pour servir à la topographie et à l'histoire de cette province* (Cambrai: Deligne, 1849)

———. *Mémoire sur les archives des églises et maisons religieuses du Cambrésis* (Lille: [n. pub.], 1852)

———. *Revue des Opera Diplomatica de Miraeus* (Brussels: Hayez, 1856)

Leven van sinte Christine de Wonderbare, in oud-dietsche rijmen, ed. by J. H. Bormans (Ghent: Annoot-Braeckman, 1850)

Lexicon of St Thomas Aquinas, ed. by Roy Deferrari and Sister M. I. Barry, 5 vols (Washington: Catholic University of America Press, 1949)

Mary of Oignies: Mother of Salvation, ed. by Anneke Mulder-Bakker (Turnhout: Brepols, 2006)

Miraeus, Aubertus, *Notitia ecclesiarum Belgii* (Antwerp: Cnobbarum, 1630)

———. and J.-Fr. Foppens, *Opera diplomatica et historica*, 4 vols (Louvain: Denique, 1723–48)

Mittellateinisches Wörterbuch (Munich: Beck, 1959–)

Monasticon belge, 8 vols (Bruges: Abbaye de Maredsous, 1890–)

Montalambert, Conte de, *The Life of Saint Elizabeth of Hungary, Duchess of Thuringia*, trans. by Mary Hackett (New York: Sadlier, 1886)

The Nine Ways of Prayer of St Dominic, trans. by Simon Tugwell (Dublin: Dominican Publications, 1978)

Other Middle Ages: Witnesses at the Margins of Medieval Society, ed. by Michael Goodich (Philadelphia: University of Pennsylvania Press, 1998)

Paris, Matthew, *Chronica Majora*, ed. by H. R. Luard, 7 vols (London: Longman, 1872–83)

Pliny the Elder, *Naturalis historia*, ed. and trans. by H. Rackham and W. H. S. Jones, 10 vols
 (London: Heinemann, 1938–63)

Réau, Louis, *Iconographie de l'art chrétien*, 3 vols (Paris: Presses Universitaires de France, 1958)

The Rule of St Augustine: Masculine and Feminine Versions, intro. and commentary by T. J. Van
 Bavel, trans. by Raymond Canning (London: Darton, Longman & Todd, 1984)

The Rule of St Benedict in Latin and English, ed. and trans. by Justin McCann (London: Burns
 & Oates, 1952)

The Rule of St Benedict: A Commentary, trans. by Justin McCann (London: Burns, Oates &
 Co., 1921; repr. Latrobe: Archabbey Press, 1950)

Sacramentarium Leonianum, ed. by C. L. Felto (Cambridge: Cambridge University Press,
 1896)

*Send Me God: The Lives of Ida the Compassionate of Nivelles, Nun of La Ramée, Arnulf, Lay
 Brother of Villers, and Abundus, Monk of Villers, by Goswin of Bossut*, ed. and trans. by
 Martinus Cawley (Turnhout: Brepols, 2003)

Sinte Lutgart, Sinte Kerstine, Nederrijns Moraalboek, ed. by Maurits Gysseling and Willy
 Pijnenburg (The Hague: Nijhoff, 1987)

Thomas Aquinas, *Commentary on Aristotle's Politics* (*In libros Politicos expositio*), trans. by
 Richard Regan (Indianapolis: Hackett, 2007)

———. *Summa theologiae*, ed. by Blackfriars, 61 vols (New York: McGraw-Hill, 1964–81)

Thomas of Cantimpré, *Bonum universale de apibus*, ed. by Georges Colvénère (Douai: Beller,
 1627)

———. *Les exemples du 'Livre des abeilles': une vision médiévale*, trans. by Henri Platelle
 (Turnhout: Brepols, 1997)

———. *Liber de natura rerum*, ed. by Helmut Boese (Berlin: De Gruyter, 1973)

———. *Vita Christinae Mirabilis*, ed. by J. Pinius, in AASS, 24 July, V, pp. 637–60

———. 'Þe Lyfe of Seinte Cristyne þe Mervelous', in 'Prosalegenden: Die Legenden des MS.
 Douce 14', ed. by Carl Horstmann, *Anglia*, 8 (1885), 119–34

———. *Vita Ioannis Cantipratensis*, in 'Une oeuvre inédite de Thomas de Cantimpré, la "Vita
 Ioannis Cantipratensis"', ed. by Robert Godding, *Revue d'histoire ecclésiastique*, 76 (1981),
 241–316 (text on pp. 257–316)

———. *Vita Lutgardis Aquiriensis*, ed. by G. Henschen, in AASS, 16 June, III, pp. 187–209

———. *Vita Margarete de Ypris*, in 'Les Frères Prêcheurs et le mouvement dévôt en Flandre
 au XIIIᵉ siècle', ed. by Gilles Meersseman, *Archivum Fratrum Praedicatorum*, 18 (1948),
 69–130 (text on pp. 106–30)

———. *Vita Mariae Oigniacensis, Supplementum*, ed. by A. Raysse, in AASS, 23 June, V, pp.
 572–81

Tractatus de Purgatorio Sancti Patricii, in *St Patrick's Purgatory*, ed. by Robert Easting, Early
 English Text Society, 298 (Oxford: New York, 1991)

Vita Ioannis de Monte-Mirabili, ed. by Constantin Suysken, in AASS, 29 September, VIII, pp.
 186–235

'Les "*Vitae Sororum*" d'Unterlinden', ed. by Jeanne Ancelet-Hustache, *Archives d'histoire
 doctrinale et littéraire du moyen âge*, 5 (1930), 317–509

William of Saint-Thierry, *Exposition on the Song of Songs*, trans. by Columba Hart (Spencer,
 MA: Cistercian Publications, 1970)

———. *The Golden Epistle: A Letter to the Brethren at Mont Dieu*, trans. by Theodore Berkeley (Kalamazoo: Cistercian Publications, 1976)

———. *On Contemplating God; Prayer; Meditations*, trans. by Sister Penelope (Kalamazoo: Cistercian Publications, 1977)

Studies

Aerts, J., 'Ridder Thimerus van Rogenier uit de Vita S. Lutgardis', *Ons Geestelijk Erf*, 43 (1969), 316–23

———. 'De schenkingen van Godefridus, Kasteelheer van Brussel en van zijn zoon Godefridus, Heer van Seneffe aan de Abdij van Aywières', *Ons Geestelijk Erf*, 42 (1968), 298–303

Akbari, Suzanne Conklin, *Seeing through the Veil: Optical Theory and Medieval Allegory* (Toronto: University of Toronto Press, 2004)

Barratt, Alexandra, 'Language and the Body in Thomas of Cantimpré's *Life* of Lutgard of Aywières', *Cistercian Studies Quarterly*, 30 (1995), 339–47

———. 'Undutiful Daughters and Metaphorical Mothers among the Beguines', in *New Trends in Feminine Spirituality: The Holy Women of Liège and Their Impact*, ed. by Juliette Dor, Lesley Johnson, and Jocelyn Wogan-Browne (Turnhout: Brepols, 1999), pp. 81–104

Bauer, Gerhard, *Claustrum animae: Untersuchungen zur Geschichte der Metapher vom Herzen als Kloster* (Munich: Fink, 1973)

Bériou, Nicole, 'Femmes et prédicateurs: La transmission de la foi au XIIᵉ et XIIIᵉ siècles', in *La Religion de ma mère: Les femmes et la transmission de la foi*, ed. by Jean Delumeau (Paris: Cerf, 1992), pp. 51–70

———. 'The Right of Women to Give Religious Instruction in the Thirteenth Century', in *Women Preachers and Prophets through Two Millennia of Christianity*, ed. by Beverly Mayne Kienzle and Pamela J. Walker (Berkeley: University of California Press, 1998), pp. 134–45

Bernards, Matthäus, 'Nudus nudum sequi', *Wissenschaft und Weisheit*, 14 (1951), 148–51

Blumenfeld-Kosinski, Renate, 'Satirical Views of the Beguines in Northern French Literature', in *New Trends in Feminine Spirituality: The Holy Women of Liège and Their Impact*, ed. by Juliette Dor, Lesley Johnson, and Jocelyn Wogan-Browne (Turnhout: Brepols, 1999), pp. 237-49

Boeren, P. C., *La Vie et les oeuvres de Guiard de Laon, 1170 env.–1248* (The Hague: Nijhoff, 1956)

Bolton, Brenda, 'Thirteenth-Century Religious Women: Further Reflections on the Low Countries "Special Case"', in *New Trends in Feminine Spirituality: The Holy Women of Liège and Their Impact*, ed. by Juliette Dor, Lesley Johnson, and Jocelyn Wogan-Browne (Turnhout: Brepols, 1999), pp. 129–57

———. '*Vitae Matrum*: A Further Aspect of the *Frauenfrage*', in *Medieval Women*, ed. by Derek Baker (Oxford: Blackwell, 1978), pp. 253–73

Bonnard, Fourier, *Histoire de l'Abbaye royale et de l'ordre des chanoines réguliers de Saint-Victor de Paris*, 2 vols (Paris: Savaète, 1904–08)

Borst, Arno, *Les Cathares* (Paris: Payot, 1974)

Bremond, Claude, Jacques Le Goff, and Jean-Claude Schmitt, *L'Exemplum*, Typologie des sources du Moyen Âge occidental, 40 (Turnhout: Brepols, 1982)

Browe, Peter, *Die eucharistischen Wunder des Mittelalters* (Breslau: Müller & Seiffert, 1938)

Bruyelle, A., 'Abbaye de Notre-Dame de Cantimpré, et église de St-Sauveur, paroissiale de Cantimpré', *Archives du Nord*, n.s. 5 (1844), 300–11

Bussels, Amandus, 'Saint Lutgard's Mystical Spirituality', in *Hidden Springs: Cistercian Monastic Women*, ed. by John Nichols and Lillian Thomas Shank, 2 vols (Kalamazoo: Cistercian Publications, 1995), I, pp. 211–23

Bynum, Caroline Walker, *Fragmentation and Redemption: Essays on Gender and the Human Body in Medieval Religion* (New York: Zone, 1991)

——. *Holy Feast and Holy Fast: The Religious Significance of Food to Medieval Women* (Berkeley: University of California Press, 1987)

——. *Jesus as Mother: Studies in the Spirituality of the High Middle Ages* (Berkeley: University of California Press, 1982)

——. *Metamorphosis and Identity* (New York: Zone, 2001)

——. *The Resurrection of the Body in Western Christianity, 200–1336* (New York: Columbia University Press, 1995)

Caciola, Nancy, *Discerning Spirits: Divine and Demonic Possession in the Middle Ages* (Ithaca: Cornell University Press, 2003)

——. 'Wraiths, Revenants and Ritual in Medieval Culture', *Past & Present*, 152 (1996), 3–45

Carruthers, Mary, *The Book of Memory: A Study of Memory in Medieval Culture* (Cambridge: Cambridge University Press, 1990; repr. 1996)

Charles, J. L., *La Ville de Saint-Trond au moyen âge: Des origines à la fin du XIVᵉ siècle* (Paris: Société d'édition 'Les Belles Lettres', 1965)

Chatillon, Jean, 'Canonici regolari di San Vittore', in *Dizionario degli Istituti de Perfezione*, 10 vols (Rome: Paoline, 1975), II, pp. 124–34

Chenu, Marie-Dominique, *La Théologie au douzième siècle* (Paris: Vrin, 1957)

——. 'The Evangelical Awakening', in *Nature, Man, and Society in the Twelfth Century*, ed. and trans. by Jerome Taylor and Lester K. Little (Chicago: University of Chicago Press, 1968), pp. 239–69

Clément-Hémery, A., 'Notice sur les communautés des femmes établies à Cambrai avant la Révolution', *Mémoires de la Société d'émulation de Cambrai*, 10 (1826), 141–83

Coakley, John, 'Friars as Confidants of Holy Women in Medieval Dominican Hagiography', in *Images of Sainthood in Medieval Europe*, ed. by Renate Blumenfeld-Kosinski and Timea Szell (Ithaca: Cornell University Press, 1991), pp. 222–46

——. 'Gender and the Authority of Friars: The Significance of Holy Women for Thirteenth-Century Franciscans and Dominicans', *Church History*, 60 (1991), 445–60

——. 'James of Vitry and the Other World of Mary of Oignies', in *Women, Men, and Spiritual Power: Female Saints and Their Male Collaborators* (New York: Columbia University Press, 2006), pp. 68–88

——. 'Thomas of Cantimpré and Female Sanctity', in *History in the Comic Mode: Medieval Communities and the Matter of Person*, ed. by Rachel Fulton and Bruce Holsinger (New York: Columbia University Press, 2007), pp. 45–55

Constable, Giles, '"Nudus nudum Christum sequi" and Parallel Formulas in the Twelfth Century: A Supplementary Dossier', in *Continuity and Discontinuity in Church History:*

Essays Presented to George Hunston Williams, ed. by F. Forester Church and Timothy George (Leiden: Brill, 1979), pp. 83–91

———. *The Reformation of the Twelfth Century* (Cambridge: Cambridge University Press, 1996)

Davy, M.-M., *Initiation à la symbolique romane (XIIᵉ siècle)* (Paris: Flammarion, 1977)

Deboutte, Alfred, 'Sint Lutgart en Magister Johannes de Liro', *Sinte Lutgart Schutsvrouwe van Vlaanderen*, 18 (1976), 46–53

———. 'The *Vita Lutgardis* of Thomas of Cantimpré', in *Hidden Springs: Cistercian Monastic Women*, ed. by John Nichols and Lillian Thomas Shank, 2 vols (Kalamazoo: Cistercian Publications, 1995), I, pp. 255–81

De Ganck, Roger, *Beatrice of Nazareth in Her Context*, Cistercian Fathers Series, 3 vols (Kalamazoo: Cistercian Publications, 1991)

d'Haenens, Albert, 'Femmes excédentaires et vocation religieuse dans l'ancien diocèse de Liège lors de l'essor urbain (fin du XIIᵉ—début du XIIIᵉ siècle). Le Cas d'Ide de Nivelles (1200–1231)', in *Hommages à la Wallonie: Mélanges d'histoire, de littérature et de philologie wallonnes offerts à Maurice A. Arnould et Pierre Ruelle*, ed. by Hervé Hasquin (Brussels: Université Libre de Bruxelles, 1981), pp. 217–35

Distant Echoes, ed. by John A. Nichols and Lillian Thomas Shank (Kalamazoo: Cistercian Publications, 1984)

Dumoutet, Edouard, *Corpus Domini: Aux sources de la piété eucharistique médiévale* (Paris: Beauchesne, 1942)

Elder, E. Rozanne, 'The Way of Ascent: The Meaning of Love in the Thought of William of St Thierry', in *Studies in Medieval Culture*, ed. by John R. Sommerfeldt (Kalamazoo: Western Michigan University, 1964), pp. 39–47

Elliott, Dyan, *Fallen Bodies: Pollution, Sexuality, and Demonology in the Middle Ages* (Philadelphia: University of Pennsylvania Press, 1999)

———. *Proving Woman: Female Spirituality and Inquisitional Culture in the Later Middle Ages* (Princeton: Princeton University Press, 2004)

———. *Spiritual Marriage: Sexual Abstinence in Medieval Wedlock* (Princeton: Princeton University Press, 1993)

Elm, Kaspar, 'Die Stellung der Frau in Ordenswesen, Semireligiösentum und Häresie zur Zeit der heiligen Elisabeth', in *Sankt Elisabeth, Fürstin, Dienerin, Heilige* (Sigmaringen: Thorbecke, 1981), pp. 7–28

Épiney-Burgard, Georgette, 'Les Béguines et l'ordre cistercien aux Pays-Bas du sud (XIIIᵉ siècle)', in *Les Mouvances laïques des ordres religieux [...]*, ed. by Nicole Bouter (Saint-Etienne: Université Jean Monnet, 1996)

Farmer, Sharon, *Surviving Poverty in Medieval Paris: Gender, Ideology, and the Daily Lives of the Poor* (Ithaca: Cornell University Press, 2002)

Frauenmystik im Mittelalter [...], ed. by Peter Dinzelbacher and Dieter R. Bauer (Ostfildern bei Stuttgart: Schwabenverlag, 1985)

Freccero, John, 'Dante's Firm Foot and the Journey without a Guide', *Harvard Theological Review*, 52 (1959), 245–81

Freed, John B., 'Urban Development and the "Cura Monialium" in Thirteenth-Century Germany', *Viator*, 3 (1972), 311–27

Fulton, Rachel, '"Taste and See that the Lord is Sweet" (Ps. 33. 9): The Flavor of God in the Monastic West', *Journal of Religion*, 86 (2006), 169–204

Galloway, Penelope, '"Discreet and Devout Maidens": Women's Involvement in Beguine Communities in Northern France, 1200–1500', in *Medieval Women in Their Communities*, ed. by Diane Watt (Toronto: University of Toronto Press, 1997), pp. 92–115

——. 'Neither Miraculous Nor Astonishing: The Devotional Practice of Beguine Communities in French Flanders', in *New Trends in Feminine Spirituality: The Holy Women of Liège and Their Impact*, ed. by Juliette Dor, Lesley Johnson, and Jocelyn Wogan-Browne (Turnhout: Brepols, 1999), pp. 107–27

Gazet, Guillaume, *L'Histoire ecclésiastique du Pays-Bas* (Arras: Guillaume de la Rivière, 1614)

Gendered Voices: Medieval Saints and Their Interpreters, ed. by Catherine M. Mooney (Philadelphia: University of Pennsylvania Press, 1999)

Gilson, Étienne, *The Christian Philosophy of Saint Augustine* (New York: Random House, 1960)

Glente, Karen, 'Mystikerinnenviten aus männlicher und weiblicher Sicht: Ein Vergleich zwischen Thomas von Cantimpré und Katherina von Unterlinden', in *Religiöse Frauenbewegung und mystische Frömmigkeit im Mittelalter*, ed. by Peter Dinzelbacher and Dieter Bauer (Cologne: Böhlau, 1988), pp. 251–64

Godding, Robert, 'Vie apostolique et société urbaine à l'aube du XIIIᵉ siècle', *Nouvelle revue théologique*, 104 (1982), 692–721

Goodich, Michael, *Vita Perfecta: The Ideal of Sainthood in the Thirteenth Century* (Stuttgart: Hiersemann, 1982)

Grégoire, Réginald, 'L'Adage ascétique "Nudus nudum Christum sequi"', in *Studi storici in onore di Ottorino Bertolini*, ed. by Ottavio Banti and others, 2 vols (Pisa: Pacini, 1972), I, pp. 395–409

Greven, Jospeh, 'Der Ursprung des Beginenwesens: Eine Auseinandersetzung mit Godefroid Kurth', *Historisches Jahrbuch*, 35 (1914), 26–58

Grisart, M., 'Le Catharisme dans le Nord de la France', *Cahiers d'études cathares*, 2ᵐᵉ sér., 3–4 (1959), 24–40

Grundmann, Herbert, *Religiöse Bewegungen im Mittelalter* (Berlin: Ebering, 1935; 2nd edn Darmstadt: Wissenschaftliche Buchgesellschaft, 1961)

——. *Religious Movements in the Middle Ages [...]*, trans. by Steven Rowan (Notre Dame: University of Notre Dame Press, 1995)

Grzebien, Thomas, 'Penance, Purgatory, Mysticism and Miracles: The Life, Hagiography, and Spirituality of Thomas of Cantimpré (1200–1270)' (unpublished doctoral dissertation, University of Notre Dame, 1989)

Haskins, Susan, *Mary Magdalen: Myth and Metaphor* (New York: Riverhead Books, 1993)

Heene, Katrien, 'Gender and Mobility in the Low Countries: Travelling Women in Thirteenth-Century Exempla and Saints' Lives', in *The Texture of Society: Medieval Women in the Southern Low Countries*, ed. by Ellen Kittell and Mary Suydam (New York: Palgrave Macmillan, 2004), pp. 31–49

——. 'Hagiography and Gender: A Tentative Case-Study on Thomas of Cantimpré', in *'Scribere sanctorum gesta': Recueil d'études d'hagiographie médiévale offert à Guy Philippart*, ed. by Étienne Renard and others (Turnhout: Brepols, 2005), pp. 109–23

Hendrix, Guido, 'Primitive Versions of Thomas of Cantimpré's *Vita Lutgardis*', *Cîteaux*, 29 (1978), 153–206

———. 'Willem van Afflighems Auteurschap van het Leven van Lutgart getoetst aan het Hoofdstuk', *Ons Geestelijk Erf*, 40 (1966), 344–49

Heynen, G., 'De Benedictinessen te Sint-Truiden en te Nonnemielen', in *Christina de Wonderbare: Gedenkboek 1150–1950*, ed. by P. Clerinx (Leuven: Bibliotheca Alfonsiana, 1950), pp. 25–30

Hollywood, Amy, *Sensible Ecstasy: Mysticism, Sexual Difference, and the Demands of History* (Chicago: University of Chicago Press, 2002)

———. *The Soul as Virgin Wife: Mechthild of Magdeburg, Marguerite Porete, and Meister Eckhart* (Notre Dame: University of Notre Dame Press, 1995)

Kantorowicz, Ernst, *Frederick the Second, 1194–1250*, trans. by E. O. Lorimer (London: Constable, 1931)

Kieckhefer, Richard, *Unquiet Souls: Fourteenth-Century Saints and Their Religious Milieu* (Chicago: University of Chicago Press, 1984)

King, Margot H., *The Desert Mothers: A Survey of the Feminine Anchoretic Tradition in Western Europe* (Toronto: Peregrina, 1989)

———. 'The Desert Mothers Revisited: The Mothers of the Diocese of Liège', *Vox Benedictina*, 5 (1988), 325–54

———. 'The Dove at the Window: The Ascent of the Soul in Thomas de Cantimpré's Life of Lutgard of Aywières', in *Hidden Springs: Cistercian Monastic Women*, ed. by John Nichols and Lillian Thomas Shank, 2 vols (Kalamazoo: Cistercian Publications, 1995), I, pp. 225–53

———. 'The Sacramental Witness of Christina *Mirabilis*: The Mystic Growth of a Fool for Christ's Sake', in *Peace Weavers*, ed. by Lillian Thomas Shank and John A. Nichols (Kalamazoo: Cistercian Publications, 1987), pp. 145–64

Kleinberg, Aviad M., *Prophets in Their Own Country: Living Saints and the Making of Sainthood in the Later Middle Ages* (Chicago: University of Chicago Press, 1992)

———. 'A Thirteenth-Century Struggle over Custody: The Case of Catherine of Parc-aux-Dames', *Bulletin of Medieval Canon Law*, n.s. 20 (1990), 51–67

Kurtz, Patricia Deery, 'Mary of Oignies, Christine the Marvelous and Medieval Heresy', *Mystics Quarterly*, 14 (1988), 186–96

Lauwers, Michel, 'Entre béguinisme et mysticisme: La Vie de Marie d'Oignies (d. 1213) de Jacques de Vitry ou la définition d'une sainteté féminine', *Ons Geestelijk Erf*, 66 (1992), 46–69

———. 'L'Expérience béguinale et récit hagiographique: À propos de la *Vita Mariae Oigniacensis* de Jacques de Vitry (vers 1215)', *Journal des savants*, 11 (1989), 61–103

———. and Walter Simons, *Béguins et béguines à Tournai au bas moyen âge: Les communautés béguinales à Tournai du XIIIᵉ au XVᵉ siècle* (Tournai: Archives du chapitre Cathédral; Louvain-la-Neuve: Université Catholique de Louvain, 1988)

Leclercq, Jean, *Initiation aux auteurs monastiques du Moyen Âge: L'amour des lettres et le désir de Dieu*, 2nd edn (Paris: Cerf, 1956)

———. *The Love of Learning and the Desire for God*, trans. by Catherine Misrahi (New York: Fordham University Press, 1960)

──. 'Medieval Feminine Monasticism: Reality Versus Romantic Images', in *Benedictus: Studies in Honour of St Benedict of Nursia*, ed. by E. Rozanne Elder (Kalamazoo: Cistercian Publications, 1981), pp. 53–70

Lefèvre, J.-B., 'Sainte Lutgarde d'Aywières en son temps (1182–1246)', *Collectanea Cisterciensia*, 58 (1996), 277–335

Le Goff, Jacques, *La Naissance du purgatoire* (Paris: Gallimard, 1981)

──. *The Birth of Purgatory*, trans. by Arthur Goldhammer (Chicago: University of Chicago Press, 1981)

──. *Your Money or Your Life: Economy and Religion in the Middle Ages*, trans. by Patricia Ranum (New York: Zone, 1988)

Lewis, Gertrud Jaron, 'The Mystical Jubilus: An Example from Gertrud of Helfta', *Vox Benedictina*, 1 (1984), 237–47

Lewy, Yochanan, *Sobria Ebrietas: Untersuchungen zur Geschichte der antiken Mystik* (Giessen: Töppelmann, 1929)

Leyser, Henrietta, *Hermits and the New Monasticism: A Study of Religious Communities in Western Europe, 1000–1150* (London: Macmillan, 1984)

Lindberg, David, *Studies in the History of Medieval Optics* (London: Variorum, 1983)

──. *Theories of Vision from al-Kindi to Kepler* (Chicago: University of Chicago Press, 1976)

Little, Lester K., *Religious Poverty and the Profit Economy in Medieval Europe* (Ithaca: Cornell University Press, 1978)

Longère, Jean, 'Pauvreté et richesse chez quelques prédicateurs durant la seconde moitié du XIIᵉ siècle', in *Études sur l'histoire de la pauvreté*, ed. by Michel Mollat, 2 vols (Paris: Sorbonne, 1974), I, pp. 255–73

Longnon, Jean, *Les Compagnons de Villehardouin: Recherches sur les croisés de la quatrième croisade* (Geneva: Droz, 1978)

Luykx, Theo, *Johanna van Constantinopel, Gravin van Vlaanderen en Henegouwen* (Antwerp: Standaard-Boekhandel, 1946)

Makowski, Elisabeth, '"Mulieres religiosae", Strictly Speaking: Some Fourteenth-Century Canonical Opinions', *Catholic Historical Review*, 85 (1999), 1–14

Mantingh, Erwin, *Een monnik met een rol: Willem van Affligem, het Kopenhaagse Leven van Lutgart en de fictie van een meerdaagse voorlezing* (Hilversum: Verloren, 2000)

Marseille, J., 'Le Couvent des dominicains de Lille de sa fondation au milieu du XVᵉ siècle', *Archivum Fratrum Praedicatorum*, 40 (1970), 73–95

McCulloch, Florence, *Mediaeval Latin and French Bestiaries* (Chapel Hill: University of North Carolina Press, 1962)

McDonnell, Ernest W., *The Beguines and Beghards in Medieval Culture, with Special Emphasis on the Belgian Scene* (New Brunswick: Rutgers University Press, 1954)

McGinn, Bernard, *The Flowering of Mysticism: Men and Women in the New Mysticism, 1200–1350* (New York: Crossroad, 1998)

McGuire, Brian Patrick, 'The Cistercians and Friendship: An Opening to Women', in *Hidden Springs: Cistercian Monastic Women*, ed. by John Nichols and Lillian Thomas Shank, 2 vols (Kalamazoo: Cistercian Publications, 1995), I, pp. 171–200

──. *Friendship and Community: The Monastic Experience, 350–1250* (Kalamazoo: Cistercian Publications, 1988)

──. 'Purgatory, the Communion of Saints, and Medieval Change', *Viator*, 20 (1989), 61–84

McNamara, Jo Ann Kay, 'Living Sermons: Consecrated Women and the Conversion of Gaul', in *Peace Weavers*, ed. by Lillian Thomas Shank and John A. Nichols (Kalamazoo: Cistercian Publications, 1987), pp. 19–37

——. 'The Need to Give: Suffering and Female Sanctity in the Middle Ages', in *Images of Sainthood in Medieval Europe*, ed. by Renate Blumenfeld-Kosinki and Timea Szell (Ithaca: Cornell University Press, 1991), pp. 199–221

——. 'The Rhetoric of Orthodoxy: Clerical Authority and Female Innovation in the Struggle with Heresy', in *Maps of Flesh and Light: The Religious Experience of Medieval Women Mystics*, ed. by Ulrike Wiethaus (Syracuse, NY: Syracuse University Press, 1993), pp. 9–27

——. *Sisters in Arms: Catholic Nuns through Two Millennia* (Cambridge, MA: Harvard University Press, 1996)

Meersseman, G., 'Les Débuts de l'Ordre des Frères Prêcheurs dans le comté de Flandre (1224–1280)', *Archivum Fratrum Praedicatorum*, 17 (1947), 5–40

——. 'Les Frères Prêcheurs et le mouvement dévot en Flandre au XIIIe siècle', *Archivum Fratrum Praedicatorum*, 18 (1948), 69–130

——. 'Jeanne de Constantinople et les Frères Prêcheurs: À propos d'un livre récent', *Archivum Fratrum Praedicatorum*, 19 (1949), 122–68

Mens, Alcantara, *L'Ombrie italienne et l'Ombrie brabançonne: Deux courants religieux parallèles d'inspiration commune* (Paris: Études Franciscaines, 1968)

——. *Oorsprong en Betekenis van de Nederlandse Begijnenen Begardenbeweging. Vergelijkende studie: XII^de–XIII^de eeuw* (Antwerp: Standaard-Boekhandel, 1947)

Merton, Thomas, *What Are These Wounds? The Life of a Cistercian Mystic, Saint Lutgarde of Aywières* (Milwaukee: Bruce, 1950)

Muessig, Carolyn, 'Paradigms of Sanctity for Thirteenth-Century Women', in *Models of Holiness in Medieval Sermons*, ed. by Beverly Mayne Kienzle (Louvain-la-Neuve: Fédération Internationale des Instituts d'Études Médiévales, 1996), pp. 85–102

——. 'Prophecy and Song: Teaching and Preaching by Medieval Women', in *Women Preachers and Prophets through Two Millennia of Christianity*, ed. by Beverly Mayne Kienzle and Pamela J. Walker (Berkeley: University of California Press, 1998), pp. 146–58

Mulder-Bakker, Anneke B., *Lives of the Anchoresses: The Rise of the Urban Recluse in Medieval Europe*, trans. by Myra Heerspink Scholz (Philadelphia: University of Pennsylvania Press, 2005)

——. 'The Prime of Their Lives: Women and Age, Wisdom and Religious Careers in Northern Europe', in *New Trends in Feminine Spirituality: The Holy Women of Liège and Their Impact*, ed. by Juliette Dor, Lesley Johnson, and Jocelyn Wogan-Browne (Turnhout: Brepols, 1999), pp. 215–36

——. 'Saints Without a Past: Sacred Places and Intercessory Power in Saints' Lives from the Low Countries', in *The Invention of Saintliness*, ed. by Anneke B. Mulder-Bakker (London: Routledge, 2002), pp. 38–57

Murray, Alexander, 'Should the Middle Ages Be Abolished?', *Essays in Medieval Studies*, 21 (2004), 1–22

Neel, Carol, 'The Origins of the Beguines', *Signs*, 14 (1989), 321–41

Newman, Barbara, 'On the Threshold of the Dead: Purgatory, Hell, and Religious Women', in her *From Virile Woman to WomanChrist: Studies in Medieval Religion and Literature* (Philadelphia: University of Pennsylvania Press, 1995), pp. 108–36

——. 'Possessed by the Spirit: Devout Women, Demoniacs, and the Apostolic Life in the Thirteenth Century', *Speculum*, 73 (1998), 733–70

——. 'What Did It Mean to Say "I Saw"? The Clash Between Theory and Practice in Medieval Visionary Culture', *Speculum*, 81 (2005), 1–43

Newman, Martha, 'Crucified by the Virtues: Monks, Lay Brothers, and Women in Thirteenth-Century Cistercian Saints' Lives', in *Gender and Difference in the Middle Ages*, ed. by Sharon Farmer and Carol Braun Pasternack (Minneapolis: University of Minnesota Press, 2003), pp. 182–209

Noonan, John T., *The Scholastic Analysis of Usury* (Cambridge, MA: Harvard University Press, 1957)

Payen, Jean Charles, 'La Pénitence dans le contexte culturel des XIIᵉ et XIIIᵉsiècles', *Revue des sciences philosophiques et théologiques*, 61 (1977), 399–428

Petroff, Elizabeth, 'Medieval Women Visionaries: Seven Stages to Power', *Frontiers*, 3 (1978), 34–45

Platelle, Henri, 'Conversions spectaculaires et langage symbolique (Cambrai XIIᵉ siècle): De la polyvalence des symboles', *Bulletin philologique et historique* (1980), 27–38

——. 'L'Image des Juifs chez Thomas de Cantimpré: De l'attrait à la répulsion', in *Mélanges à la mémoire de Marcel-Henri Prévost: Droit biblique, interprétation rabbinique, communautés et société* (Paris: Presses Universitaires de France, 1982), pp. 283–306

——. 'Le Recueil des miracles de Thomas de Cantimpré et la vie religieuse dans les Pays-Bas et le Nord de la France au XIIIᵉ siècle', in *Actes du 97e Congrès national des sociétés savantes, Nantes, 1972*, 2 vols (Paris: Bibliothèque nationale, 1977–79), I, pp. 469–98

——. 'Vengeance privée et réconciliation dans l'oeuvre de Thomas de Cantimpré', *Tijdschrift voor Rechtsgeschiedenis*, 42 (1974), 269–81

Powicke, Maurice, *The Thirteenth Century, 1216–1307* (Oxford: Clarendon Press, 1953)

Purity of Heart in Early Ascetic and Monastic Literature: Essays in Honour of Juana Raasch, O.S.B., ed. by Harriet Luckman and Linda Kulzer (Collegeville, MN: Liturgical Press, 1999)

Reinecke, Wilhelm, *Geschichte der Stadt Cambrai bis zur Erteilung der Lex Godefridi (1227)* (Marburg: Elwert, 1896)

Reypens, L., 'Een derde Beatrijs in onze dertiendeeuwse letteren? Beatrijs van Dendermonde', *Ons Geestelijk Erf*, 37 (1963), 419–22

——. 'Sint Lutgarts mystieke opgang', *Ons Geestelijk Erf*, 20 (1946), 7–49

Riehle, Wolfgang, *The Middle English Mystics* (London: Routledge & Kegan Paul, 1981)

Roisin, Simone, 'L'Efflorescence cistercienne et le courant féminin de piété au XIIIᵉ siècle', *Revue d'histoire ecclésiastique*, 39 (1943), 342–78

——. *L'Hagiographie cistercienne dans le diocèse de Liège au XIIIᵉ siècle* (Louvain: Bibliothèque de l'Université, 1947)

——. 'La Méthode hagiographique de Thomas de Cantimpré', in *Miscellanea Historica in Honorem Alberti de Meyer*, 2 vols (Louvain: Bibliothèque de l'Université, 1946), I, pp. 546–57

————. 'Sainte Lutgarde d'Aywières dans son ordre et dans son temps', *Collectanea O.C.R.*, 8 (1946), 161–72

Savary, Louis M., *Psychological Themes in the Golden Epistle of William of Saint-Thierry* (Salzburg: Analecta Cartusiana, 1973)

Saward, John, *Perfect Fools: Folly for Christ's Sake in Catholic and Orthodox Spirituality* (Oxford: Oxford University Press, 1980)

Schleusener-Eichholz, Gudrun, *Das Auge im Mittelalter*, 2 vols (Munich: Fink, 1985)

Schmitt, Jean-Claude, *Ghosts in the Middle Ages: The Living and the Dead in Medieval Society*, trans. by Teresa Lavender Fagan (Chicago: University of Chicago Press, 1998)

Schulman, Nicole, *Where Troubadours Were Bishops: The Occitania of Folc of Marseille, 1150–1231* (New York: Routledge, 2001)

Sigal, André, *L'Homme et le miracle dans la France médiévale (XIᵉ–XIIᵉ siècle)* (Paris: Cerf, 1985)

Simons, Walter, 'The Beguine Movement in the Southern Low Countries: A Reassessment', *Bulletin de l'Institut Historique Belge de Rome*, 54 (1989), 63–105

————. *Cities of Ladies: Beguine Communities in the Medieval Low Countries, 1200–1565* (Philadelphia: University of Pennsylvania Press, 2001)

————. 'Reading a Saint's Body: Rapture and Bodily Movement in the *Vitae* of Thirteenth-Century Beguines', in *Framing Medieval Bodies*, ed. by Sarah Kay and Miri Rubin (Manchester: Manchester University Press, 1994), pp. 10–23

————. 'Staining the Speech of Things Divine: The Uses of Literacy in Medieval Beguine Communities', in *The Voice of Silence: Women's Literacy in a Men's Church*, ed. by Thérèse de Hemptinne and Maria Eugenia Góngora (Turnhout: Brepols, 2004), pp. 85–110

Stephenson, C., 'The Origin and Nature of the Taille', *Revue belge de philologie et d'histoire*, 5 (1926), 801–70

Stracke, D. A., 'Proza Fragmente van S. Lutgarts Leven', *Ons Geestelijk Erf*, 11 (1937), 281–99

Sweetman, Robert, 'Christine of Saint-Trond's Preaching Apostolate: Thomas of Cantimpré's Hagiographical Method Revisited', *Vox Benedictina*, 9 (1992), 67–97

————. 'Thomas of Cantimpré, *Mulieres Religiosae*, and Purgatorial Piety: Hagiographical *Vitae* and the Beguine "Voice"', in *A Distinct Voice: Medieval Studies in Honor of Leonard E. Boyle, O.P.*, ed. by Jacqueline Brown and William P. Stoneman (Notre Dame: University of Notre Dame Press, 1997), pp. 606–28

————. 'Thomas of Cantimpré: Performative Reading and Pastoral Care', in *Performance and Transformation: New Approaches to Late Medieval Spirituality*, ed. by Mary Suydam and Joanna Ziegler (New York: St Martin's Press, 1999), pp. 133–67

————. 'Visions of Purgatory and Their Role in the *Bonum universale de apibus* of Thomas of Cantimpré', *Ons Geestelijk Erf*, 67 (1993), 20–33

Teetaert, Amédée, *La Confession aux laïques dans l'église latine depuis le VIIIᵉ siècle jusqu'au XIV siècle: Étude de théologie positive* (Paris: Gabalda, 1926)

Thompson, Sally, 'The Problem of the Cistercian Nuns in the Twelfth and Early Thirteenth Centuries', in *Medieval Women*, ed. by Derek Baker (Oxford: Blackwell, 1978), pp. 227–52

Vandecan, Suzanne, 'L'histoire du Trésor d'Oignies', in *Autour de Hugo d'Oignies*, ed. by Robert Didier and Jacques Toussaint, Musée des Arts anciens du Namurois, 25 (Namur: Société archéologique de Namur, 2003), pp. 47–57

Vauchez, André, *Les Laïcs au moyen âge: pratiques et expériences* (Paris: Cerf, 1987)

————. *The Laity in the Middle Ages: Religious Beliefs and Devotional Practices*, ed. by Daniel Bornstein, trans. by Margery Schneider (Notre Dame: University of Notre Dame Press, 1993)

————. *La Sainteté en occident aux derniers siècles du moyen âge d'après les procès de canonisation et les documents hagiographiques* (Paris: Diffusion de Boccard, 1981)

————. *Sainthood in the Later Middle Ages*, trans. by Jean Birrell (Cambridge: Cambridge University Press, 1997)

————. 'Saints admirables et saints imitables: les fonctions de l'hagiographie ont-elles changé aux derniers siècles du moyen-âge?', in *Les Fonctions des saints dans le monde occidental (IIIᵉ–XIIIᵉ siècle)*, intro. by Jean-Yves Tilliette (Rome: École Française de Rome, 1991), pp. 161–72

————. *Saints, prophètes et visionnaires: Le pouvoir surnaturel au Moyen Âge* (Paris: Michel, 1999)

Vaughan, Richard, *Matthew Paris* (Cambridge: Cambridge University Press, 1958)

Vicaire, M.-H., *Saint Thomas and His Times*, trans. by Kathleen Pond (London: Darton, Longman & Todd, 1964)

Wack, Mary, *Lovesickness in the Middle Ages: The 'Viaticum' and Its Commentaries* (Philadelphia: University of Pennsylvania Press, 1990)

Waddell, Chrysogonus, 'Simplicity and Ordinariness: The Climate of Early Cistercian Hagiography', in *Simplicity and Ordinariness*, ed. by John Sommerfeldt (Kalamazoo: Cistercian Publications, 1980), pp. 1–47

Ward, Benedicta, *Miracles and the Medieval Mind: Theory, Record and Event, 1000–1215*, rev. edn (Philadelphia: University of Pennsylvania Press, 1987)

Waters, Claire, *Angels and Earthly Creatures: Preaching, Performance, and Gender in the Later Middle Ages* (Philadelphia: University of Pennsylvania Press, 2004)

Wiethaus, Ulrike, 'The Death Song of Marie d'Oignies: Mystical Sound and Hagiographical Politics in Medieval Lorraine', in *The Texture of Society: Medieval Women in the Southern Low Countries*, ed. by Ellen Kittell and Mary Suydam (New York: Palgrave Macmillan, 2004), pp. 153–79

Wolff, Robert Lee, 'Baldwin of Flanders and Hainaut, First Latin Emperor of Constantinople: His Life, Death, and Resurrection, 1172–1225', *Speculum*, 27 (1952), 281–322

Ziegler, Joanna, 'Reality as Imitation: The Role of Religious Imagery Among the Beguines of the Low Countries', in *Maps of Flesh and Light: The Religious Experience of Medieval Women Mystics*, ed. by Ulrike Wiethaus (Syracuse, NY: Syracuse University Press, 1993), pp. 112–26

MEDIEVAL WOMEN: TEXTS AND CONTEXTS

All volumes in this series are evaluated by an Editorial Board, strictly on academic grounds, based on reports prepared by referees who have been commissioned by virtue of their specialism in the appropriate field. The Board ensures that the screening is done independently and without conflicts of interest. The definitive texts supplied by authors are also subject to review by the Board before being approved for publication. Further, the volumes are copyedited to conform to the publisher's stylebook and to the best international academic standards in the field.

Titles in series